INSIDE

ISAPI

KEVIN CLEMENTS

CHRIS WUESTEFELD

JEFFREY TRENT

JIM CLEMENS

New
Riders

New Riders Publishing, Indianapolis, Indiana

Inside ISAPI

By Kevin Clements, Chris Wuestefeld, Jeffrey Trent, and Jim Clemens

Published by:
New Riders Publishing
201 West 103rd Street
Indianapolis, IN 46290 USA

Printed in the United States of America 1 2 3 4 5 6 7 8 9 0

Library of Congress Cataloging-in-Publication Data

CIP data available upon request

Warning and Disclaimer

This book is designed to provide information about ISAPI. Every effort has been made to make this book as complete and as accurate as possible, but no warranty or fitness is implied.

The information is provided on an "as is" basis. The author(s) and New Riders Publishing shall have neither liability nor responsibility to any person or entity with respect to any loss or damages arising from the information contained in this book or from the use of the disks or programs that may accompany it.

Publisher	*Don Fowley*
Associate Publisher	*David Dwyer*
Marketing Manager	*Mary Foote*
Managing Editor	*Carla Hall*

Product Development Specialist
Brad Jones

Acquisitions Editor
Danielle Bird

Senior Editors
Sarah Kearns
Suzanne Snyder

Development Editor
Chris Cleveland

Project Editor
Brad Herriman

Copy Editor
Malinda McCain

Technical Editors
David Fritsche
Jacob Smith
Christophe Wille

Software Specialist
Steve Flatt

Software Acquisitions
Pete Bitar

Acquisitions Coordinator
Stacy Merkel

Administrative Coordinator
Karen Opal

Cover Designer
Sandra Schroeder

Cover Illustration
© James Endicott/SIS

Cover Production
Aren Howell

Book Designer
Anne Jones

Production Manager
Kelly Dobbs

Production Team Supervisors
Laurie Casey
Joe Millay

Graphics Image Specialists
Steve Adams, Debi Bolhuis,
Kevin Cliburn, Sadie Crawford,
Wil Cruz, Tammy Graham,
Dan Harris, Oliver Jackson

Production Analyst
Erich J. Richter

Production Team
Janelle Herber, Malinda Kuhn,
Rowena Rappaport,
Maureen West

Indexer
Brad Herriman

About the Authors

Kevin Clements is a software developer who's been working in C since 1985 and C++ since 1991. He has been developing software for the Microsoft Windows platforms since 1991, and has moved with them into the brave new world of Internet development. He is currently Manager of Internet Development at Software House International (http://www.shi.com), where he is currently building web sites for business-to-business electronic commerce. He is a proud graduate of the North Carolina School of Science and Mathematics (NCSSM), class of '83. He can be contacted at kmclemen@eclipse.net.

Chris Wuestefeld is a programmer/analyst from Alexandria, New Jersey. He has several years of experience in object oriented design and programming, including the Booch method, and C++ and Java. He is currently working as a Senior Software Engineer for Software House International, developing electronic commerce applications for the Internet. You can contact him at chrisw@blast.net.

Jeffrey Trent is an independent consultant developing Internet applications primarily in ISAPI, Java, and JavaScript. He specializes in Windows and C++ development and has contributed to several commercial products for various software development companies. Jeff has a B.A. in Computer Science from Rutgers University. His interests include hiking, camping, kite flying, and other outdoor activities. He is a certified EMT and enjoys volunteering for the rescue squad in his free time. Jeff is the President of Structure Software, Inc. His company's website can be found at: http://www.structsoft.com. He can be contacted via e-mail at: jtrent@structsoft.com.

Jim Clemens received his Bachelor of Science in Music from the University of Colorado in 1984. Shortly afterward, he bought his first PC clone in an effort to save time when printing his orchestral compositions. He began programming with the idea in mind that he would someday write a better music program which he finally achieved by writing Winsong 3.0 for Softronics Inc. He currently is a composer, systems consultant and Director of Research and Development at Electronic Storefronts, Inc., a firm that specializes in high-end Web sites and Internet Solutions. He can be reached at: jrc@electricstores.com.

Trademark Acknowledgments

All terms mentioned in this book that are known to be trademarks or service marks have been appropriately capitalized. New Riders Publishing cannot attest to the accuracy of this information. Use of a term in this book should not be regarded as affecting the validity of any trademark or service mark.

Dedications

Kevin Clements   This book is dedicated to the women in my life: my wife Sally, and non-human family members Heidi and Greta. They kept me sane, and were quite supportive during much of the time I was writing this book. See, I told you it would be finished soon...

Chris Wuestefeld   This book is dedicated to the idea that the technology it describes, and more generally the entire Internet, will be used to improve communication between its users. Its potential to promote understanding between people of all cultures, races and religions is enormous; don't let the politicians interfere.

Jeffrey Trent   I would like to dedicate my work on this book to my first born, Sarah, who was born this last July. She has brought incredible joy into my life and to my wife Melissa, who I would also like to thank for supporting me throughout the writing of this book.

Jim Clemens   I would like to dedicate the book to my family for everything they've done along the way.

Acknowledgments

Kevin Clements   I'd like to thank the editors at New Riders, who put up with a quartet of authors new to the world of publishing. Special thanks are due to Chris Cleveland and Danielle Bird, who kept everything on track, and Malinda McCain, who translated my prose into something resembling standard English.

I'd also like to thank the people at my old alma mater, the North Carolina School of Science and Math (NCCSM), where I had the opportunity to learn to program computers, and a great deal more. Special thanks to Dr. Stephen Davis, who taught me my first real programming language.

Finally, I'd like to thank everyone at Software House, who has given me the opportunity to build a web site from the ground up. Much of what you see in this book was originally developed for use at SHI.

Chris Wuestefeld   First and foremost, I'd like to thank my wife Cathy, who (with the help of our dog Buster) kept the house in order, the bills paid, and me sane, while I spent all my time in front of the computer working on this book rather than with her. All she got in return was a cranky husband waking her up in the middle of the night.

Secondly, I'd like to thank the participants in the ISAPI-L newsgroup. These people provided the answers to many important questions, and posed many others, unwittingly providing much of the direction for this book.

Finally, the editors at New Riders Publishing provided much badly needed help in getting through the publishing process. In particular, Christopher Cleveland's guidance contributed much value to the book's content. He knows more about programming than any editor should (we'll make a programmer out of you yet!).

Jeffrey Trent   I want to thank Danielle Bird and Christopher Cleveland for their excellent work and dedication in making this book a success. Finally, I would like to acknowledge my parents and my younger brother, Daniel, who I know will get a kick over the mention of his name in a book.

Jim Clemens   I would like to acknowledge Danielle Bird for her patience with me, Ruth Garriott for her hard work for ESI, Ken Knoll, Sue Lynch, and Jeff Oliver for their support and advice, and Scott and Lynn at Softronics for putting up with me while I was there.

Contents at a Glance

Table of Contents

3   Presenting an IDC Sample Application   53

4   Basic Form Processing in MFC   109

Introduction

Welcome to *Inside ISAPI* ! This book is intended to help experienced developers build state-of-the-art interactive web sites to be executed on Microsoft's IIS (Internet Information Server).

The Internet is perhaps the most quickly growing field of technology in the world today. A very short time ago the applications that started the excitement were largely static presentations, perhaps with a few graphics thrown in to brighten things up.

The audience has rapidly become more sophisticated and hard to please, demanding applications that are more appealing and interactive. At the same time, the numbers of these users has increased exponentially; thus, the new, more sophisticated applications must be able to serve more users without losing any responsiveness.

Under any other circumstances this would be a programmer's nightmare—a user base demanding ever more features from increasingly over-taxed hardware; however, the application platforms and development tools have been keeping pace with the upheaval. In particular, server software has become increasingly sophisticated, delivering optimum performance while providing simplified programming to developers.

These changes have created an entirely different problem for developers. It is now all they can do to keep up with technology's pace. By the time a programmer is able to gain significant expertise in a system, all the rules will have changed yet again.

One of the newest Internet servers is Microsoft's IIS . The release of this software set new standards for performance and increased competition among the other suppliers of web servers, including Netscape, O'Reilly, Process Software, and others. The result is certain to be higher-quality, better-performing servers, regardless of who comes out on top.

IIS also brought forth ISAPI (Internet Server Application Programming Interface), a new architecture for the development of interactive web-based applications. Thus, the rules have changed for developers again: they must learn a whole a new approach.

You, as a developer, can benefit if you are willing to learn how to use ISAPI. This architecture provides the basis for developing web applications that are both higher performance and more flexible than ever before.

Intended Audience

This book is written for developers who find themselves caught up in this whirlwind of progress—developers who need to produce an application to run on Microsoft IIS and find that the requirements for such development are different from previous experience.

Intermediate-to-Advanced Windows Developers

Most of this book is intended for experienced developers. The reader is assumed to be familiar with a number of programming concepts, such as the following:

- **Windows programming:** a number of things otherwise specific to Windows GUI programming are important in ISAPI programming as well. A programmer who knows how to write a multithreaded GUI application in Windows should be able to write a similar application for the web after reading this book.

- **CGI programming:** the ISAPI programming model is not revolutionary; it is clearly evolved from the CGI (Common Gateway Interface) model. Knowledge of CGI, and of the HTTP protocol in particular, will serve you well as an ISAPI programmer. If you are new to this, new books dealing with the topic are appearing on the shelves every day.

◆ **Object-Oriented programming:** most of the programming discussed in the book uses either C++ or Borland's Delphi programming languages. Both of these languages are object-oriented, and in many cases, this attribute is exploited extensively.

The exceptions to these programming concepts are Chapter 2, "Using the Internet Database Connector," and Chapter 3, "Presenting an IDC Sample Application." These chapters should be accessible not only to experienced programmers but also to less experienced people charged with providing access to data on a corporate or departmental intranet.

Internet and Intranet Developers Designing Interactive Web Sites

The concepts in this book are focused on developing applications for intranets and the Internet. You're not likely to find the content of much use outside of this area.

Goals of This Book

The book is narrowly focused on a particular set of tools on a particular platform: Microsoft Internet Information Server on the Windows NT platform, using the ISAPI programming interfaces to interact with the server.

We have attempted to provide three key benefits for developers on this platform:

◆ solutions for common problems

◆ background for solving other ISAPI problems

◆ coherent documentation

The book should be taken as a guide to constructing applications by using this architecture, on this platform. It is not a general treatise on web application development, but on the use of this model to build web sites and applications. General background material is included with the chapters where necessary, but the book is not intended to be a tutorial on the web server itself.

The book's basic approach is to illustrate a number of development techniques applicable to the IIS server and the ISAPI interfaces, using real-world examples selected for their broad applicability. The goal is to provide a text that can be read cover-to-cover as a broad reference for this type of development, yet can be consulted quickly and easily for information on how to build solutions to a set of common problems.

Ideally, someone who needs to build a form-processing application should be able to grab this book, read the chapters covering form processing, and feel well prepared to tackle the job at hand. The same is true for enhanced usage logs, redirectors, retrieval of graphics, and so forth.

To us, the authors, this is a vital attribute of the book. We, and many programmers we know, seem to look for books like this when encountering a specific problem: we know we must produce a solution on the IIS platform, and we want to know how to display graphics we have in our databases. The book's approach of pairing portions of ISAPI with specific problems should appeal to solution-oriented developers.

Provide Solutions for Common Problems

Not only is the world of web application programming changing at a breakneck pace, but the time available to build these applications is decreasing just as rapidly. Clients and employers demand solutions ever more quickly to avoid lagging behind their competitors—a vicious cycle.

On one hand, developers want to research new technology so they can employ it better. On the other hand, not enough time is available to obtain the necessary experience and expertise for effectively preparing a project ahead of time. A book full of theory and descriptions of function prototypes and structures is of little use, because the developer has no time to digest its contents.

As a result, the developer obtains knowledge from the school of hard knocks. If the developer is lucky, the result will be a workable application, albeit with sloppy design due to an incomplete understanding of the factors at play. If the developer is unlucky, the project will fail because there was insufficient information available to make the critical decisions correctly.

This book is not going to buy you additional time to complete your project. It might, however, give you solutions for some of the problems you're likely to encounter in building typical web applications. After implementing these as described in the book, you're more likely to have enough knowledge to develop reasonable designs for the unique parts of your application.

We have found, based on our personal experience and conversations on Internet mailing lists and in Usenet newsgroups, that ISAPI developers often encounter very similar problems. For example, requests for instructions on retrieving multimedia information and controlling access to application resources are posted frequently. Although every application has its quirks, the solutions to many of these problems use ISAPI in similar ways.

The first goal of this book is to lay out a set of problems many ISAPI programmers are likely to encounter. This set must be sufficiently broad so the book illustrates the use of the important features of ISAPI.

Provide Background for Solving Other ISAPI Problems

The second goal of this book is to provide depth for the solutions it presents. Developers need to understand how to adapt a particular approach to the quirks of their specific needs. This book's chapters present not only the source code to the solution, but a detailed analysis of *why* and *how* the solution works.

Reading the other parts of the book—whether or not you expect to encounter the particular problems described—will give a comprehensive view of how ISAPI works and how to turn it to your advantage.

Provide Coherent Documentation

Because the field of ISAPI programming is so new, it can be very difficult to find the information necessary to understand the technology. Documentation is hard to come by, and what does exist is frequently mixed up or incorrect.

For example, the filter notification *SF_NOTIFY_END_OF_REQUEST* is new and not yet documented in any of Microsoft's literature at the time of this writing. Another example is the confusion caused by the documentation of the *ServerSupportFunction()*. In some documentation, Microsoft seems to mix explanations of the use of these functions in the context of filters and extensions (these are two distinct functions, despite sharing the same name).

Our goal is to help you take advantage of ISAPI to the greatest extent possible. You should be able to do this with a minimum of frustration and hair loss—hopefully the receding hair lines of the authors has been sufficient price to pay for the knowledge.

Tools Needed

Internet applications are constantly becoming more demanding in both the hardware and software required to execute the applications and the tools used to build them. Developers who hope to build these applications require well-equipped machines and up-to-date tools.

Hardware Requirements

The primary requirement for building Internet applications on this platform is a machine capable of running Microsoft Windows NT 4.0. A minimum of 32 megabytes of RAM is recommended; more will improve the speed of development. If the machine is to be running SQL Server as well, more memory becomes even more important.

Software Requirements

The solutions in this book generally require the following software:

- **Windows NT 4.0 or later:** the Server edition is required for deploying the application. Development can be done on the Workstation edition instead (in conjunction with Peer Web Services) if desired

- **Internet Information Server 2.0 or later:** (or Peer Web Services for development on NT Workstation)

- **Microsoft Visual C++ 4.2:** all C++ code presented in this book is written with this compiler. Previous versions differ in ISAPI support and implementation of the Standard Template Library. Presumably, future versions will offer some degree of compatibility with applications written for version 4.2

> **Note**
>
> Some minor changes to the source code will be required for users of Visual C++ 5.0. In particular, the re-implementation of the Standard Library now is (correctly) within the *std* namespace.
>
> As a result, any reference to components from that library need to be resolved to the correct namespace. This can be done simply by placing *std::* before each reference (e.g., std::string), or by using a namespace directive to bring the definitions into the current namespace (e.g., using namespace std;).

Chapters 2 and 3, dealing with the Internet Database Connector, do not require any compiler. Chapters 12 and 13 on Delphi require Borland Delphi 2.0 or later.

CHAPTER 1

Internet Information Server Programming Options

Among a very competitive field, Microsoft's IIS (Internet Information Server) is one of the highest performing web servers available on the Windows NT platform today—possibly the highest performing, depending on whose marketing propaganda you believe. Because of the widespread use of Windows NT in business today, and because of the price of IIS (free), it's definitely worth your while to investigate the use of this server for your web site.

IIS offers all the more traditional means of delivering content. Naturally, the retrieval of static web pages is well supported. In addition, dynamic web sites can be implemented through the CGI (Common Gateway Interface). A few new twists are added as well, with more coming down the pike in future versions.

For basic applications requiring only the dynamic creation of simple pages based on the contents of a database, an IDC (Internet Database Connector) is provided. This requires little programming expertise to create an application rapidly.

For more complex applications, IIS provides an industrial strength framework. Programming with ISAPI (Internet Server Application Program Interface) enables the creation of extremely high performance applications. Writing these might take more time than using the IDC or writing with CGI and Perl, for example, but the benefits can be enormous. The performance of a well-written ISAPI extension can exceed that of a similar CGI application by an order of magnitude. Moreover, the flexibility of ISAPI allows things that simply can't be accomplished any other way.

There are also other ways of writing dynamic web applications for IIS. Some third-party programs will enable you to program in Visual Basic. Microsoft's ActiveX and OLE technology are emerging as particularly powerful third-party programs for use on your web server as well. In particular, IIS version 3 supports Active Server Pages, in which you can script the interaction of ActiveX objects running on the server.

CGI (Common Gateway Interface)

If a field as young as web application development can be considered to have a traditional approach, then programming by using the CGI must be it. In many ways, this approach offers the worst features of all other options. Performance is poor, a good deal of knowledge of the HTTP protocol is required, and CGI applications are less flexible than ISAPI applications.

The term CGI actually refers to the architecture of the approach, rather than a particular tool or language to be used. Although Perl is by far the most popular for this purpose, a CGI application can be written in virtually any language. Several variations of the gateway are available as well. One in particular, WinCGI, is reported to improve performance beyond what can normally be expected from CGI.

In the CGI approach, the web server executes an external program to handle each applicable request. The server parses the contents of the request and passes this information to the CGI program. This program can act on the input information as necessary. It outputs data to the client simply by writing to the standard output device. The web server intercepts this output and pipes it to the client.

The most significant disadvantage to CGI is its slow performance. The CGI architecture requires the server to run the external program for each request received for it. This involves creating a new process in the operating system, loading the executable image from disk, and flushing it all out upon completion. In addition, resources such as database connections must be reestablished at each invocation; they cannot be cached and reused because the process does not persist between calls.

In some cases this may not be a problem. When usage is expected to be low so that performance will not be critical, and shortening the time taken for implementation is tantamount, CGI may well be the appropriate choice.

The IDC (Internet Database Connector)

You can publish your database—allow users to view and interact with the data—by using the IDC. This requires only a minimal amount of coding from a developer. Instead of complex coding, you provide SQL queries, which IDC executes on the database, and templates, which describe how the data is to be presented to (and collected from) the user.

Implementing an IDC application does not require any knowledge of C++, DLLs, or similar programming concepts, which are ubiquitous in ISAPI and, to a lesser extent, CGI. It does require knowledge of HTML and SQL. This simplicity comes at the price of much of the application's robustness and flexibility. You give up a good deal of control over the user interface as well as almost any capability to validate data.

This tradeoff is appropriate for many applications. For example, a simple application to be used only by members of your department might not need to be particularly pretty, and you should be able to require its users to understand the effect of the information they are supplying, alleviating worry about data validation.

Thus, there is a class of applications to which the IDC lends itself well. For more complex or robust requirements, you might need to look to other tools.

Alternative Development Tools

Deciding which approach to take in developing a web application requires consideration of a number of factors. These factors include:

- **Performance of the application:** how quickly can the application respond to user requests, and how many users can it support?

- **Difficulty of implementing the application:** what is the learning curve associated with the technology, and how much code does the approach require?

- **Robustness:** can the application withstand special circumstances, including error conditions and hackers?

- **Reusability of its components:** can the work invested in the application be leveraged for other applications in the future—and can legacy code can be employed in this application?

All of these factors present the opportunity for making tradeoffs. Many developers, including Microsoft, have developed alternatives to web application development which excel in some areas and suffer in others.

ISAPI excels in all categories except implementation. CGI is somewhat easier to implement, but offers poor performance. Code written for the IDC is not robust and cannot be leveraged to other platforms.

In addition to using CGI, the IDC, or ISAPI, several alternatives are available for writing interactive web applications.

OLEISAPI

OLEISAPI is an interface between IIS and OLE servers. It enables you to develop your web applications as OLE servers, using tools such as Visual Basic.

OLEISAPI was originally provided by Microsoft as an example of interaction between ISAPI and OLE. As a stripped-down sample program, it is not appropriate for a mission-critical system. The original code was buggy and unable to handle large amounts of data. Several people have debugged and enhanced that original sample.

Many people report success in using OLEISAPI on their servers, but this is not recommended for serious development. In particular, now that Active Server Pages are available there is a far more robust and powerful way to leverage your OLE servers.

Active Server Pages

The primary new feature in IIS version 3 is ASP (Active Server Pages). This technology provides several significant benefits to developers, as described in the following list.

- ◆ **Server Side Scripting:** developers can now dynamically generate web pages by using VBScript. This avoids the need to learn more complex computer languages such as C++.

- ◆ **Access to ActiveX Objects:** the scripts might tie together ActiveX controls, which you can write yourself. A number of controls are provided, including those necessary for database access.

- ◆ **Automatic Session Tracking:** one of the more annoying problems for all web developers is tracking which requests come from what user session; ASP takes care of this automatically.

These benefits are compelling. Performance of ASP is likely to be somewhat worse than ISAPI (although the technology is too new to quantify this).

Third-Party Solutions

A number of third-party tools are available to help you create interactive web applications. Most of these aim to improve on CGI development in one or more of the following areas:

◆ **Performance:** "traditional" CGI applications tend to be slow relative to other development models.

◆ **Complexity:** CGI development also tends to require a lot of knowledge of the HTTP protocol and various programming concepts.

◆ **Reuse of existing code:** until the recent release of ASP, there was no industrial strength way to use existing Visual Basic code on your web site.

Typically, these tools are designed to handle individual requests only. That is, they only offer a means of handling *vertical* slices of functionality, where a single request is handled beginning-to-end by a single component. No means is offered for implementing *horizontal* functionality, where a component implements a part of the functionality for the entire system (such as validation and security). For a more complete explanation on this, see the information on extension DLLs and filters in the "ISAPI-Based Solutions" section. Figures 1.1 and 1.2 depict these differing ways to slice the functionality of the application.

A few of these third-party products are worthy of mention. Each offers a somewhat different approach toward solving the problems with CGI. Of course, they might or might not be appropriate for your application; if the following descriptions seem promising, you should seek out more information at the addresses given. Other products exist as well; if you need, for example, to use existing Visual Basic code, you might want to look around.

webAction

webAction is a product from classTools, Inc. The product consists of a set of tools enabling improvement in the performance of legacy CGI code. Its primary goal is to help you develop new applications that enjoy the same performance gains, using a development environment you're already familiar with, such as Visual Basic or Borland Delphi 2.0. An additional advantage is speedier application development when using their library of high-level functions.

These performance gains and integration with Visual Basic and Delphi are accomplished by an ISAPI server extension and filter. The cornerstone of the mechanism is an OLE automation interface. This interface can load and cache your OLE automation servers, invoking them as necessary. This approach offers significant advantages over CGI programming, but will still be less efficient than a program written natively in ISAPI, due to the inefficiencies of the interface used by OLE automation. You can visit classTools, Inc., at:

```
http://www.classtools.com/
```

Tornado

Tornado has a number of similarities to webAction in that it is designed to enable integration of programs written in Visual Basic and other languages; however, it was developed with some different goals in mind. The most significant difference is that webAction emphasizes rapid development of new applications (through the use of libraries and custom OLE automation interfaces). Tornado emphasizes leveraging existing applications and site administration.

Tornado is implemented through an ISAPI extension, which communicates with a server application. You can turn your own applications into servers (in the OLE sense) by adding a special OCX control to that application. The documentation claims it will work with any development tool that can use an OCX.

The disadvantages of this approach are that it is intrusive and might not scale well. Existing applications need to be modified to include the Tornado OCX. This is a simple operation, but it means you must be able to modify the source code. Also, the scheme Tornado uses—IIS communicating with a server application—might not scale well to large sites with many concurrent users. In addition, Tornado suffers from the same performance issues as webAction: placing an extra communication layer between server and application degrades performance in comparison to a native ISAPI implementation. You can get more information on Tornado at:

```
http://www.eudev.com/tornado.htm
```

WebHub

WebHub, from HREF Tools Corp., follows a rather different approach than the previous two tools. Although some capability is provided for creating applications without writing code, WebHub is designed primarily for developing interactive web applications in Borland Delphi.

By sacrificing the flexibility of integration with heterogeneous environments, WebHub is able to achieve far tighter coupling with its single target platform. Delphi developers are able to build their web applications in the same way they are already accustomed to building Windows applications. This is achieved by implementing the components of WebHub as Visual Component Library components. For more information about WebHub, visit HREF Tools Corp. at:

```
http://www.href.com
```

ISAPI-Based Solutions

ISAPI is far more powerful than traditional CGI in two key respects:

◆ **Performance:** well-designed ISAPI extensions can improve performance by an order of magnitude over a similar CGI application.

◆ **Flexibility:** ISAPI extensions enjoy a close integration with the server, which enables some actions to be executed more cheaply; ISAPI filters enable operations that couldn't be implemented in any other way.

This power does not come free, however. ISAPI programming requires more sophistication from the developer. In particular, it requires a greater understanding of the operation of the server and stronger programming skills in general.

An understanding of the way the client and server communicate is important as well. This is not specific to ISAPI programming, though—CGI programmers need expertise in this as well. The HTTP specification describes such things as the types of requests that might be made, how data is encoded, and how to respond to requests. The current version of the HTTP specification is 1.0 and is described in RFC 1945. Version 1.1 is currently being considered. Both of these texts are included on the companion CD.

Most obviously, you must learn ISAPI concepts before you can use them. This means understanding how and when to use extensions and filters, the two types of architectural components defined by ISAPI.

Note You should be aware of an unfortunate problem with the terminology used by the Microsoft documentation. The particular terms chosen can be confusing.

The terms *application* and *extension* both refer to the same thing: an ISAPI DLL that is invoked to handle a particular request. Neither refers to an ISAPI filter. This is confusing for two reasons.

First, in the more general context of Windows programming, both ISAPI filters and ISAPI extensions would be considered extensions. They are both implemented as DLLs, which are loaded by the server to extend its functionality.

Second, in the broader sense of the word application—a tool employed by the end user to accomplish a task—the services of many ISAPI extensions and filters might combine to provide all the necessary functionality.

Throughout the rest of this book, the word *filter* will be used to refer to ISAPI filters; the words *application* and *extension* will both be used for ISAPI extension .DLLs, just as in the Microsoft documentation.

After you can plan the architecture of your system, you need to be able to use the API itself. Depending on the tools you will use, this could mean learning the functions and data structures defined in the ISAPI headers. If you are using C++ with MFC or Delphi in conjunction with the framework presented in Chapter 13, "Using the Delphi ISAPI Framework," you need to understand the way the framework abstracts the interface.

Finally, the architecture of ISAPI in the context of the IIS will force you to approach some of your programming a bit differently, giving much more careful consideration to issues you might have glossed over in other types of projects. For example, debugging ISAPI is more complicated than standard Windows applications. Also, the fundamentally multithreaded nature of ISAPI forces you to always keep synchronization in mind. Finally, because your objective is almost certainly a server that can function unattended for extended periods, you must be more careful with memory management than you otherwise might.

The following sections will explore the ISAPI architecture in more detail. The benefits of ISAPI programming, including its potential for extremely high performance and great flexibility will be discussed. The roles of filters and extensions are explained, and various approaches to programming ISAPI components are explored.

Performance

The nature of ISAPI extensions enables them to be executed much more quickly than an equivalent application written to use the CGI interface. This is primarily due to the way they are invoked. An ISAPI extension is implemented as a DLL that is generally loaded only once by the server and called in memory each time it needs to service a request.

In contrast, CGI applications are loaded each time they are called. The obvious cost is that of creating a new process and loading the executable from disk for each use. In practice, it is likely the CGI application will be held in a disk cache, but this still leaves the expense of copying the image from cache and performing address fix-ups as necessary.

In addition to automatically avoiding these costs, a well-planned ISAPI extension can benefit from its memory residency. It is possible for the extension to cache frequently used and expensive-to-create resources such as database connections. A strategy of using database connections from a pool created at start-up can significantly speed an application in many cases. Designs like these require very careful attention to the synchronization of multiple threads and to memory management issues, so greatly improved performance does come at some cost.

Flexibility

Both ISAPI applications and filters are, in effect, extensions to the server itself. This close relationship allows a cooperation between the architectural components that can only be duplicated in CGI at a great expense, or not at all.

For example, an ISAPI extension can easily redirect the user to an alternate resource on the server, transparently as far as the user is concerned. A similar action in CGI requires either a redirect response to the user's browser or special provisions to obtain or execute that alternate resource. In either case, the ISAPI solution is superior in simplicity and performance.

ISAPI filters, which will be discussed later in this chapter in more detail, offer a whole class of operations otherwise difficult or impossible. For example, directing users to different pages depending on the type of their browser is simple in ISAPI. It requires implementing only a single filter. With CGI, however, this would require either user intervention (requiring the user to select a link to the alternate resource) or complex redirection code that also interrupts the user's direct access to the system.

Extension DLLs

ISAPI Extension DLLs are the more frequently used of the two types of ISAPI components. They usually take the place of CGI scripts in more traditional web applications and are invoked to service a particular request from the user. For example, the user might click on a hyperlink that would send a request to the server to retrieve an image from a database. More commonly, an extension is sent, the contents of an HTML form filled in by the user.

ISAPI Extensions are used to provide a vertical slice of functionality (see figure 1.1). They completely implement the handling of a single request.

Calling an Extension

When the server receives a request, it first determines what to do with that request. This is based on several things, including the file name extension of the requested resource (by looking in its table of extension mappings), the type of request (GET or POST), and the content of the request (a GET with a question mark indicates an executable). In general, a POST request or a GET request with a question mark following the resource (for a resource with a file name extension of .DLL) is an indication to execute an ISAPI extension.

If the server determines an ISAPI extension is to be executed, it first checks whether that extension has already been loaded into its cache. If not, the DLL is loaded. Its location is determined by the request itself. The URL is converted by the server from a logical directory name to the physical location on disk.

After the DLL has been physically loaded, the server calls the extension's *GetFilterVersion()* function. This allows the server and extension to ensure compatibility by comparing the version of the ISAPI specification they implement. It also provides an opportunity for the extension to initialize any shared resources.

Figure 1.1

ISAPI applications provide vertical slices of functionality.

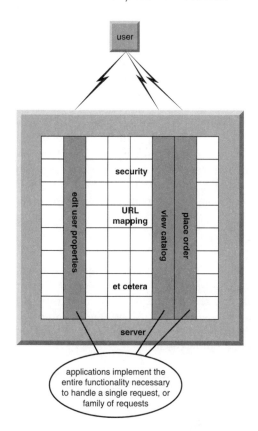

Processing the Request

With the DLL in memory, the request is serviced by calling the function *HttpExtensionProc()* in the DLL. This is where you, the ISAPI programmer, place the logic that actually performs the desired operation. The server will pass to this function all the necessary information, including the contents of the request itself. It will also pass callback functions you can use to send data to the user, obtain the values of any information sent with the request, and perform a number of other operations.

It's very important to keep in mind the potential for many users on the server simultaneously requesting processing from the same extension. The server might start multiple threads to handle all these requests, causing the extensions to execute in several different threads simultaneously. Failure to account for this can cause data corruption and crashes. For more information on this, see the section "Multi-threading."

Filters

Filters are a new concept in programming Internet applications, with no direct analog in traditional CGI programming. This feature in particular contributes to the flexibility of ISAPI programming. Whereas ISAPI extensions are designed to service a particular request, filters interact with the server in a completely different way. A filter is called by the server every time an event occurs that the filter is interested in, regardless of the resource being requested.

ISAPI Filters are used to provide a horizontal slice of functionality (see figure 1.2). They implement a single facet of functionality for all requests.

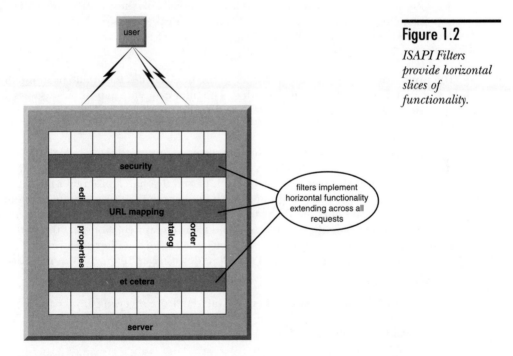

Figure 1.2

ISAPI Filters provide horizontal slices of functionality.

For example, a filter can request to be notified each time a request—*any* request—is received by the server. The filter can then inspect the request itself and change it if desired. It can use this for many purposes.

One possible use is to route the request to different directory structures depending on the language the user speaks. For example, English speakers get pages with

English text, while Spanish speakers can read Spanish pages. The desired language can be determined by examining the *Accept-Language* header from some browsers, or by setting a cookie. Depending on the result, the filter can alter the requested URL to point to the appropriate language-specific directory hierarchy.

Because of their differing nature, filters are invoked in a different manner from extensions. Filters are loaded by IIS at the time the server starts up. The server determines which DLLs to load based on a list found in the system registry.

As each filter is loaded, its *GetFilterVersion()* function is called. As with extensions, this allows the server and filter to verify compatibility and allows the filter to perform any initialization. However, the filter must also indicate to the server which events it would like to be notified of, and with what priority—that is, whether it should be notified before or after other filters.

The server builds lists of the filters that should be called for each type of event. Then, as events occur in the course of processing, the server calls the *HttpFilterProc()* function belonging to the interested filters. Each filter is called in turn. The order is determined by the priority the filter requested; ties are resolved by the order in which the filters appeared in the registry.

The notification is passed from one filter to the next. Each filter should examine the notification and decide what to do with it. The filter can react to it in various ways, for example, by appending to a log or by changing the data it received (as described previously).

After it has completed its business, the filter returns control to the server along with an indication of how the notification has been handled. This is similar to the way a message from the Windows message queue is passed through a program's message handler function. The filter might indicate it has handled the event completely and that no subsequent filters should be triggered. More frequently, though, the filter allows any downstream filters a chance to see the event as well. Note that the return status value is not necessarily related to the type of action the filter performed. The filter might act on a notification and still allow downstream filters their own chance at it.

A filter can subscribe to a variety of events, ranging from receiving any data to authenticating a user. For a complete list and explanation of these, see Chapter 7, "Understanding ISAPI Filters."

Programming with ISAPI

The benefits of using ISAPI were already described, along with the caveat that these advantages come at a price, collected in the implementation of the system. A programmer needs to spend time learning the ISAPI specification. Even after becoming experienced with it, there will be a number of issues to be accounted for, which are likely to increase the time necessary for implementation.

Although C++ is usually the language used in ISAPI programming, ISAPI presents a language-neutral interface. Any development tool capable of producing a 32-bit DLL to export functions with C linkage can be used to create ISAPI extensions and filters. Many developers are successfully using Borland's Delphi 2.0 to build web sites employing ISAPI. If you want to use other languages, you will first need to obtain the appropriate declarations for the interface; the interface for Delphi is included on this book's companion CD-ROM (see Chapter 12, "ISAPI Programming Using Borland Delphi 2.0" for more information).

You can approach ISAPI programming in different ways. The most obvious, the "SDK" approach, simply employs the ISAPI interface directly with no additional help. C++ programmers can use MFC, which simplifies some of the chores. Delphi programmers can use the framework presented in Chapter 13, "Using the Delphi ISAPI Application Framework." Regardless of the approach chosen, there are some considerations that you must pay special attention to.

SDK Approach

ISAPI programming at its lowest level involves communicating with the web server by using a protocol specified by Microsoft. C++ programmers can find this specification included with Visual C++ or in the Win32 SDK. There are two important files, httpext.h and httpfilt.h. The former declares the interfaces for extensions and the latter declares the interfaces for filters.

A server following the ISAPI protocol will load your DLL and call the prescribed entry point when appropriate. The specification also defines a number of data structures that will be passed. This process is fairly straightforward in the case of extensions. Filters, on the other hand, must cope with a large number of data structures and callback functions, depending on the types of notifications they receive.

Despite how this sounds, using the ISAPI protocol is not rocket science. It doesn't take any longer to learn than other feature-rich APIs, and it's generally easy to employ once it's understood.

MFC Approach

Visual C++ ISAPI developers have at their disposal a powerful tool for developing ISAPI extensions and filters. MFC provides many useful services for ISAPI developers. Because it provides a higher level of abstraction for both ISAPI and HTTP communication, it is easier to learn than the bare SDK approach.

The Visual C++ environment also helps you create ISAPI extensions and filters. There is an ISAPI AppWizard that will create a project containing an application, a filter, or both. Unfortunately, this is not as well integrated as other parts of the environment. In particular, you would expect the Class Wizard to add request handlers automatically (just as message handlers can be added today). Hopefully, this support will improve in future versions.

After you have learned how to use MFC for ISAPI, it will help you develop your applications more quickly as well. The framework will determine which functions should be called for handling a request. It handles all interactions between the server and the user's browser, and it parses form requests automatically, within certain limitations. Most of this work is pure drudgery—by freeing the developer from having to deal with it manually, MFC supports greater productivity.

MFC does not solve all your problems, though. In particular, the mechanism MFC uses to parse the contents of a request and dispatch the appropriate function call is quite limited. In particular, it breaks down when used with multiple-select list boxes and dynamically generated forms. Chapter 11, "Advanced Form Processing," discusses these problems and presents a class library you can use in these situations.

Special Considerations

Regardless of whether you're creating a filter or an extension, using MFC or not, or using C++, Delphi, or another language, there are special considerations you must keep in mind. The context in which your DLLs are used forces you to emphasize some factors you might not be accustomed to considering. In all these cases, though, the issues are not insurmountable. Moreover, as you gain experience, these issues will become part of your normal course of thought so you won't notice the difference.

These important issues are

- ◆ **Debugging:** requires some special preparation

- ◆ **Multithreaded:** execution requires that you protect shared resources to avoid crashes and corrupted data

- ◆ **Memory Management:** is necessary to avoid memory leaks and overwrites, to ensure maximum availability of the server

Debugging ISAPI DLLs by Using VC++

Debugging ISAPI extensions and filters requires some special techniques. Ordinary Windows programs can be debugged directly in the context in which they will be run. In contrast, interactively debugging your ISAPI DLL will result in an execution environment that differs from the DLL's natural habitat. Specifically, under normal operation, IIS runs as a Windows NT system service, so your DLLs are running on behalf of the system rather than a particular user. When you debug, though, they will be running on your behalf.

As a result of this, running your extension or filter might result in problems that don't occur while you're debugging. For example, if your ODBC datasource is accessed through a User DSN rather than a System DSN, the data access will fail when run normally, but succeed when you try to debug it.

Chapter 14, "Debugging ISAPI Filters," is devoted to describing how to debug ISAPI code, including related issues.

Multithreading

IIS is able to service many simultaneous requests by handling each request in a separate thread. If multiple simultaneous requests happen to involve your ISAPI code, your code might find itself executing simultaneously in many different threads. This is true of both applications and filters.

Most Windows programs are written with only a modest amount of multithreading, if any at all. Consequently, most programmers are not accustomed to building programs that are completely threadsafe. Failing to do so in your ISAPI applications or filters virtually guarantees your code will fail.

In practice, this means you must do two things in your programming:

> You should eliminate global or static data, unless that data is constant.

> You must synchronize access to all remaining shared resources.

With regard to access synchronization, you might want to perform all database access through a single connection. You must implement a scheme to prevent multiple simultaneous access to the database object (because MFC is not threadsafe at the object level). One approach is to use a critical section to surround the section of code that accesses the database. These issues are covered in more detail in Chapter 5, "Extracting Multimedia Images from a Database."

Memory Management

Memory management is an issue all programmers should pay careful attention to; however, memory leaks and overwrites go unnoticed many times in everyday application programs. In ISAPI programming, one objective of which is a high-availability server, such errors have a longer time to manifest themselves. In addition, such problems can snowball. For example, if each execution of your ISAPI extension leaks just a small amount, the wasted memory can become significant after many thousands of executions.

 The implementation of the C++ Standard Template Library delivered with Visual C++ 4.2 and earlier has a number of memory leaks. For example, each time you instantiate a map container, you will lose several bytes of memory.

Visual C++ 5.0 resolves these problems. This significant improvement is itself enough to upgrade. The new version also adds support for the keywords *mutable*, *explicit*, and *bool*, so hard-core C++ programmers will find a lot to enjoy in it.

Tools are available to detect and isolate these problems. One such program is BoundsChecker, produced by Nu-Mega Technologies (www.numega.com). This tool not only alerts you to the presence of memory leaks, but also shows you the source code line on which the memory was allocated.

Summary

A number of options are available for creating interactive web applications to run on the Microsoft IIS platform. All these options involve tradeoffs between performance, flexibility, and ease of programming. If the application demands maximum performance and flexibility, the hands-down winner is native ISAPI programming, the subject of most of the rest of this book.

ISAPI applications are implemented as DLLs so they can be loaded as extensions to IIS itself. They are loaded once and execute within the server's address space. Following the initial load, each subsequent invocation is accomplished by a simple function call. The result of this is the potential for blazing performance from a well-designed application.

The flexibility of the ISAPI architecture exceeds that of any architecture for developing interactive web applications and is influenced by two factors. First, ISAPI is tightly integrated with the server. This allows some functions to be implemented that would be less efficient or even impossible with another architecture. Second, ISAPI filters offer a completely different approach for designing web applications than has previously been possible.

The ISAPI architecture specifies two different types of components, each with quite different uses. ISAPI applications are analogous to CGI scripts: they provide the services for handling a single request (or a family of requests) in its entirety. In contrast, ISAPI filters each provide a part of the processing for *every* request received by the system. Applications provide vertical slices of functionality; filters provide horizontal slices.

All this comes at a price, though. Creating ISAPI-based solutions is demanding in terms of programming skills. The most obvious of these demands is the necessity of learning the ISAPI architecture itself, which can be alleviated in part by using an object-oriented class library to provide higher-level abstractions of common tasks. The Microsoft Foundation Classes offer such a library; this book presents one for use by Delphi developers.

The secondary demands on the skill of a programmer can be significant. These demands are realized in a programming environment that can be harder to manage. ISAPI applications are heavily multithreaded—a headache even for programmers experienced in its use, and few programmers have the necessary experience. Also, proper management of memory and other resources is crucial. To complicate the whole affair, debugging ISAPI systems requires some special techniques.

One alternative to the complexity of ISAPI programming is the IDC (Internet Database Connector), which is described in the next two chapters.

CHAPTER 2

Using the Internet Database Connector

The IDC (Internet Database Connector) is a feature of the IIS (Internet Information Server) that enables some applications to be written quickly and easily. Before you start programming with it, you need to determine whether your applications are among those that can be written effectively using this tool.

To make an informed decision, you should understand what the IDC is and the cost of the simplicity that it delivers. The beginning of this chapter will describe the strengths and weaknesses of the IDC and enumerate the situations in which it is particularly effective or ineffective so that you'll have the information you need to decide whether the IDC is effective for you.

The chapter will then describe how to write an IDC application. Basic IDC Programming is introduced first. This presents the components of an IDC application and how to put them together to accomplish simple tasks. This is followed by an explanation of the concepts necessary for Advanced IDC Programming. This adds some more complex features of the IDC and describes how to put everything together to solve more intricate programming problems.

What the Internet Database Connector Is

The IDC provides a simple way to publish and interact with the contents of your databases on the Internet. It is an ISAPI application that is included with IIS.

Users can produce interactive database applications by writing only minimal code. Instead, they provide SQL queries that IDC executes on the database, and templates that describe how the data is to be presented to (and collected from) the end user.

Implementing an IDC application does not require any knowledge of C++, DLLs and similar programming concepts. It does require knowledge of HTML (HyperText Markup Language) and SQL (Structured Query Language). Even then, some users might even be able to get by with minimal SQL expertise by using the visual query generator that is part of Microsoft Access (or a similar tool) to write the code, and cut-and-paste it into their IDC scripts.

When to Use the IDC

Writing IDC applications is simple, quick, and relatively inflexible. Their simplicity comes from the freedom from strong programming skill requirements, as described previously. This makes IDC applications a good choice for someone who is not necessarily a programming professional, but has a need to allow many people access to his database.

Programming in IDC also frees you from ISAPI's typical development cycle:

1. Test

2. Shutdown service

3. Compile and link

4. Restart service

The files making up an IDC application are interpreted, providing the quick cycle time and feedback that Visual Basic programmers enjoy. However, the simplicity of IDC programming eliminates the performance degradation typically associated Visual Basic, PowerBuilder, and other interpreted languages. Combine all of this with the simplicity of writing the application in the first place, and it's clear that you can build an IDC application in a fairly short time compared to traditional client/server programming or ISAPI development.

You pay for this simplicity by sacrificing a good deal of flexibility. You give up a good deal of control over the user interface, in both the design of each page and the flow from one page to another. You give up almost any capability to validate data, other than what you can describe via referential integrity or stored procedures—and that requires more programming expertise. You give up the capability to tie related data through the user interface, such as enabling and disabling controls depending on the setting of checkboxes, unless you do extra programming in VBScript or another scripting language.

IDC applications work well in the following program environments:

◆ **Simple applications:** many basic applications, such as guest books, message bases (as illustrated in the following chapter), and presentation of product specifications, demand neither a complex user interface and *data validation* nor flashy presentation.

◆ **Departmental applications:** although you're generally not able to craft an application as well tuned, integrated, or visually appealing as you could with a full-blown ISAPI application, this is not always called for in a program intended solely for internal use. If you need a means for checking warehouse inventory or customer history, you might be able to satisfy all of your needs with IDC applications.

◆ **Prototyping:** whether or not your final requirements demand more than IDC can deliver, you may still find it useful to use in prototyping. IDC applications can help you by quickly putting your data model into use so that you can verify its design and performance. You can also lay out sample pages with real data to give your users a taste of what you plan to implement for them.

◆ **Data Entry:** you can easily write a quick and dirty data entry program to populate your database. Even if you plan to throw out the program after you're done with it, you've still got a good way to enter the data that your *real* program will eventually access.

IDC Programming Basics

Programming the IDC is straightforward, but requires a different mindset than other methods of programming. This section will show how an IDC application is constructed and how to put the components together into a practical application. The components of an IDC application belong to two groups of files: .IDC files and .HTX files.

The .IDC file that is requested specifies the actions that are to be taken on the database. The results of these actions are then processed with the .HTX file, together creating the HTML code that is the response to the user.

It's extremely important to understand the order in which elements of the request are processed, and by whom. It can be difficult to keep this in mind because you will be looking at the .HTX file, which appears to draw the entire operation together. In fact, this is quite the opposite of the truth—the .IDC file is what drives the process, which is performed in discrete steps.

1. The user requests data. This is done in the form of an HTTP GET or POST request referring to the .IDC file that handles the query.

2. IIS recognizes that .IDC files are to be processed by an ISAPI application called HTTPODBC.DLL. This is loaded if necessary; however, the process is easier to understand if you overlook these details and imagine that the .IDC and .HTX files themselves are doing the job. It retrieves any variables that may have been sent with the request as HTML form elements and passes them to the requested .IDC file.

3. The .IDC file is scanned for references to variables. When one is found, the reference is replaced with the value that was retrieved in the previous step.

4. After the query has been determined, a connection to the specified database is made and the query is passed to it.

5. When the result set is returned to the .IDC file it is packaged and sent to the specified .HTX file along with any variables that were passed into the .HTX file.

6. The .HTX file is scanned, looking for variable references and keywords. These determine the HTML page that is generated.

7. The generated HTML page is sent back to the user.

IDC Files

The .IDC file is what is requested by the user, and is effectively the agent driving the production of the web page to be returned to the user. It specifies for the Internet Database Connector all of the information necessary for accessing the database, as well as the .HTX file to be used to format the information that's retrieved as shown in figure 2.1.

The file consists of a list of field names and their values.

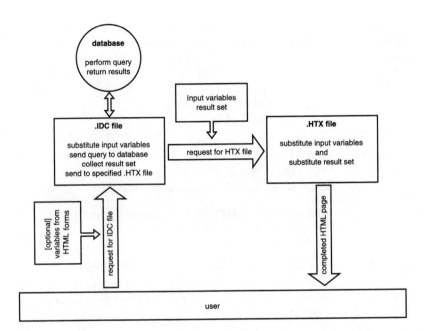

Figure 2.1

The processing of an IDC appli-cation is a cycle of discrete steps.

IDC Fields

Each field (except for the SQL statement) is on its own line, and has the form

```
Fieldname: Value[, Value][...]
```

The exception is the SQLStatement field, which may need to be many lines long. The continuation of lines is indicated by a plus sign ('+') as shown in the following lines of code

```
SQLStatement:
+SELECT UserID, UserName, UserEMail, UserPassword
+FROM Users
```

Table 2.1 lists the fields that can be specified in an .IDC file. Any unrecognized field names result in an error message returned to the user. Since this error message is oriented towards debugging rather than helping the user, you'll want to avoid it. The error message will look something like this:

```
Error Performing Query
The query file contains an unrecognized field BadField: BadValue.
```

Where *BadField* is the unrecognized field name, and *BadValue* is the value that you tried to assign to it.

The first three items in the table, Datasource, Template, and SQLStatement are always required; the remaining fields need only be provided if you need options other than the defaults.

Table 2.1
IDC Fields

Field	Description
Datasource	The ODBC System Data Source Name indicating the database to which the query is to be executed.
Template	The name of the .HTX file that describes how the data should be formatted. Note that this can be determined by a variable.
SQLStatement	The SQL statement to execute; this field may be defined more than once if multiple statements are necessary. (Please refer to Cross Reference following this table.)
DefaultParameters	A comma-delimited list of default parameters and their values: each pair is given as *ParamName=value.* Quotation marks are not necessary.
Expires	The number of seconds for which the page can be cached before it must be refreshed. The default is 0 and shouldn't be cached.
MaxFieldSize	The maximum size of any field; the default is 8 KB. Overflows result in truncation.
MaxRecords	The maximum number of rows that can be retrieved. The default is unlimited.
ODBCConnection	Can be set to pool to improve performance by using database connections from a pool of resources when desirable. The default is normally nopool, but can be changed with the registry setting HKEY_LOCAL_MACHINE\SYSTEM \CurrentControlSet\Services\W3SVC\ Parameters\PoolIDCConnections.
ODBCOptions	Allows special settings for the ODBC driver: see the following section for descriptions.
Password	The password for the specified Username. It may be omitted if the password is null.

Field	Description
RequiredParameters	A list of parameters that must be supplied for the query. If any are omitted, IDC returns an error message to the user, avoiding possible errors from the database (Please refer to the Tip following this table.)
Translationfile	The name of a file containing a list of mappings from special characters to their HTML equivalents.
Username	A valid username for the System Data Source Name specified by the Datasource field.
Content-type	A valid *MIME* type for the text returned to the user. This defaults to "text/html."

See "Using Multiple Database Queries" under "Advanced IDC Programming" in this chapter for more information about using multiple SQLStatements.

Cross Reference

 It's a good idea to use the RequiredParameters field to list all of the parameters that the corresponding .HTX file needs in addition to those used here in the .IDC. You'll find this documentation can save you from a good deal of debugging headaches.

There are several sub-fields that you can put into the ODBCOptions field. Reasonable defaults are provided, so you only need to specify one of these sub-fields if your needs differ from the defaults; if you have no out-of-the-ordinary ODBC needs, you need not include the ODBCOptions field at all.

These sub-fields and their values are be given in a list following the ODBCOptions field. They are given as *OptionName=value*. For example,

```
ODBCOptions: SQL_ACCESS_MODE=1, SQL_MAX_ROWS=10
```

The set of options that can be specified for the ODBCOptions field are described in table 2.2.

Table 2.2
Advanced ODBC Fields

Option Name	Value	Description
SQL_ACCESS_MODE	0=R/W 1=Read	The locking mode for the query. This allows you to improve performance by optimizing database locking strategies.

continues

Table 2.2, Continued
Advanced ODBC Fields

Option Name	Value	Description
SQL_LOGIN_TIMEOUT	Integer	The number of seconds to allow before disconnecting an uncompleted logon request. The default is driver dependent. If 0, timeout is disabled and a connection request can wait indefinitely.
SQL_OPT_TRACE	0=Off 1=On	Flag enabling a log feature that writes each ODBC function's call to a text file. Default is 0.
SQL_OPT_TRACEFILE	Filename	The file name used by the trace function enabled by SQL_OPT_TRACE.
SQL_PACKET_SIZE	Integer	The network packet size in bytes that is used when transferring data between the database and the IDC.
SQL_TRANSLATE_DLL	Filename	The name of a .DLL file used by the ODBC driver for character set translation.
SQL_TRANSLATE_ OPTION	Integer	A value defined by the translation DLL that specifies the features to be used.
SQL_TXN_ISOLATION	1=Read Uncommitted 2=Read Committed 4=Repeatable Read 8=Serializable 16=Versioning	Defines the SQL isolation level to be used for the query. This provides another option for performance tuning.
SQL_MAX_LENGTH	Integer	The maximum number of bytes that can be returned to IDC by the database. You will normally want to use the same value as MaxFieldSize.
SQL_MAX_ROWS	Integer	The maximum number of rows that the database will return to IDC. If your

Option Name	Value	Description
		ODBC driver implements it, it is preferable to using MaxRecords because it limits the amount of data that must be transferred between the database and IDC.
SQL_NOSCAN	0=Scan 1=Don't scan	Flag enabling a small performance increase by not scanning the query string for variables.
SQL_QUERY_TIMEOUT	Integer 1=No timeout	The number of seconds to allow before canceling an uncompleted query. The default is 0, meaning that timeout is disabled and a request may wait indefinitely.
Integer	Driver Specific	A list of driver-specific option numbers and their values, given as Number=value.

Other than the last one listed, none of these fields are themselves specific to a particular ODBC driver. However, different drivers may interpret or implement some of the values differently, as noted.

IDC Variables

Before any of the fields are interpreted, they are scanned for variable references. The values are substituted, and then the contents of the fields are examined. These variables and their values come to the .IDC file from fields in a form on the web page that requested the .IDC file.

You can make substitutions into any of the fields. Typically, you will only do this to specify values in the SQLStatement. For example, you may want to provide the values for an insert statement like this:

```
SQLStatement:
+ INSERT INTO Employees ( Name, ID )
+ VALUES ( '%EmployeeName%', %EmployeeID% )
```

Notice that the variable names are delimited with percent signs ("%") on either side. This indicates to the .IDC parser that the string they delimit is the name of a variable whose value should be substituted at this location.

When using variables in this manner, it's important to delimit the values the way your ODBC driver expects. The previous example assumes that the Name column is a string type and the ID column is numeric.

The *Access* database expects date values to be delimited with number signs ("#").

Although most of your SQL statements will look something like the previous example, you're not limited to substituting the values of columns. You can substitute any part of the statement, if you like. In fact, a perfectly legal .IDC file could contain the field:

```
SQLStatement: %Statement%
```

assuming that you provide a suitable value for the Statement variable at runtime.

The preceding SQL statement might have been initiated by a web page containing this bit of code:

```
<FORM METHOD=POST ACTION="sample.idc">
  Insert a new employee:<BR>
  Name: <INPUT TYPE=TEXT NAME="EmployeeName"><BR>
  ID: <INPUT TYPE=TEXT NAME="EmployeeID"><BR>
  <INPUT TYPE=SUBMIT>
</FORM>
```

The NAME attribute of the form's fields determines the names of the variables that will be available in the .IDC file.

You may also use server variables here. For more information on these, see the following section on .HTX files.

.HTX Files

The .HTX file is a template that describes the formatting to be applied to the data supplied by the .IDC file. In fact, the .IDC file itself specifies which .HTX file to use (by the value of the Template field, as described in the IDC Fields section), and this file name may be represented by a variable.

The contents of the .HTX file is normal HTML-formatted text with special HTX tags embedded within it. These HTX tags cause the system to alter the output in various ways. Once again, it is important to realize that this processing occurs after the execution of the database queries in the .IDC file, and before the user's web browser renders the HTML for display.

The HTX tags allow you to dynamically generate the web page based on the .HTX template by substituting variable data and by conditionally including or excluding information based on that data.

All of the statements peculiar to .HTX files are identified by a specific format. They all begin with <% and end with %>. There are two types of these statements that you can use in .HTX files:

◆ Variables

◆ Keywords

.HTX Variables

When used directly within HTML code, variables are recognized by the format <%*VariableName*%>. When the server recognizes a pattern like this, it will substitute the value of the named variable in the place of the tag.

 When using a variable to supply the value of a field in a form, it's a good idea to enclose the variable in double quotes, for example,

```
<INPUT TYPE=TEXT NAME="EmployeeName" VALUE="<%EmployeeName%>">
```

If you fail to do this, and the value contains embedded spaces or other special characters, the value might be truncated. See the section "Advanced IDC Programming" in this chapter for more information about translating these special characters.

Note Within a keyword, the variable name itself is recognized—you don't need the <% and %> delimiters. For example, <%if UserName EQ "Administrator"%> tests to see if the UserName variable is Administrator. In this case, the value is used by the keyword, rather than output to the client.

Within an .HTX file, all variables are read-only. You have no opportunity to alter their values, only to request them. In addition, no computations can be performed on variables or constants.

Variables fall into four categories:

◆ Query Results

◆ IDC Parameters

◆ Special

◆ HTTP

Query Result Variables

The values of Query Result variables are taken from the results of the query described by .IDC file's SQLStatement field. These appear within a section delimited by *begindetail* and *enddetail* (which are discussed later, in the "Detail Block Delimiters" section).

For example, suppose that an .IDC file included this SQL statement:

```
SQLStatement:
+SELECT UserID, UserName, UserEMail, UserPassword
+FROM Users
```

The .HTX file that formats the results will be able to reference variables named UserID, UserName, UserEmail, and UserPassword within a detail block.

IDC Parameter Variables

The values of IDC parameters are taken from the values of the variables passed into the .IDC file that retrieved the .HTX file. A prefix of *idc.* always identifies these variables as such. These variables are useful for propagating values from one page to the next.

For more information on why it is important to have access to IDC Parameters, see the section "Planning for the Flow of Pages" in this chapter.

In the following example, the HTX file will be able to reference variables named *idc.EmployeeName* and *idc.EmployeeID*. These references can appear anywhere within the HTX file, in or out of a detail block, because the values are not associated with the result set.

```
<FORM METHOD=POST ACTION="sample.idc">
  Insert a new employee:<BR>
  Name: <INPUT TYPE=TEXT NAME="EmployeeName"><BR>
  ID: <INPUT TYPE=TEXT NAME="EmployeeID"><BR>
  <INPUT TYPE=SUBMIT>
</FORM>
```

Special Variables

Special variables can only be referenced within an < *%if%* > statement. They are useful for altering the resulting web page that will be returned to the user depending upon the number of rows in the result set. There are two of these variables:

◆ CurrentRecord

◆ MaxRecords

CurrentRecord identifies the row of the result set that is currently being processed within a *begindetail...enddetail* block. At the close of the block, its value is equal to the number of rows that were returned.

The following code shows how you can take advantage of CurrentRecord to test to see if the results of a query were not found. Following the < *%enddetail%* > statement, CurrentRecord contains the row number of the last row processed. If this is equal to zero, then no records were returned. For example:

```
Here are all of the employees:
<UL>
  <%begindetail%>
    <LI>%EmployeeName%
  <%enddetail%>
</UL>
<%if CurrentRecord EQ 0 %>
  Sorry, no records were found
<%endif%>
```

MaxRecords returns the value of the MaxRecords field in the .IDC file. This *would* be useful if its value was MaxRecords–1, so that you could perform special processing for the last row. However, the way it has been implemented, the feature is essentially useless.

HTTP Variables

HTTP variables provide access to some server variables and all of the data in the header of the initial CGI request that results in processing the .HTX file. HTTP variables are not frequently needed, but when they are, you'll be very happy that they are available.

These variables fall into two categories:

◆ **Server variables:** these variables are defined by the server itself. They are listed in Appendix D, "Server Variables."

◆ **Header variables:** these variables are set by server depending upon the values of headers in the request. You can derive the names of these variables by adding the string "HTTP_" to the beginning of the name and changing all dashes to underscores.

The names of these variables are case sensitive. They must be given entirely in capital letters.

Cross
Reference

For a list of server variables that can be retrieved, see the Appendix.

.HTX Keywords

The Internet Database Connector provides a few ways to control the way that .HTX template files are processed. Using HTX tags containing keywords enables you to control the way the .HTX file is interpreted or the way the values of variables are presented. There are three families of keywords:

♦ detail block delimiters

♦ conditional processing

♦ value escaping

Detail Block Delimiters

The detail block delimiters are the keywords begindetail and enddetail. A detail block is a section of the .HTX template that receives the values of Query Result variables.

The result set of a SQL query might contain many rows. The begindetail and enddetail statements bracket the section of the template that should receive each row. You can think of this as a loop: while there are still rows in the result set, apply the values of the next row to the variables within this block; repeat with the next row. Although this is frequently used with queries that result in many rows of output to produce a list of the data, they are also required even if only a single row is expected.

Suppose that your database contains an *Employees* table with a column named *EmployeeName.*

If your .IDC file contains

```
SQLStatement: SELECT EmployeeName from Employees
```

and your .HTX file contains

```
Here are the employees:
<ul>
  <%begindetail%>
    <li><%EmployeeName%>
  <%enddetail%>
</ul>
```

then the HTML generated for the user might be:

```
Here are the employees:
<ul>
    <li>Jane Doe
    <li>John Smith
</ul>
```

because the detail block is repeated twice, once for each employee found.

Conditional Processing Keywords

The conditional processing keywords include if, else, and endif. You can choose different blocks of text to include in the generated web page by using these directives. The *<%if%>* statement enables you to test the value of a variable (although you can't do any computation). If the result is true, the block of text up to the matching *<%else%>* or *<%endif%>* will be processed. If the result is false, that block will be ignored and the block from the *<%else%>* to the *<%endif%>* will be chosen instead, if present.

For example, suppose that you want to display a warning message if a certain value is set. You might include the following block within your .HTX file:

```
<TABLE>
  <TR>
    <TH>Item</TH>
    <TH>Price</TH>
    <TH>Comments</TH>
  </TR>
  <%begindetail%>
  <TR>
    <TD><%ItemName%></TD>
    <TD><%ItemPrice%></TD>
    <TD>
      <%if ItemStatus EQ "S"%>
        This item is on sale!
      <%endif%>
    </TD>
  </TR>
  <%enddetail%>
</TABLE>
```

The result of this will be a table displaying the names and prices of items (assuming that these are retrieved into variables named *ItemName* and *ItemPrice*, respectively). Additionally, if the value of the variable *ItemStatus* is equal to *S*, a message will be output so that the user will know that the item's on sale. Otherwise, that column will be left empty.

There are only a few comparison operators that you can use with the conditional processing keywords:

TABLE 2.3
Comparison Operators

Operator	Tests
EQ	equality
LT	for less than
GT	for greater than
CONTAINS	to see if the right operand is contained anywhere within the left operand

There is no "not equals," "less than or equal to," nor other operators. What's more, there is no negation, so you can't even use boolean algebra to create these.

You can, however, get the effect of a negation operator by using the *<%else%>* clause of the statement. For example, you can test to see if the current row is not zero like this:

```
<%if CurrentRecord EQ 0 %>
<%else%>
  This is not record #0!
<%endif%>
```

Value Escaping Keyword

The only value escaping keyword in IDC is "%z". It can be used to translate the value of a variable so that it is suitable for use in an URL. In particular, the spaces in the value are converted to "%20". For example, if the value of MyVariable is *"Hello World"*, the value resulting from *<%"%z",MessageText%>* would be *"Hello%20World"*.

This is useful when you must synthesize a GET request as a link. For example, you might use an expression like

```
<A HREF="HTTP://www.mysite.com/myapp.idc?MYFIELD=<%"%z",MyValue%>">
Get the data for <%MyValue%>
</A>
```

in order to invoke myapp.idc with the value MyValue as a parameter. This is necessary when MyValue might contain spaces or other non-alphanumeric characters, because these characters are not allowed in URLs. For a more complete definition of URLs, see RFC 1738, a copy of which can be found on the companion CD.

Advanced IDC Programming

Now you understand the basic concepts behind the Internet Database Connector. However, as is frequently the case, this is probably not enough to build a real-world application without some glue to hold it all together.

This section attempts to provide this glue in the form of practical knowledge that you'll find is mostly lacking from the description of IDC programming presented above as well as the documentation provided with the Internet Information Server. You will be presented with practical approaches to common IDC problems as well as topics that illustrate concepts that differentiate IDC programming from conventional approaches.

Understanding the Order of IDC Processing

It can be difficult to understand the processing of an IDC request because of the way that the steps are partitioned into separate files and even different machines. You should make the effort because a proper understanding will give you much more flexibility in your applications.

The important thing to remember is that generating the query, creating the web page from the template, and rendering the web page are separate, discrete steps performed in the .IDC file, the .HTX file, and the user's browser, respectively.

The most significant implication here is that the control structures used by the .HTX file and the browser appear to intermingle, although in fact they are entirely disconnected and independent. Realizing this frees you from the compulsion to enforce proper nesting of these structures, allowing greater flexibility in design options.

For example, the following section of code seems odd because the < %if... % > is nested within a table, whereas its matching < %else% > and < %endif% > statements are outside of the table. In fact, the HTML tables and other structures are completely independent of the .HTX processing. They are treated as simple text, so you are free to use the < %if... % > statement as necessary.

LISTING 2.1—SAMPLE OF COMPLEX USAGE OF <%IF%>

```
01 <FORM>
02 <TABLE>
03   <TR>
04     <TD ALIGN=CENTER BGCOLOR=#D0FFFF>
05       <%begindetail%>
06         <H3>Welcome, <%UserName%>.</H3>
07         <INPUT TYPE=HIDDEN NAME="UserID" VALUE=<%UserID%>>
08       <%enddetail%>
09       <! If no userids were found, give error message >
10       <%if CurrentRecord EQ 0 %>
11         <FONT COLOR=RED>
12           <H3>Sorry, your account was not found. Please
13           <A HREF="MessageBase.htm">try again.</A></H3>
14         </FONT>
15     </TD>
16   </TR>
17 </TABLE>
18 </FORM>
19 <%else%>  <! If a userid was found, give them choices >
20     </TD>
21   </TR>
22   <TR>
23     <TD ALIGN=CENTER>
24       <BR><H4>View a conference's messages</H4><BR>
25       <SELECT NAME="ConferenceName">
26         <%begindetail%>
27           <OPTION><%ConferenceName%>
28         <%enddetail%>
29       </SELECT>
30       <INPUT TYPE=SUBMIT VALUE="View">
31     </TD>
32   </TR>
33 </TABLE>
34 </FORM>
35 <%endif%>
```

You still must ensure that the HTML that results from your template will be valid. Notice that whichever path is selected by the conditional expression, the closing tags for the <TD>, <TR>, <TABLE>, and <FORM> tags must still be provided. Thus, there are two separate sets of those tags, only one of which will be chosen at a time. Either the table and form will end with the statements from lines 11–18, or 20–34.

Planning for the Flow of Pages

Using the Internet Database Connector does not isolate you from the stateless nature of HTTP. This means that you can't retrieve a value from the database and expect it to remain when the user's next request comes in. If you know that you'll be needing a value again in the future, you'll either need to retrieve it again or arrange to have it passed through each request.

The flow of pages through a web site tends to fan out like a tree, starting from one welcome page through a number of paths to many leaf pages. You may typically want to gather data early in the path so that you can use it later on. A simple example is keeping track of the user's identity. He probably enters this at the very beginning, but you'll want to remember it for later so that you can put his identity on the orders he places with your application.

If you go back and look at Figure 2.1, you can see that a cycle is implied. The IDC is able to keep its part of the cycle, moving information from the request through the .IDC file and into the .HTX file. However, the user's browser is unable to hold up its part without some explicit help on your part.

You can provide this help through hidden fields on each successive page. Hidden fields resubmit the field as a new variable when the user submits the form. Here's an example:

```
<FORM ACTION="/Scripts/MyApp/SomePage.idc" METHOD=POST>
  Give me data: <INPUT TYPE=TEXT NAME="TheData">
  <INPUT TYPE=HIDDEN NAME="UserID" VALUE="<%UserID%>">
  <INPUT TYPE=SUBMIT>
</FORM>
```

 Notice that the sample will create a variable called UserID, the value of which will be the previous version of UserID. Your life will be *much* easier if you always do it this way, or you'll have a maintenance nightmare ahead of you.

If you already have some knowledge of CGI applications, you're probably wondering why you can't just use cookies for this purpose? This is of course what you'd like to do, but it turns out that it's generally impractical to use cookies in an IDC application.

It's possible to set cookies in an IDC application by using a META tag in the .HTX file. You can retrieve the cookies too, by referencing the HTTP variable HTTP_COOKIE (see the section "HTTP Variables" in this chapter). However, it turns out that this is of limited use because you'll get a string like *MyCookie=MyValue* (or even *MyCookie1=MyValue1*; *MyCookie2=MyValue2* if you used two cookies!). The IDC gives you no way at all of parsing that string to obtain the values that it contains.

Before you decide to use hidden fields in this manner, you should consider the nature of the data that they will be carrying. The user can view their values simply by asking his or her web browser to display the source HTML for the page. Also, it will be transmitted through the network in clear text unless you're using a secure connection.

If any of the data in question is sensitive, you'll probably need to find another approach for your application. This might very well rule out using IDC. See Chapter 10, "Authentication with Filters," for more information on controlling access to your data.

In the preceding form example you gather some data and pass it in a request to SomePage.idc. At the same time you make sure that the previous value of UserID is passed on so that the next can use it, even if SomePage.idc doesn't need it itself.

Using More Than One Database Query

It is possible to use multiple database queries in a single .IDC file. There are two ways to do this. If your database supports batch queries (such as Microsoft SQL Server does), all of the queries can be listed within a single SQLStatement field, like this:

```
SQLStatement:
+ SELECT EmployeeName, EmployeeID FROM Employees
+ SELECT DepartmentName, DepartmentID FROM Departments
```

If you are using a database such as Microsoft Access (that is, the Jet database engine that is used by Access and Microsoft Visual Basic), batched queries are not supported. Instead, you should put each query into a separate statement, like this:

```
SQLStatement:
+ SELECT EmployeeName, EmployeeID FROM Employees
SQLStatement:
+ SELECT DepartmentName, DepartmentID FROM Departments
```

The batched method is preferable because it enables the database to make better use of concurrency (that is, it may be able to improve efficiency by performing multiple tasks simultaneously, if it's capable). Whichever method you choose should be transparent—it should make no difference to the rest of your application.

In order to retrieve the values that were selected, you need to have a separate detail block for each query. The queries above might be intended to supply data to a .HTX file like the following query does:

```
01.<FORM ACTION="/Scripts/MyApp/SomePage.idc" METHOD=POST>
02.   <SELECT NAME="EmployeeID">
```

```
03.    <%begindetail%>
04.       <OPTION VALUE="<%EmployeeID%>"><%EmployeeName%>
05.    <%enddetail%>
06.  </SELECT>
07.  <SELECT NAME="DepartmentID">
08.    <%begindetail%>
09.       <OPTION VALUE="<%DepartmentID%>"><%DepartmentName%>
10.    <%enddetail%>
11.  </SELECT>
12.  <INPUT TYPE=SUBMIT>
13.</FORM>
```

Here, the first detail section retrieves values from the first result set and the second block retrieves values from the second result set. Note that it is impossible to interleave the values. The detail sections must be separate, and there is no way to "pause" one while retrieving from the other. In addition, once a result set has been exhausted, there is no way to "reset" it to the beginning, short of executing two identical queries in the .IDC file.

 Notice that only *SELECT* statements return result sets. *INSERT, UPDATE, CREATE TABLE,* and other statements do not generate result sets, and therefore should not have corresponding detail blocks in the .HTX file. The implication of this is that it's impossible to return to the user any indication of the success of a data manipulation operation, short of fancy programming in stored procedures.

Retrieving the Values of Calculated Fields

So far, retrieving variables from the database has been pretty straightforward: select a column, and then request its value by referencing the column's name as a variable. In real life situations, there is frequently another wrinkle.

Suppose that you want to display to the user the total annual sales for a given year, but sales in the database are recorded separately for each day. Because it's impossible to perform any calculations in the Internet Database Connector, you must have the database perform them. This is simple enough. You might write this query:

```
SELECT SUM(Sales) FROM DailySales WHERE Year = %RequestedYear%
```

You'll quickly discover that your .HTX file is *not* receiving any variables named Sales. The reason for this is that the database is no longer returning a column by that name; instead, it's returning a calculated column whose name you don't know. In order to get at the value, you must tell the database what the name of this calculated field is.

If your database is in Access, this is done with an AS clause to specify the name that you'd like the column to be given, so you might rewrite your query like this:

```
SELECT SUM(Sales) AS AnnualSales FROM DailySales
    WHERE Year = %RequestedYear%
```

You can now retrieve a variable named AnnualSales in your .HTX file.

Using Multiple-Valued Variables

Every example so far has illustrated forms that return values from either an input field or a single-select list. HTML also offers a form element that enables the user to select multiple values from a listbox.

The designers of the Internet Database Connector saw this discrepancy, and also noted that it's a potentially very useful feature. They attempted to allow the user to have multiple values substituted into the .IDC file for a single variable reference. It would be nice to allow the user to write queries such as this:

```
SQLStatement:
+SELECT EmployeeName, EmployeeID FROM Employees
+WHERE DepartmentName IN ('%RequestedDepartments%')
```

Where the user selects a *list* of departments whose employees they'd like displayed. The following sections will present ways of handling this situation.

How to Use <SELECT MULTIPLE>

When the .IDC processor discovers a variable containing multiple values, it expands those values into a comma-separated list. What's more, if the variable reference is contained within single quotes, it will individually quote each of the values.

Suppose that the user is browsing a web page containing the following form:

```
01.<FORM ACTION="/Scripts/MyApp/ShowEmployees.idc" METHOD=POST>
02.   What departments would you like to display?
03.   <SELECT MULTIPLE NAME="RequestedDepartments">
04.     <! You could have generated this list >
05.     <! from a previous query, of course >
06.     <OPTION>Accounting
07.     <OPTION>MIS
08.     <OPTION>Shipping
09.   </SELECT>
10.   <INPUT TYPE=SUBMIT VALUE="View">
11.</FORM>
```

When the user clicks the *View* button, the value returned for the field *RequestedDepartments* will be some combination of *Accounting, MIS,* and *Shipping.* If the user selects all three departments, then when these values are substituted into the previously shown SQLStatement, the resultant query will look like this:

```
SQLStatement:
+SELECT EmployeeName, EmployeeID FROM Employees
+WHERE DepartmentName IN ('Accounting','MIS','Shipping')
```

Notice that each value is placed in the *IN* clause separately.

Why the Built-In Solution Won't Always Work

Within the scope of a single .IDC request, the solution described in the preceding section works quite well; however, if you try to pass the list of departments to subsequent pages, you'll be disappointed. The second time around the cycle, the system will forget the multi-value nature of the variable.

If the .HTX file receiving the results of the sample query looked like this:

```
01.<FORM ACTION="/Scripts/MyApp/ShowOneEmployee.idc" METHOD=POST>
02.  Which employee would you like to display?
03.  <SELECT NAME="EmployeeID">
04.    <%begindetail%>
05.      <OPTION VALUE="<%EmployeeID%>"><%EmployeeName%>
06.    <%enddetail%>
07.  </SELECT>
08.  <INPUT TYPE=HIDDEN
          NAME="RequestedDepartments"
          VALUE="'<%idc.RequestedDepartments%>'">
09.  <INPUT TYPE=SUBMIT VALUE="View">
10.</FORM>
```

then the value of RequestedDepartments would become *'Accounting,MIS,Shipping'*. Note that the single quotes are surrounding the entire string because you put them there, and the system did not insert individual quotes for you like it did last time around.

There is a solution to this. Instead of retaining the DepartmentName strings, you can set the Value attribute of the original OPTION statements so that RequestedDepartments contains a list of IDs (which are presumably numeric) instead of names. If the values are numeric, then there's no need for the single quotes in any case, so the problem is circumvented.

Here is a sample piece of an IDC application that addresses the problem:

In the .HTX file the <SELECT> field will receive values corresponding with the *DepartmentIDs* rather than their names:

```
01.<FORM ACTION="/Scripts/MyApp/ShowEmployees.idc" METHOD=POST>
02.  What departments would you like to display?
03.  <SELECT MULTIPLE NAME="RequestedDepartments">
04.    <! You could have generated this list >
05.    <! from a previous query, of course >
06.    <OPTION VALUE="1">Accounting
07.    <OPTION VALUE="2">MIS
08.    <OPTION VALUE="3">Shipping
09.  </SELECT>
10.  <INPUT TYPE=SUBMIT VALUE="View">
11.</FORM>
```

In the .IDC file you can now select the based numeric ID rather than the names, so that you have no need to insert the quotation marks:

```
SQLStatement:
+SELECT EmployeeName, EmployeeID FROM Employees
+WHERE DepartmentID IN (%RequestedDepartments%)
```

Translating Entities for HTML Compliance

The HTML and HTTP standards do not provide for all possible characters to be transmitted raw to the user. Because of the way these standards are defined, some characters must be escaped or translated to "entities."

In particular, the HTML standard requires that certain characters be transmitted as entities. These include the characters representing double quotes, ampersands, and angle brackets. When rendered by the user's browser, they are displayed as the appropriate character. Furthermore, HTTP requests might not function properly with certain characters such as spaces in the URL.

The Internet Database Connector provides ways for addressing some, but not all, of these issues. It is possible to translate most characters coming from the database to arbitrary strings defined by the programmer. The .HTX file can also contain directives causing the values of variables to selectively be translated appropriately for use in an URL.

On the other hand, the Internet Database Connector does not provide a means of translating characters coming *from* an IDC request coming from the user's browser.

The facility for bulk translation of database output is Translation Files. More selective translation for use in URLs can be applied through the %z keyword.

Translation Files

An .IDC file may optionally contain a field named Translationfile. If present, this gives the name of a file that specifies a mapping from characters retrieved from the database to strings substituted in the values of the variables. If the file name does not include a path, it is assumed to reside in the same directory as the .IDC file.

The translation file contains one line for each character to be translated. The first character on the line is the character to look for. This is followed by an equals sign, and then the string (of any length) that is to replace the character. A typical translation file will contain these mappings:

```
"=&quot;
<=&lt;
>=&gt;
&=&amp;
```

You can also specify mappings for accented *international characters*. Unfortunately, the syntax of this file clearly won't allow you to specify a translation for a carriage return. For some reason, you cannot give one for a space, either. There are no workarounds known for these deficiencies.

Translating Values for Use in URLs

The %z keyword in an .HTX file enables you to selectively translate values so that their values may be used in an URL. For example, you may want to allow the user to issue a request by clicking on a hyperlink rather than pushing a submit button. In order to implement this, you must hand-code the GET request that would be sent if the request were sent by a form. If there is a possibility that the data in this request might contain spaces or other "special" characters, you must translate those characters to the proper escapes. The %z keyword enables you to do this.

For example, suppose that you want a page that lists the names of all of your products. Clicking on one should send a request to display the specifications for that product. You could implement this in your .HTX file like this:

```
Select a product to view:
<UL>
  <%begindetail%>
    <LI><A HREF="SpecSheet.idc?ProductName=<%"%z",ProductName%>">
        <%ProductName%>
        </A>
  <%enddetail%>
</UL>
```

There are two key differences between translating this way and with translation files. Most significantly, %z enables you to translate spaces, which can't be done from a translation file. Also, %z can be applied selectively on a per-reference basis; translation files apply to all of the data retrieved by the .IDC file. You can see this difference in the example code: the first reference to ProductName will have its spaces changed to %20 and any other translations necessary; the second is left in plain text.

Securing Your System

There are two aspects to security that you'll need to consider. Your database needs to be protected from prying eyes and unauthorized alterations. You also need to protect your application, the .IDC files in particular, because they may contain usernames and passwords to access the database.

Protecting Your Scripts

The .IDC and .HTX files that make up your application can be hidden from view by placing them in a directory whose rights are set to Execute Only for any of the people who will have access to the server.

Protecting Your data

Your data will be best protected if you are using *Microsoft SQL Server* as a database, because of its tight integration with Windows NT system security. If this is the case, the Username and Password fields of the .IDC file will be ignored. Instead, the system will ask the user to log in (if he hasn't already) using his own user name and password.

If you use Access or other database, the situation is more complicated. You'll be hardcoding a Username and Password in the .IDC file, and you must look elsewhere for a means to control access.

A very simple means of controlling access is to include a table of authorized users and their passwords in your database. As the first step in your application, require users to enter this data, and compare the entered data to that in the database before allowing the user to proceed. This might not be satisfactory for a number of reasons. Most significantly, a hacker could gain unauthorized entry simply by jumping directly to the second page on your site, after authentication has been performed, unless you recheck the id and password with *every* database access—which is sure to adversely affect performance. Also, it may not be acceptable to transmit userids and passwords as clear text through the network.

If these security concerns are an issue, you can employ other means of controlling access, some of which are discussed in Chapter 10, "Authentication with Filters."

Differences Between IIS 1.x and 2.0

Microsoft has been moving very quickly to catch up with Netscape and other competitors in the Internet server market. IIS 2.0 followed 1.x very closely, even by the standards of the software industry. As a result, many users are still working with older versions for a variety of reasons.

If you are using the older version, there are two very important differences you'll see in version 2.0's Internet Database Connector. You should be aware of these before considering use of the IDC, because they make a profound difference in the way you'll build an IDC application.

There is no question that these updates are sufficient justification for upgrading your system. Each difference is so significant that either one would warrant migrating to version 2.0 if you plan on using the Internet Database Connector at all.

Multiple Database Queries

Prior to version 2.0, an .IDC query could only contain a single result set. This means that your .HTX file could contain only one detail block as well. You could use multiple queries by issuing *SET COUNT OFF* and *SET COUNT ON* commands in the SQLStatement, surrounding all queries except the one whose result set you want to return.

The early adopters of IDC developed an ugly, but mostly effective approach to circumvent this shortcoming. The technique involves combining *all* of the desired queries into a single one by using a *UNION* to concatenate the results into a single result set. Each part of the query sets its particular value in a special selector column, so that <*%if%*> statements can separate the data belonging to the sub-queries from the large result set. Obviously, this also requires a lot of planning to get a superset of columns to allow all results to be returned. This method is not for the faint of heart.

Proper Nesting of Conditionals

Versions of IDC before 2.0 could not properly nest <*%if%*> statements. For example, this code fragment would have been illegal:

```
<%if Var1 EQ "X" %>
  <%if Var2 EQ "Y" %>
    do something
  <%endif%>  <! Ends BOTH if statements! >
<%endif%>
```

In this case, the first < *%endif%* > ends *both* < *%if%* > statements, making the second an error.

There were techniques to deal with this problem as well, but none were completely effective.

Summary

This chapter dealt with programming the Internet Database Connector. After reading it you should understand what the IDC is and when it is advantageous to use it (as well as when it's not), and how to write applications effectively using this platform.

The roles of the .IDC and .HTX files that make up an IDC application should be clear. You should understand the process flow of an IDC application and you should be conversant with the fields in the .IDC file and the special tags in the .HTX file. You should understand how detail block delimiters access the results of the SQLStatement in the IDC file, and how the conditional processing keywords allow you to tailor the way those results are presented.

CHAPTER 3

Presenting an IDC
Sample Application

This chapter presents a practical application written entirely by using the Internet Database Connector. The chapter serves two purposes. First, it presents real-life examples of the information presented in Chapter 2, "Using the Internet Database Connector," so users can obtain more than a purely academic understanding. Second, it provides an application useful in its own right, whether used in its entirety or taken apart so its components can solve similar problems in other applications.

Application Objective

A message base application is frequently used on both bulletin boards and corporate intranets. The program is very general, lending itself to applications ranging from bug reporting to car pools.

The objective in this chapter is to build a message base suitable for use in any of these contexts. It will allow users to log on and prevent entry by unauthorized users. It will organize messages into conferences and allow them to be viewed in a threaded format. A user will be able to enter new topics or follow up an existing message. A user will be able to search some subset of conferences for a desired string to be found in the message subject lines.

To be effective for the uses mentioned previously, there are a few features that must be included.

1. Organization — Various topics of discussion should be divided into separate conferences. Messages within a conference should be presented so that the thread of a conversation can easily be followed.

2. Posting — Users should be able to easily post a new message that either continues the thread of an existing discussion or begins a new one.

3. Searching — Users should be able to quickly locate messages discussing subjects in which they are interested.

4. Security — The program should limit access to only those people authorized to use it.

Message Organization

Messages are posted to distinct conferences. Within these conferences, messages fall into *threads*, which means responses to a particular message appear to be associated with that message. This is done by rendering a conference's list of messages as an outline, with related responses indented below each message. To see how this will appear, see figure 3.5.

New Message Posting

From a conference's message list, the user is able to post a new topic. A new topic comes at the root of the thread hierarchy; it is not a follow-up to any other message. This new topic belongs to the conference whose messages are being viewed.

A user who is viewing a particular message can respond to that message by posting a follow-up. This follow-up is listed later, when the conference's message list is displayed, below the original message and indented.

Subject Searches

The user can search for an arbitrary substring in the Subject field of the messages. The scope of the search can be narrowed by selecting the set of conferences to be examined.

For example, the search feature allows the user to get a list of all messages that include the word "Internet" in their subject. Specifying a search string of %Internet% can do this. Note the percent signs appear on either side of the search string. This is provided so that an exact match is not required; any subject that contains the search string anywhere within itself will satisfy the condition.

Such a search can potentially yield a large number of matches. This large set is divided into groups of ten. The user can step through these pages one at a time.

Security

In the interest of simplicity, only a modicum of security will be implemented. This might not be sufficient for your application. If not, you should consider using SQL Server as a database, which will allow you to use its own security, or look to another security mechanism as discussed in Chapter 10, "Authentication with Filters."

Message Base Application Data Model

The most important part of any application is to identify the data it must handle. In this program you need a means of storing the messages. The obvious answer to this requirement is to design a database for the purpose.

The database will be implemented in Microsoft Access. Most databases that can provide an ODBC datasource will, with minor changes, work in its place.

The application's database consists of four tables.

◆ Messages: stores all of the actual messages

◆ Conferences: lists the various conferences that the user can read

◆ Users: contains information about the system's users

◆ Spacing: provides the indentation necessary for thread display

There are a number of relationships tying together the entities stored in these tables.

- ◆ Messages belong to a conference

- ◆ Messages are posted by a user

- ◆ The nesting depth of a message is depicted by a string retrieved from the spacing table

Figure 3.1

The data model consists of four related entities.

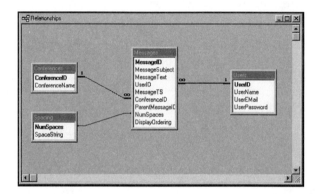

Messages

This being a message base, the Messages table is the center point of the data model. All of the information relating to the message itself is stored in this table, including the text of the message itself, its subject, and other information. The columns are described in table 3.1.

Messages contain the following information:

TABLE 3.1
Message Table Columns

Column Name	Data Type	Description
MessageID	AutoNumber; Primary key	Unique identifier for the message
MessageSubject	Text; Required; Allow 0 length	The subject of the message
MessageText	Memo; Required; Allow 0 length	The message itself

Column Name	Data Type	Description
UserID	Number; Required	Reference to the user who posted the message
MessageTS	Date/Time	Indication of when the message was posted
ConferenceID	Number; Required; Indexed; Duplicates OK	Reference to the conference to which the message belongs
Parent-MessageID	Number; Required; Indexed; Duplicates OK	If this message is a follow-up to another, a reference to that parent message
NumSpaces	Number; Required	The depth this message is nested to. A new topic is nested to a depth of zero; a follow-up to it is nested to a depth of one.
Display Ordering	Number; Required; Indexed; Duplicates OK	A mechanism for ordering a conference's messages

Because this is a relational database, the *references* described in table 3.1 actually contain the ID of the entity. In each case, the appropriate table is consulted to locate the entity itself. Thus, the name of the message's author can be retrieved by looking for a User whose ID is equal to the UserID stored with the message.

As you can see in figure 3.1, there are referential integrity constraints imposed on the relationships with the Conferences, Users, and Spacing tables. Also notable is the omission of a relationship with itself via the ParentMessageID. This is not enforced, because a New Topic message does not have a parent. In these cases the value will be 0; otherwise, it should contain a valid MessageID.

Conferences

Conferences serve to partition the database into separate topics. One might contain a discussion of marketing plans, while another conference serves as a suggestion box. Each *conference* contains the information described in table 3.2.

TABLE 3.2
Conference Table Columns

Column Name	Data Type	Description
ConferenceID	AutoNumber; Primary key;	Unique identifier for the conference
ConferenceName	Text; Required; Indexed	The name of the conference

This table is queried to obtain a list of conferences so users can select the one they want to view.

Users

Records in the *Users* table describe the attributes of a user. In the message base application, this serves two purposes.

◆ **Security:** this table lists all of the users that are authorized to access the message base, and stores the passwords they must use to log in.

◆ **Contact Information:** information such as the user's email address is retained so that other users can easily send private email to a user in response to a message. When a user logs on, this table is queried to check if the UserID/ Password combination is valid. Note that there is a potential problem if two users have identical UserNames and Passwords. The security exposure is minimal, considering the weak security already inherent in the application. The solution to this problem is to either force user names to be unique, or create a unique composite index on the combination of UserName and Password—which is not supported by Access. Neither of these solutions have been implemented here.

The Users table is also used to retrieve a message author's name and email address when the message is displayed. The table's data is stored in the columns described in table 3.3.

TABLE 3.3
Users Table Columns

Column Name	Data Type	Description
UserID	AutoNumber; Primary key;	Unique identifier for the user

Column Name	Data Type	Description
UserName	Text; Required; Indexed; Duplicates OK	The user's real name
UserEmail	Text	The user's email address, if any
UserPassword	Text	The user's password

Spacing

The spacing table is an implementation artifact, used to provide threaded display feature. It bridges from the abstract requirement to indicate message threading depth to the implementation need to depict threading by indenting the message.

A spacing table contains the information described in table 3.4.

TABLE 3.4
Spacing Table Columns

Column Name	Data Type	Description
NumSpaces	AutoNumber; Primary key;	The amount of spacing in the string
SpaceString	Text; Required; Allow 0 length	A string with the appropriate number of spaces

This table seems strange at first, but it's really quite necessary for implementation of the application's message-threading feature. Remember that there is no way to perform any calculations in your .IDC or .HTX files as stipulated in Chapter 2. The only alternative is to have the database do it for you. That is exactly what's happening here. By asking this table for a string of n spaces, you can get the same effect as generating one yourself.

Message Base Application User Interface

Before you start coding .IDC and .HTX files, you should lay out a static web site to plan the flow of the application. Later, these pages are used as a baseline for creation of your .HTX files.

Using plain HTML web pages which link together in a simulation of the web site's operation, you can quickly prototype your user interface. Once you've got the user interface layed out the way you want it, you need to look at where data is obtained and where it's used. You'll need to plan a means of carrying data from the place at which its value is first determined to the places that it is used.

For example, the very first thing that the message base will do is to obtain the user's name by requiring a logon. This information needs to be used later, to record the identity of the user when a message is posted. Clearly, a means must be provided to carry the user's identity from one page to the next.

Figure 3.2 shows the flow through the message base application. Each box represents a web page; along each line or arc you need to write an .IDC file to do the following:

1. Perform any database manipulation requested by the previous page

2. Gather the information necessary to display on the subsequent page

Figure 3.2

The message base application consists of a number of web pages that can be accessed in a well-defined sequence.

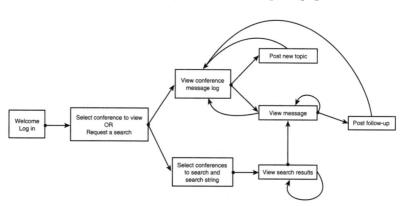

The first step is always to welcome users to the application and invite them to log in. A successful login brings them to the main screen. Here they can select a conference to view or perform a search.

If a user opts to view a conference, a list of messages in the conference is displayed. From here, the user can either select a message to view or post a new topic. The latter choice accesses a New Topic page. After posting, the user is returned to the Message List. After selecting a message for display, the user is brought to the View Message page and can return to the Message List, view the next or previous message (thus coming right back to the View Message page), or post a follow-up. Anyone who chooses to post a follow-up will go to the Post Message page, after which they will return to the Message List.

Users who request a search will get the Search page, which asks them to select the conferences they are interested in and the string they would like to search for. Once the criteria has been submitted, the Search Results screen appears. Users can cycle through this page many times, viewing each subset of matches. When users locate a conference that interests them, they can open it, bringing the View Message page described earlier.

Message Base Application Implementation Issues

Having designed the application's data model and user interface, there are several issues you'll have to resolve before you can jump into implementation.

1. Patching the Access ODBC driver: the driver supplied with Access 7.0 has bugs; a replacement is available from Microsoft.

2. Configuring the system: a System DSN and a Scripts directory must be created for the server to access your database and scripts, respectively.

3. The application's specifications and design present some challenges. You should plan your attack before actually starting.

Access Bug Patch

The Jet drivers, delivered with Microsoft Access 7.0 and Microsoft Visual Basic, have a bug that surfaces very frequently when used in conjunction with the IIS (Internet Information Server). If you're using an Access database, get error messages in response to your queries for no apparent reason, and the World Wide Web Publishing Service shuts down, you might be experiencing this problem.

A patch is available from Microsoft. It can be downloaded from Microsoft online at the following URL:

```
http://www.microsoft.com/kb/softlib/mslfiles/MSJTWNG.EXE
```

Configuring Your System

In order for the server to make your application available to users, it needs to be able to access the components making up the application. The database needs to be represented by a System Data Source Name so that the ODBC drivers can locate and communicate with it. Similarly, the .IDC and .HTX files should have a home of their own so that you can keep track of the various applications hosted on your server.

Supplying a System Data Source Name

The .IDC files in the application must be supplied with a data source against which they perform their SQL Statements. After you have created your database, it needs to be given a System DSN (Data Source Name).

The source code presented here assumes you have created a System DSN of *dbMessageBase*. After this has been done, the actual database files can be located anywhere that the user (IUSR_*machinename*, unless you're using another means of security) has access. In the case of this Access database, that means that the user needs access to the actual .MDB file containing the database. In the case of SQL Server databases, the user needs an account on the requested database server and privileges to access the data.

Cross Reference

For instructions on creating a System DSN, see Appendix B, "Creating a System Data Source Name."

Creating a Scripts Directory

You will need to locate a place to store the application's source code. You will want a directory with Execute Only permissions. The default configuration of IIS has such a directory, but you will want to create one of your own to keep all your applications organized. The source code in this chapter assumes the files are stored in a directory called */Scripts/MessageBase/*.

Cross Reference

See the Internet Information Server online documentation for instructions on mapping virtual directories for use by IIS. This information can be found in Chapter 6, "Developing an E-Mail Gateway," and is by default installed into the URL "iisadmin/htmldocs/06_iis.htm."

Providing Starting Data in the Database

This application does not contain any administrative tools, so if you're entering this program by hand rather than from the companion CD-ROM, you must enter any Users and Conferences into the database manually.

You will also need to add appropriate values to the Spacing table. When using Access, this turns out to be a bit easier said than done. Access queries seem to treat fields in which the user only enters spaces as null strings, so you need to use another vehicle to set the values. For example, if you create a number of records with *NumSpaces* equal to 0 through 15, a query for setting them to strings of spaces having appropriate lengths (actually two spaces for each increment of *NumSpaces*—it looks nicer):

```
UPDATE spacing
SET spacing.SpaceString =
    Left('                                ',[NumSpaces]*2);
```

Propagating Values Through the Program

After you have figured out how web pages progress through the system (see fig. 3.2), you need to consider what values need to persist through the system (discussed in Chapter 2, in the section on "Planning for the Flow of Pages").

There are three items that need special attention in this regard:

◆ The most significant item to retain is the UserID, from the point of its retrieval onward

◆ After the user selects a Conference on the main screen, this value is required on every page below it

◆ After the user requests a list of conferences and a string to search for, these should be retained as the user steps through the search results

Threading Message Responses

Perhaps the most challenging aspect of implementing the application is threading message responses. It proves to be very difficult to provide enough information to allow messages to be ordered so a newly inserted follow-up is placed after the last follow-up posted, rather than after the parent message.

There is a solution, but it involves some complicated SQL statements and the addition of the *DisplayOrdering* field. The feature is so useful that it's worth going to the trouble.

There are two sides to the threading problem. The first is displaying the messages in a threaded format. The second, and more complex, is supplying the necessary information to that displayer.

Displaying a Threaded Message List

The first part of the solution is to assume two things: the *DisplayOrdering* field provides the correct ordering for messages belonging to a particular conference, and the correct amount of indentation can be obtained by selecting the SpaceString corresponding to the message's level of indentation. The space string is prepended to the message subject into a calculated field. Here is the SQL statement that retrieves a list of messages with the proper ordering and indentation for the threaded display:

```
SELECT DISTINCTROW '+' & [SpaceString] & [MessageSubject] AS Expr1,
Users.UserName, Messages.MessageTS, Messages.MessageID, '<%UserID%>'
FROM Users INNER JOIN
   (Conferences INNER JOIN
     (Spacing INNER JOIN
```

```
       Messages ON Spacing.NumSpaces = Messages.NumSpaces
     ) ON Conferences.ConferenceID = Messages.ConferenceID
   ) ON Users.UserID = Messages.UserID
WHERE (((Conferences.ConferenceName)='%ConferenceName%'))
ORDER BY Messages.DisplayOrdering
```

Expr1 now contains a string with the correct number of spaces to show the indentation properly, but HTML is working against you—unless told not to, it compresses all the spaces into a single one. To deal with this, you must place the reference to Expr1 within a preformatted text tag (*<PRE>*).

An alternative to retrieving the SpaceString from the Spacing table for each message is to generate the string of spaces dynamically. This can be accomplished by using an expression similar to the one shown in the earlier "Providing Starting Data in the Database" section; however, this precludes any simple changes to the spacing string. With the given design, the number of spaces can be changed easily by altering the database; no code changes are necessary. You could also use periods rather than spaces, for example, making the *<PRE>* tag unnecessary.

Posting Threaded Messages

Now you must ensure the validity of the two preceding assumptions. The easy part is to keep the indentation level (NumSpaces) accurate. At first, this seems difficult because the IDC doesn't enable calculations to be performed, and it's necessary to use a value equal to the parent's NumSpaces incremented by 1. In this case, you can circumvent the problem by having the database perform the calculation for you, albeit in a sneaky way. You can set the value of the nesting depth equal to the parent's plus 1, like this:

```
<INPUT TYPE=HIDDEN NAME="NestDepth" VALUE="<%NumSpaces%>+1">
```

Now, if the parent's value of NumSpaces is 1, the value of NestDepth is, literally, *1+1*. When this value eventually finds its way to the database, this string is evaluated by the database engine as 2.

This leaves the thorny problem of keeping the *DisplayOrdering* values accurate. The objective is to give the new message a *DisplayOrdering* value equal to 1 greater than the greatest *DisplayOrdering* among the parent messages and all the other messages sharing that same parent. Also, you need to increment the value for all messages in the conference with values greater than or equal to the value you want to use, to free a spot for the new message.

This is a mouthful, and it takes two SQL statements to implement it:

1. Allocate a new spot in the middle of the message list

2. Insert the new message into that free spot

The first statement must begin by calculating the desired value for *DisplayOrdering*. This is accomplished by retrieving the highest value possessed by either the parent or its other children. Then the value is incremented for any message in that conference with a *DisplayOrdering* value that puts it at that place in the list or later.

```
UPDATE messages SET displayordering=displayordering+1
WHERE conferenceid=%ConferenceID%
AND displayordering>
  (SELECT MAX(displayordering) FROM messages
    WHERE parentmessageid=%ParentID% OR MessageID=%ParentID%
  )
```

Now that a spot has been allocated for the new message, you must execute a second statement to insert it. Unfortunately, there is no way (short of using stored procedures) to remember the desired value of *DisplayOrdering* calculated previously, so you must calculate it again. This value, together with all the other attributes of the new message, is inserted into the Messages Table.

```
INSERT INTO messages
(MessageSubject,UserID,messagets,conferenceid,
parentmessageid,numspaces,messagetext,displayordering)
SELECT '%MessageSubject%',%UserID%,Now(),%ConferenceID%,
 %ParentID%,%NestDepth%,'%MessageText%', 1+MAX(displayordering)
 FROM Messages
 WHERE parentmessageid=%ParentID% OR MessageID=%ParentID%
```

Note that adding new topics requires a slightly different approach. Because there is no parent message, the SQL statements must be written a bit differently. This case is actually somewhat simpler than posting a response, though.

The query will also fail for the first message added to a conference because *MAX (DisplayOrdering)* evaluates to null, and the column is non-nullable. To work around this problem, you must always add an initial message to each conference that you create. As noted previously, these administration functions haven't been implemented for you. You'll have to do it manually, or implement the administrations functions yourself.

Implementing Multi-Page Search Results

It's actually quite easy to implement a feature such as multi-page search capabilities, so long as the data being searched meets some criteria:

◆ There must be a single value that can be used to identify the current location in the results (the primary key is the usual choice, if it is a single column).

MessageID fulfills this requirement. If you are implementing another application with this feature, it should be easy to add such a field if one does not already exist. This value is referred to as the key field in the following explanation.

◆ The search must be sorted according to the key field that satisfies the first requirement. This is unfortunate, because it would be nice to be able to sort according to the Conference or Subject string. Still, the message base application is able to fulfill this requirement.

Three things must be done to implement the multi-page search feature:

1. Limit the number of matches returned per query

2. Sort the result set by a single unique key field

3. Maintain a cursor to track the current position in the result set

The first step is to limit the number of matches retrieved at a given time. This is simple to do: just set the value of *SQL_MAX_ROWS* in the ODBCOptions field of the .IDC file, as follows:

```
ODBCOptions: SQL_MAX_ROWS=10
```

Now only ten rows will be returned at a time.The second step is to order the results by the field used as the key. This is done with a SQL *ORDER BY* clause to sort by the field being used as the cursor. Without this sorting, there would be no way to ensure that each matching message is retrieved once, without being repeated.

The final hurdle is to maintain a *cursor* that always has the last value selected of the key described previously. The cursor should start with an initial value of zero on the page that initiates the search. You can get your .HTX file to capture subsequent values for this with just a bit of finagling, as shown in the following code:

```
<%if CurrentRecord EQ 9%>
  <TR>
    <TD COLSPAN=5 ALIGN=CENTER>
      <FORM ACTION="/Scripts/MessageBase/SearchResults.idc"
            METHOD=POST>
        <INPUT TYPE=HIDDEN NAME="MaxMsg" VALUE="<%MessageID%>">
        <INPUT TYPE=HIDDEN NAME="UserID" VALUE="<%idc.UserID%>">
        <INPUT TYPE=HIDDEN NAME="SeldConferences"
               VALUE="<%idc.SeldConferences%>">
        <INPUT TYPE=HIDDEN NAME="SearchText" VALUE="<%idc.SearchText%>">
        <INPUT TYPE=SUBMIT VALUE="Next Page">
      </FORM>
```

```
    </TD>
  </TR>
<%endif%>
```

You can see the preceding code in context in the "View Search Results Page" section later in this chapter.

This inserts a form only if the current record is 9 (where counting begins at 0). Because the number of rows returned was previously limited to ten, the form will only be created once, during processing of the last record. Moreover, if the last page comes up with fewer than ten matches, the *Next Page* button won't be generated at all—a nice benefit at no additional cost.

In this special "last record" form, you capture the MessageID of this record into the variable MaxMsg, which is used for the cursor.

If the user presses the *Next Page* button, this value will be submitted to the search query and used to determine the starting point for the next set of matches. Here is the SQL statement that implements this:

```
SELECT DISTINCTROW '+' & [SpaceString] & [MessageSubject] AS Expr1,
Users.UserName, Messages.MessageTS,
Messages.MessageID, Conferences.ConferenceName
FROM Users INNER JOIN
  (Conferences INNER JOIN
    (Spacing INNER JOIN
      Messages ON Spacing.NumSpaces = Messages.NumSpaces
    ) ON Conferences.ConferenceID = Messages.ConferenceID
  ) ON Users.UserID = Messages.UserID
WHERE Messages.MessageID > %MaxMsg%
 AND Messages.MessageSubject LIKE '%SearchText%'
 AND Conferences.ConferenceID IN (%SeldConferences%)
ORDER BY Messages.MessageID
```

The important parts of this query are the *WHERE* and *ORDER BY* clauses. The *WHERE* clause includes a condition that the rows selected must be greater than MaxMsg, which is the cursor. On the first visit to this query, its value should be zero, so the first matches are selected. On subsequent visits, the value of MaxMsg will be equal to that of the last message retrieved by the previous iteration, and because the query only retrieves those messages that are greater, the results will begin with the next matching message on the list.

Message Base Application Implementation

This section presents the actual source code implementing the application that is discussed in this chapter. It is also available on the CD accompanying this book. Each page of the application is presented individually, along with the .HTML, .IDC, and .HTX files that implement it and comments explaining what it does and how it works.

Here is a list of the pages making up the application:

◆ Welcome/Login: welcomes the user and requests a name and password for login

◆ Main Page: presents the user with the two main options in the application: view a conference or search for a subject

◆ Conference Message List: shows the threaded list of messages for the selected conference

◆ View Message: displays a message

◆ Post a Follow-Up: provides a form into which the user can enter a new message in response to an existing message

◆ Post a New Topic: provides a form into which the user can enter a new message on a new topic

◆ Search Request: allows the user to request a search for a string in the subject field of the existing messages

◆ View Search Results: displays the results of the user's search request

Welcome/Login Page

The Welcome/Login page gathers the user's name and password (see fig. 3.3). When the user presses the Submit button, the system sends this information to the application's main page for verification.

This is actually a simple form that leads into the IDC aspects of the application. As such, it's nothing more than a vanilla HTML form.

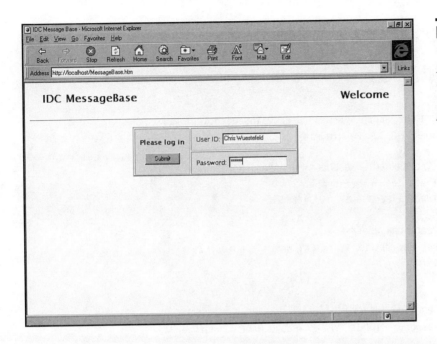

Figure 3.3
The Welcome/ Login page collects the user's name and password.

LISTING 3.1—MessageBase.htm

```
01.<!doctype html public "-//IETF//DTD HTML//EN">
02.<HTML>
03.
04.<HEAD>
05.
06.<TITLE>IDC Message Base</TITLE>
07.
08.</HEAD>
09.
10.<BODY BGCOLOR=#FFFFF7>
11.
12.<DIV ALIGN=CENTER>
13.<TABLE WIDTH=95%>
14.   <TR>
15.    <TD ALIGN=LEFT>
16.      <H2>IDC MessageBase</H2>
17.    </TD>
18.    <TD ALIGN=RIGHT>
19.      <H2>Welcome</H2>
20.    </TD>
```

continues

Listing 3.1—MessageBase.htm, Continued

```
21.  </TR>
22.</TABLE>
23.<HR>
24.
25.<FORM ACTION="/Scripts/MessageBase/MainScreen.idc" METHOD=POST>
26.<TABLE BORDER=2 CELLPADDING=10>
27.  <TR>
28.    <TH VALIGN=CENTER BGCOLOR="#D0FFD0" ROWSPAN=2>
29.       Please log in<br><br>
30.        <INPUT TYPE=SUBMIT NAME="Submit">
31.    </TH>
32.    <TD BGCOLOR="#D0FFFF">
33.       User ID: <INPUT TYPE=TEXT NAME="InputUserID">
34.    </TD>
35.  </TR>
36.  <TR>
37.    <TD BGCOLOR="#D0FFFF">
38.       Password: <INPUT TYPE=PASSWORD NAME="InputUserPW">
39.    </TD>
40.  </TR>
41.</TABLE>
42.</DIV>
43.</FORM>
44.</BODY>
45.
46.</HTML>
```

This is a simple form for entry of the user's name and password. When the user submits this data, the first .IDC request of the application is initiated.

Main Page

This page has two functions, as follows:

1. Validating the user

2. Presenting the user with a choice of viewing a particular conference or searching for a message (see fig. 3.4)

Figure 3.4 depicts the Main page. There are three main features on it:

♦ The Welcome message shows the full name of the user that has logged on; had the logon been incorrect, the only feature on the page would be an error message indicating an invalid login

♦ The combobox and *View* button that allow the user to select a conference for viewing

♦ The *Search* button allows the user to invoke the application's search feature

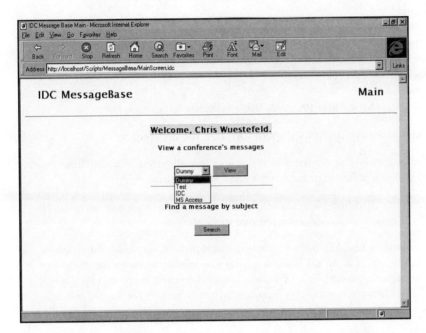

Figure 3.4

The Message Base Main page.

The Main page of the application, like most elements of an IDC program, consists of an .IDC file that retrieves the desired data and a single .HTX file for displaying that data.

IDC File for the Main Page

Listing 3.2 presents the .IDC file that results in the creation of the Main page. Its file name is MainScreen.idc and is located on the companion CD.

LISTING 3.2—MAINSCREEN.IDC

```
01.Datasource: dbMessageBase
02.Username: sa
03.Template: MainScreen.htx
```

continues

Listing 3.2—MainScreen.idc, Continued

```
04.ODBCOptions: SQL_ACCESS_MODE=1
05.RequiredParameter: InputUserID, InputUserPW
06.SQLStatement:
07.+SELECT UserID, UserName, UserEmail, UserPassword
08.+FROM Users
09.+WHERE UserName='%InputUserID%' AND UserPassword='%InputUserPW%'
10.SQLStatement:
11.+SELECT ConferenceID, ConferenceName
12.+FROM Conferences
13.SQLStatement:
14.+SELECT UserID AS UserID2
15.+FROM Users
16.+WHERE UserName='%InputUserID%' AND UserPassword='%InputUserPW%'
```

Three SQL statements are performed when this .IDC file is executed.

The first statement, at line 6, determines if the user is authorized. If a matching name and password pair is not found, it means the user is not authorized.

The second statement, at line 10, retrieves the list of conference names and IDs. This will be used by the user to choose a conference to view.

The final statement, at line 13, looks at first to be redundant: it retrieves the same information as the first statement. This illustrates one of the common headaches of IDC programming—the same piece of information is required twice on this page. Their use needs to be separated by an intervening query, so you are forced to re-query for the same information.

Don't be confused by the different names used on lines 9 and 16 for the information determining the user's identity. Internally the user's identity is actually tracked by a numeric identifier, but the user shouldn't be burdened with remembering a number. At the same time, the identifier that the user gives is not necessarily his name, and calling it that could cause confusion. Thus, there is a discrepancy between what the user sees and what the implementation does under the covers. This file bridges the difference between the two domains.

HTX File for the Main Page

Listing 3.3 presents the .HTX file that specifies the appearance of the Main page. Its file name is MainScreen.htx and is located on the companion CD.

LISTING 3.3—MAINSCREEN.HTX

```
01.<!doctype html public "-//IETF//DTD HTML//EN">
02.<HTML>
03.
04.<HEAD>
05.
06.<TITLE>IDC Message Base Main</TITLE>
07.
08.</HEAD>
09.
10.<BODY BGCOLOR=#FFFFF7>
11.
12.<DIV ALIGN=CENTER>
13.<TABLE WIDTH=95%>
14.  <TR>
15.    <TD ALIGN=LEFT>
16.      <H2>IDC MessageBase</H2>
17.    </TD>
18.    <TD ALIGN=RIGHT>
19.      <H2>Main</H2>
20.    </TD>
21.  </TR>
22.</TABLE>
23.<HR>
24.
25.<FORM ACTION="/Scripts/MessageBase/ViewConfMessages.idc" METHOD=POST>
26.<TABLE>
27.  <TR>
28.    <TD ALIGN=CENTER BGCOLOR=#D0FFFF>
29.      <%begindetail%>
30.      <H3>Welcome, <%UserName%>.</H3>
31.      <INPUT TYPE=HIDDEN NAME="UserID" VALUE=<%UserID%>>
32.      <%enddetail%>
33.      <%if CurrentRecord EQ 0 %>
34.      <FONT COLOR=RED>
35.        <H3>Sorry, your account was not found. Please
36.      <A HREF="MessageBase.htm">try again.</A></H3>
37.      </FONT>
38.    </TD>
39.  </TR>
40.</TABLE>
41.</FORM>
```

continues

LISTING 3.3—MAINSCREEN.HTX, CONTINUED

```
42.<%else%>
43.    </TD>
44.  </TR>
45.  <TR>
46.    <TD ALIGN=CENTER>
47.      <BR><H4>View a conference's messages</H4><BR>
48.      <SELECT NAME="ConferenceName">
49.        <%begindetail%>
50.          <OPTION><%ConferenceName%>
51.        <%enddetail%>
52.      </SELECT>
53.      <INPUT TYPE=SUBMIT VALUE="View">
54.    </TD>
55.  </TR>
56.  <TR>
57.    <TD>
58.      <HR>
59.    </TD>
60.  </TR>
61.</TABLE>
62.</FORM>
63.<FORM ACTION="/Scripts/MessageBase/Search.idc" METHOD=POST>
64.  <H4>Find a message by subject</H4><br>
65.  <%begindetail%>
66.    <INPUT TYPE=HIDDEN NAME="UserID" VALUE=<%UserID2%>>
67.  <%enddetail%>
68.  <INPUT TYPE=SUBMIT VALUE="Search">
69.</FORM>
70.
71.<%endif%>
72.
73.</DIV>
74.
75.</body>
76.</html>
```

The first purpose of this page, validation of the user, is taken care of on lines 29–42. The first result set contains the user's personal information if a match is found for the name and password. In this case the user is greeted by the message on line 30. Also, the user's ID is propagated to the Message List page by the input field on line 31.

If no match for the user is found, the condition on line 33 tests true, and the user gets an error message. Otherwise, the <%else%> on line 42 allows the rest of the page to be displayed.

The next order of business is to provide the user with a list of conferences that can be viewed. The second result set received by this file contains this information. Lines 48–52 set up the combo box from which the user can make a choice. Note that since the request must contain the user's ID, the form was started even before the first detail block. Thus the first UserID found in the search for the user can be used in the request to view a conference.

The user can get to the application's search feature by pressing the button presented by the third feature on this page, the form on lines 63–69. Because an action different from View is required, this second form must be created. To pass the UserID on this form as well, it is necessary to select it a second time in the .IDC file.

Note that the <%else%> is placed in the middle of a table. When you do this, you must be sure that either path contains the appropriate tags to properly close the currently open control structures. Thus, the tags on lines 38–41 serve exactly the same function as those on lines 59–62, depending on how the conditional expression is evaluated.

Conference Message List Page

The user views the threaded message list on the Conference Message List page, with the option of opening any message listed for display or adding a message on a new topic. This page contains the implementation of the threaded message display feature, discussed in the "Threading Message Responses" section earlier in this chapter.

Figure 3.5 depicts the Conference Message List page. There are three features of note on this page:

◆ A *Refresh List* button allows the user to update the list. This is useful to see if other users have added messages since the page was last shown.

◆ A *Post New Topic* button allows the user to post a message on a new topic to the conference.

◆ The list of messages in the conference, each with an *Open* button that the user can click to open the message for viewing.

The Conference Message List page consists of an .IDC file that retrieves the desired data and a single .HTX file for displaying that data.

Figure 3.5

*The Conference
Message List
page.*

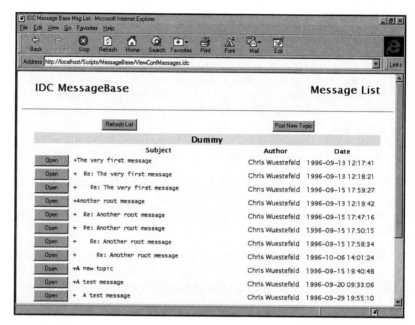

IDC File for the Conference Message List Page

Listing 3.4 presents the .IDC file that results in the creation of the View Conference Message List page. Its file name is ViewConfMessages.idc and is located on the companion CD.

LISTING 3.4—VIEWCONFMESSAGES.IDC

```
01.Datasource: dbMessageBase
02.Username: sa
03.Template: ViewConfMessages.htx
04.RequiredParameters: UserID, ConferenceName
05.ODBCOptions: SQL_ACCESS_MODE=1, SQL_MAX_ROWS=0
06.SQLStatement:
07.+SELECT DISTINCTROW '+' & [SpaceString] & [MessageSubject] AS Expr1,
08.+Users.UserName, Messages.MessageTS, Messages.MessageID,
➥'<%UserID%>'
09.+FROM Users INNER JOIN
10.+  (Conferences INNER JOIN
11.+   (Spacing INNER JOIN
12.+     Messages ON Spacing.NumSpaces = Messages.NumSpaces
13.+   ) ON Conferences.ConferenceID = Messages.ConferenceID
```

```
14.+  ) ON Users.UserID = Messages.UserID
15.+WHERE (((Conferences.ConferenceName)='%ConferenceName%'))
16.+ORDER BY Messages.DisplayOrdering
```

The .IDC file in listing 3.4 contains a single query that retrieves all the messages in the conference, sorted in the order in which they're meant to be displayed. Along with the message field, other data relating to the author is retrieved: the name of the author and the spacing string necessary to show threading. For an explanation of the threading mechanism, see the "Threading Message Responses" section earlier in this chapter.

HTX File for the Conference Message List Page

Listing 3.5 presents the .HTX file that specifies the appearance of the Conference Message List page. Its file name is ViewConfMessages.htx and is located on the companion CD. Don't be fooled by the length of the listing; it's actually straightforward.

LISTING 3.5—VIEWCONFMESSAGES.HTX

```
01.<!doctype html public "-//IETF//DTD HTML//EN">
02.<HTML>
03.
04.<HEAD>
05.
06.<TITLE>IDC Message Base Msg List</TITLE>
07.
08.</HEAD>
09.
10.<BODY BGCOLOR=#FFFFF7>
11.
12.<DIV ALIGN=CENTER>
13.<TABLE WIDTH=95%>
14.   <TR>
15.     <TD ALIGN=LEFT>
16.       <H2>IDC MessageBase</H2>
17.     </TD>
18.     <TD ALIGN=RIGHT>
19.       <H2>Message List</H2>
20.     </TD>
21.   </TR>
22.</TABLE>
23.<HR>
```

continues

LISTING 3.5—VIEWCONFMESSAGES.HTX, CONTINUED

```
24.
25.<TABLE WIDTH=95%>
26.  <TR>
27.   <TD WIDTH=50% ALIGN=CENTER>
28.     <FORM ACTION="/Scripts/MessageBase/ViewConfMessages.idc"
29.           METHOD=POST>
30.     <INPUT TYPE=HIDDEN NAME="UserID" VALUE="<%idc.UserID%>">
31.     <INPUT TYPE=HIDDEN NAME="ConferenceName"
32.           VALUE="<%idc.ConferenceName%>">
33.     <INPUT TYPE=SUBMIT VALUE="Refresh List">
34.     </FORM>
35.   </TD>
36.   <TD WIDTH=50% ALIGN=CENTER>
37.     <FORM ACTION="/Scripts/MessageBase/NewTopic.idc"
38.           METHOD=POST>
39.     <INPUT TYPE=HIDDEN NAME="UserID" VALUE="<%idc.UserID%>">
40.     <INPUT TYPE=HIDDEN NAME="ConferenceName"
41.           VALUE="<%idc.ConferenceName%>">
42.     <INPUT TYPE=SUBMIT VALUE="Post New Topic">
43.     </FORM>
44.   </TD>
45.  </TR>
46.</TABLE>
47.
48.<TABLE WIDTH=95%>
49.  <TR>
50.   <TD COLSPAN=4 ALIGN=CENTER BGCOLOR=#D0FFFF>
51.     <H3><%idc.ConferenceName%></H3>
52.   </TD>
53.  </TR>
54.  <TR>
55.   <TH>
56.   </TH>
57.   <TH>
58.     Subject
59.   </TH>
60.   <TH>
61.     Author
62.   </TH>
63.   <TH>
64.     Date
65.   </TH>
```

```
66.  </TR>
67.  <%begindetail%>
68.  <TR>
69.    <TD>
70.      <FORM ACTION="/Scripts/MessageBase/ViewMessage.idc"
71.           METHOD=POST>
72.        <INPUT TYPE=SUBMIT VALUE="Open">
73.        <INPUT TYPE=HIDDEN NAME="MessageID" VALUE="<%MessageID%>">
74.        <INPUT TYPE=HIDDEN NAME="UserID" VALUE="<%idc.UserID%>">
75.      </FORM>
76.    </TD>
77.    <TD>
78.      <PRE><%Expr1%></PRE>
79.    </TD>
80.    <TD>
81.      <%UserName%>
82.    </TD>
83.    <TD>
84.      <%MessageTS%>
85.    </TD>
86.  </TR>
87.  <%enddetail%>
88.</TABLE>
89.
90.</DIV>
91.
92.</BODY>
93.</HTML>
```

Although this is a relatively long .HTX file, most of the hard work is done by the large query in the .IDC file that invoked it.

There are many forms on this screen. Note that unlike the main screen, multiple queries to retrieve the UserID for each of these are not required. Because the UserID is passed into the .IDC file, it can be accessed directly by using *<%idc.UserID%>*.

The first two forms on the screen are relatively static. The first simply refreshes the page by re-invoking ViewConfMessages.idc, passing it the conference name and, of course, the UserID. The second passes the same information to an IDC request that enables the user to post a new topic.

Each message in the conference results in the creation of a separate form. In each case the action, the submit field, and the UserID field are identical. The MessageID field conveys to the ViewMessage.idc the identity of the message to be opened.

An alternative to this approach is to make the subject string a hyperlink. This can be accomplished by synthesizing a GET request using these values and using this string as the link destination. For more information on dynamically creating URLs, as this alternative would require, see the section "Value Escaping Keyword" in Chapter 2.

View Message Page

The View Message page presents a message and all its related information (see fig. 3.6). The user has the option of paging to the previous or next message in the conference, following up the message with a reply, or returning to the list of conference messages.

Figure 3.6 depicts the View Message page. The page contains a number of features:

◆ *Next* and *Previous* buttons allow the user to view multiple messages in the conference in turn, without needing to return to the Conference Message List page.

◆ A *Follow up* button allows the user to post a response to the displayed message.

◆ A *Return to list* button allows the user to return to the Conference Message List page.

◆ The message itself — this includes not only the details of the message itself, but also a *mailto* hyperlink allowing the user to send private email to the message's author, if an email address is available.

Figure 3.6

The View Message page.

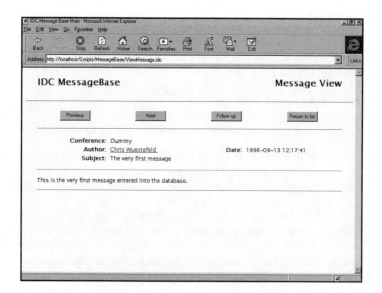

IDC Files for the View Message Page

Several .IDC files participate in the View Message Page. This is necessary because the function is available from several places in the program, each one of which needs to determine the data to be used differently:

◆ Initial Request — Retrieves the page's data when called from either the Conference Message List page or the View Search Results page

◆ Next Message — Retrieves the page's data when called as a result of pressing the View Message page's own *Next* button

◆ Previous Message — Retrieves the page's data when called as a result of pressing the View Message page's own *Previous* button

Initial Request

Listing 3.6 presents one of the .IDC files that result in the creation of the View Message page. This particular file is called by the Conference Message List page and the View Search Results page. Its file name is ViewMessage.idc and is located on the companion CD.

LISTING 3.6—VIEWMESSAGE.IDC

```
01.Datasource: dbMessageBase
02.Username: sa
03.Template: ViewMessage.htx
04.ODBCOptions: SQL_ACCESS_MODE=1
05.Translationfile: xlatfile.txt
06.RequiredParameter: UserID, MessageID
07.SQLStatement:
08.+SELECT DISTINCTROW Messages.MessageSubject, Messages.MessageText,
09.+Users.UserName AS AuthorName, Users.UserEmail AS AuthorEmail,
10.+Messages.MessageTS, Conferences.ConferenceID,
11.+Conferences.ConferenceName, Messages.NumSpaces,
12.+Messages.DisplayOrdering, Messages.MessageID
13.+FROM Conferences INNER JOIN
14.+  (Users INNER JOIN
15.+    Messages ON Users.UserID = Messages.UserID
16.+  )
17.+  ON Conferences.ConferenceID = Messages.ConferenceID
18.+WHERE (((Messages.MessageID)=%MessageID%))
```

Although the SQL query seems long, it's actually straightforward. All the fields of the message itself are retrieved, based on the MessageID provided. In addition, the name of the conference, the name of the message author, and the author's email addresses are retrieved.

Note one feature that hasn't been used elsewhere: a translation file specified in line 5. The contents of this file are shown in the "Translation Files" section of Chapter 2.

The translation file is required because the message text could contain virtually anything. If the message included characters with special meaning to the user's web browser (such as "<", for example), the result could prevent proper viewing of the message. The translation file will translate those characters to entities that will be display the same as the character the same, but will not affect the browser ("<" will be translated to "<", for example).

Next Message

Listing 3.7 presents one of the .IDC files that result in the creation of the View Message page. This particular file is called by the View Message page itself, in response to the user clicking the *Next* button. Its file name is NextMessage.idc and is located on the companion CD.

LISTING 3.7—NEXTMESSAGE.IDC

```
01.Datasource: dbMessageBase
02.Username: sa
03.Template: ViewMessage.htx
04.ODBCOptions: SQL_ACCESS_MODE=1, SQL_MAX_ROWS=1
05.RequiredParameter: UserID, ConferenceID, MessageID
06.SQLStatement:
07.+SELECT DISTINCTROW Messages.MessageSubject, Messages.MessageText,
08.+Users.UserName AS AuthorName, Users.UserEmail AS AuthorEmail,
09.+Messages.MessageTS, Conferences.ConferenceID,
10.+Conferences.ConferenceName, Messages.NumSpaces,
11.+Messages.DisplayOrdering, Messages.MessageID
12.+FROM Conferences INNER JOIN
13.+   (Users INNER JOIN
14.+     Messages ON Users.UserID = Messages.UserID
15.+   )
16.+   ON Conferences.ConferenceID = Messages.ConferenceID
17.+WHERE Conferences.ConferenceID=%ConferenceID%
18.+ AND Messages.DisplayOrdering >
19.+   (SELECT DisplayOrdering FROM Messages WHERE MessageID=%MessageID%)
20.+ ORDER BY Messages.DisplayOrdering ASC
```

This IDC request is invoked when the user presses the *Next* button. It is very similar to ViewMessage.idc but has an added wrinkle of determining which message is next. This is accomplished by lines 18 and 19, which request only those messages in the conference that have a display ordering greater than the current message. This request might return many rows; the set is limited on line 4 where an *ODBCOption* for *SQL_MAX_ROWS* is set so only a maximum of one row can be retrieved.

Previous Message

Listing 3.8 presents one of the .IDC files that result in the creation of the View Message page. This particular file is called by the View Message page itself, in response to the user clicking the *Previous* button. Its file name is PrevMessage.idc and is located on the companion CD.

LISTING 3.8—PREVMESSAGE.IDC

```
01.Datasource: dbMessageBase
02.Username: sa
03.Template: ViewMessage.htx
04.ODBCOptions: SQL_ACCESS_MODE=1, SQL_MAX_ROWS=1
05.RequiredParameter: UserID, ConferenceID
06.SQLStatement:
07.+SELECT DISTINCTROW Messages.MessageSubject, Messages.MessageText,
08.+Users.UserName AS AuthorName, Users.UserEmail AS AuthorEmail,
09.+Messages.MessageTS, Conferences.ConferenceID,
10.+Conferences.ConferenceName, Messages.NumSpaces,
11.+Messages.DisplayOrdering, Messages.MessageID
12.+FROM Conferences INNER JOIN
13.+  (Users INNER JOIN
14.+    Messages ON Users.UserID = Messages.UserID
15.+  )
16.+  ON Conferences.ConferenceID = Messages.ConferenceID
17.+WHERE Conferences.ConferenceID=%ConferenceID%
18.+ AND Messages.DisplayOrdering <
19.+  (SELECT DisplayOrdering FROM Messages WHERE MessageID=%MessageID%)
20.+ ORDER BY Messages.DisplayOrdering DESC
```

This IDC request is invoked when the user presses the *Previous* button. It is identical to nextmessage.idc (discussed in the previous section) with the exception of two lines: line 18 changes the > to < and line 20 changes *ASC* to *DESC*.

Rather than placing these very similar requests in separate .IDC files, you could combine them into one. The two elements that differ could be represented by variables whose values the requesting forms would set accordingly. For example, lines 17–20 could read:

```
+WHERE Conferences.ConferenceID=%ConferenceID%
+ AND Messages.DisplayOrdering %RelationOp%
+  (SELECT DisplayOrdering FROM Messages WHERE MessageID=%MessageID%)
+ ORDER BY Messages.DisplayOrdering %SortOrder%
```

HTX File for the View Message Page

While several .IDC files retrieve data for this feature, they all lead to the same .HTX file to present a consistent user interface.

Listing 3.9 presents the .HTX file that specifies the appearance of the View Message page. Its file name is ViewMessage.htx and is located on the companion CD. This is another long listing that is actually quite simple.

LISTING 3.9—VIEWMESSAGE.HTX

```
001.<!doctype html public "-//IETF//DTD HTML//EN">
002.<HTML>
003.
004.<HEAD>
005.
006.<TITLE>IDC Message Base Main</TITLE>
007.
008.</HEAD>
009.
010.<BODY BGCOLOR=#FFFFF7>
011.
012.<DIV ALIGN=CENTER>
013.<TABLE WIDTH=95%>
014.  <TR>
015.    <TD ALIGN=LEFT>
016.      <H2>IDC MessageBase</H2>
017.    </TD>
018.    <TD ALIGN=RIGHT>
019.      <H2>Message View</H2>
020.    </TD>
021.  </TR>
022.</TABLE>
023.<HR>
024.
025.<%begindetail%>
026.<TABLE WIDTH=95%>
027.  <TR>
```

```
028.    <TD COLSPAN=4>
029.      <TABLE WIDTH=100%>
030.        <TR>
031.          <TD ALIGN=CENTER WIDTH=25%>
032.            <FORM ACTION="/Scripts/MessageBase/PrevMessage.idc"
033.              METHOD=POST>
034.              <INPUT TYPE=HIDDEN NAME="UserID"
035.                VALUE="<%idc.UserID%>">
036.              <INPUT TYPE=HIDDEN NAME="ConferenceID"
037.                VALUE="<%ConferenceID%>">
038.              <INPUT TYPE=HIDDEN NAME="MessageID"
039               VALUE="<%MessageID%>">
040.              <INPUT TYPE=SUBMIT VALUE="Previous">
041.            </FORM>
042.          </TD>
043.          <TD ALIGN=CENTER WIDTH=25%>
044.            <FORM ACTION="/Scripts/MessageBase/NextMessage.idc"
045.              METHOD=POST>
046.              <INPUT TYPE=HIDDEN NAME="UserID"
047.                VALUE="<%idc.UserID%>">
048.              <INPUT TYPE=HIDDEN NAME="ConferenceID"
049               VALUE="<%ConferenceID%>">
050.              <INPUT TYPE=HIDDEN NAME="MessageID"
051.                VALUE="<%MessageID%>">
052.              <INPUT TYPE=SUBMIT VALUE="Next">
053.            </FORM>
054.          </TD>
055.          <TD ALIGN=CENTER WIDTH=25%>
056.            <FORM ACTION="/Scripts/MessageBase/Follow-up.idc"
057.              METHOD=POST>
058.              <INPUT TYPE=HIDDEN NAME="UserID"
059.                VALUE="<%idc.UserID%>">
060.              <INPUT TYPE=HIDDEN NAME="ConferenceID"
061.                VALUE="<%ConferenceID%>">
062.              <INPUT TYPE=HIDDEN NAME="ConferenceName"
063.                VALUE="<%ConferenceName%>">
064.              <INPUT TYPE=HIDDEN NAME="ParentID"
065.                VALUE="<%MessageID%>">
066.              <INPUT TYPE=HIDDEN NAME="ParentDispOrder"
067.                VALUE="<%DisplayOrdering%>">
068.              <INPUT TYPE=HIDDEN NAME="MessageSubject"
069.                VALUE="<%MessageSubject%>">
070.              <INPUT TYPE=HIDDEN NAME="NestDepth"
```

continues

LISTING 3.9—VIEWMESSAGE.HTX, CONTINUED

```
071.                    VALUE="<%NumSpaces%>+1">
072.                <INPUT TYPE=SUBMIT VALUE="Follow up">
073.              </FORM>
074.            </TD>
075.            <TD ALIGN=CENTER WIDTH=25%>
076.              <FORM ACTION="/Scripts/MessageBase/ViewConfMessages.idc"
077.                METHOD=POST>
078.                <INPUT TYPE=HIDDEN NAME="UserID"
079.                  VALUE="<%idc.UserID%>">
080.                <INPUT TYPE=HIDDEN NAME="ConferenceName"
081.                  VALUE="<%ConferenceName%>">
082.                <INPUT TYPE=SUBMIT VALUE="Return to list">
083.              </FORM>
084.            </TD>
085.          </TR>
086.        </TABLE>
087.        <HR>
088.      </TD>
089.  </TR>
090.  <TR>
091.    <TH ALIGN=RIGHT>
092.      Conference:
093.    </TH>
094.    <TD COLSPAN=3>
095.      <%ConferenceName%>
096.    </TD>
097.  </TR>
098.  <TR>
099.    <TH ALIGN=RIGHT>
100.      Author:
101.    </TH>
102.    <TD>
103.      <%if AuthorEmail EQ "" %>
104.        <%AuthorName%>
105.      <%else%>
106.        <A HREF="mailto:<%AuthorEmail%>">
107.          <%AuthorName%>
108.        </A>
109.      <%endif%>
110.    </TD>
111.    <TH ALIGN=RIGHT>
```

```
112.      Date:
113.    </TH>
114.    <TD>
115.       <%MessageTS%>
116.    </TD>
117.  </TR>
118.  <TR>
119.    <TH ALIGN=RIGHT>
120.      Subject:
121.    </TH>
122.    <TD COLSPAN=3>
123.       <%MessageSubject%>
124.    </TD>
125.  </TR>
126.  <TR>
127.    <TD COLSPAN=4>
128.      <HR>
129.      <%MessageText%>
130.      <HR>
131.    </TD>
132.  </TR>
133.</TABLE>
134.
135.</DIV>
136.
137.<%enddetail%>
138.<%if CurrentRecord EQ 0 %>
139.<CENTER>
140.  <FONT COLOR=RED>
141.    <H3>No message found!</H3>
142.  </FONT>
143.</CENTER>
144.<%endif%>
145.</body>
146.</html>
```

A couple of features are worthy of note in this file, as shown in listing 3.9.

First, notice how lines 70 and 71 set up the nesting for a follow-up message, if any. Because the Internet Database Connector cannot perform any calculations of its own, the form assigns a value to the NestDepth variable equal, literally, to the nesting depth (NumSpaces) of the current message, "+1". When this value is eventually replaced and sent to the database engine, the expression is evaluated there.

Second, lines 103–109 check for the availability of an email address for the author. If one is retrieved, a mail to hyperlink is placed around the author's name so users can send email directly. This is accomplished by checking whether the variable contains a null string.

Finally, in the event the message is not found (which might occur if the user presses Next or Previous too many times), the user receives an error message. This is handled on lines 138–144. If, after the message details are supposed to have been written, the current record equals 0 (it is normally 1 at this point), a message is output.

Post a Follow-Up Page

The Post a Follow-Up page enables the user to post a message in reply to an existing topic. Only one action can be performed here: posting the message (see fig. 3.7).

Figure 3.7 depicts the Post a Follow-Up page. The page contains two features:

◆ A form that the user enters the message into. Note that the conference, author, and date fields are filled automatically and not editable, while the subject field defaults to the same subject as the message that the follow-up is in response to

◆ A *Post* button that the user presses to post the message once the form has been completed

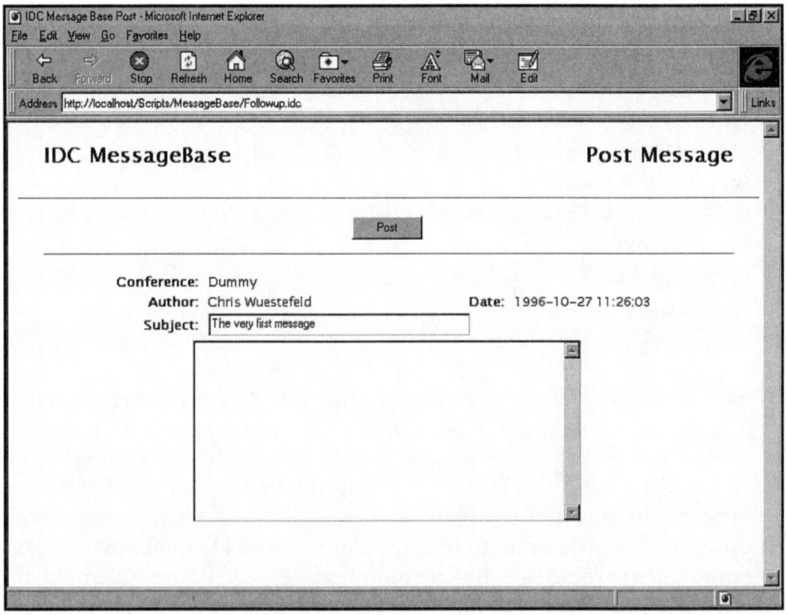

Figure 3.7

The Post a Follow-Up page.

The Post a Follow-Up page consists of an .IDC file that retrieves the desired data and a single .HTX file for displaying that data.

IDC Files for the Post a Follow-Up Page

Implementing the feature to post follow-up messages requires two .IDC files. Unlike the View Message page, this is not because different paths must be taken to obtain the data. Here one file gets the data for the page, while the second .IDC file stores data when commanded by the user and retrieves the data necessary to return to the Message List.

Setting Up the Follow-Up Message

Listing 3.10 presents the .IDC file that supplies the input data to the Post a Follow-Up page. This file's name is Followup.idc and is located on the companion CD.

LISTING 3.10—FOLLOWUP.IDC

```
1.Datasource: dbMessageBase
2.Username: sa
3.Template: Followup.htx
4.ODBCOptions: SQL_ACCESS_MODE=1
5.RequiredParameter: UserID, ConferenceID, ConferenceName
6.SQLStatement:
7.+SELECT DISTINCTROW UserName, Now() AS CurrTS
8.+FROM Users
9.+WHERE UserID = %UserID%
```

The request for the follow-up page is almost trivial. Two values are requested from the database: the user's name and the current time. Both of these will simply be displayed on the page and discarded; neither is used in the actual posting of the message.

Note that while the SQL query here only uses the UserID variable, there are entries in the *RequiredParameter* field for ConferenceID and ConferenceName. These are given because the template file, follow-up.htx, expects values for these variables. Because the processing of the entire request requires all these values, it's a good idea to list them here so the IDC can enforce the requirement, as well as for documentation purposes.

Posting the Follow-Up Message

Listing 3.11 presents the .IDC file that actually posts the follow-up message for the Post a Follow-Up page. This file's name is PostMessage.idc and is located on the companion CD. The request to post a message is issued when the user presses the *Post* button on the Post a Follow-Up page.

LISTING 3.11—POSTMESSAGE.IDC

```
01.Datasource: dbMessageBase
02.Username: sa
03.Template: ViewConfMessages.htx
04.ODBCOptions: SQL_MAX_ROWS=0
05.Translationfile: xlatfile.txt
06.RequiredParameter: UserID, ConferenceID, ConferenceName, ParentID, NestDepth
07.SQLStatement:
08.+UPDATE messages SET displayordering=displayordering+1
09.+WHERE conferenceid=%ConferenceID%
10.+AND displayordering>
11.+   (SELECT MAX(displayordering) FROM messages
12.+    WHERE parentmessageid=%ParentID% OR MessageID=%ParentID%
13.+   )
14.SQLStatement:
15.+INSERT INTO messages
16.+(MessageSubject,UserID,messagets,conferenceid,
17.+parentmessageid,numspaces,messagetext,displayordering)
18.+SELECT '%MessageSubject%',%UserID%,Now(),%ConferenceID%,
19.+ %ParentID%,%NestDepth%,'%MessageText%', 1+MAX(displayordering)
20.+ FROM Messages
21.+ WHERE parentmessageid=%ParentID% OR MessageID=%ParentID%
22.SQLStatement:
23.+SELECT DISTINCTROW '+' & [SpaceString] & [MessageSubject] AS Expr1,
24.+Users.UserName, Messages.MessageTS, Messages.MessageID
25.+FROM Users INNER JOIN
26.+   (Conferences INNER JOIN
27.+     (Spacing INNER JOIN
28.+       Messages ON Spacing.NumSpaces = Messages.NumSpaces
29.+     ) ON Conferences.ConferenceID = Messages.ConferenceID
30.+   ) ON Users.UserID = Messages.UserID
31.+WHERE (((Conferences.ConferenceID)=%ConferenceID%))
32.+ORDER BY Messages.DisplayOrdering
```

This file has two tasks:

Post the message that was just entered

Return to the conference message list

The first task is carried out by the statements in lines 7–21. The message is inserted into the database, and threading information is adjusted according to the algorithm described in the "Posting Threaded Messages" section earlier in this chapter.

The second task is to set up and call ViewConfMessages.htx. This is done by the query on lines 22–32, which are actually identical to those in ViewConfMessages.idc.

HTX File for the Post a Follow-Up Page

Listing 3.12 presents the .HTX file that specifies the appearance of the Post a Follow-Up page. Its file name is Followup.htx and is located on the companion CD.

LISTING 3.12—FOLLOWUP.HTX

```
01.<!doctype html public "-//IETF//DTD HTML//EN">
02.<HTML>
03.
04.<HEAD>
05.
06.<TITLE>IDC Message Base Post</TITLE>
07.
08.</HEAD>
09.
10.<BODY BGCOLOR=#FFFFF7>
11.
12.<DIV ALIGN=CENTER>13.<TABLE WIDTH=95%>
14.   <TR>
15.     <TD ALIGN=LEFT>
16.       <H2>IDC MessageBase</H2>
17.     </TD>
18.     <TD ALIGN=RIGHT>
19.       <H2>Post Message</H2>
20.     </TD>
21.   </TR>
22.</TABLE>
23.<HR>
24.
25.<%begindetail%>
26.<FORM ACTION="/Scripts/MessageBase/PostMessage.idc" METHOD=POST>
27.<TABLE WIDTH=95%>
28.   <TR>
29.     <TD COLSPAN=4 ALIGN=CENTER>
30.       <INPUT TYPE=HIDDEN NAME="UserID" VALUE="<%idc.UserID%>">
31.       <INPUT TYPE=SUBMIT VALUE="Post">
32.       <HR>
33.     </TD>
```

continues

LISTING 3.12—FOLLOWUP.HTX, CONTINUED

```
34.  </TR>
35.  <TR>
36.   <TH ALIGN=RIGHT>
37.    Conference:
38.   </TH>
39.   <TD COLSPAN=3>
40.    <%idc.ConferenceName%>
41.    <INPUT TYPE=HIDDEN NAME="ConferenceID" VALUE="<%idc.ConferenceID%>">
42.    <INPUT TYPE=HIDDEN NAME="ConferenceName" VALUE="<%idc.
➥ConferenceName%>">
43.   </TD>
44.  </TR>
45.  <TR>
46.   <TH ALIGN=RIGHT>
47.    Author:
48.   </TH>
49.   <TD>
50.    <%UserName%>
51.   </TD>
52.   <TH ALIGN=RIGHT>
53.    Date:
54.   </TH>
55.   <TD>
56.    <%CurrTS%>
57.    <INPUT TYPE=HIDDEN NAME="MessageTS" VALUE="<%CurrTS%>">
58.   </TD>
59.  </TR>
60.  <TR>
61.   <TH ALIGN=RIGHT>
62.    Subject:
63.   </TH>
64.   <TD COLSPAN=3>
65.    <INPUT TYPE=TEXT NAME="MessageSubject" MAXLENGTH=100 SIZE=50
66.      VALUE="<%idc.MessageSubject%>">
67.   </TD>
68.  </TR>
69.  <TR>
70.   <TD COLSPAN=4>
71.    <CENTER>
```

```
72.      <TEXTAREA NAME="MessageText" WRAP=OFF COLS=80 ROWS=12></TEXTAREA>
73.     </CENTER>
74.    </TD>
75.   </TR>
76.</TABLE>
77.
78.<INPUT TYPE=HIDDEN NAME="ParentID" VALUE="<%idc.ParentID%>">
79.<INPUT TYPE=HIDDEN NAME="NestDepth" VALUE="<%idc.NestDepth%>">
80.</FORM>
81.<%enddetail%>
82.</DIV>
83.
84.</body>
85.</html>
```

You should not find any surprises here. The preceding listing is a very straightforward .HTX template, despite the fact that it calls a remarkably complex .IDC file. One issue you may want to note is on line 72. You should place the ending of the <TEXTAREA> tag immediately following the start tag, or any intervening characters will be interpreted as a default value for the field.

Post a New Topic Page

The intent of the Post a New Topic page is very similar to that of the Follow-Up page: to add a new message to the database and return to the Conference Message list. There is only difference visible to the user. The Follow-Up page supplies a default message subject, while a message on a *new* topic obviously won't have such a default. On the other hand, there are important differences in the implementation.

You can see the Post a New Topic page depicted in Figure 3.8.

Figure 3.8

*Post a New
Topic page.*

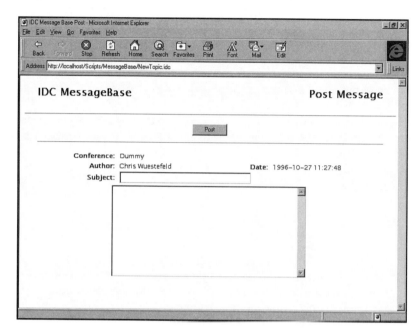

IDC Files for the Post a New Topic Page

Just as when you posted a follow-up message, there are two .IDC files involved in the Post a New Topic page: one to get the initial data, and one to store the results and return to the Message List.

Setting up the New Message

This request retrieves the data necessary for display on the message-editing page. The only difference between this and followup.idc (previously discussed in the section "Setting Up the Follow-Up Message") is the need to retrieve the ID of the conference by this request; in the case of followup.idc it was already known.

Listing 3.13 presents the .IDC file that supplies the input data to the Post a New Topic page. This file's name is NewTopic.idc and is located on the companion CD.

LISTING 3.13—NewTopic.idc

```
01.Datasource: dbMessageBase
02.Username: sa
03.Template: NewTopic.htx
04.ODBCOptions: SQL_ACCESS_MODE=1
05.RequiredParameter: UserID, ConferenceName
```

```
06.SQLStatement:
07.+SELECT DISTINCTROW ConferenceName, ConferenceID
08.+FROM Conferences
09.+WHERE ConferenceName = '%ConferenceName%'
10.SQLStatement:
11.+SELECT DISTINCTROW UserName, Now() AS CurrTS
12.+FROM Users
13.+WHERE UserID = %UserID%
```

Line 4 is noteworthy. The *SQL_ACCESS_MODE* option is set to 1, which means "Read." By doing this in queries that do not require any data changes (most of the queries in this application), performance can be improved by not requiring write locks on the tables.

Posting the New Message

As in postmessage.idc (discussed in the section "Posting the Follow-Up Message"), this request has two goals:

Get the new message into the database.

Prepare to view the conference message list again.

Listing 3.14 presents the .IDC file that posts the new message when invoked as a result of the user clicking the *Post* button on the Post a New Topic page. This file's name is PostNew.idc and is located on the companion CD.

LISTING 3.14—POSTNEW.IDC

```
01.Datasource: dbMessageBase
02.Username: sa
03.Template: ViewConfMessages.htx
04.ODBCOptions: SQL_MAX_ROWS=0
05.Translationfile: xlatfile.txt
06.RequiredParameter: UserID, ConferenceID
07.SQLStatement:
08.+INSERT INTO messages
09.+(MessageSubject,UserID,messagets,conferenceid,
10.+parentmessageid,numspaces,messagetext,displayordering)
11.+SELECT '%MessageSubject%',%UserID%,Now(),%ConferenceID%,
12.+ 0,0,'%MessageText%', 1+MAX(displayordering)
13.+ FROM Messages
14.+ WHERE ConferenceID=%ConferenceID%
15.SQLStatement:
16.+SELECT DISTINCTROW '+' & [SpaceString] & [MessageSubject] AS Expr1,
```

continues

LISTING 3.14—POSTNEW.IDC, CONTINUED

```
17.+Users.UserName, Messages.MessageTS, Messages.MessageID
18.+FROM Users INNER JOIN
19.+  (Conferences INNER JOIN
20.+    (Spacing INNER JOIN
21.+      Messages ON Spacing.NumSpaces = Messages.NumSpaces
22.+    ) ON Conferences.ConferenceID = Messages.ConferenceID
23.+  ) ON Users.UserID = Messages.UserID
24.+WHERE (((Conferences.ConferenceID)=%ConferenceID%))
25.+ORDER BY Messages.DisplayOrdering
```

The insertion of the new message is a bit different than the query used to post a follow-up (see listing 3.11). The fact that this is a new topic (that is, not a follow-up to anything) allows some simplification of the query because certain assumptions can be made. In particular, the new message goes at the end of the list, so no other messages need their DisplayOrdering values adjusted. Thus, the insertion can be performed in a single statement in which the DisplayOrdering is set to 1 greater than the highest value currently used.

This comes with a small price: if no messages yet exist within the conference, the value of *MAX (displayordering)* will be *NULL*, and *1+NULL* is still *NULL*. When this value is inserted, an error will occur because DisplayOrdering is a required field. Because of this, any new conference must have an initial message manually inserted by the system administrator.

A more complex query could probably be written to take this into account, but such a query would slow the system down a bit. In the interest of preserving performance of the web server, a better solution is the requirement that upon creation of a new conference, an initial message must be inserted manually.

HTX File for the Post a New Topic Page

Listing 3.15 presents the .HTX file that specifies the appearance of the Post a New Topic page. Its file name is NewTopic.htx and is located on the companion CD.

LISTING 3.15—NEWTOPIC.HTX

```
01.<!doctype html public "-//IETF//DTD HTML//EN">
02.<HTML>
03.
04.<HEAD>
05.
06.<TITLE>IDC Message Base Post</TITLE>
07.
```

```
08.</HEAD>
09.
10.<BODY BGCOLOR=#FFFFF7>
11.
12.<DIV ALIGN=CENTER>
13.<TABLE WIDTH=95%>
14.  <TR>
15.    <TD ALIGN=LEFT>
16.      <H2>IDC MessageBase</H2>
17.    </TD>
18.    <TD ALIGN=RIGHT>
19.      <H2>Post Message</H2>
20.    </TD>
21.  </TR>
22.</TABLE>
23.<HR>
24.
25.<%begindetail%>
26.<FORM ACTION="/Scripts/MessageBase/PostNew.idc" METHOD=POST>
27.<TABLE WIDTH=95%>
28.  <TR>
29.    <TD COLSPAN=4 ALIGN=CENTER>
30.      <INPUT TYPE=HIDDEN NAME="UserID" VALUE="<%idc.UserID%>">
31.      <INPUT TYPE=SUBMIT VALUE="Post">
32.      <HR>
33.    </TD>
34.  </TR>
35.  <TR>
36.    <TH ALIGN=RIGHT>
37.      Conference:
38.    </TH>
39.    <TD COLSPAN=3>
40.      <%begindetail%>
41.      <%idc.ConferenceName%>
42.      <INPUT TYPE=HIDDEN NAME="ConferenceID" VALUE="<%ConferenceID%>">
43.      <INPUT TYPE=HIDDEN NAME="ConferenceName" VALUE="<%idc.
➥ConferenceName%>">
44.      <%enddetail%>
45.    </TD>
46.  </TR>
47.  <%begindetail%>
48.  <TR>
49.    <TH ALIGN=RIGHT>
```

continues

LISTING 3.15—NewTopic.htx, Continued

```
50.      Author:
51.    </TH>
52.    <TD>
53.      <%UserName%>
54.    </TD>
55.    <TH ALIGN=RIGHT>
56.      Date:
57.    </TH>
58.    <TD>
59.      <%CurrTS%>
60.      <INPUT TYPE=HIDDEN NAME="MessageTS" VALUE="<%CurrTS%>">
61.    </TD>
62.  </TR>
63.  <%enddetail%>
64.  <TR>
65.    <TH ALIGN=RIGHT>
66.      Subject:
67.    </TH>
68.    <TD COLSPAN=3>
69.      <INPUT TYPE=TEXT NAME="MessageSubject" MAXLENGTH=100 SIZE=50>
70.    </TD>
71.  </TR>
72.  <TR>
73.    <TD COLSPAN=4>
74.      <CENTER>
75.      <TEXTAREA NAME="MessageText" WRAP=OFF COLS=80
➥ROWS=12></TEXTAREA>
76.      </CENTER>
77.    </TD>
78.  </TR>
79.</TABLE>
80.
81.</FORM>
82.<%enddetail%>
83.</DIV>
84.
85.</body>
86.</html>
```

There are two small differences between this template and followup.htx (see listing 3.12). The more obvious of these differences is no default message subject offered on line 69. The second, more subtle difference is on line 42. Although follow-up was able to retrieve the Conference ID from the input to the IDC request, in this file you must have a detail block and retrieve the value from the result set.

Search Request Page

On the Search Request page, the user is given a list of conferences that might be searched for the specified string. Pressing the *Search* button causes those conferences to be searched for messages having subject strings matching the input criteria.

Figure 3.9 depicts the Search Request page. On this page you can see three items:

◆ A list box from which a set of conferences to search can be chosen

◆ An entry field into which the user can enter the string to search for

◆ A *Search* button that the user presses to execute the search

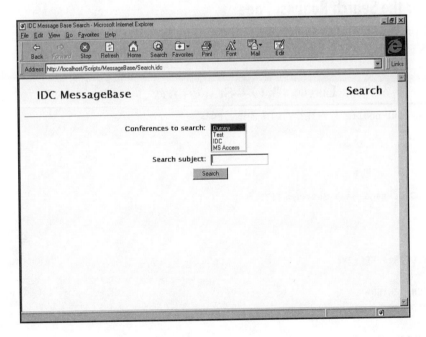

Figure 3.9

The Search Request page.

The Search Request page consists of an .IDC file that retrieves the desired data and a single .HTX file for displaying that data.

IDC File for the Search Request Page

Listing 3.16 presents the .IDC file that results in the creation of the Search Request page. Its file name is Search.idc and is located on the companion CD.

LISTING 3.16—SEARCH.IDC

```
1.Datasource: dbMessageBase
2.Username: sa
3.Template: Search.htx
4.ODBCOptions: SQL_ACCESS_MODE=1
5.RequiredParameter: UserID
6.SQLStatement:
7.+SELECT ConferenceID, ConferenceName
8.+FROM Conferences
```

This is a simple request. It serves to retrieve the list of conferences (and their IDs) in the system, to present to the user in the page's conference listbox.

Simply retrieve a list of all the conferences, along with their IDs.

HTX File for the Search Request Page

Listing 3.17 presents the .HTX file that specifies the appearance of the Search Request page. Its file name is Search.htx and is located on the companion CD.

LISTING 3.17—SEARCH.HTX

```
01.<!doctype html public "-//IETF//DTD HTML//EN">
02.<HTML>
03.
04.<HEAD>
05.
06.<TITLE>IDC Message Base Search</TITLE>
07.
08.</HEAD>
09.
10.<BODY BGCOLOR=#FFFFF7>
11.
12.<DIV ALIGN=CENTER>
13.<TABLE WIDTH=95%>
14.    <TR>
15.      <TD ALIGN=LEFT>
16.        <H2>IDC MessageBase</H2>
17.      </TD>
18.      <TD ALIGN=RIGHT>
19.        <H2>Search</H2>
20.      </TD>
21.    </TR>
```

```
22.</TABLE>
23.<HR>
24.
25.<FORM ACTION="/Scripts/MessageBase/SearchResults.idc" METHOD=POST>
26.<TABLE WIDTH=95%>
27.   <TR>
28.      <TH ALIGN=RIGHT VALIGN=TOP WIDTH=50%>
29.         Conferences to search:
30.      </TH>
31.      <TD ALIGN=LEFT VALIGN=TOP WIDTH=50%>
32.         <SELECT MULTIPLE NAME="SeldConferences">
33.           <%begindetail%>
34.             <OPTION VALUE="<%ConferenceID%>"><%ConferenceName%>
35.           <%enddetail%>
36.         </SELECT>
37.      </TD>
38.   </TR>
39.   <TR>
40.      <TH ALIGN=RIGHT VALIGN=TOP>
41.         Search subject:
42.      </TH>
43.      <TD ALIGN=LEFT VALIGN=TOP>
44.         <INPUT TYPE=TEXT NAME="SearchText">
45.      </TD>
46.   </TR>
47.   <TR>
48.      <TD COLSPAN=2 ALIGN=CENTER>
49.         <INPUT TYPE=HIDDEN NAME="UserID" VALUE="<%idc.UserID%>">
50.         <INPUT TYPE="SUBMIT" VALUE="Search">
51.      </TD>
52.   </TR>
53.</TABLE>
54.</FORM>
55.
56.
57.</DIV>
58.
59.</body>
60.</html>
```

Notice line 34, which enumerates the conferences available to be searched. A simpler approach to implementing this might use only the conference names (without the corresponding IDs). This won't work as expected due to problems in the way the IDC handles multiple-valued variables. (For further explanation, see the section "Using Multiple-Valued Variables" in Chapter 2.) To get the desired results, you need to give the conference IDs as values corresponding to the names.

View Search Results Page

This page is designed to deliver the results of the search function in a presentation as similar as possible to the Conference Message list (of course, commands such as posting a new topic don't make sense here).

The content of the page varies depending upon the number of matches that are left to be displayed. If more results are available, a *Next Page* button should be displayed below the list of matches, so that the user can get to the next set of matches. This is depicted in figure 3.10. If there are no further matches to be displayed, the user sees a message indicating the search has been completed. This is depicted in figure 3.11. For a discussion of the algorithm for paged search results, see "Implementing Multi-Page Search Results," earlier in this chapter.

The page also contains a *New Search* button for the user to click if they want to narrow the search criteria, for example. Just below that button is a colored bar displaying the search text that the user entered.

Figure 3.10

When more than ten matches remain, the user can request another page of results.

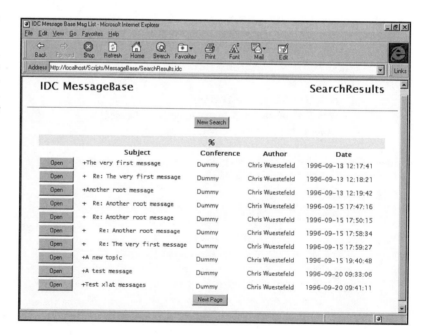

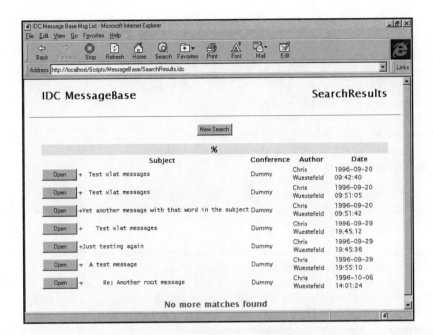

Figure 3.11

When fewer than ten matches remain, the user is informed that no more matches are available.

The View Search Results page consists of an .IDC file that retrieves the desired data and a single .HTX file for displaying that data.

IDC File for the View Search Results Page

Listing 3.18 presents the .IDC file that results in the creation of the View Conference Message List page. Its file name is Search.idc and is located on the companion CD.

LISTING 3.18—SEARCHRESULTS.IDC

```
01.Datasource: dbMessageBase
02.Username: sa
03.Template: SearchResults.htx
04.RequiredParameters: UserID, SeldConferences
05.DefaultParameters: MaxMsg=0
06.ODBCOptions: SQL_ACCESS_MODE=1, SQL_MAX_ROWS=10
07.SQLStatement:
08.+SELECT DISTINCTROW '+' & [SpaceString] & [MessageSubject] AS Expr1,
09.+Users.UserName, Messages.MessageTS,
10.+Messages.MessageID, Conferences.ConferenceName
11.+FROM Users INNER JOIN
12.+  (Conferences INNER JOIN
```

continues

LISTING 3.18—SEARCHRESULTS.IDC, CONTINUED

```
13.+   (Spacing INNER JOIN
14.+      Messages ON Spacing.NumSpaces = Messages.NumSpaces
15.+   ) ON Conferences.ConferenceID = Messages.ConferenceID
16.+   ) ON Users.UserID = Messages.UserID
17.+WHERE Messages.MessageID > %MaxMsg%
18.+ AND Messages.MessageSubject LIKE '%SearchText%'
19.+ AND Conferences.ConferenceID IN (%SeldConferences%)
20.+ORDER BY Messages.MessageID
```

Most of this query looks very much like ViewConfMessages.idc. Lines 17–20 contain some changes that result in search functionality rather than selection of a particular message by ID.

Even more confusing is the code necessary to implement paging through the set of matches—enabled by the *MaxMsg* variable. Its value is always equal to the ID of the last match retrieved. On the first invocation, the *DefaultParameters* field supplies a starting value of 0. The query can therefore start retrieving at the first value following the ending of the previous set. The results are limited to a page size equal to the value specified for the *SQL_MAX_ROWS* ODBCOption.

HTX File for the View Search Results Page

Listing 3.19 presents the .HTX file that specifies the appearance of the Search Results page. Its file name is SearchResults.htx and is located on the companion CD.

LISTING 3.19—SEARCHRESULTS.HTX

```
001.<!doctype html public "-//IETF//DTD HTML//EN">
002.<HTML>
003.
004.<HEAD>
005.
006.<TITLE>IDC Message Base Msg List</TITLE>
007.
008.</HEAD>
009.
010.<BODY BGCOLOR=#FFFFF7>
011.
012.<DIV ALIGN=CENTER>
013.<TABLE WIDTH=95%>
014.  <TR>
015.    <TD ALIGN=LEFT>
016.      <H2>IDC MessageBase</H2>
```

```
017.    </TD>
018.    <TD ALIGN=RIGHT>
019.      <H2>SearchResults</H2>
020.    </TD>
021.  </TR>
022.</TABLE>
023.<HR>
024.
025.<FORM ACTION="/Scripts/MessageBase/Search.idc" METHOD=POST>
026.  <INPUT TYPE=HIDDEN NAME="UserID" VALUE="<%idc.UserID%>">
027.  <INPUT TYPE=SUBMIT VALUE="New Search">
028.</FORM>
029.
030.
031.<TABLE WIDTH=95%>
032.  <TR>
033.    <TD COLSPAN=5 ALIGN=CENTER BGCOLOR=#D0FFFF>
034.      <H3><%idc.SearchText%></H3>
035.    </TD>
036.  </TR>
037.  <TR>
038.    <TH>
039.    </TH>
040.    <TH>
041.      Subject
042.    </TH>
043.    <TH>
044.      Conference
045.    </TH>
046.    <TH>
047.      Author
048.    </TH>
049.    <TH>
050.      Date
051.    </TH>
052.  </TR>
053.  <%begindetail%>
054.  <TR>
055.    <TD>
056.      <FORM ACTION="/Scripts/MessageBase/ViewMessage.idc" METHOD=POST>
057.      <INPUT TYPE=HIDDEN NAME="MessageID" VALUE="<%MessageID%>">
058.      <INPUT TYPE=HIDDEN NAME="UserID" VALUE="<%idc.UserID%>">
059.      <INPUT TYPE=SUBMIT VALUE="Open">
```

continues

LISTING 3.19—SEARCHRESULTS.HTX, CONTINUED

```
060.      </FORM>
061.    </TD>
062.    <TD>
063.      <PRE><%Expr1%></PRE>
064.    </TD>
065.    <TD>
066.      <FONT SIZE=-1>
067.        <%ConferenceName%>
068.      </FONT>
069.    </TD>
070.    <TD>
071.      <FONT SIZE=-1>
072.        <%UserName%>
073.      </FONT>
074.    </TD>
075.    <TD>
076.      <FONT SIZE=-1>
077.        <%MessageTS%>
078.      </FONT>
079.    </TD>
080.  </TR>
081.  <%if CurrentRecord EQ 9%>
082.    <TR>
083.      <TD COLSPAN=5 ALIGN=CENTER>
084.        <FORM ACTION="/Scripts/MessageBase/SearchResults.idc"
085.          METHOD=POST>
086.        <INPUT TYPE=HIDDEN NAME="MaxMsg" VALUE="<%MessageID%>">
087.        <INPUT TYPE=HIDDEN NAME="UserID" VALUE="<%idc.UserID%>">
088.        <INPUT TYPE=HIDDEN NAME="SeldConferences"
➥VALUE="<%idc.SeldConferences%>">
089.        <INPUT TYPE=HIDDEN NAME="SearchText"
➥VALUE="<%idc.SearchText%>">
090.        <INPUT TYPE=SUBMIT VALUE="Next Page">
091.        </FORM>
092.      </TD>
093.    </TR>
094.  <%endif%>
095.  <%enddetail%>
096.</TABLE>
097.<%if CurrentRecord LT 9%>
098.<FONT COLOR=RED>
099.  <H3>No more matches found</H3>
```

```
100.</H3>
101.<%endif%>
102.</DIV>
103.
104.</BODY>
105.</HTML>
```

The interesting code here is the implementation of multi-page search results, accomplished in cooperation with the .IDC query. The most important part is found on lines 81–94. This block implements the form requesting the next page and communicates the new value of MaxMsg, the ID of the last message returned, so the query knows where to start retrieving again.

The conditional that begins this block ensures it is only inserted following the last message retrieved on the page. For this to work, the number specified must always be equal to 1 less than the value of the *SQL_MAX_ROWS* ODBCOption specified in the .IDC file. The value of MaxMsg is then saved in a hidden form field, along with other relevant information. Note that the last page completes with a value too low to trigger the conditional, and the *Next Page* button is not placed on the form.

Lines 97–101 contain the code that generates the message to appear when all search data has been returned. If the preceding detail block completed with a value less than 9 (again, this must be the same value used in the conditional just discussed and 1 less than the number of rows the .IDC query is allowed to return), this must be the last page of results. A message is generated indicating there is no more data available.

Note that if the number of matches is exactly a multiple of 10, then a *Next Page* button will be placed after the last match, leading to a page that displays nothing but the "No more matches found" message. This is because what's actually being tested is not whether there are any more, but whether the current set was full or not. The convoluted logic to avoid this is probably not worth the trouble.

Summary

After reading this chapter you should have a clearer understanding of the way IDC concepts can be applied to solve a practical problem. You should also understand how to implement solutions to common problems, such as carrying data from page to page and multi-page search results.

This application was implemented without resorting to C++ or any other complex language. Instead, all that was required was an understanding of .IDC and .HTX files, along with the ability to write SQL queries, either on your own or with the help of a tool such as Microsoft Access or Microsoft Query.

You should be able to see how this technology can be used to build useful, real-world applications. It allows you to enable access to your database through the Internet or Intranet quickly and without a large amount of programming experience. On the other hand, you've also seen how these advantages sometimes come at the expense of robust error checking or security.

CHAPTER 4

Basic Form Processing in MFC

In the early '90s, the vast majority of the World Wide Web was a network of static HTML pages. It provided a platform for presenting and organizing information across networks and operating systems, but was lacking a critical component: behavior. Although the web provided at least a partial solution to the problems of distribution and presentation over a wide number of systems, it didn't provide a way to make applications "live" on the net.

The answer to this problem was the introduction of the CGI (Common Gateway Interface). CGI provides a structure for extending web servers to add behavior beyond simply fetching HTML pages. CGI defines the standard for connecting HTTP servers to external programs, implemented in any language that runs on the computer hosting your web server. CGI applications interact with the web server through a combination of environment variables; the standard input and standard output streams.

CGI defines how the web server connects to external components to service requests from the browser. The HTTP <form> tags define a method for connecting a series of fields on a web page to a script or program on the server that knows how to process those fields. The fields might be edit controls, list boxes, check boxes, or buttons.

Microsoft's NT-based HTTP Server, IIS (Internet Information Server) supports the CGI standard; you can develop applications for the server in Perl, as stand-alone C programs, or any language you choose. It also supports an alternative: the ISAPI (Internet Server Application Programming Interface). ISAPI supports the same form processing capabilties supplied by CGI, but packages the code as DLLs (dynamic link libraries). This allows the form-handling code to be loaded once and reused with each incoming request, significantly improving the performance of the web server. This chapter will talk about what the ISAPI interfaces can do for you, how you can use them, and why you should care.

The first thing in the chapter is an introduction to web forms, ISAPI extensions, and the support for each of them in the MFC (Microsoft Foundation Class) library.

Web Forms

Web forms provide a way to interact with users. They provide a packaged mechanism for collecting input from the user, triggering an action on the web server, and getting a response from the user. They are the web's equivalent to a Windows dialog box, and are used almost any time a web-based application needs to collect data from a user. Some common used forms include:

◆ **Data Entry Forms:** including surveys, registration forms, order forms, and more

◆ **Interfaces to Search Engines:** that allow users to define the conditions for their search

◆ **Navigators:** these user interface elements allow the user to navigate through the web site. They may not look like forms but may use push-buttons or other input controls to trigger navigation

Forms are less fashionable than newer tools such as Java, JavaScript, or VBScript, but they offer one advantage over these newer tools: They work across a much larger portion of the web. Java only works on recent versions of some web browsers, and only when running from operating systems that support multi-threading. JavaScript (and compatibles, such as JScript) is also limited to a few browsers and can be somewhat quirky across versions of those browsers. Forms are defined to the browser in standard HTML and work virtually everywhere.

Advantages of ISAPI for Form Processing

Prior to the development of ISAPI, form processing was generally implemented by using CGI programs or scripts. In the CGI model, a request is handled by launching the target program with standard input and output streams connected to the web server for interaction with the browser. If multiple users submit the same form at the same time, separate copies of the program are launched for each request.

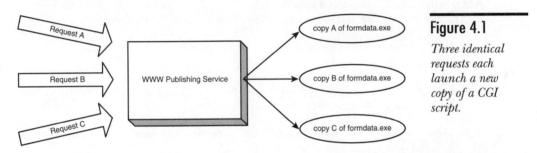

Figure 4.1

Three identical requests each launch a new copy of a CGI script.

In the ISAPI model, requests are handled through DLLs (Dynamic Link Libraries). Form-processing requests are handled by ISAPI extension DLLs. The server loads an extension the first time a page is referred to by a request. The extension remains in memory until the server is shut down.

As requests arrive for processing by the extension, the web server calls the DLL, passing it data corresponding to the user's request. If multiple requests for an extension arrive simultaneously, the server spawns a new thread and calls into the same copy of the extension DLL.

This model offers important advantages over the CGI model on the NT platform. Because the extension remains resident after it has been loaded, the server does not need to load a copy of the program to service each request. Individual requests to the extension cause the server to spawn a thread instead of launching a process. This is a much less expensive operation.

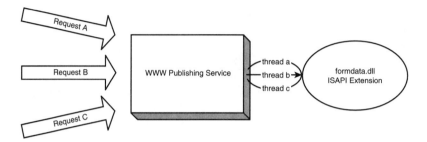

Figure 4.2

Three identical requests share a single copy of an ISAPI extension.

When Windows NT launches a process, it has to perform a great deal of "housekeeping" before the process can begin executing. This housekeeping may include:

♦ Create a new entry in the task database to mananage resource allocation, and so on.

♦ Create a virtual machine to execute the process; correctly populating descriptor table to map virtual memory to physical memory.

♦ Load the process' executable into RAM or re-map a program already in memory into the new virtual machine.

♦ Load or remap all DLLs used by the program.

♦ Allocate a new heap for the program, and initialize non-constant global data.

♦ Create and initialize standard input/output and standard error streams.

♦ Initialize the C run-time library for the process.

♦ Spawn the first thread of execution for the process.

A thread describes a path of execution through a program. Every process contains at least one thread; it begins executing a program's *main()* or *WinMain()* method as soon as the process' initialization is complete. A thread's context consists of:

♦ The pointer to the next byte of code to be executed by the thread

♦ The contents of the CPU registers the code executes

♦ A stack to hold local data, function parameters, and function return addresses

The thread is the unit of work the operating system uses to schedule processor time. By making a copy of the thread's context, the operating system can save the task in a ready-to-run state, and restore that state when the thread's turn to execute comes around again.

Initializing a thread requires much less work than initializing a process because it only requires enough work to create a new thread context; this basically boils down to allocating a new stack and a set of bookkeeping structures in the run-time library and the operating system. Launching a second thread in an existing process does not require that the operating system allocate a new heap, or that the run-time environment be reinitialized.

Remember that every process contains at least one thread, so a process launch will also always entail a thread launch. Since a thread launch avoids the other baggage of process launch and initialization, it is guaranteed to be a cheaper operation.

Advantages of Using MFC in ISAPI Forms

Since its release, the MFC (Microsoft Foundation Class) library has been accepted as the standard platform for developing Windows applications. By providing a cleaner, simpler interface to the Windows API, MFC helps developers write code more quickly and easily.

With the release of Visual C++ 4.1, MFC has been extended to help develop ISAPI applications. A number of new classes have been added to the MFC to support ISAPI extensions. These classes help automate the parsing and mapping of data on the form into C++ variables and the dispatching of commands to C++ member functions.

The new classes added to MFC to support ISAPI are:

◆ CHttpServer

◆ CHttpServerContext

◆ CHttpFilter

◆ CHttpFilterContext

◆ CHtmlStream

Most of the arguments in favor of using MFC for Windows application development apply to the use of MFC for ISAPI form-processing extensions. MFC enables the programmer to write less code, thus improving productivity and quality by reducing the potential for error. The MFC support classes for ISAPI development provide a programming model very similar to that provided for normal Windows applications. This makes it easy for developers who understand the MFC message map model to pick up the fundamentals of ISAPI PARSEMAPs.

There are trade-offs in the use of MFC. MFC applications are typically larger than applications that don't use MFC. There is also some run-time overhead involved in the *PARSEMAP* mechanism (see the sections "A Simple PARSEMAP" and "MFC PARSEMAPs Inside and Out," later in this chapter for more information). Linking to the MFC libraries is also infamous for bringing in large amounts of code not necessarily required for the specific application at hand, due to the monolithic design of pieces of MFC.

There are factors that ameliorate these problems somewhat. Microsoft has packaged the MFC support classes in a separate module from the rest of the class library; this means that the decision to use the MFC ISAPI classes can be made independently of the decision to use any other MFC classes.

The memory footprint of the full MFC library can also be reduced by controlling the way the library is linked to your extension. If the extension is linked to the DLL version of the MFC library, a single copy of the library can be reused by multiple extensions. It is also possible to use the "smart linking" features of the linker; these features will allow you to ensure that only those functions actually required by the extension will be brought in from the MFC libraries.

Developers need to consider these factors when deciding whether to use MFC for ISAPI applications. The overhead incurred by the use of the libraries is offset by the reduction in the amount of code the developer must write (and debug!), and the implications for development, speed, and quality. In general, you will find that for all but the largest sites, the advantages that come from the use of MFC will outweigh the disadvantages easily.

A Simple ISAPI Extension for Form Processing

The rest of this chapter discusses the development of a couple of ISAPI extensions in MFC. It will work through two forms and the ISAPI code to support them, including the HTML, the C++ source, and a detailed breakdown of how they work together. This chapter also discusses some places where the MFC ISAPI model presents problems and makes life harder.

This section begins with a simple example of form processing. The goal is to construct a form for building a profile of one of the users of a web site. The form collects user information on the following:

◆ Name

◆ Age

◆ Gender

◆ Email address

◆ Connection speed

To enable this profile builder, you will design a form, then write the ISAPI extension to process the data.

Designing the Form

Designing a form for the WWW is a great deal like designing any other GUI dialog box or window. The goal is to design a form that is attractive, easy to use, and effective. HTML forms support a variety of data entry controls, analogous to the standard controls available in Windows, OS/2, or other graphical user interfaces.

The first step in creating the form is to select the form elements for representing each field. For simplicity, the example will use just a few of them. The criteria for deciding which control to use in which place is simple—pick the control that makes it easiest for the user to do the right thing. In the example form, the choices are fairly straightforward:

◆ **Name:** a simple free-form text field or edit control.

◆ **Age:** a simple free-form text field.

◆ **Gender:** the gender attribute can only take on two values: female and male. When the number of options is small (less than five), it makes sense to use a control that forces the user to pick one or the other.

◆ **Email address:** another free form text field.

◆ **Connection speed:** the user needs to choose from a list of available options, which might expand over time. To avoid the need to change the form layout as faster modems are released, this form uses a selection list or combo box.

Selecting these elements produces a form that looks like figure 4.3.

This form isn't as aesthetically pleasing as users expect from their experience in Windows, OS/2, or other modern GUIs. The HTML language, unlike a Windows dialog box, does not provide any way to specify a position for a control. There are no attributes for specifying the X and Y positions of the fields. HTML is designed to represent the structure of the data, not the details of its presentation.

Figure 4.3

*A rough layout
for a data entry
form.*

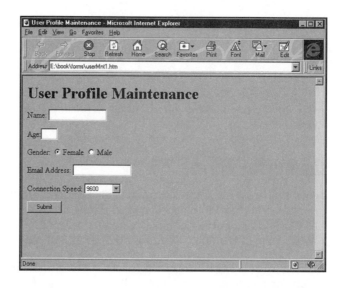

Various techniques can be used to deal with positioning, including the use of HTML
tables. Tables can be used to arrange elements into rows and columns, providing an
imperfect coordinate system. The addition of a table specification improves the
appearance of the table, making it look more like the interface in figure 4.4.

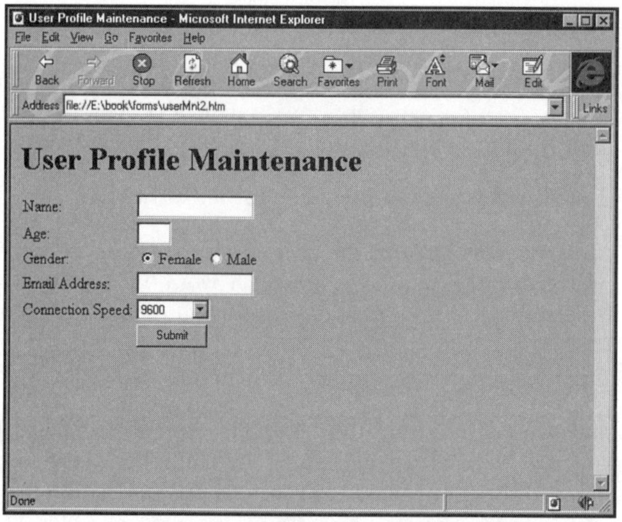

Figure 4.4

*A data entry form
using tables to
align the fields.*

Because more attractive forms are generally preferable, most users will prefer the
version of a form that uses tables. The form in figure 4.4 will be used for the remainder of this example.

The new HTML standards for style sheets should improve the look and feel of a form. Style sheets address HTML's biggest weakness by focusing on the presentation of the data.

HTML for the Form

The HTML used to implement the form shown in figure 4.4 is as follows:

LISTING 4.1—THE HTML FOR THE FORM FROM FIGURE 4.4

```
01.<html>
02.
03.<head><title>User Profile Maintenance</title></head>
04.<body>
05.<h1>User Profile Maintenance</h1>
06.<form action="Scripts/UserProfile.dll?SetProfile" method="POST">
07.  <table>
08.   <tr>
09.    <td>Name:</td>
10.    <td><input type=text size=20 name="Name"></td>
11.   </tr>
12.   <tr>
13.    <td>Age:</td>
14.    <td><input type=text size=3 name="Age"></td>
15.   </tr>
16.   <tr>
17.    <td>Gender:</td>
18.    <td><input type=radio checked name="Gender" value="F">Female
19.      <input type=radio name="Gender" value="M">Male</td>
20.   </tr>
21.   <tr>
22.    <td>E-mail Address:</td>
23.    <td><input type=text size=20 maxlength=20 name="e-mail"></td>
24.   </tr>
25.   <tr>
26.    <td>Connection Speed:</td>
27.    <td><select name="ConnectSpeed" size=1>
28.      <option selected>9600</option>
29.      <option>14400</option>
30.      <option>28800</option>
31.     </select></td>
```

continues

LISTING 4.1—THE HTML FOR THE FORM
FROM FIGURE 4.4, CONTINUED

```
32.  </tr>
33.  <tr>
34.    <td></td>
35.    <td><input type=submit name="Submit" value="Submit"></td>
36.  </tr>
37. </table>
38.</form>
39.</body>
40.
41.</html>
```

The portions of the HTML that define the table used to lay out the form can be
ignored for this discussion. They are included in the listing to illustrate the way a
form is likely to be defined in a real-world form.

An ISAPI Extension to Process the Form Data

The data input from the form is handled by an ISAPI extension. The extension
presented here doesn't do anything particularly sophisticated; it simply unpacks the
data and sends a response back to the user to convey that the data was correctly
received. While it is simple, it does show the three basic steps in the development of
an ISAPI form processing application:

♦ Defining a PARSEMAP to support the commands and their parameters.

♦ Getting the data entered into the form by the user.

♦ Generating a response to the user.

A Simple PARSEMAP

A PARSEMAP is a data structure that defines the mapping between a HTML form and
a command handler routine. The data structure is defined with a set of macros
provided by MFC; they make it simple to build the data structure. A PARSEMAP is
used to define the commands supported by an extension, and the sets of parameters
used by those commands.

The PARSEMAP relates a command to a command handler function. The handler is
a C++ member function with a parameter list matching the contents of the form.

A PARSEMAP for the form in figure 4.4 might look like this:

LISTING 4.2—A SIMPLE PARSEMAP

```
1.BEGIN_PARSE_MAP(CUserProfileExtension, CHttpServer)
2.   ON_PARSE_COMMAND(SetProfile, CUserProfileExtension,
3.           ITS_PSTR ITS_I4
4.           ITS_PSTR ITS_PSTR
5.           ITS_PSTR)
6.   ON_PARSE_COMMAND_PARAMS("Name Age
7.               Gender e-mail
8.               ConnectSpeed")
9.END_PARSE_MAP(CUserProfileExtension)
```

The ON_PARSE_COMMAND macro defines a map for the command *SetProfile()*. The map contains a parameter map, indicating that the function takes 5 parameters: 4 strings and a long integer.

The next macro, ON_PARSE_COMMAND_PARAMS, associates names with the parameters listed in the ON_PARSE_COMMAND macro. The names and parameter types are mapped based on position in the list, so Name is a character string, Age is a long integer, and so on.

For more information on PARSEMAPs, see the section "MCF PARSEMAPs Inside and Out."

Getting Data from the Form

The data entered by the user reaches the ISAPI extension as parameters to the command function. The data is parsed and converted to the data types specified in the PARSEMAP. To find the data entered by the user, simply examine the matching variables. The ISAPI framework will handle any translation required to move from an encoded set of data to a standard presentation using C++ data types.

The next section shows how the data is presented for this example.

Responding to the User

After the command handler function has been called, it should generate a response to send back to the client. The key to the response is the CHttpServerContext object passed as the first parameter of the command handler.

LISTING 4.3—THE SETPROFILE() COMMAND HANDLER FUNCTION

```
01.Void CUserProfileExtension::SetProfile(CHttpServerContext * pCtxt,
02.                LPCTSTR pName,
03.                long  age,
04.                LPCTSTR pGender,
05.                LPCTSTR pAddress,
06.                LPCTSTR pSpeed)
07.{
08.   StartContent(pCtxt);
09.   WriteTitle(pCtxt);
10.   *pCtxt << "Thank you for registering, " << pName << "\r\n";
11.   *pCtxt << "   Your registration information will be sent to: " <<
➥pAddress << "\r\n";
12.   EndContent(pCtxt);
13.}
```

The context object is passed to the StartContent, WriteTitle, and EndContent
member functions. These are used to set up the HTML for the response. It is also
used as the recipient of the overloaded << operator when sending data back to the
end user.

Form Processing Logistics

To demonstrate exactly what happens during the processing of a form, this section
presents a sample set of data for the user registration form. The explanations that
follow assume the user fills out the form as in figure 4.5.

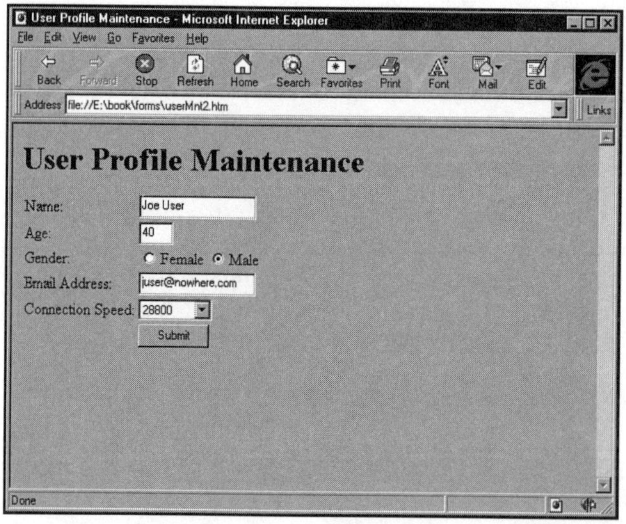

Figure 4.5

*A sample HTML
form with user
input.*

How the Browser Sends Data

When the user clicks on the Submit button, the browser creates a request message. The packet it creates consists of the query method and URL from the form's action statement, a variety of environmental information about the browser and the workstation it runs on, and an encoded version of the form data. A copy of the message sent for the form data shown in figure 4.5 is listed in the following example:

LISTING 4.4—THE DATA TRANSMITTED BY THE BROWSER FOR THE FORM IN FIGURE 4.5

```
01.POST./Scripts/UserProfile.dll?SetProfile.HTTP/1.0
02.Accept: image/gif, image/x-xbitmap, image/jpeg, image/pjpeg, */*
03.Referer: http://localhost/usermnt2.htm
04.Accept-Language: en
05.Content-Type: application/x-www-form-urlencoded
06.UA-pixels:.800x600
07.UA-color:.color8
08.UA-OS:.Windows NT
09.UA-CPU:.x86
10.User-Agent: Mozilla/2.0 (compatible; MSIE 3.0; Windows NT)
11.Host: localhost
12.Connection: Keep-Alive
13.Content-Length: 72
14.Pragma:.No-Cache
15.
16.Name=Joe+User&Age=40&Gender=M&e-mail=juser@nowhere.com&ConnectSpeed=28800
```

Note that the last section of the packet contains the data from the form. Each field is packaged as a name/value pair; the pairs are separated by ampersands (&). In addition, an escape character (+) replaces the space in the Name value.

How the Response Function Is Called

When the request is received, the Internet Information Server examines the URL and determines that a request is being made to the UserProfile DLL. The Internet Information Server loads the DLL (if it is not already resident) and calls into the DLL on the function *HTTPExtensionProc()*.

From this point on, the process is in the hands of the MFC ISAPI support module. MFC examines the URL for the name of a command; it also examines the PARSEMAP for a default command and the query for the special parameter mfcISAPICommand. The MFC ISAPI support module uses a command from any of these places to search the PARSEMAP for an entry for the requested command.

If a PARSEMAP for the command is found, MFC attempts to map the fields on the form to variables to be passed to the command handler function. If an ON_PARSE_ COMMAND_PARAMS map is present for the command, fields are matched by name; if not, they are matched by position. If default values are specified for any fields not sent by the browser, they are used to fill in the missing values.

MFC converts the data from the form transmitted by the browser to the form specified in the PARSEMAP. This includes translating the data from the *application/x-www- form-urlencoded* form of the data back into standard character data and performing required conversions into floating point or integer data types based on the PARSEMAP.

After this process is complete, the MFC ISAPI code checks to ensure all mandatory fields were supplied. It also checks to see if any specified form fields are not handled by the command function. If either situation occurs, the MFC ISAPI support code reports an error and will *not* call the command handler.

If the incoming field data and PARSEMAP definitions match, the data will be pushed onto the stack and your function will be called.

How the Form Fields Are Presented to the Function

By the time the command handler function is called, the data has been decoded, parsed, and converted to the appropriate data type. For the sample under discussion, the function parameters will be as follows:

TABLE 4.1
Variable Contents in Command Handler

Variable	Value
pName	Joe User
age	40
pGender	M
pE-mail	juser@nowhere.com
pSpeed	28800

How the Reply Is Sent to the User

This command handler begins with a call to the *StartContent()* function. This function adds a "content-type: text/html" header to the beginning of the response stream.

The documentation for the *StartContent()* function provided with Visual C++ 4.1 and 4.2 is incorrect; it indicates that it also sends the HTML for the <html> and <body> tags. This is performed by *WriteTitle()*.

The second statement in the function is a call to *WriteTitle()*. This function adds the HTML for the <html>, <title>, and <body> tags. *WriteTitle()* calls the extension's *GetTitle()* function to obtain the text to place between the <title> and </title> tags. After calling this function, the CHttpServerContext object is properly set up to receive the body of the response.

After the context is set up, the extension can generate its response by using the overloaded << operators defined for the CHttpServerContext class. These operators enable the extension to add data to a CHtmlStream object embedded in the CHttpServerContext object. The ISAPI support classes define overloaded operators for several common data types, including the following:

◆ **Void operator<<(LPCTSTR psz):** outputs a null terminated string to the stream contained in the context

◆ **Void operator<<(WORD w):** outputs an unsigned short integer to the stream

◆ **Void operator<<(DWORD dw):** outputs a doubleword to the stream

Other data types should be sent to the stream by converting them into a supported type; the *CString:Format()* function is frequently useful for doing so.

Note The CString class's *Format()* member function is analogous to the ANSI C *printf()* function. It takes a format string, and a variable set of data as parameters. For example, a call to the function may look like this:

```
CString text;

text.Format("The average score was %4.2f", average);
```

This will create a string containing some text and the value of the float variable named *average*. This is a convenient way to convert data from a type that is not supported by the CHttpStream class into a CString, which is supported. See the MFC documentation with your compiler for more information.

The data sent to the HTML stream is accumulated in a buffer managed by the stream object. The MFC framework sends the data after the command handler function exists; no data is sent via the CHtmlStream object until all other processing is complete. The stream manages the memory required to buffer the response as it is accumulated during the function call; sufficient memory must be available to hold all of the accumulated response. This can be a factor when transferring the data from very large reports or graphics; the exact point depends on the configuration of your server and its level of activity.

Note It is possible to transmit data immediately by using the CHttpServerContext object passed to the command handler. The object provides a function named *WriteClient()* which may be used to send data without the normal MFC caching behavior. This function should be used sparingly; it is much more efficient to send the data in a single transmission than as multiple small transmissions.

A common use for *WriteClient()* is the transfer of non-textual data, such as graphic or sound files.

The response function ends with a call to EndContent. This function simply appends the </body> and </html> tags to the end of the stream.

Forms in HTML

Web page forms are defined by using a <form> tag and one or more data entry elements. The tags relevant to form processing are as follows:

◆ **<form>:** defines the region of the HTML page that constitutes a form, and the manner in which the data is encoded and transmitted.

◆ **<input>:** used to define a number of types of data entry fields, including single-line text fields, check boxes, radio buttons, hidden fields, images, submit buttons, reset buttons, and password fields.

◆ **<select>:** defines selection lists, which appear as list boxes or drop-down list boxes. Used to select one or more values from a set of several.

◆ **<option>:** a subtag used to define an option within <select> tags.

◆ **<textarea>:** defines a multi-line text entry control.

Before going on to a more advanced example of forms processing, you'll take a look at each of these tags and how they interact with ISAPI extension modules and PARSEMAPs.

Note The reference information provided in this section comes from the HTML standard. Individual browsers may support additional tags, or more commonly, additional attributes on standard tags. See the documentation for your favorite browsers if you need browser-specific extension information.

The Form

The <form> and </form> tags define a region of an HTML page that constitutes a form. The data entry elements between the two tags are sent to the server as a group when one of the Submit buttons in the form is chosen. The <form> tag has the following attributes:

- ◆ **ACTION—URL:** the ACTION attribute specifies the URL of the ISAPI extension module (or other script or program) responsible for handling the data from the form. The ACTION attribute is mandatory; the form must be processed by something.

- ◆ **METHOD—GET or POST:** the METHOD attribute specifies the way the data will be transmitted to the server. If the method is Get, the data is encoded as part of the URL sent to the server. If the method is POST, the data is sent as the body of the message, and the URL is left as specified. This attribute will default to GET if not specified.

- ◆ **EncType—mime-type:** encType specifies the manner in which the data is encoded. This value defaults to "x-www-form-urlencoded." The only alternative value in commercial use today is "multipart/form-data," supported only by the Netscape Navigator browser. This attribute can generally be omitted; the ISAPI support classes assume "x-www-form-urlencoded" encoding.

 The HTML 3 standard adds a new attribute to the <form> tag: SCRIPT. This tag associates a client-side script with the form to be used for processing and updating the input elements on the form. This feature is not yet implemented by any commercial browsers.

Input Fields

The <input> tag defines a fairly wide variety of data entry elements. The type of interface element used to collect the input from the users is dependent on the "type" attribute; several of the attributes are specific to one input type or another.

The <input> tag takes the following form

```
<INPUT [attribute-list]>
```

The attribute list contains zero or more of the attributes described in the following sections. The following sections discuss those attributes common to all forms of the tag, then discuss those specific to each specific input type.

The types of input supported by the input tag are:

♦ Text input

♦ Password input

♦ Radio button

♦ Check box

♦ Image input

♦ Hidden fields

♦ Submit buttons

♦ Reset buttons

♦ File input elements

Common Attributes

The following attributes are common to all forms of the <input> tag:

♦ **NAME—text-string:** assigns a name to the data element. Information is transmitted to the server in the form name=value; this same name should be specified if you are using named parameters via the ON_PARSE_COMMAND_ PARAMS macro.

♦ **VALUE—text-string:** sets the default or initial value of the element.

♦ **TYPE—checkbox, file, hidden, image, password, radio, reset, submit, or text:** determines the type of input element to be placed in the form.

Text Input

Text entry controls are created by specifying an input type of text and are generally represented by single-line edit controls.

The attributes specific to text-input elements are as follows:

♦ **MAXLENGTH—n:** specifies the maximum number of characters to accept

♦ **SIZE—n:** sets the physical size of the displayed edit control, with "n" indicating the number of characters of data to be displayed in the field

It's a good idea to specify the MAXLENGTH and SIZE attributes for fields. If you allow users to enter more characters than can be displayed, it can be hard for users to tell there's more data than they can see. Because this is a single-line edit control, no horizontal scroll bars are visible to indicate the presence of more text. It's generally best to use MAXLENGTH = SIZE to ensure that the user cannot enter more characters than can be shown at one time.

Password Field Input

Password fields are created by specifying an input type of "password." These elements display asterisks in place of the characters a user enters into the field, thus obscuring the entered data from casual "over-the-shoulder" observation.

It's important to remember that the data entered is transmitted in the clear when sent to the web server. The data will not be encrypted as it is transmitted unless you take other steps to protect the data. If you are trying to implement secure password entry, you might want to use the HTTP authentication mechanisms and let the browser handle the username/password entry. (See Chapter 10 for more information about security and authetication.)

Password elements accept the same attributes as text elements.

Radio Button Input

These input elements force users to pick one value from a group of choices. To create a set of radio buttons that are linked together, define an input element for each possible value. Assign the same name to each button in the set, giving each button a different value.

When the data for the form is transmitted to the server, the value associated with the currently checked button is used.

The only attribute specific to the radio button input element is CHECKED, which indicates a given input element is checked. Use this attribute to specify that a button will be checked button when the set of buttons is initially displayed. Only one radio button in a set can be checked.

Check Box Input

Check boxes present users with an *on* or *off* condition. If the box is checked, its name and value are transmitted to the host. If the box is not checked, nothing will be transmitted for the field.

It is possible to define multiple check boxes with a given name. If more than one check box exists with a particular name and more than one is checked, multiple name=value pairs are transmitted to the server. This tends to be a problem under MFC's ISAPI extension support, which is oriented around single-valued elements. You should avoid this situation when using MFC PARSEMAPS.

The check box element supports the same "checked" attribute as a radio button, but multiple elements with the same name can be checked.

Image Input

Input elements using some type of image provide the equivalent of graphical submit buttons. Clicking on the image submits the form data to the web server, along with the coordinates of the position the user clicked on within the image.

The position is specified as the number of pixels from the top left corner of the image and is transmitted to the server via two name/value pairs. The names are generated by appending ".x" and ".y" to the value supplied in the "name" attribute.

For example, if the name of the image element is Start, the values will be transmitted in the attributes "start.x" and "start.y."

 A common use of these elements is creating a button with an image to replace the submit button for a form. If you do so, remember to define parameters in your PARSEMAP to hold the position values. Otherwise, your PARSEMAP might not work as you expect.

A number of attributes are specific to image elements. These include the following:

- **ALIGN—top, middle, or bottom:** specifies the alignment of the image relative to the surrounding text. "Bottom" aligns the bottom of the image with the baseline of the surrounding text; "middle" aligns the middle of the image with the baseline of the text, and "top" aligns the top of the image with the top of the tallest thing on the line.

- **SRC—URL:** specifies an URL to act as the source for the image.

Hidden Input

If the type=hidden, no user interface element is displayed on the web form. At first glance, this might seem nonsensical; why create an input element the user cannot see or modify? In reality, hidden fields can be extremely useful.

Hidden fields are a way to pre-fill values on the form so they will be available to the ISAPI extension when the form is submitted for processing. Any type of information can be pre-filled in this fashion; session identifiers, command codes, or other useful values. A good example of a value you might choose to pre-fill is the mfcISAPICommand variable, described later in the chapter in the section "The mfcISAPICommand Parameter."

 Don't use hidden fields to hold human-readable versions of secure data. Users can see hidden fields by using the View Source command on their browser, even though the field is not shown on the form.

Submit Input

Elements with a type of "submit" define submit buttons. When the user clicks on one of these buttons, the data from the form is transmitted. A form can have multiple submit buttons, each with a different name/value pair; the browser will only send the pair from the button the user actually chooses.

The value attribute is displayed to the user as the caption of the button. There are no attributes specific to the submit input element.

Reset Input

A "reset" input element enables the user to set a form back to its initial state. Each of the input elements in the form is returned to the value specified in its value attribute.

There are no attributes specific to a reset input element.

File Input

The file input type is currently only supported by the Netscape browser. This tag should cause the browser to display a file selection widget of some kind or another; when the file is selected, the contents of the file will be uploaded to the host.

This input type is not directly supported by ISAPI extensions and is mentioned here only for thorough coverage of the topic.

Selection Lists

Selection lists place list boxes or drop-down lists on a form. They enable the user to select one or more values from a list of options.

Lists that support the selection of multiple values do not work well with ISAPI PARSEMAPs. The data is sent from the browser to the server via multiple name=value pairs, which is not handled gracefully. This is a limitation of the MFC ISAPI support code, not of ISAPI itself. If support for multi-value lists is important, it will be necessary to use an alternative mechanism to manage the data. One such mechanism is presented in Chapter 11.

Selection lists are implemented via two HTML tags: <select> and <option>. The list takes the following general form:

```
1.<select attribute="x">
2.<option attribute="x">Option 1</option>
3.<option attribute="x">Option 2</option>
4....
5.<option attribute="x">Option 3</option>
6.</select>
```

The <select> Tag

The selection list itself is defined by the <select> tag. The range of available options is governed by the set of <option> tags within the <select> and </SELECT> tags; no other text or tags should be found within these tags.

The following attributes are valid for the <select> tag. Only the NAME attribute is mandatory.

- ◆ **NAME—name:** specifies the name used to identify the value (or values) when sent to the server.

- ◆ **MULTIPLE:** when this attribute is present, the user is able to select multiple values from the list. The values are transmitted by using multiple *name=value* pairs. If this attribute is not present, only a single value can be selected.

- ◆ **SIZE—n:** specifies the number of items displayed to the user. If the value is 1, the selection list is typically displayed as a drop-down list box or a pull-down menu; if it is >1, it is typically a list box. If the multiple attribute is set, the size should not be set to 1. In this situation, the browser will increase the size to 2 or more to allow for multiple selections.

The <option> Tag

The <option> and </option> tags define the value displayed in the selection list. The <option> tag can take the following general form:

```
<option attribute-list>Item</option>
```

The Item text contains the data displayed in the list. The </option> tag is optional; if you don't include the end tag, the text is terminated by the start of the next <option> tag or the terminating </SELECT> tag.

Both attributes of this tag, described here, are optional:

- **VALUE—value string:** specifies the value to be sent to the server when this option is selected. If this is omitted, the item text is used as the value.

- **SELECTED:** indicates whether or not the value is initially selected. If the enclosing <select> tag has the multiple attribute set, multiple options can have this attribute set; if not, only one option can have the select attribute set.

Text Areas

The <textarea> tag defines a text field that accepts multiple lines of text. These fields should always be rendered by using a fixed-pitch font, allowing the display area to be sized in terms of rows and columns of text.

Text area fields render text literally; they do not interpret HTML markup found within the text. Normally, the element does not wrap text; lines are terminated by carriage return/linefeed pairs entered by the user or transmitted by the server. The <textarea> tag takes the following form:

```
<TEXTAREA attribute-list> text </textarea>
```

The *attribute-list* contains the mandatory and/or optional attributes described in the following section, and the text between the <textarea> and </textarea> tags defines the initial value of the text area.

The following attributes are defined for the <textarea> tag. All these attributes are mandatory, with the exception of the WRAP tag.

- **NAME—name:** specifies the name used to identify the value when sent to the server.

- **COLS—n:** the width of the display rectangle, specified in columns. Note that the width of each line of text might be greater than this value; this only specifies the amount of data to be displayed.

- **ROWS—n:** the physical height of the displayed edit control, indicating the number of rows of character data to be displayed in the field.

- **WRAP—off, virtual, or physical:** controls the way text is wrapped in the TextArea. When wrapping is "off," text is only wrapped in response to new line characters included in the data. If wrap is set to "virtual," the TextArea wraps text to ensure it fits within the available width of the element, but newline characters are *not* included in the data. If wrap is "physical," the browser wraps text as it does for "virtual" mode, but includes the generated new lines in the data.

MFC PARSEMAPs Inside and Out

An MFC PARSEMAP is a data structure that defines the mapping between an HTML form and a command handler routine. The data structure is defined with a set of five macros provided by MFC; they make it simple to build the data structure. These are discussed in more detail later in this section.

A PARSEMAP is used to define the commands supported by an extension and the sets of parameters used by those commands. It relates a command to a command handler function. The handler is a C++ member function with a parameter list matching the contents of the form.

MFC PARSEMAP macros are:

- ◆ BEGIN_PARSE_MAP

- ◆ ON_PARSE_COMMAND

- ◆ ON_PARSE_COMMAND_PARAMS

- ◆ DEFAULT_PARSE_COMMAND

- ◆ END_PARSE_MAP

These macros describe the commands implemented in your extension module, the parameters taken by the command handlers, and the handler to be invoked when none is specified.

The following sections describe each of these macros and its use in an MFC ISAPI extension.

BEGIN_PARSE_MAP

This macro defines the start of the PARSEMAP. It takes two parameters: the name of the extension class and the name of the base class. The syntax of this macro is as follows:

```
BEGIN_PARSE_MAP(MyExtension, BaseClass)
```

MyExtension denotes the extension being defined and *BaseClass* denotes the C++ base class for *MyExtension* (generally CHttpServer).

ON_PARSE_COMMAND

This macro defines a command supported by your extension, including the parameters the extension will accept. There should be an occurrence of the ON_PARSE_

COMMAND macro for each command implemented in the extension. It is extremely important to ensure that the parameter list defined with this macro exactly matches the parameters of the command handler function.

If the parameters in the paramList do not match those in the C++ function definition, the compiler will not generate any error or warning messages. The nature of the macro extension prevents the compiler from detecting the problem. The first symptom of a mismatch will generally be a strange protection fault or system crash. The syntax of this macro is as follows:

```
ON_PARSE_COMMAND(className, funcName, paramList)
```

The *className* denotes the name of the ISAPI extension module being defined. The *funcName* gives the name of the command function being implemented. This is also the name of the command as exposed to the HTML form. The function must be a member function of class *className*. The paramList is a list of one or more codes defining the parameter list for the function. The set of available codes is as follows:

- ◆ **ITS_PSTR:** a pointer to a null-terminated string; the matching C++ data type is an LPCSTR, or a *const char * const.* The memory associated with the string is owned by the ISAPI framework.

- ◆ **ITS_I2:** a 2-byte integer; corresponds to a *short int* in C++.

- ◆ **ITS_I4:** a 4-byte integer; usually a *long int* in C++.

- ◆ **ITS_R4:** a 4-byte floating point number, represented by a float in C++.

- ◆ **ITS_R8:** an 8-byte floating point number, represented by a double in C++.

- ◆ **ITS_EMPTY:** a special code used to denote an empty parameter list. The paramList cannot be null; use this value when there are no other parameters.

 Tip A paramList is a string containing one or more of these codes, separated by spaces. Don't try and use commas to separate the codes; this will produce a number of fairly strange compiler error messages.

ON_PARSE_COMMAND_PARAMS

This macro defines parameter names and/or default values, changing the way fields are mapped to command function parameters. Without the macro, parameters are mapped to parameters based on their position in the form; with it, they are mapped based on the value of the name attribute. The macro can also be used to assign default values for attributes on the form.

Naming Parameters

Naming parameters via this macro have advantages and disadvantages. The largest advantage is that of improved reliability and flexibility.

If your command handler does not use named parameters, MFC will attempt to match incoming parameters in a GET or POST request to the parameters of the command handler, based on their sequence within the form. This requires the extension and its form to be quite tightly coupled: simply rearranging the fields on the form can break your extension. Anytime the sequence of fields within the form is changed, it is necessary to modify the function definition to match.

When parameters are named, they are bound to the fields on the HTML form by the "name" attribute of the data entry elements. The sequence of fields on the form is irrelevant; the only required matches are between field and parameter names. Naming a parameter also makes a parameter mandatory, unless the field is also assigned a default value.

Default Values for Parameters

The ON_PARSE_COMMAND_PARAMS macro can be used to assign default values to the parameters that have been specified for the command. The default value will be used if no value is transmitted by the browser.

This feature does not always behave in exactly the manner you would expect. Under Visual C++ 4.*x*, the default value will only be used if the browser passes no value. This is *not* the same as saying it will be used if the user does not enter a value. For example, if a form contains the following HTML:

```
01.<html>
02.<title>Sample Menu</title>
03.<body>
04.<form action="/scripts/DefaultValues.dll" method=POST>
05.<input type="hidden" name="mfcISAPICommand" value="Test">
06.<INPUT TYPE=TEXT NAME="FIELD1">
07.<INPUT TYPE=SUBMIT VALUE="Test">
08.</form>
09.</body>
10.</html>
```

and is handled by the following PARSEMAP:

```
1.…
2.ON_PARSE_COMMAND(CTestExtention,Test, ITS_LPSTR)
3.ON_PARSE_COMMAND_PARAMS("FIELD1=~")
4.…
```

The browser will send the string "FIELD1=" if the user does not fill in the field. This will result in the command-handling function getting a pointer to an empty string for this parameter, not a string containing ~.

The default value will not be used to replace bad data, either. For example, if a PARSEMAP specifies a parameter as numeric (via an ITS_I4, for instance) and the user enters a nonnumeric value in the string (such as "DOG"), the parameter will be passed a value of 0.

DEFAULT_PARSE_COMMAND

The default command macro is used to specify one of the commands handled by the extension as the default command. It is called if the form or URL passed by the browser does not contain a command name. The command must be specified in an ON_PARSE_COMMAND clause. The syntax for this macro is as follows:

```
DEFAULT_PARSE_COMMAND(funcName,className)
```

The *funcName* is the name of the default function, and *className* is the name of the extension being defined.

END_PARSE_COMMAND

This macro denotes the end of the PARSEMAP and takes only the following parameter, where *MyExtension* is the name of the extension class being defined:

```
END_PARSE_COMMAND(MyExtension)
```

A More Advanced Form Processing Example

This section presents a more advanced example, adding techniques for validation and error reporting to the form. This version of the form logic checks the data sent to users and sends back the form with appropriate messages for correction if the data doesn't meet the validation requirements.

Forms and Validation

Validation of the data being entered into a form can be handled in many different ways. This example validates the data in the ISAPI form processing extension. If there are any problems with the data, the extension sends a list of problems back to the user to be corrected.

In addition, when the extension sends the list of problems back to the browser, the list is combined with a copy of the form containing the data the user submitted for processing. The problems to be corrected are seen on the same page as the fields containing the bad data, making it easier for the user to correct the problems, as there is no need to page back and forth between an error list and a form.

The Process

To make this work, the form won't be stored in an HTML file on the server. Instead, it will be generated from the ISAPI extension, ensuring that the form initially sent to the user matches the form used to correct errors.

When the form is submitted, it is checked for errors. The errors are accumulated in memory until all validation is completed. If any errors are encountered, they are sent to the user en masse, along with a copy of the form and user data. This new page points back to the same function within the ISAPI form processing function. Because the error message added to the form won't affect the fields on the form, they won't make any difference to the ISAPI command function.

The two commands that must be implemented to support the new version of the form are as follows:

◆ **ShowForm:** responsible for generating the blank form and sending it to the browser

◆ **ProcessForm:** responsible for processing the user's data and sending any necessary feedback

An ISAPI PARSEMAP for these two functions is shown in listing 4.5:

LISTING 4.5—THE **PARSEMAP** FOR THE USER PROFILE EXTENSION

```
1.BEGIN_PARSE_MAP(CUserProfileExtension, CHttpServer)
2.   ON_PARSE_COMMAND(ShowForm, CUserProfileExtension, ITS_EMPTY)
3.   ON_PARSE_COMMAND(SetProfile, CUserProfileExtension,
4.          ITS_PSTR ITS_I4
5.          ITS_PSTR ITS_PSTR
6.          ITS_PSTR)
7.   ON_PARSE_COMMAND_PARAMS("Name=~ Age=0 Gender=~ e-mail=~ ConnectSpeed=9600")
8.END_PARSE_MAP(CUserProfileExtension)
```

The details of the *ShowForm()* and *SetProfile()* functions and their implementations will be given later in this chapter, under the headings "Handling the ShowForm Command" and "Handling Input for the User." The general flow of the process is indicated in figure 4.6.

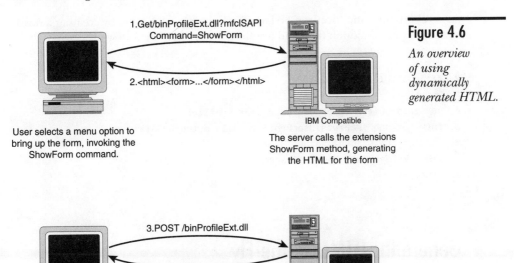

1.Get/binProfileExt.dll?mfcISAPI
Command=ShowForm

2.<html><form>...</form></html>

IBM Compatible

User selects a menu option to
bring up the form, invoking the
ShowForm command.

The server calls the extensions
ShowForm method, generating
the HTML for the form

Figure 4.6

*An overview
of using
dynamically
generated HTML.*

3.POST /binProfileExt.dll

4.Either an acknowledgement or a
copy of the form with feedback

IBM Compatible

The user fills out the form, and
hits the Submit button, sending
the data to the server.

The server calls the extensions
SetProfile function to handle the
data. The data is validated, and
feedback is sent to the user.

Invoking the Form

Because the HTML form is generated by the ISAPI extension, you will need to provide a way to trigger the initial display of the form. You can accomplish this easily by defining an operation or command in the extension that simply sends out the initial form.

To trigger the form, the web site needs to invoke the extension's *ShowForm* method from a link or a button. This can be accomplished by constructing an URL for a GET request in place of an URL for a standard page. The HTML for a page with a menu option that would trigger the function might look like the following:

```
1.<html>
2.<title>Sample Menu</title>
3.<body>
```

```
4.<a href="/scripts/UserProfiles.dll?mfcISAPICommand=ShowForm">
5.Show the form</a>
6.</body>
7.</html>
```

As an alternative, the form can be launched with a push button by creating a form that consists of a hidden field and a submit button like the following:

```
1.<html>
2.<title>Sample Menu</title>
3.<body>
4.Push this button to update your user profile:
5.<form action="/scripts/UserProfiles.dll" method=POST>
6.<input type="hidden" value="ShowForm">
7.<INPUT TYPE=SUBMIT VALUE="Search">
8.</form>
9.</body>
10.</html>
```

Generating HTML On-the-Fly

As described earlier in the "The Process," generating HTML on-the-fly requires the ISAPI extension to generate the HTML form dynamically. There are two situations when the form must be generated: when initially rendering the form, and when sending feedback in response to errors.

When initially rendering the form, no data from the user must be preserved. The extension generates a blank form; the only field data presented should represent a set of reasonable default values for the particular form being implemented by the extension.

When sending feedback in response to errors, the extension feeds the user's data back to the browser in place of the defaults. This enables the user to correct the problems reported by the editing login in the extension, without re-entering all the other fields.

To ensure identical presentation of the form in each case, the extension should implement a single routine to generate the HTML for either case. This routine will not generate any of the framing elements of the page (<HTML>, <TITLE>, <BODY>, and so on); it should only generate the region from the <form> tag to the </form> tag, maximizing the capability to reuse the routine, maintain it separately from error reporting mechanisms, and so forth.

This technique for generating the form means the ShowForm command described earlier is implemented in two parts: an ISAPI command function to handle the actual request and an auxiliary routine to output the form itself. These implementation parts are discussed in the following sections.

Handling the ShowForm Command

The *ShowForm()* function itself is very straightforward. The form's responsibilities are as follows:

◆ **Comply with requirements of an ISAPI handler:** the function must match the footprint for an ISAPI command handler.

◆ **Set default values:** the form output function is responsible for sending to the browser the values passed to the form; this function is responsible for setting reasonable defaults.

◆ **Output framing HTML:** the function is responsible for generating the HTML to frame the form. This includes the usual HTML page tags (<HTML>, <BODY>, and so on), as well as any other desired HTML. In this case, additional HTML includes outputting the title and applying an <h1> heading tag.

One possible implementation of the *ShowForm()* function is as follows:

LISTING 4.6—THE CUSERPROFILEEXTENSION:: SHOWFORM() FUNCTION

```
01.void CUserProfileExtension::ShowForm(CHttpServerContext* pCtxt)
02.{
03.   // Add "Content-Type: text/html" to the header. Note that
04.   // the MFC 4.x docs claim this sends the <Body> and <HTML>
05.   // tags into the document; it doesn't.
06.   StartContent(pCtxt);
07.
08.   // Outputs the "<html><head><title>" tags, then the text
09.   // returned by the overloaded GetTitle() function,
10.   // then the </title></head><body> tag sequence.
11.   WriteTitle(pCtxt);
12.
13.   // Output some framing HTML, including an <h1> header tag
14.   *pCtxt << _T("<h1>User Profile Maintenance</h1>\r\n");
15.
16.   // Output the actual form
17.   OutputFormHTML(pCtxt, szEmpty, 0, _T("F"), szEmpty, _T("9600"));
```

continues

LISTING 4.6—THE CUSERPROFILEEXTENSION: SHOWFORM() FUNCTION, CONTINUED

```
18.
19.   // Outputs the closing "</body></html>" tags
20.   EndContent(pCtxt);
21.}
```

The function starts by sending the standard header, title, and introductory HTML to the browser via lines 3–15. On line 17, it calls the *OutputFormHTML()* function to actually send the form to the browser. When *OutputFormHTML()* is called, it is passed a set of reasonable default values for each of the fields on the form. *ShowForm()* finishes its work by sending the standard page-closing tags to the browser via the *EndContent()* function call on line 20.

Generating the Form

The *OutputFormHTML()* function is responsible for building the HTML for the form, and sending it to the browser. The declaration for the *OutputFormHTML()* is as follows:

```
1.void CUserProfileExtension::OutputFormHTML(CHttpServerContext* pCtxt,
2.                    LPCTSTR pName,
3.                    long  age,
4.                    LPCTSTR pGender,
5.                    LPCTSTR pEmail,
6.                    LPCTSTR pSpeed)
```

The first parameter represents the server context that receives the form; it is the value passed to the ISAPI command handler requesting the form. The remaining parameters contain the values for the data entry fields on the form. When called by the *ShowForm()* method, these will be the default values; when called from *SetProfile()* (discussed in the following section "Handling Input from the User") they will contain the values entered by the user.

Generating the Form Header

The *OutputFormHTML()* function begins by defining the form and a table to align the labels and fields, as shown in listing 4.7.

LISTING 4.7—GENERATING THE HEADINGS
AND TABLE IN OUTPUTFORMHTML()

```
01.{
02.  //
03.  // send the <form> tag
04.  //
05.  *pCtxt << _T("<form ");
06.  *pCtxt << _T("action=\"/Scripts/UserProfile.dll\" ");
07.  *pCtxt << _T("method=\"POST\">\r\n");
08.
09.  //
10.  // Use the mfcISAPIcommand hidden variable to specify the
11.  // command safely.
12.  //
13.  *pCtxt << _T("<input type=hidden name=\"mfcISAPICommand\"";
14.  *pCtxt << _T(" Value=\"SetPlatform\">\r\n");
15.
16.  //
17.  // open a table to align the labels and fields
18.  //
19.  *pCtxt << _T("<table>\r\n");
```

Lines 2–7 output the <form> tag, and specify the name of the extension that will be handling the input from this form. The name of the command that will be passed to the extension is defined on lines 13 and 14 using the mfcISAPICommand parameter (see the section entitled "The mfcISAPICommand Parameter" for more information.) The table that will be used to align the fields is generated on line 19.

Generating the HTML for the Name Field

The function continues by generating the HTML for the field labels and the fields. Each field is generated within a row of the table, with the label sent in the first cell and the input element in the second. The value clause is used to pass the default value.

The "name" attribute is the simplest of the input fields. It consists of a label and a text element; this is shown in listing 4.8.

LISTING 4.8—GENERATING THE NAME FIELD IN OUTPUTFORMHTML()

```
1.  //
2.  // Output the name label and field.
3.  //
4.  *pCtxt << _T("<tr>\r\n");
5.  *pCtxt << _T("<td>Name:</td>\r\n");
6.  *pCtxt << _T("<td><input type=text size=20 name=\"Name\"
7.  *pCtxt << _T(" Value=\"" << pName << "\"></td>\r\n");
8.  *pCtxt << _T("</tr>\r\n");
```

Note that the value is enclosed in quotation marks in the output stream; this is required if the field might contain spaces or other punctuation.

Generating the HTML for the Age Field

The age field is only slightly more complicated. The age attribute is an integer, but HTML does not contain any particular support for numeric fields. The field doesn't require any complicated support, but it would be nice to replace 0 values with a blank field. If the user enters bad data in the field, or leaves it blank, the ISAPI support code converts it to a 0 when converting it to the ITS_I4 parameter type. This is illustrated in listing 4.9.

LISTING 4.9—GENERATING THE AGE FIELD IN OUTPUTFORMHTML()

```
01.//
02.// Output the age label and field.
03.//
04.CString   ageWord;
05.*pCtxt << _T("<tr>\r\n");
06.*pCtxt << _T("<td>Age:</td>\r\n");
07.if (age > 0)
08.ageWord.Format(" value = \"%0d\"",age);
09.*pCtxt << _T("<td><input type=text size=3 name=\"Age\""
10.<< (LPCSTR)ageWord << "></td>\r\n");
11.*pCtxt << _T("</tr>\r\n");
```

Generating the HTML for the Gender Field

The gender field presents a minor complication; because it has been implemented by using checkboxes; the value cannot be set via the "value" attribute. Instead, it is necessary to set the "checked" attribute for the checkbox whose value corresponds to the pGender parameter. This can be done as shown in listing 4.10.

Listing 4.10—Generating the Gender Field in OutputFormHTML()

```
01.  //
02.  // Output the gender label and field.
03.  //
04.  const _TCHAR *pChecked;
05.  *pCtxt << _T("<tr>\r\n");
06.  *pCtxt << _T("<td>Gender:</td>\r\n");
07.  *pCtxt << _T("<td>");
08.  pChecked = (*pGender == _T('F')) ? szChecked : szEmpty;
09.  *pCtxt << _T("<input type=radio name=\"Gender\" value=\"F\" " << pChecked
     << " >Female \r\n");
10.  pChecked = (*pGender == _T('M')) ? szChecked : szEmpty;
11.  *pCtxt << _T("<input type=radio name=\"Gender\" value=\"M\" " << pChecked
     << " >Male\r\n");
12.  *pCtxt << _T("</td></tr>\r\n");
```

In this example, the extension sends the common elements of the HTML for the control, including the row start tags and labels. The value of the pGender parameter is compared to "F" to conditionally initialize a variable to the string "checked" or to a blank string. This variable is then used to build the HTML for the first of the gender check boxes. The procedure is repeated for the value "M," corresponding to the Male check box.

Generating the HTML for the E-Mail Field

The e-mail address element is another simple element; it is handled in exactly the same manner as the name field. All that the OutputFormHTML() function must do is generate a table row containing a label and a text input element; this is illustrated in list 4.11.

Listing 4.11—Generating the E-mail Address Field in OutputFormHTML()

```
1.  //
2.  // Output the e-mail address and field.
3.  //
4.  *pCtxt << _T("<tr>\r\n");
```

continues

LISTING 4.11—GENERATING THE E-MAIL
ADDRESS FIELD IN OUTPUTFORMHTML(), CONTINUED

```
5.  *pCtxt << _T("<td>E-mail Address:</td>\r\n");
6.  *pCtxt << _T("<td><input type=text size=20 maxlength=20 name=\"e-mail\"
➥value=\"" << pE-mail [ccc]<< "\"></td>\r\n");
7.  *pCtxt << _T("</tr>\r\n");
```

Generating the HTML for the Connection Speed Field

The remaining field, connectionSpeed, is implemented via a selection list. Selection lists are similar to groups of check boxes; the current value of the field is not passed via the "value" attribute. Instead, it is passed by setting the "selected" attribute on the element corresponding to the desired value.

In order to set the default value for the form, it is necessary to figure out which tag corresponds to the default value, and output the word "selected" when generating the HTML for that element. Code that does so is shown in listing 4.12.

LISTING 4.12—GENERATING THE CONNECTION SPEED
FIELD IN OUTPUTFORMHTML()

```
01.  //
02.  // Output the connection speed label and field.
03.  //
04.  const _TCHAR *pSelected;
05.  *pCtxt << _T("<tr>\r\n");
06.  *pCtxt << _T("<td>Connection Speed:</td>\r\n");
07.  *pCtxt << _T("<td><select name=\"ConnectSpeed\" size=1>\r\n");
08.  pSelected = (_tcscmp(pSpeed,_T("9600"))==0) ? szSelected : szEmpty;
09.  *pCtxt << _T("<option " << pSelected <<">9600</option>\r\n");
10.  pSelected = (_tcscmp(pSpeed,_T("14400"))==0) ? szSelected : szEmpty;
11.  *pCtxt << _T("<option " << pSelected <<">14400</option>\r\n");
12.  pSelected = (_tcscmp(pSpeed,_T("28800"))==0) ? szSelected : szEmpty;
13.  *pCtxt << _T("<option " << pSelected <<">28800</option>\r\n");
14.  *pCtxt << _T("</select></td>\r\n");
15.  *pCtxt << _T("</tr>\r\n");
```

Generating the Remainder of the HTML Form

The remainder of the function is straightforward; it consists of adding a submit button, and then closing the table and form tags. The code for this process is shown in listing 4.13.

Lines 1–8 are responsible for generating the HTML for the the submit button. The button is positioned by enclosing it in a table row, just as all of the other elements have been positioned. The button is moved to the right-hand column by including a blank cell before the button; this can be seen on lines 6 and 7.

LISTING 4.13—COMPLETING THE HTML FORM IN OUTPUTFORMHTML()

```
01.  //
02.  // Output the submit button; use a blank cell to fill the first
03.  // column
04.  //
05.  *pCtxt << _T("<tr>\r\n");
06.  *pCtxt << _T("<td></td>\r\n");
07.  *pCtxt << _T("<td><input type=submit value=\"Submit\"></td>\r\n");
08.  *pCtxt << _T("</tr>\r\n");
09.
10.  //
11.  // end the table, and the form.
12.  //
13.  *pCtxt << _T("</table>\r\n");
14.  *pCtxt << _T("</form>\r\n");
15.}
```

Handling Input from the User

Once the user has completed the form sent in the previous section, the extension will be called again to process the input. The basic process can be broken down into three steps:

- ◆ Getting the user's input

- ◆ Validating the user's input

- ◆ Generating a response to the user

The remainder of this section will break the process of handling the user input into these three steps. An overall roadmap of the process can be seen in figure 4.7.

Figure 4.7

A roadmap to handling user input in the SetProfile() function.

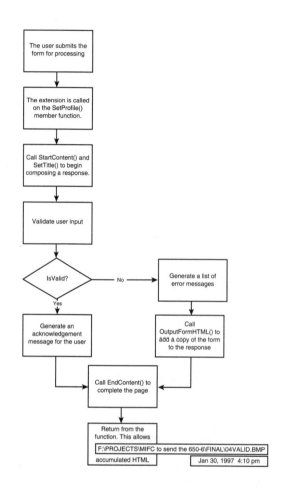

Getting the User's Input

The process for getting the information entered by the user response is fairly simple. The data is parsed by the MFC support code prior to the call to the command handler. When the handler is called, the data entered by the user is converted to the proper data type and passed to the handler.

The function declaration for the SetProfile() function is as follows:

```
1.void CUserProfileExtension::SetProfile(CHttpServerContext* pCtxt,
2.                LPCTSTR pName,
3.                long  age,
4.                LPCTSTR pGender,
5.                LPCTSTR pE-mail,
6.                LPCTSTR pSpeed)
```

The first parameter defines the context for the call; the remaining parameters carry the values entered by the user or merged from the defaults defined in the PARSEMAP.

 Note   It is important to remember that in VC 4.1 and 4.2 the default values will only be used in cases where the browser does not submit an entry for the field in the form. If the browser defines a text input field and the user happens to leave the field blank, the default will *not* be used.

Validating User Input

The response handler begins by validating the data passed by the user. This example has very rudimentary validation requirements: it checks to make sure the user has entered a name and email address and the age field contains a value greater than zero. These values are checked and flags are set to indicate the validity (or lack thereof) of the data.

The code that implements this validation is shown in listing 4.14.

LISTING 4.14—VALIDATING THE FIELDS IN SETPROFILE()

```
01.{
02.   BOOL bNameValid = TRUE;
03.   BOOL bAgeValid = TRUE;
04.   BOOL bE-mailValid = TRUE;
05.
06.
07.   if ((_tcscmp(pName,"~")==0) || (_tcslen(pName)==0))
08.     bNameValid = FALSE;
09.   if ((_tcscmp(pE-mail,"~")==0) || (_tcslen(pE-mail)==0))
10.     bE-mailValid = FALSE;
11.   bAgeValid = (age > 0);
```

A number of flags that indicate the state of the validation are initialized on lines 2–4. The flags are initialized to TRUE, reflecting the assumption that the data is valid until shown to be invalid.

On lines 7–10 the name and e-mail address field values are tested to ensure that the user has entered something into the field; if they are missing, the validation flags are set appropriately. The validation takes two forms: the field is tested for the default value, "~" specified in the parse map, and are checked to make sure they contain at least one character.

Tip A string field's value will only be set to the default value if the field is not present in the incoming form data. Most browsers will send data from empty text data fields in the form "name=." In these cases, the command handler function will receive a pointer to an empty string for these fields, rather than the default.

Responding to the User

Once the extension has acquired and validated the user's input, it is ready to generate some form of response. The exact set of actions taken will depend on the validity of the data.

Composing a Response to the User

The first step in generating the response is to output the normal page start HTML, including the <html>, <title>, and <body> tags. The page headers are the same for valid and invalid data, so this is a simple process; it can be seen in listing 4.15.

LISTING 4.15—GENERATING THE PAGE HEADER AND TITLE IN SETPROFILE()

```
1.  //
2.  // Output the standard headers and title.
3.  //
4.  StartContent(pCtxt);
5.  WriteTitle(pCtxt);
```

Providing Feedback to the User

The actions that should be taken at this point depend on the validity of the data entered by the user. There are only two possibilties:

◆ **The information is valid:** the extension should process the data and send the user some acknowledgement telling them that the information has been accepted.

◆ **The data is invalid:** the extension should notify the user and provide an opportunity to correct the problem.

Responding to Valid Input

If the data is valid, this extension simply sends a page notifying the user that the data has been accepted. In a real application, this is the point at which the data would be saved in a database or some other object store. In our example, the extension simply sends the user an acknowledgement thanking them for their entry.

The code to implement this behavior is shown in listing 4.16. In the first line of the listing, the function examines the validation flags set in listing 4.14. If the flags indicate that the data is valid, lines 2–9 are used to process the data and add an acknowledgement to the HTML that will be returned to the browser.

LISTING 4.16—ACKNOWLEDGING VALID INPUT IN SETPROFILE()

```
1.  if ( bNameValid && bAgeValid && bE-mailValid)
2.  {
3.     // Note: In a real application, we'd probably like to
4.     // save the data into a database, or perform some other
5.     // useful operation.
6.     *pCtxt << _T("<h1>User Profile Maintenance</h1>\r\n");
7.     *pCtxt << _T("<p>Thank you for updating ");
8.     *pCtxt << _T("<p>your profile...\r\n");
9.  }
```

Returning an Error Message to the User

If the data is not valid, matters are slightly more complicated. In this case, the extension sends the user a list of errors and sends a copy of the form with the data they submitted back for correction. The code used to accomplish this is shown in listing 4.17.

LISTING 4.17—HANDLING INVALID DATA IN SETPROFILE()

```
01.else
02.  {
03.     *pCtxt << _T("<h1>User Profile Maintenance</h1>\r\n");
04.     *pCtxt << _T("<h2>Errors during processing</h2>\r\n");
05.     *pCtxt << _T("<p>The following problem(s) were found \r\n");
06.     *pCtxt << _T("during processing:</p>\r\n");
07.     *pCtxt << _T("<ul>\r\n");
08.     if (!bNameValid)
09.       *pCtxt << _T("<li>You must enter a name.</li>\r\n");
10.     if (!bAgeValid)
11.       *pCtxt << _T("<li>You must enter an age > 0.</li>\r\n");
12.     if (!bE-mailValid)
13.       *pCtxt << _T("<li>You must enter an e-mail address.</li>\r\n");
14.     *pCtxt << _T("</ul>");
15.
16.     // Output the form & user's data
17.     OutputFormHTML(pCtxt, pName, age,
18.                    pGender, pE-mail, pSpeed);
19.}
```

Lines 3–4 add page headings to the returned HTML via <h1> and <h2> tags; these provide the user with some warning that problems were encountered. The heading text is continued with lines 5 and 6 by adding a paragraph that acts as a heading for the list of errors that follows.

The extension then generate a list of the encountered problems, formatted as a bulleted list. The list is opened on line 7 by generating the <ul> tag. On lines 8–12, the function checks each of the validation flags, and generates a list item for each error found in the incoming data. The error list is closed on line 14 via a </ul> tag.

Once the error list has been added to the accumulated HTML page, the extension adds a copy of the orignal data entry form. This copy of the entry form incorporates the data entered by the user, allowing the the user to correct the problems in place. This is done via a call to the same *OutputFormHTML()* on line 17. This is the same *OutputFormHTML()* function used to generate the form originally during the *ShowForm()* function.

 The data sent back to the user isn't necessarily exactly the same as the data entered. For example, if the user enters nonnumeric data in the age field, the data will be "lost" when the MFC ISAPI support code converts it from a string to a long integer. The extension will receive a zero as the value of this field, which the user will see as a blank field when the form is presented for correction.

Completing the Response

Finally, the *SetProfile()* function ends with a call to the *EndContent()* member function, which will properly end the page by generating a </body></html> pair.

```
1.  EndContent(pCtxt);
2.  }
```

Strengths and Weaknesses of Generating HTML On-the-Fly

The biggest strength of this approach is enabling integration of the form, data, and feedback to the user in a single page. This makes the form look like a more traditional GUI form application and makes it easier for the user to correct problems.

The biggest drawback to this approach is that the HTML form isn't conveniently located in an HTML file for editing and revision with web page editors. The result is a trade-off between the convenience of using HTML editors and the capability to programmatically generate a page combining user input and feedback by moving the creation of the page into code.

Using an HTML editor to perform the initial design of the form is frequently a good idea. When you're comfortable with the layout of the form, it's easy to cut and paste the HTML into the ISAPI extension. The HTML file can then be discarded, or maintained as a convenient place to experiment with revisions in the future.

 Here is a technique used in Perl scripts and other development environments to allow easy editing of the HTML for the form: the HTML is stored externally to the program in an HTML file and parsed by the program at run-time. In this approach, the ISAPI module would parse the file, looking for added tags to tell it where to output error message, data fields, and form data.

This allows the use of HTML editors but introduces the complexity of a run-time parser and markup syntax to indicate the location of information the extension will output onto the page.

I generally find it simpler to output the HTML from the C++ code, as illustrated in this the section "Generating HTML On-the-Fly," earlier in this chapter.

Potential Form-Processing Problems

Although it is important to learn how to design and write extensions, it's equally important to learn how to fix them when they go wrong. The following section describes some problems commonly encountered when building and running the applications, techniques to diagnose them, and solutions for getting around them.

Troubleshooting ISAPI Extensions

A number of problems that might be encountered when running the extension sometimes present symptoms and error messages inaccurate in describing what happened to the extension. Some of the most common problems are presented in the following sections, with a description of what actually happened and some suggestions for fixing the problems.

Module Not Found Errors

The "Module Not Found" message indicates the ISAPI extension specified in the action clause could not be located. Frequently, it means exactly that: the module's name or path is incorrectly specified.

The message is also displayed, however, if the command name given via the URL or mfcISAPICommand parameter is not present in the extension module. When this message is displayed, it is generally a good idea to check the PARSEMAP and the form to ensure an *exact* match of the names.

Module Cannot Be Loaded Errors

The "Module Cannot Be Loaded" message generally occurs when moving an ISAPI extension from a development machine to a production machine, or from one production system to another. It usually occurs when one or more DLLs required by the module are not present on the new hosts.

Diagnosing this problem requires finding the DLL not present on the new system, which might be a module directly linked to the ISAPI extension or a DLL referred to by another DLL. Check to see if all required modules are present and located in a path to be searched by the loader when it processes the ISAPI extension.

A useful tool for searching out these dependencies is the *dumpbin* utility included in Visual C++. Use the following command line:

```
dumpbin /imports myExtention.dll
```

This yields a list of all DLLs implicitly linked to the extension. If all those modules are present, repeat the process on the DLLs listed in the report generated by dumpbin.

Crashes Upon Return from the Handler

A common problem during development of an ISAPI module is the command handler that appears to work perfectly but causes a general protection fault after returning control to MFC. This problem is often caused by a mismatch between the number or type of parameters listed in the ON_PARSE_COMMAND macro and the actual command handler function.

When MFC processes an incoming command in an ISAPI extension, it dynamically generates a stack frame containing the parameters to the command handler based on those specified in the matching ON_PARSE_COMMAND macro. If the macro's parameter list does not match the parameters declared in the matching member function, the wrong number of bytes of data will be popped off the stack when the handler returns. This causes a protection fault after the function returns.

Form Has No Data Errors

The "Form Has No Data" message frequently indicates a failure of the ISAPI extension to handle a C++ exception. In the absence of any local handler, the exception will be caught by a try/catch block in the MFC ISAPI support module.

Many routines an ISAPI module might call can throw exceptions to indicate an error. In particular, MFC classes generally use exceptions to signal errors. Frequent culprits are the MFC CDatabase and CRecordset classes; they use exceptions to report errors quite extensively. A wide variety of database problems may be reflected by generating exceptions; these include problems that occur during the processing of stored procedures or triggers.

To handle these errors, it is frequently desirable to place a try/catch block around the entire handler. This duplicates some work code present in the MFC support module, but affords an extension the capability to generate a sensible error message.

GET Command Problems

Many forms can be implemented equally well as either a GET or a POST request. The GET command is limited to handling only 1024 bytes of data and can have problems when using the ISAPI command handlers.

When writing ISAPI extensions to support forms, it is recommended that you use the POST method and the MFC 4.2 mfcISAPICommand feature described in the next section.

The mfcISAPICommand Parameter

The MFC PARSEMAP mechanism provides a standardized model for combining multiple functions in a single ISAPI extension DLL. Although it's certainly possible to develop your own mechanism to do similar things, the MFC classes provide a standard, simple model for handling the commands.

Prior to the release of Visual C++ 4.2, there was a potential problem with the mechanism used to implement the MFC command handlers. The MFC PARSEMAPs relied on a somewhat unusual URL using a second question mark to separate the command and parameters.

For example, assume you're building a form to enable retrieval of one of the user profiles built in the form in the beginning of this chapter. It would be convenient to package the search form in the same module as the form used to update the data, thus producing a set of HTML that looks something like the following code:

```
1.<FORM ACTION="Scripts/UserProfiles.dll?FindProfile" METHOD=GET>
2.Enter the name of the user to search for: <INPUT NAME="SearchTarget">
3.<INPUT TYPE=SUBMIT VALUE="Search">
4.</form>
```

When the user chooses the Search button, one would expect to get called on the *UpdateProfile()* function of the CHttpServerExtension class. Unfortunately, this doesn't always work.

The culprit is the way some browsers handle the two question marks in the URL. Not surprisingly, everything works correctly under Microsoft Internet Explorer. When the user clicks on the Search button, Explorer sends a request such as the following:

```
http://www.test.com/scripts/Scripts UserProfiles.dll?FindProfile?SearchTarget
➥=Clements
```

All is well. If you do the same thing from a Netscape 2.0 or 3.0 browser, however, there is a problem. Netscape sends something that looks like this:

```
http://www.test.com/scripts/Scripts/UserProfiles.dll?SearchTarget=Clements
```

The Netscape browser sends an URL that ends with a question mark and only contains one question mark. The command name, "FindProfile," is not transmitted. This tends to cause problems, because the PARSEMAP is defined to dispatch a call to the correct function.

This problem is solved by adding the special parameter *mfcISAPICommand*. If the first parameter in the HTML form is named mfcISAPICommand, the MFC ISAPI module uses the string found there as the name of the command. Thus, if the form is modified to look like the following HTML code, the mfcISAPICommand variable added to the beginning of the form takes the place of the command clause in the URL.

```
1.<FORM ACTION="Scripts/UserProfiles.dll?" METHOD=POST>
2.<INPUT TYPE=HIDDEN NAME="mfcISAPICommand" VALUE="FindProfile">
3.Enter the name of the user to search for: <INPUT NAME="SearchTarget">
4.<INPUT TYPE=SUBMIT VALUE="Search">
5.</form>
```

When this form is submitted, both the Netscape and Microsoft browsers send the following, which is correctly dispatched to the command handler:

```
http://www.test.com/scripts/UserProfiles.dll?mfcISAPICommand=FindProfile&
SearchTarget=Clements
```

 The mfcISAPICommand parameter will only be interpreted as a command if it is the *first* field on the form. In any other position, it's treated the same as any other field.

When Parse Maps Don't Work

The MFC PARSEMAP mechanism is generally a useful structure for invoking the code required to handle a form. It handles parameter parsing and data-type conversion automatically, and makes function dispatching equally convenient. For 90 percent of the code you'll be writing in ISAPI extensions, PARSEMAPs are an invaluable tool.

Unfortunately, PARSEMAPs can sometimes make your life more difficult than necessary. It's important to learn to recognize these situations and to use other tools to handle them. This section discusses a number of situations that usually cause problems in ISAPI applications.

Forms with Variable Content

The MFC PARSEMAP mechanism is designed around forms with fixed numbers of parameters and with fairly predictable content. They require you to know what your form is going to contain at the time you code the PARSEMAP: what the fields will be, what the data types of the fields will be, and how many instances of each field there will be.

For some applications, such as a typical shopping cart e-commerce application, the fixed parameter-count model doesn't quite fit. For these forms, you need to support a variable number of fields. An example of such a form is shown in figure 4.8.

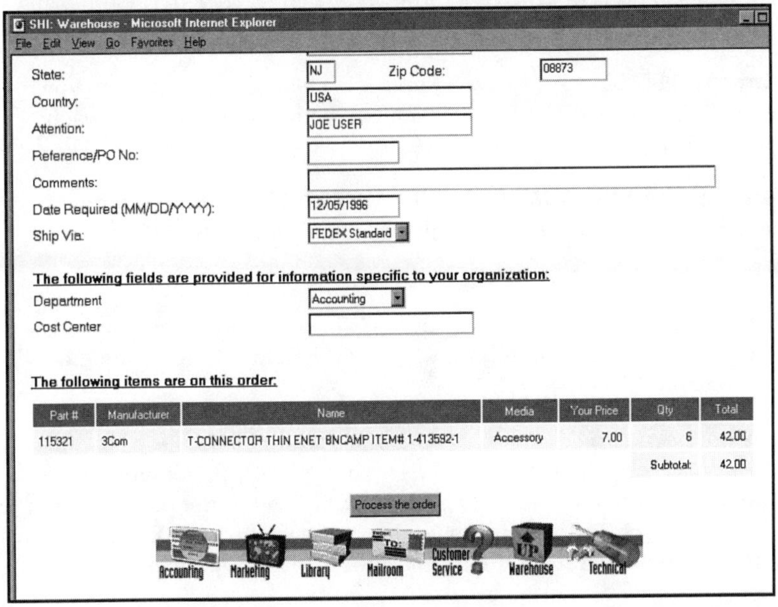

Figure 4.8

An order form supporting customized fields.

The form in figure 4.8 has a further complication: it shows a variable number of fields specific to a particular customer. At the time the form is coded, you don't know how many of these fields there might be, which makes defining the PARSEMAPs difficult.

When faced with such forms, you might find PARSEMAPs doing more harm than good. They're a tool like any other and, as such, aren't always the right tool for the job. If you're designing the code to generate the form and pick up the data, you might find it's simpler to parse the data yourself. For another set of techniques to help with this problem, see Chapter 11, "Advanced Form Processing."

Remember, this doesn't mean it's impossible to use PARSEMAPs for these situations; it simply means they aren't necessarily the best tools for the job. Some developers have suggested working around the problem by defining a large number of generic fields that might or might not be present; this will certainly solve the problem for some forms. The question to ask is whether the PARSEMAPs are making things harder or simpler.

Fields with Multiple Values

The PARSEMAP mechanism makes one assumption that seems safe enough: that a field has a single value. This is not the case, however, when faced with the following situations:

♦ **Check boxes:** HTML supports use of multiple check boxes with the same name but differing values. The browser sends a "name=value" pair for each "checked" control.

♦ **Select elements with MULTIPLE:** if the MULTIPLE attribute is set on a select element, the browser sends a name=value pair for each of the selected options.

The PARSEMAP support classes tend to act strangely in cases where there are multiple values. The exact behavior depends on whether the fields of the command handler have been named.

If the fields have not been named, the extra values are added to the list of parameters. This causes a problem when the number of parameters supplied does not match the number of parameters specified in the PARSEMAP. If the parameters have been named, the support code finds multiple values for a single PARSEMAP, causing the MFC code to reject the data from the form on the basis of a faulty parameter map.

The actual behavior exhibited when one of these problems occurs depends on whether the extension has been loaded prior to the bad invocation. The extension might display an "invalid command" message or simply send a blank page back to the browser.

If you have a need for these types of forms, you'll need to look beyond the standard MFC ISAPI support code. The problem does not lie in ISAPI, but in the MFC PARSEMAP mechanism. An alternative method of handling multi-valued field data is implemented in Chapter 11 "Advanced Form Processing."

Summary

This chapter has presented the basic building blocks for implementing form handling ISAPI using MFC. It showed a simple form without any validation, and a more advanced form with validation and user feedback; these should provide models for implementing form processing.

It also provided reference material useful to the developer creating HTML forms and extensions to support them, including coverage of:

◆ Forms in the HTML standard

◆ Details of the MFC PARSEMAP mechanism

◆ Common problems that may been encountered when developing forms applications

CHAPTER 5

Extracting Multimedia Images from a Database

MFC programmers will undoubtedly find that ISAPI programming is easy. The new Class Wizard introduced in Visual C++ version 4.1 makes generating an ISAPI extension a breeze. Don't get too comfortable, though. Special complications are present if you plan to use MFC database support from within ISAPI response functions. This chapter will teach you the techniques needed for advanced MFC development of ISAPI modules that use an ODBC database. In addition, this chapter will outline a general approach for dealing with shared resources (such as a database) in a multithreaded environment.

This chapter goes well beyond what you might see in most introductory level books on MFC database development. If you are new to MFC or ISAPI programming, you should start by reading at least Chapter 4, "Basic Form Processing in MFC." The information contained here in Chapter 5 builds on the material in Chapter 4. The current chapter also covers some advanced Win32 concepts including multithreading, process synchronization, and database design, using ODBC and MFC recordsets. For a good review of Windows multithreaded programming, see Jeff Richter's book titled *Advanced Windows NT* (pay particular attention to Chapter 5 of Richter's book, which covers thread synchronization). You can also find his book in MSDN Books Online. A review of MFC recordsets can be found in either MSDN's Books Online or in the MSVC help files.

As in the rest of this book, the core concepts of this chapter are taught within the framework of a programming problem you could actually face. Although the example used here might not be of the utmost interest to you, it will illustrate many issues related to ISAPI and database development.

By the end of this chapter, you should understand most of the complex issues related to MFC ISAPI response functions using ODBC. If nothing more, you will at least have mmGet.dll, which you can use in your own development to generate images from a database on the fly.

The first couple of sections will lay out the problem of dynamic image extraction from an ODBC database in more depth. Then the chapter will jump around a bit to give you the background necessary for understanding the mechanics used in the remainder of the chapter. The "Image Extraction Module" section gets into the pertinent issues related to ODBC access from an ISAPI response function. Even if you consider yourself a seasoned veteran to MIME types, HTML, and the nature of the HTTP GET request, you are encouraged to read the introductory sections of the chapter.

Dynamic, Multimedia Web Page Creation

Multimedia images such as GIFs and JPEGs are conventionally kept as files on the web server. HTML pages referencing these images typically refer to them by using the image source tag (for example, <IMG SRC="/Images/logo.gif">). This method presents certain difficulties if your images are dynamic in nature.

Suppose, for instance, you are asked to write an online auction. One of the objectives might be keeping the uploaded images in a database associated with their corresponding items instead of keeping them in their own separate files. Accomplishing this goal would require you to have a mechanism in place for extracting the images when the web server is requested to render an item from the auction onto a web page. This chapter will present a fully functional ISAPI extension program to accomplish this task.

The code for the example has been written by using MFC 4.2b, using ODBC recordsets and Microsoft Access '97 as the database. At the time of writing, DAO is not considered to be thread-safe and will not be discussed in this chapter for that reason.

Archive More Than Just Graphics in Database

You will discover that you can do more than store graphic images for dynamic web page creation. In fact, it is possible to dynamically render any MIME-type image from a database. This includes but is not limited to audio formats, video formats, Java scripts, Zip files, and Word documents. The word *render* is used here loosely. Audio formats, Zip files, and Word documents are obviously handled differently by your web browser than graphic and video formats. As you will see, this does not preclude your using them on your web page and keeping them in the database. This means the auction could even be equipped to map sound bytes beside the pictures of auctioned items.

Throughout the rest of this chapter, the word *image* will mean any type of multimedia file or binary data stream you wish to keep in your database.

The Populator Tool

A utility program named POPULATE has been included on the sample CD-ROM in the projects\chap05\populate directory with source code. It is an MFC 4.2b application that was written to facilitate importing files into the image database. The Access database images.mdb has been pre-populated with various MIME type files for demonstration in the samples included in this chapter. You will undoubtedly find this utility handy for importing your own images into the database. You will need to run Access, however, if you wish to manipulate the database extensively. POPULATE.EXE is only an importing tool at this point. A web page to house the latest revisions of this tool has been added to our corporate web site at:

```
http://www.structsoft.com/isapi.htm
```

Remember to set up an ODBC datasource before you attempt to use the POPULATE application. Follow the directions on "ODBC Datasource Preparation" later in this chapter. For additional information, see the readme.txt file in the mmGet directory on the CD-ROM. The readme.txt file contains important information not available for inclusion in the book at the time of printing.

MIME Types

Perhaps you are wondering what a MIME type is. A MIME type, simply stated, informs a web browser what type of data it can expect to be retrieving, before the data is actually sent to it. To put it another way, it gives meaning to binary images. Without MIME types, all data sent to your browser would be nothing more than streams of bytes—not too beneficial, as you can imagine. MIME types enable the display of images and the playback of audio streams.

Your web browser is configured to process files according to their MIME types. When files with unknown MIME types are encountered your browser reacts by displaying a Save As dialog box. You may have noticed your browser behaves differently when retrieving known MIME types such as audio streams. Known MIME types are fluently handled according to their type. Audio streams, for example, are automatically played (provided that you have the necessary hardware of course). Consequently, the same rule applies to graphic style MIME types. JPEG, GIF, and BMP need to each be treated differently because of differences in file formats; therefore, each is assigned their own MIME type so that the browser can easily determine which drawing routine should be called to correctly render the image within the browser.

You might conclude from this that the file extension plays a role in determining how the file is handled by the browser. Although this is true in some cases, many web browsers first attempt to handle the downloaded image by its MIME type, which is sent directly in the header preceding the image stream. In the case of an executable file, the header typically contains the string "Content-Type: application/octet-stream." *Application/octet-stream* is a MIME type representing general binary images. Most browsers are configured to respond to this MIME type by presenting the Save As dialog box. Other examples include video/x-msvideo for AVI files, audio/x-pn-realaudio for RealAudio encoded streams, and image/gif and image/jpeg for GIF and JPEG image types.

The numbered procedure that follows shows how most browsers communicate with a remote web server. If you are using Netscape's browser, look at Options, General Preferences, Helpers in the main menu. The file-type column on that screen lists all the MIME types your Netscape browser recognizes. For any MIME type your browser is configured to recognize, the browser will perform special actions whenever it is retrieving that type of data. Using Internet Explorer 3, you can find the same information under View, Options, Programs, File Types from the main menu.

1. HTML is read by the browser:

```
<html>
…
<img src="image.xyz">
…
</html>
```

2. Browser converts HTML to a Server GET request:

```
GET image.xyz
```

3. The Web Server responds by sending the content-type and data in response:

```
Content-Type: image/gif
{binary image data sent from reading image.xyz file}
```

You can see from the preceding procedure that each image source tag (<IMG SRC=...>) in an HTML file resolves to a GET request into the web server. The GET requests happen behind the scenes without user interaction. The server responds to each GET request by sending the content-type (MIME type) in the header response before the image is returned. Understanding how a web browser interacts with a web server and how Microsoft's IIS interacts with your extension DLL is extremely important for a complete understanding of the concepts discussed in the remainder of this chapter.

 RFCs are published by the IETF (Internet Engineering Task Force). They are used to set standards on a wide range of topics related to the Internet.

More on MIME Types: The Call to StartContent()

You might have noticed that most standard MFC ISAPI response functions begin with a call to *StartContent()*. The default implementation of StartContent() from MFC 4.2b is shown in listing 5.1.

LISTING 5.1—EXCERPTS FROM ISAPI.CPP IN MFC VERSION 4.2B. STARTCONTENT() CONVENTIONALLY INITIATES MOST STANDARD ISAPI RESPONSE FUNCTIONS

```
1.static const TCHAR szContentType[] = _T("Content-Type: text/html\r\n");
2.…
3.void CHttpServer::StartContent(CHttpServerContext* pCtxt) const
4.{
5.    AddHeader(pCtxt, szContentType);
6.}
```

It is interesting to note that this function returns a MIME type header. As you can see in this listing, "text" is a valid MIME type as well.

Don't be misled by the word "image" in the image source tag (<IMG SRC=...>). It is entirely acceptable for <img src="image.xyz"> to return a text stream. Remember, the image tag can refer to any external element, whether it's text, graphic, audio, video, or whatever. If the server handles the GET requests by first sending the appropriate MIME type name back to the client's browser, and if the client's browser knows what to do with that type of MIME type data, everything should work the way you would expect—graphics and video are rendered, audio is played, binary files are saved, and so on.

MIME stands for Multipurpose Internet Mail Extension. It was actually developed to associate meaning with file attachments in Internet mail messages. See http://www.oac.uci.edu/indiv/ehood/MIME/MIME.html or RFC 1521 & 1522 for exhaustive presentation of the MIME standard.

Embedded ISAPI Response Calls

The previous section demonstrated how you could use the image source tag to refer to any type of external file, providing the two requirements are met:

1. The server responds with the correct MIME type

2. The client's browser knows how to deal with the returned image type

We can modify our example slightly now to refer to an ISAPI extension DLL instead of a file named image.xyz (see line 3 in listing 5.2). Every image requested by the browser would ultimately be serviced by separate calls into the mmGet.dll ISAPI extension module instead of file retrieval at the server.

Don't try this example yet. The ultimate goal is to have an ISAPI response function return various images extracted from a database. You address this issue by assigning a unique, generated, long-integer value to all images kept in the database; therefore, given that image.xyz has a unique record ID of 20, the final embedded image source becomes <IMG SRC="mmGet.dll?20">. This is the method mmGet will use to extract images dynamically from the database.

 Tip   This method can also serve as an alternative to SSIs (Server-Side Includes) .

LISTING 5.2—EMBEDDED CALL TO AN ISAPI RESPONSE FUNCTION
INSTEAD OF AN EXTERNAL FILE ELEMENT

```
1.<html>
2.…
3. <img src="mmGet.dll">
4.…
5.</html>
```

Storing BLOBs in an ODBC Database

If you are a veteran to database programming, you already know that storing or retrieving BLOBs (binary large objects) in databases is not much fun—especially if you are working with ODBC. MFC and ODBC impose limits of 64K for binary field sizes, further complicating the issue. Addressing this limit resulted in the database schema for mmGet presented here.

Note Recordsets can actually handle fields larger than 64K if you use CLongBinary. CLongBinary will read fields up to available memory; however, Microsoft states in the MSVC help files that this approach is "prohibitively expensive." See tech note #45 in *Visual C++ Books Online* for more information on this subject.

The Database Schema

Table 5.1 contains the definition for the Images table. An Access database named images.mdb is included on the CD-ROM containing a table also named images. Remember to setup an ODBC system data source name from the control panel before you try to refer to it or run the ISAPI extension presented in the next section.

Table 5.1
Images Table Definition

Field Name	Type	Size
ID	long integer (indexed)	
SEQUENCE	long integer	
MIMETYPE	text	60 bytes
IMAGESRC	text	255 bytes
IMAGELEN	long integer	
IMAGE	binary object	

The ID alone represents the logical image entity. The ID and SEQUENCE fields are combined to form a primary, unique key for each record. The IMAGESRC field is used for informational purposes only. The POPULATOR program provided on the CD-ROM uses this field to indicate the file name used as the source when importing the image into the database. IMAGELEN represents the number of bytes kept in the IMAGE field on the same record. The POPULATOR program chunks up the imported data into 4K increments; therefore, the value of IMAGELEN should range between 1 and 4096 bytes.

For an example, take image.xyz, which has a file size of 10,000 bytes. Loading this image via the POPULATOR application will result in entries like the following:

id	sequence	mimetype	imagesrc	imagelen	image
20	0	image/gif	C:\images\image.xyz	4096	...
20	1	image/gif	C:\images\image.xyz	4096	...
20	2	image/gif	C:\images\image.xyz	1904	...

 There is nothing magic about using 4K as the IMAGELEN setting. You can feel free to change this value in both the POPULATOR and mmGet projects if you desire. If you are so inclined, you should re-create the image database from scratch since it has been included on the CD-ROM pre-populated with data in 4K chunks. The average size of the binary objects kept in your database should be the basis for deciding on a good IMAGELEN value if you decide to make this change.

ODBC Datasource Preparation

You will need to install the ODBC drivers for Access if you haven't done so already. At the time of this writing, a patch is necessary to successfully use the Access drivers under NT 4.0. You can find this patch on FTP at:

```
ftp://ftp.microsoft.com/Softlib/MSLFILES/Msjtwng.exe
```

Follow the installation instructions in the readme file contained in the self-extracting executable. After you have the Access driver installed, you will be able to check its version by clicking on the *Drivers* button inside the ODBC-32 control panel applet. mmGet has been developed and tested by using version 3.40.2829 of the Access Driver.

Use the ODBC-32 control panel applet to set up a datasource for the mmGet extension. ODBC-32 is automatically installed with many software packages, including VC 4.2. Begin by copying the images.mdb file from the CD-ROM's \mmGet directory into a directory somewhere on your local drive. You do not necessarily need to copy this file in a directory specified by Microsoft's ISM (Internet Service Manager).

ISAPI extensions require a system DSN setup instead of a User Datasource. System datasources are visible by all users accessing the machine. Add a new system datasource named "Images" if you have not already done so. Be sure to select the copy of images.mdb residing on your local drive.

The Image Extraction Module

By this point you should have an understanding of MIME types and the interactions that transpire between a web browser, the IIS server, and an ISAPI extension module.

If you have been following along on your computer, you should also have a system datasource named Images installed in ODBC-32.

Now you need to examine the workings of the mmGet.dll ISAPI extension module in depth. The sample files listed in this section can be found on the CD-ROM under projects\chap05\step1.

Recall from the database schema that the image table uses a unique primary key named ID to reference images. A response function must therefore be written that accepts a long binary integer and then dynamically extracts that image from the database to send back to the client's web browser. Only one response function is needed to load any image from the database. The *Default()* response function created by the ClassWizard is a perfect candidate to serve this purpose. It has been changed slightly from its original (generated) form to accommodate one long-integer parameter passed to it. The *Default()* handler is called whenever a response function name is omitted from the URL. The usage syntax changes from listing 5.2 to become "/mmGet.dll?1" or /mmGet.dll?<ID> in that general case.

LISTING 5.3—MMGET.H

```
01.// MMGET.H - Header file for your Internet Server
02.//    mmGet Extension
03.
04.class CmmGetSet;
05.
06.class CMmGetExtension : public CHttpServer
07.{
08.public:
09.    CMmGetExtension();
10.    ~CMmGetExtension();
11.
12.virtual BOOL initialize();
13.
14.// Overrides
15.    // ClassWizard generated virtual function overrides
16.        // NOTE - the ClassWizard will add and remove member functions
➡here.
17.        //    DO NOT EDIT what you see in these blocks of generated code !
18.    //{{AFX_VIRTUAL(CMmGetExtension)
19.    public:
20.    virtual BOOL GetExtensionVersion(HSE_VERSION_INFO* pVer);
21.    //}}AFX_VIRTUAL
```

continues

LISTING 5.3—MMGET.H, CONTINUED

```
22.
23.     // mmGet's one and only response function handler
24.     void Default(CHttpServerContext* pCtxt, int imageId);
25.
26.     DECLARE_PARSE_MAP()
27.
28.     //{{AFX_MSG(CMmGetExtension)
29.     //}}AFX_MSG
30.
31.protected:
32.CmmGetSet     *m_pImageSet;
33.};
```

LISTING 5.4—MMGET.CPP. IMPLEMENTATION FOR THE MMGET ISAPI EXTENSION PROGRAM

```
001.// MMGET.CPP - Implementation file for your Internet Server
002.//     mmGet Extension
003.#include "stdafx.h"
004.#include "mmGet.h"
005.#include "mmGetSet.h"
006.#include "resource.h"
007.
008.///////////////////////////////////////////////////////////////////
009.// command-parsing map
010.
011.BEGIN_PARSE_MAP(CMmGetExtension, CHttpServer)
012.     ON_PARSE_COMMAND(Default, CMmGetExtension, ITS_I4)
013.     ON_PARSE_COMMAND_PARAMS("ID")
014.     DEFAULT_PARSE_COMMAND(Default, CMmGetExtension)
015.END_PARSE_MAP(CMmGetExtension)
016.
017.///////////////////////////////////////////////////////////////////
018.// The one and only CMmGetExtension object
019.
020.CMmGetExtension theExtension;
021.
022.///////////////////////////////////////////////////////////////////
023.// CMmGetExtension implementation
024.
025.CMmGetExtension::CMmGetExtension()
```

```
026.{
027.    m_pImageSet = NULL;
028.}
029.
030.CMmGetExtension::~CMmGetExtension()
031.{
032.    delete m_pImageSet;
033.}
034.
035.BOOL CMmGetExtension::initialize()
036.{
037.    BOOL bSuccess;
038.
039.    TRY
040.    {
041.        if (m_pImageSet)
042.        {
043.            bSuccess = TRUE;
044.        }
045.        else
046.        {
047.            m_pImageSet = new CmmGetSet;
048.            if (!m_pImageSet)
049.                return FALSE;
050.
051.            bSuccess = m_pImageSet->Open(CRecordset::snapshot);
052.        }
053.
054.        ASSERT_VALID(m_pImageSet);
055.    }
056.    CATCH(CDBException, e)
057.    {
058.        ISAPITRACE0(e->m_strError);
059.    }
060.    CATCH_ALL(e)
061.    {
062.        bSuccess = FALSE;
063.    }
064.    END_CATCH_ALL
065.
066.    return bSuccess;
067.}
```

continues

**LISTING 5.4—MMGET.CPP. IMPLEMENTATION FOR
THE MMGET ISAPI EXTENSION PROGRAM, CONTINUED**

```
068.
069.BOOL CMmGetExtension::GetExtensionVersion(HSE_VERSION_INFO* pVer)
070.{
071.    // Call default implementation for initialization
072.    CHttpServer::GetExtensionVersion(pVer);
073.
074.    // Load description string
075.    TCHAR sz[HSE_MAX_EXT_DLL_NAME_LEN+1];
076.    ISAPIVERIFY(::LoadString(AfxGetResourceHandle(),
077.            IDS_SERVER, sz, HSE_MAX_EXT_DLL_NAME_LEN));
078.    _tcscpy(pVer->lpszExtensionDesc, sz);
079.    return TRUE;
080.}
081.
082.////////////////////////////////////////////////////////////////////
083.// CMmGetExtension command handlers
084.
085.void CMmGetExtension::Default(CHttpServerContext* pCtxt, int imageId)
086.{
087.    if (!initialize())
088.    {
089.        OnParseError(pCtxt, HTTP_STATUS_SERVER_ERROR);
090.    }
091.    else
092.    {
093.        if (m_pImageSet->accessId(imageId))
094.        {
095.            AddHeader(pCtxt, CString(_T("Content-Type: ")) +
096.                            m_pImageSet->getMimeType() +
097.                                _T("\r\n"));
098.            *pCtxt << *m_pImageSet;
099.        }
100.        else
101.        {
102.            StartContent(pCtxt);
103.            *pCtxt << _T("Missing Image\r\n");
104.            EndContent(pCtxt);
105.        }
106.    }
107.}
```

```
108.
109.// Do not edit the following lines, which are needed by ClassWizard.
110.#if 0
111.BEGIN_MESSAGE_MAP(CMmGetExtension, CHttpServer)
112.    //{{AFX_MSG_MAP(CMmGetExtension)
113.    //}}AFX_MSG_MAP
114.END_MESSAGE_MAP()
115.#endif    // 0
```

The *Default()* handler begins by calling the *initialize()* function on line 87. The first call to *initialize()* opens the recordset and continues to use the same recordset until the server stops or unloads the mmGet extension DLL. This method appears to be fairly efficient and is probably the approach many MFC developers would take to achieve the stated goal of dynamic image retrieval using ODBC. Unfortunately, this method is not acceptable, because it is destined to crash IIS with less than a moderate amount of usage!

Can you see the potential problem in the code? Here is a hint—the alternative is to open the recordset at the onset of each call to *Default()* and close the recordset before you leave the call to *Default()*. However, this alternative is not very palatable, because it could cause the database to be opened and closed several hundred times per minute on an active web server. ODBC is notoriously slow in opening databases and recordsets.

If you guessed that the problem relates to concurrent access to line 93 in listing 5.4 then you are correct. An attempt will be made, therefore, to address the issues in the first approach—open the database in the module initialization code. First, we will finish looking at the rest of the *Default()* function and the recordset source.

Using a CRecordset for Image Extraction

A call to *Default()* (line 85 in listing 5.4) passes the image ID as an argument. This ID is used to query the database in a m_pImageSet->accessId(imageId) call. On a successful image access (SQL query), the content type is retrieved and sent to the CHttpServerContext, followed by the image stream. Notice the use of the stream operator in statement *pCtxt << *m_pImageSet found on line 98. This syntax does not come for free. Listing 5.5 and 5.6 details how this is accomplished.

LISTING 5.5—DEFINITIONS FOR THE IMAGE RETRIEVING RECORDSET. SEE MFC HELP ON CHTMLSTREAM FOR FURTHER DETAILS

```
01.// mmGetSet.h : header file
02.//
03.
```

continues

LISTING 5.5—DEFINITIONS FOR THE IMAGE RETRIEVING RECORDSET. SEE MFC HELP ON CHtmlStream FOR FURTHER DETAILS, CONTINUED

```
04.//////////////////////////////////////////////////////////////////////
/
05.// CmmGetSet recordset
06.
07.#define    IMAGE_LOAD_INCREMENT 4096
08.
09.class CmmGetSet : public Crecordset, public CHtmlStream
10.{
11.public:
12.     CmmGetSet(CDatabase* pDatabase = NULL);
13.     DECLARE_DYNAMIC(CmmGetSet)
14.
15.// Field/Param Data
16.     //{{AFX_FIELD(CmmGetSet, CRecordset)
17.     long     m_id;
18.     long     m_sequence;
19.     CString     m_mimetype;
20.     CString     m_imagesrc;
21.     long     m_imagelen;
22.     CByteArray     m_image;
23.     //}}AFX_FIELD
24.
25.     long     m_findId;
26.
27.     // Returns TRUE if image was successfully located in database
28.     virtual BOOL accessId(int id);
29.
30.     virtual LPCSTR getMimeType();
31.
32.// Overrides
33.     // ClassWizard generated virtual function overrides
34.     //{{AFX_VIRTUAL(CmmGetSet)
35.     public:
36.     virtual CString GetDefaultConnect();    // Default connection string
37.     virtual CString GetDefaultSQL();    // Default SQL for Recordset
38.     virtual void DoFieldExchange(CFieldExchange* pFX);  // RFX support
39.     //}}AFX_VIRTUAL
40.
```

```
41.// Implementation
42.#ifdef _DEBUG
43.     virtual void AssertValid() const;
44.     virtual void Dump(CDumpContext& dc) const;
45.#endif
46.};
47.
48.inline LPCSTR CmmGetSet::getMimeType()
49.{
50.     return m_mimetype;
51.}
```

CmmGetSet is multiply derived from both CRecordset and CHtmlStream. This is perfectly reasonable to do since the CHtmlStream class is a base class. We can safely derive from both CRecordset and CHtmlStream without ambiguous references to CObject. See the sidebar note on this.

Note The use of multiple derivation in listing 5.5 might get a few developers a little squeamish. Actually, this is a perfect candidate for multiple inheritance. Here's the scoop. Microsoft once decided to derive everything from CObject (evident in earlier versions of MFC). This might seem okay from an object-oriented, purist point of view; however, C++ has big problems if you use multiple inheritance where any classes are derived (either directly or indirectly) non-virtually from a common base class such as CObject (the case with most of the MFC library). You probably know about this stuff already, so this chapter won't bore you with details (see the *Annotated C++ Reference Manual* if you are unfamiliar with this topic). Fortunately, later versions of MFC have been breaking from this tradition of ever-deepening derivations off of CObject. Fortunately for us, CHtmlStream is one of those exceptions. It is not derived from CObject thereby making reference to it non-ambiguous. See Tech Note #16 In *Visual C++ Books Online* for further information on this subject.

Deriving off of CHtmlStream, coupled with a little bit of coding found in listing 5.6, enables you to stream images the same way you would stream a string or an integer to a CHttpServerContext.

LISTING 5.6—IMPLEMENTATION OF THE IMAGE RETRIEVING RECORDSET

```
001.// mmGetSet.cpp : implementation file
002.//
003.
```

continues

LISTING 5.6—IMPLEMENTATION OF
THE IMAGE RETRIEVING RECORDSET, CONTINUED

```
004.#include "stdafx.h"
005.#include "mmGet.h"
006.#include "mmGetSet.h"
007.
008.#ifdef _DEBUG
009.#define new DEBUG_NEW
010.#undef THIS_FILE
011.static char THIS_FILE[] = __FILE__;
012.#endif
013.
014.//////////////////////////////////////////////////////////////////////////
➥//
015.// mmGetSet
016.
017.IMPLEMENT_DYNAMIC(CmmGetSet, CRecordset)
018.
019.CmmGetSet::CmmGetSet(CDatabase* pdb)
020.    : CRecordset(pdb)
021.{
022.    //{{AFX_FIELD_INIT(CmmGetSet)
023.    m_id = 0;
024.    m_sequence = 0;
025.    m_mimetype = _T("");
026.    m_imagesrc = _T("");
027.    m_imagelen = 0;
028.    m_nFields = 6;
029.    //}}AFX_FIELD_INIT
030.    m_nDefaultType = snapshot;
031.
032.    m_findId = -1;
033.}
034.
035.
036.CString CmmGetSet::GetDefaultConnect()
037.{
038.    return _T("ODBC;DSN=Images");
039.}
040.
041.CString CmmGetSet::GetDefaultSQL()
042.{
```

```
043.    m_strSort = _T("sequence");
044.    m_strFilter.Format(_T("id=%ld"), m_findId);
045.    return _T("[images]");
046.}
047.
048.void CmmGetSet::DoFieldExchange(CFieldExchange* pFX)
049.{
050.    //{{AFX_FIELD_MAP(CmmGetSet)
051.    pFX->SetFieldType(CFieldExchange::outputColumn);
052.    RFX_Long(pFX, _T("[id]"), m_id);
053.    RFX_Long(pFX, _T("[sequence]"), m_sequence);
054.    RFX_Text(pFX, _T("[mimetype]"), m_mimetype);
055.    RFX_Text(pFX, _T("[imagesrc]"), m_imagesrc);
056.    RFX_Long(pFX, _T("[imagelen]"), m_imagelen);
057.    RFX_Binary(pFX, _T("[image]"), m_image, IMAGE_LOAD_INCREMENT);
058.    //}}AFX_FIELD_MAP
059.}
060.
061.///////////////////////////////////////////////////////////////////////
//
062.// mmGetSet diagnostics
063.
064.#ifdef _DEBUG
065.void CmmGetSet::AssertValid() const
066.{
067.    CRecordset::AssertValid();
068.}
069.
070.void CmmGetSet::Dump(CDumpContext& dc) const
071.{
072.    CRecordset::Dump(dc);
073.}
074.#endif //_DEBUG
075.
076.BOOL CmmGetSet::accessId(int id)
077.{
078.    TRY
079.    {
080.        if (m_findId != id)
081.        {
082.            m_findId = id;
083.            m_strFilter.Format(_T("id=%ld"), m_findId);
084.
```

continues

**LISTING 5.6—IMPLEMENTATION OF
THE IMAGE RETRIEVING RECORDSET, CONTINUED**

```
085.            if (!Requery())
086.                THROW(new CDBException);
087.
088.            //
089.            //  Ready our CHtmlStream half for usage
090.            //
091.            CHtmlStream::Reset();
092.
093.            int skipCount = 0;
094.            while (!IsEOF())
095.            {
096.                if (m_imagelen > 0)
097.                    CHtmlStream::Write(m_image.GetData(), m_imagelen);
098.                MoveNext();
099.                ++skipCount;
100.            }
101.
102.            // reverse our movements back to first record in sequence
103.            while (skipCount— > 0)
104.                MovePrev();
105.        }
106.    }
107.    CATCH_ALL(e)
108.    {
109.        return FALSE;
110.    }
111.    END_CATCH_ALL
112.
113.    return (!IsEOF());
114.}
```

The call to *accessId()* does most of the work by repeatedly calling the protected member *Write()* in the CHtmlStream base class shown on line 97 in listing 5.6. Currently, the code is hard-wired to retrieve up to 4K binary blocks per record. You can increase this amount if you desire; just remember to change the POPULATOR source as well if you decide to make this change.

The rest of the mmgetSet should be self-explanatory to developers familiar with MFC recordset. Notice the special attention to trap exceptions. This is good practice in general, but even more important in ISAPI extension programs, where you run the risk of crashing IIS in addition to your extension DLL when exceptions and assertions are not handled appropriately. See the "Troubleshooting" section near the end of this chapter for details.

Test Driving the mmGet Extension

If you don't feel like building the project for step 1, you can copy the mmGet.dll from the CD-ROM to your IIS script's (or cgi-bin) directory. Start IIS and ensure proper directory access settings if you haven't already done so. Type in the location/URL of:

```
http://<your server>[/<scripts directory/>]mmGet.dll?1
```

There might be a slight delay after you press enter—IIS is loading the DLL and symbol tables into memory as well as opening the ODBC datasource. You should then see something like figure 5.1 if everything went smoothly (see the "Troubleshooting" section near the end of this chapter if you had problems).

Change the image value from 1 to another number. The images in the database are a mix of sample MIME types; therefore, changing to another number might result in the browser rendering a different image, or video clip, or playing an audio file. If you type an image value not recognized by mmGet, you will receive the message "Missing image."

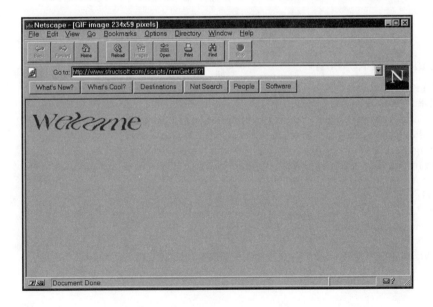

Figure 5.1

Image produced from the database.

If you are daring enough and you don't mind crashing your IIS server, you could try loading the HTML page in listing 5.7—but I don't recommend it. The problem is related to the method of ODBC access and a few topics mentioned previously—the concurrency issue. Basically, the failure stems from the timing of communications between the web browser, IIS, and your extension program. The problem will become more evident if you revisit figure 5.1 to account for the flow of events for accessing an HTML page such as the one shown in listing 5.7.

LISTING 5.7—HTML WHICH MAY CAUSE STEP1 OF THE MMGET EXTENSION TO FAIL DUE TO CONCURRENCY ISSUES. STEP2 OF MMGET ENABLES THIS HTML TO LOADED WITHOUT ANY PROBLEMS

```
01.<html>
02.<body>
03.    <P>Image 1 = <img src=/scripts/mmGet.dll?1>
04.    <P>Image 2 = <img src=/scripts/mmGet.dll?2>
05.    <P>Image 3 = <img src=/scripts/mmGet.dll?3>
06.    <P>Image 4 = <img src=/scripts/mmGet.dll?4>
07.    <P>Image 5 = <img src=/scripts/mmGet.dll?5>
08.    <P>Invalid Image results in returning <img src=/scripts/mmGet.dll?10000>
09.</body>
10.</html>
```

Multithreaded GET Requests

Typical HTTP communication sessions involve opening a socket on port 80 (web), sending a GET request to the server, and then waiting for a response back from the server. The concurrency problem stems from the fact that this process usually happens in parallel during the page-loading process. This means the HTML found in listing 5.7 might result in up to five overlapped calls to the *Default()* response function handler in mmGet.dll (graphically depicted in figure 5.2). ODBC as a whole has been thread-safe for some time now. ODBC access on a common handle including portions of MFC, however, are not thread-safe. Consequently, the recordset code shown in listing 5.6 either returns unanticipated results or dies altogether, depending on the timing of events—mileage may vary.

Step 2 in the refinement of mmGet involves using the Win32 thread synchronization to guarantee the common ODBC handle is not accessed in parallel from multiple GET requests.

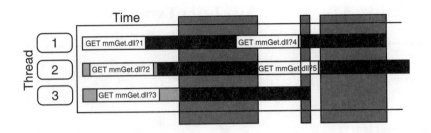

Figure 5.2

A graphical depiction of overlapped calls into IIS and mmGet.dll. This example has the browser employing three threads to do GET requests into the Internet Server.

Thread-Safe Image Extraction

Enter the critical section. Critical sections provide Win32 developers a means to synchronize thread activity. In this example, you will use a critical section to synchronize image extraction from the shared recordset (ODBC resource). Your Windows application can use as many critical sections as are warranted, which in this case is only one. A thread has a binary, *In or Out*, relationship to every critical section created in your application. After a thread enters a critical section, all other threads attempting to enter are blocked until the first thread leaves the critical section. Note, however, that critical sections do not work between separate processes. This is okay, because all extension modules run in the same process space as IIS. IIS creates new threads for each GET request it receives, but each thread uses the same process space.

Note   A *mutex* is an alternative to a critical section. Mutexes are named and can also be referenced between processes. According to Microsoft, however, critical sections are frequently much more efficient than mutexes. Only critical sections will be utilized in our examples.

The CmmGetSet class does not change with the introduction of critical sections. Listings 5.8 and 5.9 contain the final changes to the mmGet header and implementation. These changes can be found on the CD-ROM under projects\chap05\step2. MMGET.H only changes by the critical section member variable declaration found on line 35. MMGET.CPP changes are more extensive.

LISTING 5.8—THREAD-SAFE IMAGE EXTRACTION IN MMGET.H

```
01.// MMGET.H - Header file for your Internet Server
02.//    mmGet Extension
03.
04.class CmmGetSet;
```

continues

LISTING 5.8—THREAD-SAFE IMAGE EXTRACTION IN MMGET.H, CONTINUED

```
05.
06.class CMmGetExtension : public CHttpServer
07.{
08.public:
09.     CMmGetExtension();
10.     ~CMmGetExtension();
11.
12.    virtual BOOL initialize();
13.
14.// Overrides
15.     // ClassWizard generated virtual function overrides
16.          // NOTE - the ClassWizard will add and remove member functions
➥here.
17.          //     DO NOT EDIT what you see in these blocks of generated code !
18.     //{{AFX_VIRTUAL(CMmGetExtension)
19.     public:
20.     virtual BOOL GetExtensionVersion(HSE_VERSION_INFO* pVer);
21.     //}}AFX_VIRTUAL
22.
23.     // TODO: Add handlers for your commands here.
24.     // For example:
25.
26.     void Default(CHttpServerContext* pCtxt, int imageId);
27.
28.     DECLARE_PARSE_MAP()
29.
30.     //{{AFX_MSG(CMmGetExtension)
31.     //}}AFX_MSG
32.
33.protected:
34.     CmmGetSet   *m_pImageSet;
35.     LPCRITICAL_SECTION    m_pCriticalSection;
36.};
```

LISTING 5.9—THREAD-SAFE IMAGE EXTRACTION IN MMGET.CPP

```
001.// MMGET.CPP - Implementation file for your Internet Server
002.//    mmGet Extension
003.#include "stdafx.h"
004.#include "mmGet.h"
```

```
005.#include "mmGetSet.h"
006.#include "resource.h"
007.
008.///////////////////////////////////////////////////////////////////
009.// command-parsing map
010.
011.BEGIN_PARSE_MAP(CMmGetExtension, CHttpServer)
012.    // TODO: insert your ON_PARSE_COMMAND() and
013.    // ON_PARSE_COMMAND_PARAMS() here to hook up your commands.
014.    // For example:
015.    ON_PARSE_COMMAND(Default, CMmGetExtension, ITS_I4)
016.    ON_PARSE_COMMAND_PARAMS("ID")
017.    DEFAULT_PARSE_COMMAND(Default, CMmGetExtension)
018.END_PARSE_MAP(CMmGetExtension)
019.
020.///////////////////////////////////////////////////////////////////
021.// The one and only CMmGetExtension object
022.
023.CMmGetExtension theExtension;
024.
025.///////////////////////////////////////////////////////////////////
026.// CMmGetExtension implementation
027.
028.CMmGetExtension::CMmGetExtension()
029.{
030.    m_pImageSet = NULL;
031.
032.    VERIFY(m_pCriticalSection = new CRITICAL_SECTION);
033.    ::InitializeCriticalSection(m_pCriticalSection);
034.}
035.
036.CMmGetExtension::~CMmGetExtension()
037.{
038.    delete m_pImageSet;
039.
040.    ::DeleteCriticalSection(m_pCriticalSection);
041.    delete m_pCriticalSection;
042.}
043.
044.BOOL CMmGetExtension::initialize()
045.{
046.    BOOL bSuccess;
047.
```

continues

LISTING 5.9—THREAD-SAFE IMAGE EXTRACTION IN MMGET.CPP, CONTINUED

```
048.    ::EnterCriticalSection(m_pCriticalSection);
049.
050.    TRY
051.    {
052.        if (m_pImageSet)
053.        {
054.            bSuccess = TRUE;
055.        }
056.        else
057.        {
058.            m_pImageSet = new CmmGetSet;
059.            if (!m_pImageSet)
060.                return FALSE;
061.
062.            bSuccess = m_pImageSet->Open(CRecordset::snapshot);
063.        }
064.
065.        ASSERT_VALID(m_pImageSet);
066.    }
067.    CATCH(CDBException, e)
068.    {
069.        ISAPITRACE0(e->m_strError);
070.    }
071.    CATCH_ALL(e)
072.    {
073.        bSuccess = FALSE;
074.    }
075.    END_CATCH_ALL
076.
077.    ::LeaveCriticalSection(m_pCriticalSection);
078.
079.    return bSuccess;
080.}
081.
082.BOOL CMmGetExtension::GetExtensionVersion(HSE_VERSION_INFO* pVer)
083.{
084.    // Call default implementation for initialization
085.    CHttpServer::GetExtensionVersion(pVer);
086.
087.    // Load description string
088.    TCHAR sz[HSE_MAX_EXT_DLL_NAME_LEN+1];
```

```
089.      ISAPIVERIFY(::LoadString(AfxGetResourceHandle(),
090.              IDS_SERVER, sz, HSE_MAX_EXT_DLL_NAME_LEN));
091.      _tcscpy(pVer->lpszExtensionDesc, sz);
092.      return TRUE;
093.}
094.
095.///////////////////////////////////////////////////////////////////
096.// CMmGetExtension command handlers
097.
098.void CMmGetExtension::Default(CHttpServerContext* pCtxt, int imageId)
099.{
100.    if (!initialize())
101.    {
102.        OnParseError(pCtxt, HTTP_STATUS_SERVER_ERROR);
103.    }
104.    else
105.    {
106.        ::EnterCriticalSection(m_pCriticalSection);
107.
108.        if (m_pImageSet->accessId(imageId))
109.        {
110.            AddHeader(pCtxt, CString(_T("Content-Type: ")) +
111.                            m_pImageSet->getMimeType() +
112.                             _T("\r\n"));
113.            *pCtxt << *m_pImageSet;
114.        }
115.        else
116.        {
117.            StartContent(pCtxt);
118.            *pCtxt << _T("Missing Image\r\n");
119.            EndContent(pCtxt);
120.        }
121.
122.        ::LeaveCriticalSection(m_pCriticalSection);
123.    }
124.}
125.
126.// Do not edit the following lines, which are needed by ClassWizard.
127.#if 0
128.BEGIN_MESSAGE_MAP(CMmGetExtension, CHttpServer)
129.    //{{AFX_MSG_MAP(CMmGetExtension)
130.    //}}AFX_MSG_MAP
131.END_MESSAGE_MAP()
132.#endif     // 0
```

Looking down from the top of the implementation, you will encounter the following statements (lines 32 and 33):

```
          VERIFY(m_pCriticalSection = new CRITICAL_SECTION);
::InitializeCriticalSection(m_pCriticalSection);
```

The constructor has been changed from step 1 so that it now initializes the critical section, which will be used to synchronize all threads calling the mmGet server extension. A critical section must be initialized before it is used. A critical section should also be destroyed before the extension DLL is unloaded. This occurs in the destructor shown on lines 40 and 41.

Continuing down the source you will find that a critical section is first used in the *initialize()* member function starting on line 48. At the onset of *initialize()*, *EnterCriticalSection*(m_pCriticalSection) is called to block other threads from entering into the initialization code simultaneously. Notice how exception handling is used here. This is important if for some reason MFC throws an exception. The *LeaveCriticalSection* (m_pCriticalSection) will still be called in any event, preventing the extension module from becoming effectively blocked due to the exception not being caught. Remember, once a thread enters a critical section, all other threads must wait until the first critical section leaves. If the exception is not caught then the critical section is never left by the first thread. It is possible that I/O related calls such as the one found on line 62 will throw an exception. Keep exception handling in mind when you develop your own ISAPI extensions.

The critical section is used again in the *Default()* handler, as you should expect. The critical section wraps the image-access portion so the shared recordset is not accessed from more than one thread simultaneously (see lines 106-122).

It's safe to go back into the water—now try the HTML from listing 5.7. The precautions in step 2 enable mmGet to handle the multithreaded GET requests appropriately. You can now implement your dynamic, image-retrieving auction web site with peace of mind.

Advanced Topics

Many of you will undoubtedly find ways to improve the code presented in this chapter even further. The level of difficulty and the amount of code have been intentionally kept to a minimum in the samples to convey the concepts effectively. Now we will deviate from the ISAPI discussion a bit to give you some ideas regarding such improvements. In particular, the following topics will be described:

◆ Scalability, using worker threads

◆ Optimizing thread access with semaphores

◆ Storing database user names and passwords in the registry

◆ Enhancing database user privilege management

◆ Use cookies to keep state

 I would like to hear from anyone who finds ways to improve further on these topics; send me mail at ideas@structsoft.com or post comments on the microsoft.public.inetserver.iis newsgroup found on msnews.microsoft.com news server for an open discussion.

Scalability, Using Worker Threads

A better solution for accessing a shared database would be to queue requests to the database as they come in. A worker thread could be written that is dedicated to monitoring the queue. The thread would continuously check the queue for new (database) requests and service them one at a time. A critical section or mutex would synchronize access to the shared queue.

This design is more scalable, because worker threads could be started either at startup or programmatically as need arises. For instance, you could check how many processors are available at runtime and spawn the appropriate number of worker threads accordingly. Each thread could keep its own recordset instance.

 Depending on the nature of the queued requests, you might find it more appropriate to use dynasets instead of snapshots. Dynasets are updated automatically when the database is changed from other activities.

The *Default()* member function would be changed to create a custom database request object and append it (packaged with the CHttpServerContext class) to queue for handling. After the worker handles the request, the worker would be responsible for clean-up of the database request object.

Optimizing Thread Access with Semaphores

A further thread enhancement would be to use a semaphore triggered by new arrivals on the queue. The semaphore would be an addition to using the critical section or mutex to synchronize access to the queue. As new arrivals are placed on the queue, the semaphore count would be raised by one. Worker threads could then go to sleep until the semaphore is set high. The number of workers waking up to service the queue would equal the number of entries waiting on the queue to be processed, not exceeding the number of worker threads created at startup.

Storing Database User Names and Passwords in the Registry

Typically, all requests processed by your ISAPI extension program are run under a thread that impersonates the user rights of IUSR_*MACHINE*. IIS provides this default login with very limited access rights. Remember to assign the necessary access privileges to the IUSR_*MACHINE* database user so ODBC errors are not generated from within your ISAPI extension.

In addition, if a login name and password are required in your environment, it is advantageous to keep the hard-code user name and password out of the DLL. If you accidentally assign read privileges to your scripts directory, that information possibly could be extracted out of the binary file and be abused without your knowledge.

Use the registry to house the IUSR_*MACHINE*'s database user name and password. This information could be queried when your ISAPI extension module is loaded. The registry code was not implemented in the sample program so the discussion could focus on the ISAPI-relevant details instead.

Enhancing Database User Privilege Management

A substantial complication can result to the database access methods if created threads are impersonating various NT user accounts. This is the case if you are using the REMOTE_USER variable and are asked to open the database handle within the REMOTE_USER context to grant varying degrees of data-view privileges. You might decide the best method would be opening a new recordset each time a response function is called; however, if your database has a limited number of licenses, this still might be an unacceptable solution.

A more sophisticated design uses a dictionary to index all worker threads running, including their user context. When a new REMOTE_USER is encountered and the dictionary has no entry for that user, a new thread with that database context is started. Each worker only handles the queue (or subset of a queue) dedicated for servicing a particular REMOTE_USER, and worker threads end after a period of inactivity or some other stopping criterion.

This topic is clearly more complicated than all the others. If speed or connection limits are not a big concern, it is advisable to stick to the easy solution of recordset instantiation by using REMOTE_USER login in each separate call to *Default()*.

Use Cookies to Keep State

The programmer's term "cookie" has been around for a while. *The New Hackers Dictionary* defines it as "a handle, transaction ID, or other token of agreement between cooperating programs." For web developers it has special significance. Typical requests to the server are considered stateless because each request is handled by the server independently from any other request. The introduction of cookies permit the server to keep a client's state throughout a session on the web site.

There are many facets of cookie use between web servers and browsers. This section will introduce only one that is applicable to this chapter. For a complete specification of HTTP cookies see

```
http://home.netscape.com/newsref/std/cookie_spec.html
```

Consider this solution: when the web browser receives a request, it checks for the presence of a session ID (cookie). The session ID could be used to determine the caller's context. A Database connection could be one element within that context. New requests received by the server without a session ID would be assigned a new session ID once a new database connection is opened on the server. Session IDs could timeout on both the server and browser after a period of inactivity. Therefore, the ISAPI extension can use the connection handle associated with the caller's session ID. This is exactly the concept behind Active Server Pages by the way!

Troubleshooting ISAPI Extensions

Troubleshooting ISAPI extensions, particularly those using ODBC, is often arduous. This section is included as a reference to common pitfalls the author has personally ran into at one time or another. Some of these problems took weeks to diagnose and correct! (There is no particular order to the items listed here.)

◆ **ODBC Access fails:** make sure you have a system datasource set up in ODBC-32. Make sure appropriate database privileges are granted, if necessary. SQL Server is said to time out on dormant connections; therefore, you might need to alter the methods presented in this chapter to compensate for this. SQL Server's temp file might have filled up, causing miscellaneous ODBC problems as well. These ODBC problems are sometimes evident in intermittent failures between queries if checkpointing is used but hasn't yet had time to perform. Do you have the latest versions of ODBC? There might be a patch available. Finally, the *CDatabase::SetSynchronousMode()* has become obsolete in MFC version 4.2; however, earlier versions of MFC require this function to be called in ODBC response functions using a CDatabase/CRecordset.

◆ **IIS hangs:** are you using try/catch blocks? You should do this for any API that might potentially throw an exception! Could your server be hung because your critical section was never left or your mutex was never released? This could be the case if any exception was thrown or an assertion has failed. As silly as this might sound, dialogs (and message boxes) should never be used in an ISAPI extension module. Make sure you have the World Wide Web service configured with the "Allow Service to Interact with Desktop" option turned on in any case, as depicted in figure 5.3. In the event an assertion failure occurs, you will see some record of it on the screen if you have this option enabled. Use the Control Panel, Services option to find the World Wide Web service.

Figure 5.3

Safeguard your IIS by "Allowing Service to Interact with Desktop."

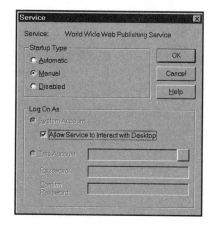

♦ **Bad data returned:** are you using a snapshot? Dynasets are automatically updated when the database is altered. Is it possible your shared (database) resource was corrupted? You should be using critical sections or mutexes to guard against this.

Summary

This chapter has addressed some core issues you are bound to face as an ISAPI developer. Database access from within an extension module is not much different than in any other Windows application. If you follow the precautions outlined in this chapter, you will probably be in good shape. Achieving maximum throughput from your database is a common goal—even more so through your ISAPI response functions if you expect heavy traffic on your web server. Hopefully, from this chapter you've acquired a few attack plans to use database connections optimally while preserving thread safety. If nothing else, you at least have an ISAPI module you can use in the future for dynamic image retrieval.

The basic, most important theme to this chapter is thread synchronization. MFC ISAPI extension modules should use critical sections or mutexes to synchronize access to *any* shared resource besides the ODBC recordsets.

CHAPTER 6

Developing an E-mail Gateway

Most web servers, small or large, require electronic mail services for one reason or another. These might be as simple as a button to press for submitting a service question from a customer, or as complicated as distribution-list messages sent automatically to report real-time events such as stock market fluctuations. There are many other reasons for incorporating email on your web server.

You might be surprised to learn, however, that the options available to you as a web page developer are limited if you're using IIS and HTML alone. Furthermore, while there are a plethora of mailer scripts designed for programming languages such as Perl, finding one optimized for Win32 platforms is extremely difficult.

This chapter will show you how to effectively incorporate electronic mail facilities on your web server. It will also give you the software needed to perform even such complicated chores as sending mail to a distribution list automatically from your ISAPI programs or other Win32 utilities. Finally, it will present an ISAPI-based, data-driven solution that can be configured to automatically send electronic mail when someone submits data on any form residing on your web server.

Structure Software, Inc., has been selling these mail utilities on our web site to developers and Internet Service Providers (ISPs) all over the world for about one year now. You can get a demonstration of the tools presented in this chapter by visiting the Structure Software home page at:

```
http://www.structsoft.com/products.htm
```

Your purchase of this book grants you a limited license to the binary forms of the utility software for educational, noncommercial use. Please contact Structure Software, Inc., for licensing information if you wish to use the binaries commercially. All the software pertaining to this chapter can be found in the Projects\Chapter6 directory on the book's CD-ROM.

This chapter is different from all the others in this book. Ninety percent of the material in this chapter focuses on how to write an SMTP mailer by using Win32. The other ten percent of the chapter focuses on how to hook the SMTP mailer up to an ISAPI extension. This chapter is included in this book because of the overwhelming number of people who have demonstrated a need for such a utility.

You might choose to skip reading this chapter if you are solely concerned with ISAPI programming techniques. The ISAPI piece that is included is extremely short and simple. If you decide to read this chapter, however, you will learn how to process form data by using MFC, while avoiding the use of MFC response macros.

SMTP Overview

SMTP is an acronym for Simple Mail Transfer Protocol, an Internet-based protocol initially proposed by Jonathan B. Postel in 1982 under RFC 821. Subsequent RFCs have extended the feature set of the SMTP protocol; however, the extended features of SMTP will not be required for this discussion. If you are interested in the complete specifications, see:

```
ftp://rs.internic.net/rfc/rfc821.txt and rfc822.txt
```

In a nutshell, SMTP establishes a sender and receiver relationship (see figure 6.3). The sender would be your web server, for instance, and the receiver would be a SMTP/mail server somewhere else on the network. After a message is delivered to the SMTP server, the server takes care of the mundane chores of relaying the message to either the recipient's mailbox or another SMTP mail server.

All communications occur over a socket layer just as in all other Internet-based protocols. Specifically, a connection-oriented socket (stream socket) is established with the SMTP server on port 25. The client sending the mail messages sends commands over port 25, which might look something like listing 6.1.

Note WINSOCK.H contains a listing of the ports used by Internet protocols such as SMTP. IPPORT_SMTP is defined to be 25.

LISTING 6.1—COMMANDS SENT TO AN SMTP SERVER

```
1.          HELO <SP> <hostname> <CRLF>
2.
3.          MAIL <SP> FROM:<reverse-path> <CRLF>
4.
5.          RCPT <SP> TO:<forward-path> <CRLF>
6.
7.          DATA <data> <CRLF><CRLF>
8.
9.          QUIT <CRLF>
```

SMTP is very polite as protocols go. A client is expected to begin the conversation by saying HELO to the SMTP server, thereby announcing its presence/readiness to the server. When the client receives the appropriate acknowledgment back from the server, this also serves the purpose of confirming that a server resides on the other end of the channel. Listing 6.1 gave a one-sided view, from only the client's perspective. The server actually echoes back a three-digit result code after every command line sent by the client. The client must parse this result code. A two-way conversation depicting hypothetical server responses is shown in listing 6.2.

LISTING 6.2—BI-DIRECTIONAL CONVERSATION BETWEEN CLIENT AND SMTP SERVER

```
01.220
02.         HELO <SP> <domain> <CRLF>
03.250
04.         MAIL <SP> FROM:<reverse-path> <CRLF>
05.250
06.         RCPT <SP> TO:<forward-path> <CRLF>
07.250
08.         DATA <data> <CRLF>.<CRLF>
09.354
10.250
11.         QUIT <CRLF>
12.221
```

All codes beginning with a 1 or a 3 represent a preliminary positive reply, a 2 represents a successful condition, and a 4 or 5 represents an error condition. Table 6.1 documents some of the more common result codes.

TABLE 6.1.
SMTP Reply Codes

SMTP Reply Code	Meaning
211	System status, or system help reply
214	Help message (Information on how to use the receiver or the meaning of a particular nonstandard command; this reply is useful only to the human user)
220	<domain> Service ready
221	<domain> Service closing transmission channel
250	Requested mail action okay, completed
251	User not local; will forward to <forward-path>
354	Start mail input; end with <CRLF>.<CRLF>
421	<domain> Service not available, closing transmission channel (This may be a reply to any command if the service knows it must shut down)
450	Requested mail action not taken: mailbox unavailable (for example, mailbox busy)
451	Requested action aborted: local error in processing
452	Requested action not taken: insufficient system storage
500	Syntax error, command unrecognized (This might include errors such as command line too long)
501	Syntax error in parameters or arguments
502	Command not implemented
503	Bad sequence of commands
504	Command parameter not implemented
550	Requested action not taken: mailbox unavailable (for example, mailbox not found, no access)
551	User not local; please try <forward-path>

SMTP Reply Code	Meaning
552	Requested mail action aborted: exceeded storage allocation
553	Requested action not taken: mailbox name not allowed (for example, mailbox syntax incorrect)
554	Transaction failed

 Note The data portion of the message is required to be in 7-bit ASCII characters. Additionally, limits are placed on individual line length up to 1000 characters, and the total number of mail recipients is limited to 100.

The Simplest Way to Send Mail from a Web Page

The simplest and fastest way to adopt electronic mail capabilities on a web page is to use the HTML tag called a *Mailto*. Chances are you have used the HTML Mailto: tag, whether you knew it or not. When you click on a Mailto: hyperlink, Netscape or Internet Explorer responds by popping up a mail dialog box similar to the one shown in figure 6.1.

The HTML specification offers no alternative for sending electronic mail besides the *mailto:: tag*. This poses special problems for the following reasons:

◆ It requires the client's web browser to support Mailto: functionality; however, browsers that don't are rare today.

◆ It requires the client's web browser to be configured properly. This problem is much more likely to occur. Many casual surfers might not know how to configure their browsers for their SMTP or POP3 server.

◆ A popup mail dialog such as the one shown in figure 6.1 is not tightly integrated with the context. It is often desirable to keep the focus on the form instead of prompting the user with a mail dialog box, because the box itself might hide essential information the user needs to refer to on the web page.

◆ An empty template such as the one shown in figure 6.1 might be unacceptable for specific needs. This is the most compelling argument against using Mailto:— it is simply impossible to configure the dialog box to include the critical information you wish to capture.

Figure 6.1

Mail dialog used to send mail from Netscape.

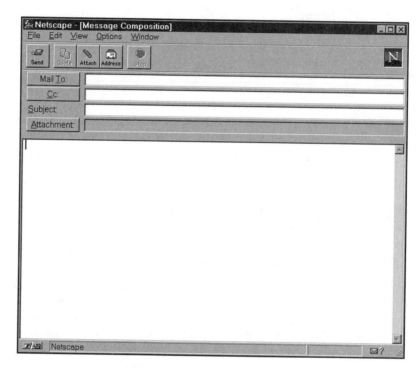

Capturing the Critical Information

The most compelling reason not to use Mailto: is its inability to capture potentially important information. For instance, if you are writing an order-entry system, you need to capture the customer's first and last name, shipping address, telephone number, and the items and quantity they are ordering. If the Mailto: tag is used, the user is responsible for remembering all the data that needs to be included in the order form. Shifting this burden onto the user not only invites errors, it is also rather rude behavior, possibly driving customers away from a site. It is much more appealing to use a system like the one shown in figure 6.2.

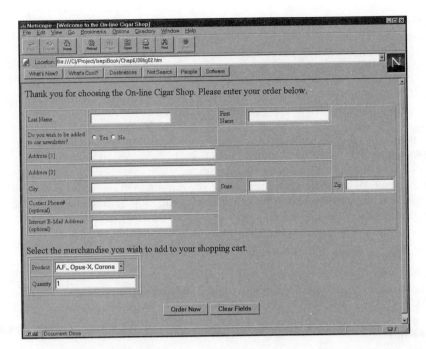

Figure 6.2

Capturing the core data to successfully process a client's order. This data is used to generate the email message.

Notice how drop-down list boxes and radio buttons are used to ease the burden on the user placing the order. Additionally, these enforce the data integrity of the entry system. It is less likely an order will arrive with an invalid item or purchase quantity when pre-populated selections are used. They also focus the user's attention on the form instead of on an external process such as the popup mail dialog box.

Implementing an SMTP Mailer DLL

The basic components of an SMTP mail message are the following:

◆ Sender's name and address

◆ Recipient's name and address

◆ Subject

◆ Text body

◆ Destination SMTP server

Therefore, the SMTP Mailer DLL needs to supply APIs that take at a minimum these fields as arguments. The SMTP protocol can handle multiple recipients (up to 100). The API will be written to provide the capability to send a message to more than one recipient simultaneously.

Finally, the SMTP Mailer will be written to work synchronously or asynchronously. Why include this in the API? There are a couple of reasons for this.

◆ SMTP uses sockets, potentially a very slow communication medium. Obviously, if you are using a T1 line, this is much less of a worry; however, in general, server load, network routing delays, and communication line speed could result in some serious delays while communicating to a remote mail server. This is especially true if a dial-up modem is somewhere in the loop. If mail is sent asynchronously, the calling process does not need to be blocked from performing other operations as it waits for the communication session to finish with the mail server.

◆ The caller might need to send mail while simultaneously servicing other events. This factor will be significant in the second part of this chapter, where we hook the SMTP Mailer into an ISAPI extension module. The extension module can't be delayed in sending a mail message while the user is waiting for a web page to become visible.

◆ The final reason for sending mail asynchronously is that there is no compelling reason not to. The act of sending mail is independent of other program activity; therefore, it makes more sense in many situations to simply send the mail message as a background task. While the use of threads to perform autonomous activity can be abused, many developers avoid its use because of perceived complexity. The source code of the SMTP Mailer should prove how easy it is to incorporate multithreaded programming techniques into your own Win32 programs.

The SMTP Mailer API

The discussion so far brings us to the set of APIs found in listing 6.3. All functions have C exports to make the APIs usable from other calling languages, such as Visual Basic or Powerbuilder. A single exported function could have been used instead of four; however, there is some trade-off between the number of APIs versus the extent of parameter usage. Using more APIs with fewer parameters means they're more easily remembered and applied.

LISTING 6.3—THE SMTP MAILER API EXPORTED FROM THE DLL

```
01.//
02.//   SMTPapi.h
03.//
04.//  (c) 1996; Structure Software, Inc. - All rights reserved.
05.//
06.#ifndef __SMTPAPI_H
07.#define __SMTPAPI_H
08.
09.#include "SMTPResult.h"
10.
11.#define MAX_SMTP_RECIPIENTS 100 // SMTP limits the number of recipients to
➥100!
12.
13.#if defined(cplusplus)
14.extern "C"
15.{
16.#endif
17.
18.//
19.//  Send mail asynchronously to a single recipient.
20.//     Returns:    0   on successful queuing of the message, or
21.//                 non-zero for miscellaneous failure
22.//
23.int AsyncMailTo(
24.               LPCTSTR szServer,    // SMTP server to negotiate with
25.               LPCTSTR szTo,        // A well-formatted e-mail recipient
➥(e.g., admin@structsoft.com)
26.               LPCTSTR szFrom,      // The e-mail address as you wish it
➥to appear to the recipient
27.               LPCTSTR szSubject,   // Message subject
28.               LPCTSTR szBody,      // Message body
29.               HWND hNotifyWnd,     // [optional] A window to notify
➥when e-mail is complete
30.               UINT nNotifyMsg      // [optional] The message Id to send
➥to the Notify Window
31.               );
32.
33.//
34.//  Send mail asynchronously to multiple recipients.
35.//     Returns:    0   on successful queuing of the message, or
```

continues

LISTING 6.3—THE SMTP MAILER API EXPORTED FROM THE DLL, CONTINUED

```
36.//                    non-zero for miscellaneous failure
37.//
38.int AsyncMailToMany(
39.                  LPCTSTR szServer,
40.                  LPCTSTR szToArr[],  // An array of well-formatted e-mail
➡recipients
41.                  unsigned uToArrSize,// The number of valid entries in
*➡the szTo array
42.                  LPCTSTR szFrom,
43.                  LPCTSTR szSubject,
44.                  LPCTSTR szBody,
45.                  HWND hNotifyWnd,
46.                  UINT nNotifyMsg
47.              );
48.
49.//
50.// Send mail synchronously to a single recipient.
51.//     Returns:   0   on successful queuing of the message, or
52.//                    non-zero for miscellaneous failure
53.//
54.IEnumMailerResult MailTo(
55.                  LPCTSTR szServer,
56.                  LPCTSTR szTo,
57.                  LPCTSTR szFrom,
58.                  LPCTSTR szSubject,
59.                  LPCTSTR szBody
60.              );
61.
62.//
63.// Send mail synchronously to multiple recipients.
64.//     Returns:   0   on successful queuing of the message, or
65.//                    non-zero for miscellaneous failure
66.//
67.IEnumMailerResult MailToMany(
68.                  LPCTSTR szServer,
69.                  LPCTSTR szToArr[],
70.                  unsigned uToArrSize,
71.                  LPCTSTR szFrom,
72.                  LPCTSTR szSubject,
73.                  LPCTSTR szBody
```

```
74.                    );
75.
76.//
77.//  Windows notifications have the following form:
78.//      WPARAM: result code from IEnumMailerResult (see SMTPResult.h)
79.//      LPARAM: (not used.  However, this build currently passes the SMTP
 server
80.//              name.  This is bound to change in future revisions!)
81.//
82.
83.#if defined(__cplusplus)
84.}
85.#endif
86.
87.#endif  //  __SMTPAPI_H
```

 Note   IEnumMailerResult, incidentally, is not an OLE interface. You may have been misled by the leading "I." It is an enumerated type found in the SMTPResult.h file.

The asynchronous APIs of the mailer shown on lines 29, 30, 45, and 56 in listing 6.3 use two additional, optional parameters, *hNotifyWnd* and *nNotifyMsg*. They are used to notify the calling process when the mail message has finished sending, including any success or failure codes. Table 6.2 contains all the possible result codes that can be sent in the *nNotifyMsg* parameter. The synchronous version waits until it has a result code before it returns; therefore, the synchronous versions of the APIs return the result code instead of notifying a window by using registered Windows messages.

 Tip   See Registered Windows Messages in MSVC Books On-Line for examples of using the two additional parameters, *hNotifyWnd*, and *nNotifyMsg*.

TABLE 6.2
Result Codes from the SMTP Mailer Routines

IEnumMailerResult	Value	Description
SUCCESS	0	Operation succeeded
STATELESS	1	Idle state

continues

TABLE 6.2, CONTINUED
Result Codes from the SMTP Mailer Routines

IEnumMailerResult	Value	Description
HIGH_CONFIDENCE	2	The thread was spawned but indeterminate whether the data can be sent
READY_TO_SEND	3	Server ready to accept data (better than HIGH_CONFIDENCE)
SOCK_ERROR	4	A socket error occurred during operation
UNDEFINED_SERVER	5	The SMTP server address was not supplied
INVALID_SERVER	6	Invalid SMTP server address
UNKNOWN_SERVER_RESPONSE	7	The server returned a result code unknown to the SMTP Mailer
UNKNOWN_RECIPIENT	8	The server wasn't able to identity the recipient
BAD_PARAMETER	9	A bad parameter was sent to the SMTP Mailer
MISC_FAILURE	10	Unknown error occurred

The interface and possible result values have now been defined. The next section completes the implementation of the SMTP Mailer API.

Implementing the SMTP Mailer

The source in listing 6.4 is very straightforward and proceeds with the following sequence of events:

1. Each exported function first validates the passed parameters.

2. Parameters are packaged into a C structure and passed to a nonexported worker function for processing.

The code should prove to you how easy it is to write multithreaded applications.

Pay special attention to how the data structure is built before its ownership is passed over to the worker function (see lines 115–149 of AsyncMailTo for an example).

This is important because the asynchronous calling routines are bound to return control to the caller well before the worker thread starts running. If the structure were deleted before the APIs returned, both asynchronous calls would cause a General Protection Fault (GPF).

LISTING 6.4—IMPLEMENTATION OF THE SMTP MAILER

```
001.//
002.//  SMTPapi.cpp
003.//
004.//  (c) 1996; Structure Software, Inc. - All rights reserved.
005.//
006.#include "stdafx.h"
007.#include "SMTPapi.h"
008.#include "SMTPClient.h"
009.
010.typedef struct tagAMT
011.{
012.    unsigned     uStructSize;
013.    LPTSTR       szServer;
014.    LPTSTR       szTo[MAX_SMTP_RECIPIENTS];
015.    unsigned     uToArrSize;
016.    LPTSTR       szFrom;
017.    LPTSTR       szSubject;
018.    LPTSTR       szBody;
019.    HWND         hNotifyWnd;
020.    UINT         nNotifyMsg;
021.} AMT, *PAMT;
022.
023.
024.static UINT workerMailTo(LPVOID pParam)
025.{
026.    CSMTPClient mailer;
027.    IEnumMailerResult result;
028.    PAMT pAMT;
029.
030.    ASSERT(pParam);
031.    if (!pParam)
032.    {
033.        TRACE0("Invalid initialization of workerMailTo!\n");
034.        result = MISC_FAILURE;
035.        goto out;
```

continues

LISTING 6.4—IMPLEMENTATION OF THE
SMTP MAILER, CONTINUED

```
036.    }
037.
038.    pAMT = (PAMT)pParam;
039.
040.    if (sizeof(AMT) != pAMT->uStructSize)
041.    {
042.        TRACE0("Invalid structure passed to workerMailTo!\n");
043.        result = BAD_PARAMETER;
044.        goto out;
045.    }
046.
047.    ASSERT(pAMT->szTo && pAMT->uToArrSize);
048.    if (!pAMT->szTo || !pAMT->uToArrSize || pAMT->uToArrSize >
➥MAX_SMTP_RECIPIENTS)
049.    {
050.        TRACE0("Invalid parameters passed to workerMailTo!\n");
051.        result = BAD_PARAMETER;
052.        goto out;
053.    }
054.
055.    result = mailer.SetServer(pAMT->szServer);
056.    if (HIGH_CONFIDENCE == result || SUCCESS == result || READY_TO_SEND ==
➥result)
057.    {
058.        if (1 == pAMT->uToArrSize)
059.        {
060.            ASSERT(pAMT->szTo[0]);
061.            result = mailer.MailTo(pAMT->szTo[0], pAMT->szFrom, pAMT-
➥>szSubject, pAMT->szBody);
062.        }
063.        else
064.        {
065.            ASSERT(pAMT->uToArrSize <= MAX_SMTP_RECIPIENTS);
066.            result = mailer.MailTo((LPCTSTR*)pAMT->szTo, pAMT->uToArrSize,
➥pAMT->szFrom, pAMT->szSubject, pAMT->szBody);
067.        }
068.    }
069.
070.out:;
071.    #ifdef _DEBUG
```

```
072.    if (SUCCESS != result)
073.    {
074.        TRACE1("AsyncMailTo Failed with result code [%d]!\n", (int)result);
075.    }
076.    #endif
077.
078.    //
079.    //  Check to see if we still have a window to notify
080.    //
081.    if (::IsWindow(pAMT->hNotifyWnd) && pAMT->nNotifyMsg)
082.    {
083.        ::SendMessage(pAMT->hNotifyWnd, pAMT->nNotifyMsg, result,
➥(DWORD)pAMT->szServer);
084.    }
085.
086.    //
087.    //  We own the AMT structure now.  Therefore, we are responsible for
➥clean-up.
088.    //
089.    delete [] pAMT->szServer;
090.    for (unsigned i = 0; i < pAMT->uToArrSize; i++)
091.        delete [] pAMT->szTo[i];
092.    delete [] pAMT->szFrom;
093.    delete [] pAMT->szSubject;
094.    delete [] pAMT->szBody;
095.    delete pAMT;
096.
097.    return result;
098.}
099.
100.//
101.// This routine is exported in the DEF file.  It is called to run a
➥"zombie"
102.// mail message sent to a single recipient.
103.//
104.int AsyncMailTo(    LPCTSTR szServer,
105.                    LPCTSTR szTo,
106.                    LPCTSTR szFrom,
107.                    LPCTSTR szSubject,
108.                    LPCTSTR szBody,
109.                    HWND hNotifyWnd, UINT nNotifyMsg
110.                )
```

continues

LISTING 6.4—IMPLEMENTATION OF THE
SMTP MAILER, CONTINUED

```
111.{
112.    if (!szServer || !szTo)
113.        return BAD_PARAMETER;
114.
115.    PAMT pAMT = new AMT;
116.    ASSERT(pAMT);
117.
118.    pAMT->uStructSize = sizeof(AMT);
119.
120.    pAMT->szServer  = new char[strlen(szServer)+1];
121.    ASSERT(pAMT->szServer);
122.    strcpy(pAMT->szServer, szServer);
123.
124.    pAMT->uToArrSize = 1;
125.
126.    pAMT->szTo[0]   = new char[strlen(szTo)+1];
127.    ASSERT(pAMT->szTo[0]);
128.    strcpy(pAMT->szTo[0], szTo);
129.
130.    pAMT->szFrom    = szFrom ? new char[strlen(szFrom)+1] : NULL;
131.    if (pAMT->szFrom)
132.    {
133.        strcpy(pAMT->szFrom, szFrom);
134.    }
135.
136.    pAMT->szSubject = szSubject ? new char[strlen(szSubject)+1] : NULL;
137.    if (pAMT->szSubject)
138.    {
139.        strcpy(pAMT->szSubject, szSubject);
140.    }
141.
142.    pAMT->szBody = szBody ? new char[strlen(szBody)+1] : NULL;
143.    if (pAMT->szBody)
144.    {
145.        strcpy(pAMT->szBody, szBody);
146.    }
147.
148.    pAMT->hNotifyWnd    = hNotifyWnd;
149.    pAMT->nNotifyMsg    = nNotifyMsg;
150.
```

```
151.    VERIFY(AfxBeginThread(workerMailTo, pAMT));
152.
153.    return 0;
154.}
155.
156.//
157.// This routine is exported in the DEF file.  It is called to run a
➥"zombie"
158.//  mail message sent to multiple mail recipients.
159.//
160.int AsyncMailToMany(
161.                    LPCTSTR szServer,
162.                    LPCTSTR szToArr[],
163.                    unsigned uToArrSize,
164.                    LPCTSTR szFrom,
165.                    LPCTSTR szSubject,
166.                    LPCTSTR szBody,
167.                    HWND hNotifyWnd, UINT nNotifyMsg
168.              )
169.{
170.    if (!szServer ¦¦ !uToArrSize)
171.        return BAD_PARAMETER;
172.
173.    if (uToArrSize > MAX_SMTP_RECIPIENTS)
174.        return BAD_PARAMETER;
175.
176.    PAMT pAMT = new AMT;
177.    ASSERT(pAMT);
178.
179.    pAMT->uStructSize = sizeof(AMT);
180.
181.    pAMT->szServer  = new char[strlen(szServer)+1];
182.    ASSERT(pAMT->szServer);
183.    strcpy(pAMT->szServer, szServer);
184.
185.    pAMT->uToArrSize = uToArrSize;
186.
187.    for (unsigned i = 0; i < uToArrSize; i++)
188.    {
189.        ASSERT(szToArr[i]);
190.        pAMT->szTo[i]  = new char[strlen(szToArr[i])+1];
191.        ASSERT(pAMT->szTo[i]);
```

continues

LISTING 6.4—IMPLEMENTATION OF THE
SMTP MAILER, CONTINUED

```
192.        strcpy(pAMT->szTo[i], szToArr[i]);
193.    }
194.
195.    pAMT->szFrom    = szFrom ? new char[strlen(szFrom)+1] : NULL;
196.    if (pAMT->szFrom)
197.    {
198.        strcpy(pAMT->szFrom, szFrom);
199.    }
200.
201.    pAMT->szSubject = szSubject ? new char[strlen(szSubject)+1] : NULL;
202.    if (pAMT->szSubject)
203.    {
204.        strcpy(pAMT->szSubject, szSubject);
205.    }
206.
207.    pAMT->szBody = szBody ? new char[strlen(szBody)+1] : NULL;
208.    if (pAMI->szBody)
209.    {
210.        strcpy(pAMT->szBody, szBody);
211.    }
212.
213.    pAMT->hNotifyWnd    = hNotifyWnd;
214.    pAMT->nNotifyMsg    = nNotifyMsg;
215.
216.    VERIFY(AfxBeginThread(workerMailTo, pAMT));
217.
218.    return 0;
219.}
220.
221.//
222.//  This routine is exported in the DEF file.  It is called to run a
➥blocking
223.//   mail message sent to a single recipient.
224.//
225.IEnumMailerResult MailTo(
226.                LPCTSTR szServer,
227.                LPCTSTR szTo,
228.                LPCTSTR szFrom,
229.                LPCTSTR szSubject,
230.                LPCTSTR szBody
```

```
231.                    )
232.{
233.    if (!szServer || !szTo)
234.        return BAD_PARAMETER;
235.
236.    PAMT pAMT = new AMT;
237.    ASSERT(pAMT);
238.
239.    pAMT->uStructSize = sizeof(AMT);
240.
241.    pAMT->szServer  = new char[strlen(szServer)+1];
242.    ASSERT(pAMT->szServer);
243.    strcpy(pAMT->szServer, szServer);
244.
245.    pAMT->uToArrSize = 1;
246.
247.    pAMT->szTo[0]   = new char[strlen(szTo)+1];
248.    ASSERT(pAMT->szTo[0]);
249.    strcpy(pAMT->szTo[0], szTo);
250.
251.    pAMT->szFrom    = szFrom ? new char[strlen(szFrom)+1] : NULL;
252.    if (pAMT->szFrom)
253.    {
254.        strcpy(pAMT->szFrom, szFrom);
255.    }
256.
257.    pAMT->szSubject = szSubject ? new char[strlen(szSubject)+1] : NULL;
258.    if (pAMT->szSubject)
259.    {
260.        strcpy(pAMT->szSubject, szSubject);
261.    }
262.
263.    pAMT->szBody = szBody ? new char[strlen(szBody)+1] : NULL;
264.    if (pAMT->szBody)
265.    {
266.        strcpy(pAMT->szBody, szBody);
267.    }
268.
269.    pAMT->hNotifyWnd   = 0;
270.    pAMT->nNotifyMsg   = 0;
271.
272.    return (IEnumMailerResult)workerMailTo((LPVOID)pAMT);
```

continues

LISTING 6.4—IMPLEMENTATION OF THE
SMTP MAILER, CONTINUED

```
273.}
274.
275.//
276.//  This routine is exported in the DEF file.  It is called to run a
➥blocking
277.//  mail message sent to multiple mail recipients.
278.//
279.IEnumMailerResult MailToMany(
280.                  LPCTSTR szServer,
281.                  LPCTSTR szToArr[],
282.                  unsigned uToArrSize,
283.                  LPCTSTR szFrom,
284.                  LPCTSTR szSubject,
285.                  LPCTSTR szBody
286.              )
287.{
288.    if (!szServer ¦¦ !uToArrSize)
289.        return BAD_PARAMETER;
290.
291.    if (uToArrSize > MAX_SMTP_RECIPIENTS)
292.        return BAD_PARAMETER;
293.
294.    PAMT pAMT = new AMT;
295.    ASSERT(pAMT);
296.
297.    pAMT->uStructSize = sizeof(AMT);
298.
299.    pAMT->szServer  = new char[strlen(szServer)+1];
300.    ASSERT(pAMT->szServer);
301.    strcpy(pAMT->szServer, szServer);
302.
303.    pAMT->uToArrSize = uToArrSize;
304.
305.    for (unsigned i = 0; i < uToArrSize; i++)
306.    {
307.        ASSERT(szToArr[i]);
308.        pAMT->szTo[i]   = new char[strlen(szToArr[i])+1];
309.        ASSERT(pAMT->szTo[i]);
310.        strcpy(pAMT->szTo[i], szToArr[i]);
311.    }
```

```
312.
313.    pAMT->szFrom     = szFrom ? new char[strlen(szFrom)+1] : NULL;
314.    if (pAMT->szFrom)
315.    {
316.        strcpy(pAMT->szFrom, szFrom);
317.    }
318.
319.    pAMT->szSubject = szSubject ? new char[strlen(szSubject)+1] : NULL;
320.    if (pAMT->szSubject)
321.    {
322.        strcpy(pAMT->szSubject, szSubject);
323.    }
324.
325.    pAMT->szBody = szBody ? new char[strlen(szBody)+1] : NULL;
326.    if (pAMT->szBody)
327.    {
328.        strcpy(pAMT->szBody, szBody);
329.    }
330.
331.    pAMT->hNotifyWnd    = 0;
332.    pAMT->nNotifyMsg    = 0;
333.
334.    return (IEnumMailerResult)workerMailTo((LPVOID)pAMT);
335.}
```

Walking through the code found in listing 6.4 you will see that all execution paths
lead to a common call to the *workerMailTo()* function (line #24). The parameters are
validated and upon successful communication with the remote SMTP Server (line
#55) the message is sent (line #66). The portions of code dealing with this communi-
cation stream (CSMTPClient class instantiated on line #26) is not shown here but can
be found in the project source files.

Listing 6.4 represents the first tier in a three-tier architecture which is also graphically
depicted in Figure 6.3. It can be referred to as the logical layer because it guides the
mailing process at a very high, abstract level. The worker function uses an instance of
CSMTPClient to tell the second tier, the control layer, of the SMTP server to use,
along with the characteristics of the message being sent. The second tier negotiates
the conversation, using protocols similar to those shown in listing 6.2. The lowest tier
is the communication layer, which only concerns itself with porting bytes in and out
over the socket.

Figure 6.3

Three-tier architecture of the SMTP Mailer.

Tier 1 - The Logical Layer

Guides the process of sending mail at a high level.
- Parameters are validated
- An CSMTPClient object is instantiated
- Methods in the CSMTPClient are called passing the server name and message data.
- Result codes are either returned or posted via a user defined windows message

Tier 2 - The Control Layer

Program logic that follows the procedure outlined in RFC 821 for SMTP.
- Check for SMTP server presence.
- Send HELO and wait for acknowledgment.
- Send message header information and wait for response.
- Send message data and wait for response.

Tier 3 - The Communication Layer

Low level socket communication code. This layer concerns itself with the actual porting of data to and from the socket connected to the local SMTP server.

The source for this section can be found on the CD.

The control layer and the communication layer are coupled to form a state machine. The discussion of state machines is outside the scope of this book. The source for these two layers is not included in this text but can be found on the enclosed CD-ROM.

 Note See *Design Patterns* by Gamma, Helm, Johnson, Vlissides, published by Addison Wesley Press (ISBN 0-201-63361-2). The chapter on state machines even covers an example applying to TCP/IP.

A Test Harness for The SMTP Mailer

Now that you have some understanding of SMTP and the mailer API, you need a test harness for testing the DLL. Figure 6.3 shows the Windows application included to test the SMTP Mailer DLL. It is a MDI (Multiple Document Interface), Win32 application built by using MSVC 4.2 with MFC. Remember, all the software in this module will only run under Win32 platforms. The sample Windows application provides the capability to send messages synchronously or asynchronously to one or more recipients.

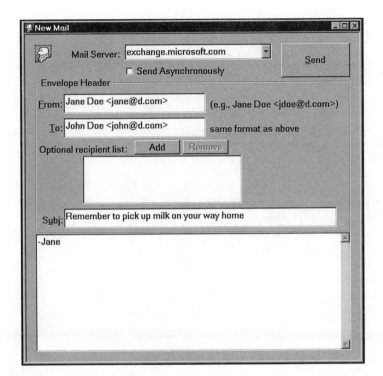

Figure 6.4

A test harness for the SMTP Mailer included in source and binary form on the CD.

Warning | It's time to give a general warning about all SMTP mailers: they can very easily be abused. The SMTP server that accepts your outgoing messages does not perform validation on the sender's name or address! One reason for this is to allow the sending of anonymous mail. An adverse side effect, however, is that people can send mail while pretending to be someone else. I strongly encourage you not to abuse the software or use it for spamming. ISPs will most certainly delete accounts when they catch up with the perpetrators of such activities.

Adopting the SMTP Mailer to ISAPI Extensions

Recapping the goal: The data collected on an HTML form is to be sent automatically to a destination mail address. The SMTP Mailer APIs can service these needs with a little bit of additional programming to overcome the following two obstacles:

◆ The need to write an ISAPI response function that can accept a variable number of field parameters

◆ The need to enable the parsing of submitted field parameters so they can be put in a readable form in the body text portion of the SMTP message

An ISAPI extension called LiteMail has been written to handle these two obstacles. In addition, LiteMail was written to be completely data-driven by the HTML form (see listing 6.5); therefore, no code changes are needed to begin using the extension module immediately.

LISTING 6.5—SAMPLE HTML FORM SUBMITTED TO LITEMAIL FOR PACKAGING AS A MAIL MESSAGE

```
01.<html>
02.</body>
03.
04. <head>
05.   <title>Sample of LiteMail and the SMTP Mailer</title>
00. </head>
07.
08. <FONT COLOR=BLUE SIZE=+2>Enter a Sample Message</FONT>
09.
10. <!-- replace the server below with your server name>
11. <!-- note: only post requests are supported>
12. <form action="http://www.structsoft.com/scripts/LiteMail.dll?sample"
[ccc]Method="post">
13.
14. <!-- this parameter tells LiteMail which SMTP server to use>
15. <input type="hidden" name="server" value="exchange.microsoft.com">
16.
17. <!-- this parameter tells LiteMail the name of the From Address>
18. <input type="hidden" name="from" value="<Anonymous@nowhere.xxx>">
19.
20. <!-- this parameter is optional and tells LiteMail what the response should
➥say after submission>
21. <input type="hidden" name="resp" value="<font size=+1 color=blue>Thank
➥you</font> for using the LiteMailer.  You can expect mail delivery shortly.">
22.
23.   <table cellspacing=1 cellpadding=3>
24.
25.   <tr>
```

```
26.    <td>
27.     <font size=+1>To: (eg. test@domain.com)</font>
28.    </td>
29.    <td>
30.     <input type="edit" name="To">
31.    </td>
32.   </tr>
33.
34.   <tr>
35.    <td>
36.     <font size=+1>Regarding:</font>
37.    </td>
38.    <td>
39.     <input type="edit" name="Subject">
40.    </td>
41.   </tr>
42.
43.   <tr>
44.    <td valign=top>
45.     <font size=+1>Enter a Message:</font>
46.    </td>
47.    <td align=left>
48.     <Textarea name="Message" value="" rows=10 cols=32>
49.     </textarea>
50.    </td>
51.   </tr>
52.
53.   <tr>
54.    <td></td>
55.    <td>
56.     <input type="SUBMIT" value="Submit"><input type="RESET" value="Reset">
57.    </td>
58.   </tr>
59.
60.  </table>
61.
62.  </form>
63.
64.</body>
65.</html>
```

Notice the use of three hidden fields in listing 6.5: *server, from,* and *resp* (line # 15, 18, and 21). Each has a default value that will be sent to the LiteMail extension without being seen by the form submitter. These fields are not required to be hidden; however, it probably doesn't make sense to permit the user to enter the SMTP server. Basically, as long as the required field names are incorporated anywhere on the submitted form, processing will occur. A listing of the required fields is found in table 6.3.

TABLE 6.3
Fields Required for LiteMail to Function

Field Name	Description
SERVER	The SMTP server to use
FROM	The sender's name and address
RESP	The response message sent back after acceptance of the mail message
TO	The recipient's name and address
SUBJECT	The subject of the message
MESSAGE	The message body text

 Note   LiteMail uses the POST method because of potential inconsistencies in the GET method between browsers. Furthermore, the GET method is limited to sending 1000 bytes. No such limitation exists for the POST method.

The LiteMail SMTP Gateway ISAPI Extension

Listing 6.6 contains the source for the ISAPI extension. Notice how parse maps are avoided in the source. Microsoft provides *CallFunction()* as a virtual function in *CHttpServer* to override the default functionality of PARSE_MAPS. This enables you to parse the EXTENSION_CONTROL_BLOCK yourself. The *CallFunction()* routine is overridden here to send the submitted data automatically to the SMTP Mailer DLL developed earlier in this chapter.

LISTING 6.6—IMPLEMENTATION OF
THE LITEMAIL ISAPI EXTENSION

```
001.//
002.// LITEMAIL.CPP
003.//
004.//  (c) 1996; Structure Software, Inc. - All rights reserved.
005.//
006.#include <afx.h>
007.#include <afxwin.h>
008.#include <afxisapi.h>
009.#include <winsock.h>
010.#include "resource.h"
011.#include "LiteMail.h"
012.#include "SMTPapi.h"
013.
014.class CISAPIService : public CWinApp
015.{
016.public:
017.// Overrides
018.    // ClassWizard generated virtual function overrides
019.    //{{AFX_VIRTUAL(CISAPIService)
020.    public:
021.    //}}AFX_VIRTUAL
022.
023.// Implementation
024.
025.    //{{AFX_MSG(CISAPIService)
026.        // NOTE - the ClassWizard will add and remove member functions
➥here.
027.        //    DO NOT EDIT what you see in these blocks of generated code !
028.    //}}AFX_MSG
029.    DECLARE_MESSAGE_MAP()
030.};
031.
032.///////////////////////////////////////////////////////////////////
➥//
033.
034.CISAPIService isapiServer;
035.
036.///////////////////////////////////////////////////////////////////
➥//
```

continues

LISTING 6.6—IMPLEMENTATION OF
THE LITEMAIL ISAPI EXTENSION, CONTINUED

```
037.
038.BEGIN_MESSAGE_MAP(CISAPIService, CWinApp)
039.    //{{AFX_MSG_MAP(CISAPIService)
040.        // NOTE - the ClassWizard will add and remove mapping macros here.
041.        //    DO NOT EDIT what you see in these blocks of generated code!
042.    //}}AFX_MSG
043.END_MESSAGE_MAP()
044.
045.//////////////////////////////////////////////////////////////////////
046.// command-parsing map
047.
048.BEGIN_PARSE_MAP(CLiteMailExtension, CHttpServer)
049.    // TODO: insert your ON_PARSE_COMMAND() and
050.    // ON_PARSE_COMMAND_PARAMS() here to hook up your commands.
051.    // For example:
052.    ON_PARSE_COMMAND(Default, CLiteMailExtension, ITS_EMPTY)
053.END_PARSE_MAP(CLiteMailExtension)
054.
055.
056.//////////////////////////////////////////////////////////////////////
057.// The one and only CLiteMailExtension object
058.CLiteMailExtension theExtension;
059.
060.//////////////////////////////////////////////////////////////////////
061.// CLiteMailExtension implementation
062.CLiteMailExtension::CLiteMailExtension()
063.{
064.}
065.
066.CLiteMailExtension::~CLiteMailExtension()
067.{
068.}
069.
070.//GetExtensionVersion
071.BOOL CLiteMailExtension::GetExtensionVersion(HSE_VERSION_INFO* pVer)
072.{
073.    // Call default implementation for initialization
074.    CHttpServer::GetExtensionVersion(pVer);
075.
076.    // Load description string
```

```
077.    TCHAR sz[HSE_MAX_EXT_DLL_NAME_LEN+1];
078.    ISAPIVERIFY(::LoadString(AfxGetResourceHandle(),
079.         IDS_SERVER, sz, HSE_MAX_EXT_DLL_NAME_LEN));
080.    _tcscpy(pVer->lpszExtensionDesc, sz);
081.    return TRUE;
082.}
083.
084.//*****************************************
085.//vitural CallFunction;
086.//Note: function has 2 return statements.
087.//*****************************************
088.int CLiteMailExtension::CallFunction(CHttpServerContext* pCtxt,
089.                                                    LPTSTR pszQuery,
➥LPTSTR pszCommand)
090.{
091.    EXTENSION_CONTROL_BLOCK *pECB = pCtxt->m_pECB;
092.
093.    if (pECB->cbAvailable > 0)
094.    {
095.        CString item(' ', 256);
096.        CString good_response(' ', 256);
097.        CString to(' ', 128);
098.        CString server(' ', 256);
099.        CString subject(' ', 256);
100.        CString body(' ', 2048);
101.        CString mail_from(' ', 128);
102.        char szRemoteHost[256];
103.        char szRemoteUser[256];
104.
105.        //Need to set the control block internal status code to OK
106.          pECB->dwHttpStatusCode = HTTP_STATUS_OK;
107.
108.        CHttpServerContext& sc = *pCtxt;
109.          ASSERT(!sc.m_pStream);
110.          sc.m_pStream = ConstructStream();
111.          sc.m_pStream->InitStream();
112.
113.        DWORD size = sizeof(szRemoteHost);
114.        if (!sc.GetServerVariable("REMOTE_HOST", (LPVOID)szRemoteHost,
➥&size))
115.            *szRemoteHost = 0;
116.        else
```

continues

LISTING 6.6—IMPLEMENTATION OF
THE LITEMAIL ISAPI EXTENSION, CONTINUED

```
117.            szRemoteHost[size] = '\0';
118.
119.        size = sizeof(szRemoteUser);
120.        if (!sc.GetServerVariable("REMOTE_USER", (LPVOID)szRemoteUser,
➡&size))
121.            *szRemoteUser = 0;
122.        else
123.            szRemoteUser[size] = '\0';
124.
125.        item            = "";
126.        good_response   = "";
127.        to              = "";
128.        server          = "";
129.        subject         = "";
130.        body            = "";
131.        mail_from       = "";
132.
133.        char nbAddr[4];
134.        nbAddr[0] = atoi(strtok(szRemoteHost,"."));
135.        nbAddr[1] = atoi(strtok(NULL,"."));
136.        nbAddr[2] = atoi(strtok(NULL,"."));
137.        nbAddr[3] = atoi(strtok(NULL,"."));
138.
139.        struct hostent *pHost = ::gethostbyaddr(nbAddr, 4, PF_INET);
140.        if (pHost && pHost->h_name && *pHost->h_name)
141.        {
142.            strcpy(szRemoteHost, pHost->h_name);
143.        }
144.
145.        if (!*szRemoteUser)
146.        {
147.            strcpy(szRemoteUser, "anonymous user");
148.        }
149.
150.        CString    from(CString(szRemoteHost) + " {" + szRemoteUser +
➡"}");
151.        body       = CString("<form ") + pszCommand + " from " + from +
➡">\r\n";
152.        mail_from  = pszCommand;
153.
```

```
154.        DWORD i = 0;
155.        while (i < pECB->cbAvailable)
156.        {
157.            item = "";
158.            while (i < pECB->cbAvailable && '=' != pECB->lpbData[i])
159.            {
160.                item += pECB->lpbData[i];
161.                ++i;
162.            }
163.            ++i;    // pass '='
164.
165.            if (0 == item.CompareNoCase("To"))
166.            {
167.                GetNext(to, pECB->lpbData, i, pECB->cbAvailable);
168.                to.TrimRight();
169.            }
170.            else if (0 == item.CompareNoCase("Server"))
171.            {
172.                GetNext(server, pECB->lpbData, i, pECB->cbAvailable);
173.                server.TrimRight();
174.            }
175.            else if (0 == item.CompareNoCase("Subject"))
176.            {
177.                GetNext(subject, pECB->lpbData, i, pECB->cbAvailable);
178.//              subject.TrimRight();    // Avoid trimming this (many
➥servers require double CRLF after subject)
179.            }
180.            else if (0 == item.CompareNoCase("Resp"))
181.            {
182.                GetNext(good_response, pECB->lpbData, i, pECB-
➥>cbAvailable);
183.            }
184.            else
185.            {
186.                body += item + "=\t[";
187.                GetNext(item, pECB->lpbData, i, pECB->cbAvailable);
188.
189.                sprintf(szRemoteHost, "%03d]:", item.GetLength());
190.                body += CString(szRemoteHost) + item + "\r\n";
191.            }
192.        }
193.
```

continues

**LISTING 6.6—IMPLEMENTATION OF
THE LITEMAIL ISAPI EXTENSION, CONTINUED**

```
194.        StartContent(&sc);
195.
196.        if (to.IsEmpty() || server.IsEmpty())
197.        {
198.            sc << "<font size=+3 color=red>Error</font>\r\n";
199.            sc << "LiteMail was unable to deliver e-mail because the
➥<strong>TO</strong> address or the ";
200.            sc << "SMTP server was not defined...\r\n";
201.        }
202.        else
203.        {
204.            AsyncMailTo(server, to, mail_from, subject, body, 0, 0);
205.
206.            if (!good_response.IsEmpty())
207.            {
208.                sc << good_response;
209.            }
210.            else
211.            {
212.                sc << "<FONT size=+2 color=BLUE>Thank you</font>\r\n";
213.                sc << "<P><font size=-1><center><A HREF=\"http://
➥www.structsoft.com\">Internet Mailer for Win32</a></center></font>\r\n";
214.            }
215.        }
216.
217.        EndContent(&sc);
218.    }
219.
220.    return callOK;
221.}
222.
223.
224.void CLiteMailExtension::Default(CHttpServerContext* pCtxt)
225.{
226.    StartContent(pCtxt);
227.    EndContent(pCtxt);
228.}
229.
230.
231.////////////////////////////////////////////////////////////////////////
```

```
232.// CLiteMailExtension command handlers
233.
234.////////////////////////////////////////////////////////////////////
235.// If your extension will not use MFC, you'll need this code to make
236.// sure the extension objects can find the resource handle for the
237.// module.  If you convert your extension to not be dependent on MFC,
238.// remove the comments around the following AfxGetResourceHandle()
239.// and DllMain() functions, as well as the g_hInstance global.
240.
241./****
242.
243.static HINSTANCE g_hInstance;
244.
245.HINSTANCE AFXISAPI AfxGetResourceHandle()
246.{
247.    return g_hInstance;
248.}
249.
250.BOOL WINAPI DllMain(HINSTANCE hInst, ULONG ulReason,
251.                    LPVOID lpReserved)
252.{
253.    if (ulReason == DLL_PROCESS_ATTACH)
254.    {
255.        g_hInstance = hInst;
256.    }
257.
258.    return TRUE;
259.}
260.
261.****/
262.
263.void CLiteMailExtension::GetNext(CString& dest, LPBYTE pBuff, DWORD&
➥offset, DWORD cbAvailable)
264.{
265.    char szHex[3];
266.    szHex[2] = '\0';
267.    int hexVal;
268.
269.    dest = "";
270.    while (offset < cbAvailable && '&' != pBuff[offset])
271.    {
272.        if ('%' == pBuff[offset])
```

LISTING 6.6—IMPLEMENTATION OF
THE LITEMAIL ISAPI EXTENSION, CONTINUED

```
273.        {
274.            szHex[0] = pBuff[offset+1];
275.            szHex[1] = pBuff[offset+2];
276.            sscanf(szHex, "%x", &hexVal);
277.            dest += (char)hexVal;
278.            offset += 3;
279.        }
280.        else if ('+' == pBuff[offset])
281.        {
282.            dest += ' ';
283.            ++offset;
284.        }
285.        else
286.        {
287.            dest += pBuff[offset];
288.            ++offset;
289.        }
290.    }
291.
292.    if ('&' == pBuff[offset])
293.        ++offset;
294.
295.    if (dest == "\r\n")
296.        dest = "";
297.}
```

Examining listing 6.6 in detail will reveal that approximately one third of the near 300 line source is Microsoft generated code. The remaining portions of custom ISAPI code are found in the *CallFunction()* and the *GetNext()* routines included on lines 88–221 and 263–297, respectively.

The *GetNext()* routine is used to parse standard formatted HTTP POST request/query into discrete elements. Deserving more attention is the *CallFunction()* routine. *CallFunction()* uses *GetNext()* to take the URL query, parse it into its component elements (such as "To" address, "From" address, etc.) and then package it up for processing by the SMTP Mailer DLL discussed earlier in the chapter.

CallFunction() is defined as a virtual function in MFC's CHttpServer class. It is used by the framework to find and execute the function associated with the command in the URL. The default functionality of *CallFunction()* uses the command parse map such as the one shown on lines 48–53 in listing 6.4 to determine the function and calling parameters. The overridden version of *CallFunction()* shown here prevents the default behavior of function lookup from taking place. Instead, it treats each query as if it were a form submission to the SMTP Mailer subsystem.

The parameters within the URL are checked against keywords such as "To," "From," "Subject," "Server," and "Resp" as they are parsed from the URL. These predefined parameters are used to build the resulting call into the SMTP Mailer DLL. All other URL parameters are considered to be part of the DATA portion of the mail message. LiteMail can handle posts with a variable number of fields as a result.

Summary

Many of the emailers available to web page developers have been written for Unix in Perl. Although these might be satisfactory for some uses, it is clearly more desirable to use binaries written specifically for the Win32 environment if you are developing ISAPI solutions. The SMTP Mailer DLL coupled with LiteMail is all you need to mail-enable your web server.

The LiteMail extension is versatile because it is completely data-driven by the form submitted to it. Applications of LiteMail have included automatically mail-forwarding submitted orders recorded online, sending product literature to a web surfer interested in receiving more information on products, and automatically sending mail based on server activity, such as new customer entries, into a database. Whatever the need, the LiteMailer with the SMTP Mailer DLL should be all you need to generate mail messages automatically from IIS and other custom Win32 applications.

CHAPTER 7

Understanding ISAPI Filters

This chapter presents a brief overview of ISAPI filters. This material is intended to serve as an introduction to concepts covered in several chapters to follow, which implement ISAPI filters demonstrating a variety of functionality. This chapter will also act as a reference to some aspects common to each of these filters.

The chapter does supply two skeletal ISAPI filters: one implemented in C and the other in C++ with MFC. These are intended to illustrate some of the basic mechanisms rather than implement application functionality. For applications of filters, see the next three chapters:

- Chapter 8, "Enhancing IIS Logging with Filters"

- Chapter 9, "Redirecting Based on Client Browser"

- Chapter 10, "Authentication With Filters"

Filters Defined

ISAPI filters are DLL (Dynamic Link Library) modules that have the opportunity to monitor and alter the processing of incoming HTTP requests. Filters have the opportunity to be called for each request made of the server; when called, they can see and modify the request or service the request without passing it back to the default IIS logic. Filters can be used to make fundamental changes to the way the IIS server operates.

 Although ISAPI is now supported by a number of non-Microsoft HTTP servers, the majority of these servers only support extensions, not filters. Check the documentation for your HTTP server before attempting to develop filters. The only non-Microsoft HTTP server supporting ISAPI filters at this time is the SpyGlass web server (www.spyglass.com). A good source for updated information on this subject is the "ISAPI Developer's Site" at **www.isapideveloper.net.** A list of of vendors supporting ISAPI and ISAPI filters may be found at **www.isapideveloper.net/isapigiven.htm.**

ISAPI Filters versus Extensions

ISAPI extensions are used to implement a piece of vertical functionality on a web server. Extensions are invoked when they are referred to as a web page; they execute some piece of application logic and return a result to the client. Extensions typically implement specific application features apparent to the end users of the system.

Filters represent a horizontal slice of functionality. They are connected to a specific event that occurs on the server, rather than to a page or part of a site. A filter can monitor all authentication requests or all data being sent from the server to the client. A filter spans the entire web server and can affect the way all parts of the server work.

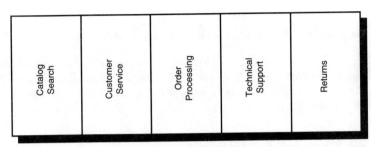

Extensions implement Vertical Functionality

Figure 7.1

Filters versus extensions.

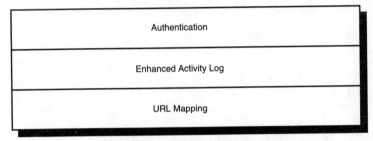

Filters implement horizontal functionality

Applications of ISAPI Filters

Servers are typically used to implement code that changes the way the entire site handles some type of request. Some commonly cited examples of features filters scanimplement are as follows:

◆ Custom authentication schemes

◆ Data compression

◆ Encryption and decryption

◆ Enhanced logging

◆ Real-time analysis of web site traffic

Filters have also been used to implement new features in IIS itself. The Microsoft support for SSL (Secure Sockets Layers) was implemented as an ISAPI filter named sspifilt.dll. The new Active Server functionality in IIS 3.0 is largely implemented via a filter named aspfilt.dll. This demonstrates rather conclusively that filters can be used to implement significant new functionality for the web server that fundamentally alters the way the server behaves.

The Life-cycle of ISAPI Filters

Before embarking on the development of ISAPI filters, it is important to understand how filters are loaded and configured. This includes some understanding of how IIS finds and loads filters, and how they communicate with the server to configure themselves for proper operation.

Loading and Unloading Filters

The HTTP server loads filters when it is started. The list of filters is read from the Registry, from the following key:

```
HKEY_LOCAL_MACHINE\CurrentControlSet\Services\W3Svc\Parameters\Filter Dlls
```

This key contains a comma-delimited list of filter DLL names, generally specified with a full path to the module. The filter is loaded as the server starts and is not unloaded until the server is shut down.

 Note   The IIS HTTP Server, W3SVC, supports an option for turning off the caching of server extensions. This makes it simpler to develop and test extensions by unloading extension DLLs after the processing for a request is complete. There is no equivalent setting to control the lifespan of an ISAPI filter. When a filter is loaded, it will remain in memory until the HTTP service is terminated.

Configuring Filters

When the server loads a filter module, it has an opportunity to supply information indicating when the server should call it. The filter must tell the server:

- ◆ **What events it will be handling:** this is done by passing the server a set of notification codes corresponding to the set of events the server would like to handle.

- ◆ **What the filter's priority will be:** this is used to determine the order in which filters will be told of each event.

It might also indicate whether it is interested in events coming in on the standard service port, the secured service port (used for SSL requests), or both.

This configuration happens during a call to the filter's *GetFilterVersion()* function; this is described in more detail later in the chapter.

Filter Notification Types

As described earlier in this chapter, an ISAPI filter has the opportunity to see everything there is to know about each request serviced by the HTTP server. This, however, is not the norm for filters. Instead, a filter is generally interested in a specific class of events. A filter is generally not written to examine everything that happens to the server but to handle all authentication events or all writes to the server log.

This is accomplished by passing a set of notification types to the server in the *GetFilterVersion()* function. The available notification types (as of IIS 3.0) are as follows:

◆ **SF_NOTIFY_READ_RAW_DATA:** indicates that the server is reading incoming data from the client. The filter has the opportunity to examine and/or alter the raw incoming data before any other processing occurs.

◆ **SF_NOTIFY_PREPROC_HEADERS:** called after the server has preprocessed the HTTP request headers; allows the filter to examine, replace, or add headers.

◆ **SF_NOTIFY_AUTHENTICATION:** fires when the server attempts to authenticate a client's identity. This notification allows the filter to replace or augment the standard authentication scheme.

◆ **SF_NOTIFY_URL_MAP:** this notification is fired when the server attempts to resolve an incoming URL to a physical file on disk. This can be used to redirect the request to a different file than the default mechanism would yield.

◆ **SF_NOTIFY_SEND_RAW_DATA:** this is called whenever data is to be sent to the client, after all other processing is complete. It can be used to monitor or alter the data being sent to the client.

◆ **SF_NOTIFY_LOG:** indicates that a record is to be written to the server log file. This is generally used to add additional information to the data being collected or to control the amount of data by filtering the records being written.

◆ **SF_NOTIFY_END_OF_NET_SESSION:** called at the end of the processing for a session. A *session* represents a sequence of communications with a remote client. It might consist of a single request and response; if the browser supports "keep-alive" connections, it might be substantially longer lived. This notification is typically used to free resources being used to support a sequence of notifications from a single client.

◆ **SF_NOTIFY_ACCESS_DENIED:** this notification was added in IIS 2.0; it is called when the server is about to return an "Access Denied" response to the client. It allows the filter to augment the normal response in some way.

◆ **SF_NOTIFY_END_OF_REQUEST:** this notification was added in IIS 3.0. It is sent at the end of processing for a single request. This can be used to manage resources on a request-by-request basis as opposed to the session level management by SF_NOTIFY_END_OF_NET_SESSION.

The SF_NOTIFY_END_OF_REQUEST notification value was added after the release of Visual C++ 4.2. To use this notification with VC 4.2 (or earlier) add the line:

```
#define SF_NOTIFY_END_OF_REQUEST 0x00000080
```

to the file "httpfilt.h". There is no data structure associated with this code.

Filter Priorities

At the same time the filter sets the notifications it is interested in receiving, it must also set its priority level. The priority level is used to set the order in which filters will be given the opportunity to see and act upon an event. This occurs during the server's call to the filter's *GetFilterVersion()* function. The IIS Server maintains an ordered list of the filters it has loaded. The filters are ordered by priority class and by the order in which they were loaded. The load order is determined by the order in which the filters are listed in the Registry.

There are four priority values available to the ISAPI filter in IIS 3.0:

◆ SF_NOTIFY_ORDER_LOW

◆ SF_NOTIFY_ORDER_MEDIUM

◆ SF_NOTIFY_ORDER_HIGH

◆ SF_NOTIFY_ORDER_DEFAULT

SF_NOTIFY_ORDER_DEFAULT is the default priority; this is the recommended value. This is currently equivalent to SF_NOTIFY_ORDER_LOW.

The sequence in which the filters are called is significant. The high-priority filters for a given notification are called first; they have the opportunity to handle the event and prevent it from passing to the next in line, or to alter the notification data before the next filter in line is called.

When faced with the opportunity to indicate the priority of their code, many programmers instinctively set the priority level as high as they can. This is a good place to curb that instinct. It's important to remember that an ISAPI filter will be called for each notification of its class not already handled by a higher priority filter. Even if your filter can quickly determine the need to handle a given request, the cost of invoking that code for every HTTP request handled by the server can add up.

If your filter is configured to be a high-priority filter, it will get all the notifications before most other filters. If the notification could have been handled by another filter, your code will be called unnecessarily. This means the filter will incur the overhead of being executed for no good reason.

Filters should always use the default priority class unless they have a good reason to do otherwise. If they have a reason to specify a priority class, they should choose the lowest priority they can to accomplish their goal.

An example of a filter that runs at high priority is a filter that provides encryption and description services. Such a filter may be processing the SF_NOTIFY_SEND_RAW_DATA and SF_NOTIFY_READ_RAW_DATA notifications to encrypt and decrypt data as it flows in and out of the web server. Since the encrypted data will be meaningless to other filters until it has been deciphered, the filter should run at high priority to ensure that it will be called before any other filters attempt to use this data. This is presumably done by the Microsoft filter which implements SSL for the IIS server, sspifilt.dll.

ISAPI Filter DLL Entry Points

Each ISAPI filter DLL exposes two functions for use by the ISAPI server.

◆ **GetFilterVersion():** used in the intialization and configuration of the filter

◆ **HttpFilterProc():** the function called by the server to deliver notifications to the filter

These functions constitute the entire exposed interface from the server to the filter. Each filter DLL must export these functions by name.

GetFilterVersion() Function

The *GetFilterVersion()* function is guaranteed to be the first call received by the ISAPI filter. The server calls this function to find out what version of the ISAPI filter interface the filter expects to use and to acquire configuration information. This function is the mechanism by which the server asks the extension which events it will handle and what precedence it should take in the chain of filters.

The declaration of this function is as follows, where pVer points to an HTTP_FILTER_VERSION structure.

```
BOOL WINAPI GetFilterVersion(PHTTP_FILTER_VERSION pVer );
```

The function return value indicates whether the filter initialized properly. If the function returns **TRUE**, the filter is assumed ready to run and will be inserted into the chain of active ISAPI filters. If it returns **FALSE**, it will be unloaded and will not receive any notification events.

The filter supplies the server with configuration information by filling in the attributes of the HTTP_FILTER_VERSION structure supplied via the parameter *pVer*. As of version 2.0 of the ISAPI specification, this structure is defined to be:

```
typedef struct _HTTP_FILTER_VERSION

{
DWORD   dwServerFilterVersion;
DWORD   dwFilterVersion;
CHAR    lpszFilterDesc[SF_MAX_FILTER_DESC_LEN+1];
DWORD   dwFlags;
} HTTP_FILTER_VERSION, *PHTTP_FILTER_VERSION;
```

The structure elements are as follows:

- **dwServerFilterVersion:** a value passed from the server to the filter, it indicates the revision level of the ISAPI specification in use by the server.

- **dwFilterVersion:** a value to be supplied by the extension; it indicates the version of the ISAPI header files and interface used when building the filter. The current revision level can be obtained from the defined symbol HTTP_FILTER_REVISION.

- **lpszFilterDesc:** a pointer to a buffer that can be used to supply the server with a description of the filter.

- **dwFlags:** a doubleword containing an OR'd set of flags. These flags allow the filter to indicate which categories of events it is interested in and at what priority it is to be inserted into the chain of filters.

Both the *GetFilterVersion()* function and the HTTP_FILTER_VERSION structure are slightly misnamed, given that the *dwFlags* parameter affects the operation of the filter to the extent it does.

As described earlier, the dwFlags attribute of the HTTP_FILTER_VERSION structure consists of a set of flags OR'd together. It should consist of:

- One or more of the notification types (such as SF_NOTIFY_PREPROC_ HEADERS or SF_NOTIFY_LOG).

- A priority code (usually SF_NOTIFY_ORDER_DEFAULT).

◆ Port connections (SF_NOTIFY_SECURE_PORT or SF_NOTIFY_
NONSECURE_PORT). These flags are optional and can be used to indicate
that the filter is only interested in secure port connections (SSL or PCT, for
example) or nonsecure port connections. If neither of these flags is set, the
filter will be notified of all requests.

 In addition to its official functions, the GetFilterVersion() function represents a useful
opportunity to perform one-time initialization of the module. At the time it is called,
the server is loaded and initialized.

HttpFilterProc() Function

The *HttpFilterProc()* is the ISAPI filter's analog of the old *WndProc()* window function.
It represents a callback function that will be called by the HTTP server whenever one
of the events specified in the dwFlags attribute of HTTP_FILTER_VERSION occurs.

This function is the core of an ISAPI filter. As an example, suppose that a filter set the
dwFlags attribute to contain the SF_NOTIFY_READ_RAW_DATA notification code in
its implementation of *GetFilterVersion()*. This means that the server will call the filter's
HttpFilterProc() function whenever the server reads raw data from an incoming
request, passing it an SF_NOTIFY_READ_RAW_DATA notification.

The footprint of this function is:

```
DWORD WINAPI HttpFilterProc(PHTTP_FILTER_CONTEXT pfc,
                     DWORD notificationType,
                     LPVOID pvNotification);
```

The parameters to the function are as follows:

◆ **PHTTP_FILTER_CONTEXT pfc:** a pointer to a filter context object. This
contains a flag indicating whether the request came from the secure port, a
pointer to user data, and a table of function pointers. This is described in more
detail later in this section.

◆ **DWORD notificationType:** a flag indicating the nature of the event that
caused the function to be called; this corresponds to one of the notification
codes set in *GetFilterVersion()*.

◆ **LPVOID pvNotification:** a pointer to a structure carrying data specific to the
notification type passed in the previous parameter. The actual structures
pointed to are as follows:

Notification Type Code	Notification Structure Type
SF_NOTIFY_ACCESS_DENIED	HTTP_FILTER ACCESS_DENIED
SF_NOTIFY_AUTHENTICATION	HTTP_FILTER AUTHENTICATION
SF_NOTIFY_END_OF_NET_SESSION	None. Pointer will be NULL.
SF_NOTIFY_END_OF_REQUEST	None. Pointer will be NULL.
SF_NOTIFY_LOG	HTTP_FILTER LOG
SF_NOTIFY_PREPROC_HEADERS	HTTP_FILTER_PREPROC_HEADERS
SF_NOTIFY_READ_RAW_DATA	HTTP_FILTER_RAW_DATA
SF_NOTIFY_SEND_RAW_DATA	HTTP_FILTER_RAW_DATA
SF_NOTIFY_URL_MAP	HTTP_FILTER_URL_MAP

HttpFilterProc() Return Values

The function return value tells the HTTP server what to do with the request when *HttpFilterProc()* returns control to the server. The return values govern whether other filters will be called and whether or not processing for the request will continue.

The valid return values for *HttpFilterProc()* are as follows:

◆ **SF_STATUS_REQ_FINISHED:** this indicates that this filter has completed processing for the request and the server should close the HTTP session.

◆ **SF_STATUS_REQ_FINISHED_KEEP_CONN:** identical to the previous return code, except the TCP/IP connection to the browser will be left open if the "keep-alive" option is set for the session.

◆ **SF_STATUS_REQ_NEXT_NOTIFICATION:** indicates that the next filters (if any) should be called for this notification. The next filter in line will see the data with any modifications made by this filter. This code should be returned to allow processing to continue normally.

SF_STATUS_REQ_HANDLED_NOTIFICATION: this return code indicates that the filter has handled this phase of the request and no additional filters are needed for this notification code for this request. Filters associated with other phases of filling the request will still be called.

◆ **SF_STATUS_REQ_ERROR:** an error has occurred during the processing of the request. In this case, the HTTP server will call after the function returns and act appropriately. This should include notifying the remote client that an error occurred.

◆ **SF_STATUS_REQ_READ_NEXT:** this is a special result used by SF_NOTIFY_ READ_RAW_DATA notifications. It indicates that the filter is handling the input stream without passing it on to the normal processing logic, and the filter needs to read an additional data block to negotiate session parameters.

HTTP_FILTER_CONTEXT Structure

An HTTP_FILTER_CONTEXT structure will be passed to the filter's *HttpFilterProc()* function each time it is called to notify it of an event. The filter context structure serves two major purposes:

◆ To provide *HttpFilterProc()* with context information via a number of data attributes

◆ To provide a table of function pointers that can be used to request other functionality from the server

Parts of the structure are intended for the use of the HTTP server itself. They are provided to the filter so the filter can pass them back to the server with other function calls. Other fields in the structure are intended for use by the filter. Those intended for the filter will be explained in this section; see Appendix A, "ISAPI Functions, Structures, and Constants," for the full structure definition.

The function pointers provided in the HTTP_FILTER_CONTEXT structure allow the filter to request services from the HTTP server. Each pointer contains the address of function providing some behavior that is of use to the server. The HTTP_FILTER_CONTEXT provides pointers to the following functions:

◆ *GetServerVariable()*

◆ *AddResponseHeader()*

◆ *WriteClient()*

◆ *AllocMem()*

◆ *ServerSupportFunction()*

These functions are discussed in more detail later in this chapter.

| Tip | Most developers are familiar with pointers to data elements, but many are unfamiliar with function pointers. Function pointers are simply pointers to a a piece that can be called later. |

Function pointers are used heavily in IIS applications because they give the server a simple, extensible way to provide functionality to filters or extensions. Instead of requiring filters to link to a library containing this code, the server provides a mechanism to obtain the server's implementation of these functions. This allows the server to be rewritten quite drastically without any changes to the filters, as long as the server still provides an implementation of these functions.

A function pointer is called using the normal syntax for dereferencing a pointer. For example, the following function takes a pointer to a filter context as a parameter. On line 4, it uses the *AllocMem()* function pointer provided in the HTTP_FILTER_CONTEXT to call the server's implementation of *AllocMem()*.

```
1. LPSTR GetMemory(PHTTP_FILTER_CONTEXT pfc, int nBytes)
2. {
3.     int nBytes = 200;
4.     return (LPSTR)(pfc->AllocMem(nBytes ,01));
5. }
```

Useful Filter Context Attributes

The filter context structure provides two data members or attributes that supply the filter with information about the event it is handling, or the environment in which it is operating. Two of these attributes are of particular use to the filter:

```
BOOL        fIsSecurePort;
PVOID       pFilterContext;
```

The first member, *fIsSecurePort*, is TRUE if the request came from a port that supports secure communications. Secure communication ports are those used to implement one of the secure protocols, such as SSL or PCT (Personal Communication Technology).

The second member, *pFilterContext*, can be used to store a pointer to filter-specific data that will be given back to the filter on subsequent notifications within the HTTP session. This can be used to pass data from one call of the filter procedure to another. For example, the filter might pick up data from an early notification, such as SF_NOTIFY_URL_MAP, and save a pointer to it by setting *pFilterContext* for use by the SF_NOTIFY_LOG function call.

Warning ISAPI guarantees that if the filter sets *pFilterContext*, it will get the pointer back for each notification in the session. It does not provide any special management of the memory pointed to by *pFilterContext*. The filter must make some provision for freeing the memory, either by using the *AllocMem* function pointer (discussed in more detail in a couple of pages) or by requesting the SF_NOTIFY_END_OF_NET_SESSION notification and freeing the memory at that time.

The GetServerVariable() Function Pointer

The first pointer is for the *GetServerVariable()* function. It allows the filter to request information that typically comes in the HTTP request header or from the operation of the server. The function declaration is as follows:

```
BOOL (WINAPI * GetServerVariable) (
        struct _HTTP_FILTER_CONTEXT * pfc,
        LPSTR                         lpszVariableName,
        LPVOID                        lpvBuffer,
        LPDWORD                       lpdwSize
```

The parameters to the function are as follows:

- **struct _HTTP_FILTER_CONTEXT * pfc:** like all functions whose pointers are passed in the filter context, this function takes a pointer back to the context as its first parameter. This allows the server to determine which request the filter function is currently processing.

- **LPSTR lpszVariableName:** pointer to the name of the variable to retrieve. Variable names include SERVER_NAME, SERVER_PORT, REMOTE_USER_NAME.

- **LPVOID lpvBuffer:** pointer to a buffer to contain the resulting values.

- **LPDWORD lpdwSiz:** pointer to a doubleword to contain the size of the data. On input, the doubleword should contain the size of the buffer; on output, it will contain the size of the data, including a terminating null.

The AddResponseHeaders() Function Pointer

The AddResponseHeaders() function pointer allows the filter to add additional headers to a response that will be sent to the remote client. The declaration of the function is:

```
BOOL (WINAPI * AddResponseHeaders) (
       struct _HTTP_FILTER_CONTEXT * pfc,
       LPSTR                         lpszHeaders,
       DWORD                         dwReserved
       );
```

This function's parameters are straightforward:

◆ **struct _HTTP_FILTER_CONTEXT * pfc:** the usual pointer to the containing filter context.

◆ **LPSTR lpszHeaders:** pointer to a null-terminated string containing the header(s) to add.

◆ **DWORD dwReserved:** must be zero.

The WriteClient() Function Pointer

The WriteClient()function pointer can be used to send data immediately. When this function is called, it sends the number of bytes of Buffer indicated by *lpdwBytes*. The data will not be buffered or combined with other pending data, and it can contain anything at all. The function footprint is as follows:

```
BOOL (WINAPI * WriteClient)  (
       struct _HTTP_FILTER_CONTEXT * pfc,
       LPVOID                        Buffer,
       LPDWORD                       lpdwBytes,
       DWORD                         dwReserved
       );
```

The parameters of the WriteClient() function pointer are:

◆ **struct _HTTP_FILTER_CONTEXT * pfc:** the usual pointer to the containing filter context.

◆ **LPVOID Buffer:** pointer to the data to write.

◆ **LPDWORD lpdwBytes:** pointer to a doubleword containing the size of the buffer to send, in bytes.

◆ **DWORD dwReserved:** must be zero.

The AllocMem() Function Pointer

The *AllocMem()* function is something of a double-edged sword. It can be used to allocate memory fro the HTTP server that will be automatically freed at the end of the network session. The declaration of the function pointer is as follows:

```
VOID * (WINAPI * AllocMem) (
        struct _HTTP_FILTER_CONTEXT * pfc,
        DWORD                         cbSize,
        DWORD                         dwReserved
        );
```

The function parameters of the *AllocMem()* function are:

◆ **struct _HTTP_FILTER_CONTEXT * pfc:** pointer to the containing filter context.

◆ **DWORD cbSize:** amount of memory to allocate, in bytes.

◆ **DWORD dwReserved:** must be zero.

Because the memory will be released automatically when the session is terminated, the filter is freed from the need to manage the life span of the memory. Unfortunately, overuse of this function can impact the performance of the filter and, thus, the server. With sufficient volume, the overhead of constant allocation and deallocation of memory can become significant, slowing the server. This function is discussed in more detail in the the "Using AllocMem() for Memory Management" section later in the chapter.

It will often be more efficient for the filter to manage a pool of buffers within the filter for this purpose. The SF_NOTIFY_END_OF_NET_SESSION notification can be used to perform the bookkeeping required to implement some other method of pooling buffers.

The ServerSupportFunction ()Pointer

ServerSupportFunction() pointer provides the filter with several useful functions, centering on transmitting request headers to the remote client. Although the function parameters are the same as those of the ISAPI extension version of *ServerSupportFunction()*, the number of functions is considerably more limited. The function signature is as follows:

```
BOOL (WINAPI * ServerSupportFunction) (
        struct _HTTP_FILTER_CONTEXT * pfc,
        enum SF_REQ_TYPE              sfReq,
        PVOID                         pData,
        DWORD                         ul1,
        DWORD                         ul2
        );
```

The parameters of ServerSupportFunction() are:

- **struct _HTTP_FILTER_CONTEXT * pfc:** the usual pointer to the containing filter context.

- **enum SF_REQ_TYPE sfReq:** a code identifying the operation the filter is requesting of the server. This code governs the action that will be taken, and the interpretation of the pData and null parameters. (See the table that follows for more information).

- **PVOID pData:** pointer to parameter data; meaning varies by request code.

- **DWORD ul1:** generic parameter; can be numeric or a pointer cast to a DWORD. The meaning varies by request code.

- **DWORD ul2:** not used; should be set to zero.

The valid values of the *sfReq* request code and the corresponding interpretations of *pData* and *ul1* are as follows:

- **SF_REQ_SEND_REQUEST_HEADER:** requests that the server sendsa complete response header to the client. The response will include the status, server version, message time, and MIME version. The *pData* parameter should be a pointer to a null-terminated string containing the server status ("401 Access Denied") or a NULL pointer. If the pointer is NULL, the default "200 OK" will be used. The *ul1* parameter might point to a string containing optional headers, followed by an extra \r\n, or a NULL pointer.

- **SF_REQ_ADD_HEADERS_ON_DENIAL:** if the server denies the HTTP request, this code adds the indicated headers to the server error response. This is designed to allow authentication filters to advertise their services by adding WWW-Authenticate headers to the response. The *pData* parameter should point to a null-terminated string containing the headers to add.

- **SF_REQ_NEXT_READ_SIZE:** this request code is only used by rawdata read filters that return a result code of SF_STATUS_READ_NEXT. The *pData* parameter is not used; *ul1* contains the number of bytes for the next read.

Notification Structures

As described earlier, one of the parameters to the *HttpFilterProc()* function is a pointer named *pvNotification*. This parameter points to a data structure specific to the notification being processed by the *HttpFilterProc()*. This structure contains data elements that are relevant to the specific notification; for example, the structure for authentication events contains attributes containing a user name and password, and the logging notification structure contains attributes corresponding to the fields to be written to the log.

The *pvNotification* pointer is declared to be a pointer to void (void *). It is actually a pointer to a notification structure. The type of structure that *pvNotification* points to for particular call to *HttpFilterProc()* can be determined from the *notificationType* paramater. The *notificationType* contains an IIS notification code, as described in table 7.1.

Each of the notification structures is described in more detail in this section.

HTTP_FILTER_ACCESS_DENIED

This structure is passed when the server is about to deny access to an URL to the remote client. The structure supplies the URL requested by the client, the physical path the URL was mapped to, and the reason the request has been denied.

The actual structure is defined as follows:

```
typedef struct _HTTP_FILTER_ACCESS_DENIED
{
const CHAR * pszURL;            // Requesting URL
const CHAR * pszPhysicalPath;   // Physical path of resource
DWORD        dwReason;          // Bitfield of SF_DENIED flags
}
```

The *dwReason* data member is defined as a set of single-bit flags. The flags are as follows:

TABLE 7.1

Flag Name	Meaning
SF_DENIED_LOGON	Denied due to a logon failure
SF_DENIED_RESOURCE	Denied due to an ACL (Access Control List) on the resource
SF_DENIED_FILTER	Access denied by a filter
SF_DENIED_APPLICATION	Denied by a CGI application or an ISAPI server extension
SF_DENIED_BY_CONFIG	Denied due to the configuration of the server

The SF_DENIED_BY_CONFIG and SF_DENIED_LOGON flags can both be set if the configuration of the server did not allow the user to log on.

HTTP_FILTER_AUTHENT

This structure is received when the server is authenticating the client. Authentication is the process by which the user name and password entered by the user are checked and potentially mapped to a different NT user name, which will be used to verify the user's access rights to resources on the server.

The actual structure used to implement this is:

```
typedef struct _HTTP_FILTER_AUTHENT
{
    CHAR *    pszUser;
    DWORD     cbUserBuff;
    CHAR *    pszPassword;
    DWORD     cbPasswordBuff;
} HTTP_FILTER_AUTHENT, *PHTTP_FILTER_AUTHENT;
```

The incoming user name and password are found in the buffers pointed to by *pszUser* and *pszPassword*, respectively; the sizes of the buffers are given in the *cbUserBuff* and *cbPasswordBuff* fields. It is important to remember that these fields indicate the size of the buffers themselves, not the length of the strings contained in the buffers. The buffers are guaranteed to be at least SF_MAX_USERNAME and SF_MAX_PASSWORD bytes in length.

If the authentication scheme in effect on the server is anything other than the basic or anonymous schemes, the user name and password fields will not be visible to the filter in a comprehensible form.

HTTP_FILTER_LOG

This structure is passed to the filter on SF_NOTIFY_LOG events. It contains copies of all the information to be written to the server log.

The following structure is used to carry the log data:

```
1.typedef struct _HTTP_FILTER_LOG
2.{
3.    const CHAR * pszClientHostName;
4.    const CHAR * pszClientUserName;
5.    const CHAR * pszServerName;
6.    const CHAR * pszOperation;
7.    const CHAR * pszTarget;
8.    const CHAR * pszParameters;
9.
10.    DWORD  dwHttpStatus;
```

```
11.    DWORD  dwWin32Status;
12.
13.} HTTP_FILTER_LOG, *PHTTP_FILTER_LOG;
```

The fields are defined in the following list:

- ◆ **pszClientHostName:** the IP address of the client's computer, in dotted number notation (127.0.0.1, for example).

- ◆ **pszClientUserName:** the client's user name, or a '-'. The user name is only valid if the HTTP status code indicates the request was successful; if the status code is "401 Unauthorized," the name has not been authenticated.

- ◆ **pszServerName:** pointer to the name of the server handling the request; this will be in dotted number form.

- ◆ **pszTarget:** pointer to the name of the resource being requested.

- ◆ **pszParameters:** pointer to the parameters for the operation. The parameter string might contain a query string, a set of coordinates for an imagemap, or whatever other parameters are relevant to the operation.

- ◆ **pszOperation:** pointer to a buffer containing the name of the operation requested, such as GET or POST.

- ◆ **dwHttpStatus:** the HTTP status code being returned to the remote client for this request.

- ◆ **dwWin32Status:** the Win32 status code resulting from processing the request. By default, this will be the code retrieved by the *GetLastError( )* after a request returns SF_STATUS_REQ_ERROR.

Unlike the other notification structures, this structure does not allow the user to update the strings passed as parameter fields. If the filter would like to replace the fields, it must replace the string pointers rather than update the strings in place.

HTTP_FILTER_PREPROC_HEADERS

Unlike the other structures, this notification structure does not contain any data elements of direct use to the user. The only data element is a reserved value, which should be left as a zero.

The structure does contain three function pointers. These functions allow the filter to get the value of a header variable, add a new header variable, or update an existing header variable. The functions each take a pointer to the filter context; this will be used by the functions to determine which request will be affected.

The function names are as follows:

◆ **GetHeader():** gets the value of a header into a-caller-supplied buffer. Passing the header name in the pszName field specifies the header. The name should include a trailing colon (:). In place of a literal name, the special values *method*, *url* and *version* can be used to retrieve specific portions of the request line.

◆ **SetHeader():** updates an existing header with a new value, supplied by the caller. To delete an existing header, pass a pointer to an empty string in the *lpsvValue* parameter.

◆ **AddHeader():** adds a new header, using the name and value specified in the call.

HTTP_FILTER_URL_MAP

This structure is passed for the SF_NOTIFY_URL_MAP event. The structure contains fields for the requested URL, the physical file on disk, and the size of the buffer containing the physical file name. The structure is as shown in the following:

```
typedef struct _HTTP_FILTER_URL_MAP
{
    const CHAR * pszURL;          // Incoming URL name
    CHAR *       pszPhysicalPath; // Buffer containing the physical file name
    DWORD        cbPathBuff;      // size of the buffer, in bytes

} HTTP_FILTER_URL_MAP, *PHTTP_FILTER_URL_MAP;
```

The filter can change the file that will be used to satisfy the request by updating the *pszPhysizalPath* attribute in place.

Threading

Threading is a fact of life for the ISAPI developer; this is especially true for the filter developer. The Microsoft IIS platform is inherently multithreaded; it spawns new threads of execution as needed to handle incoming requests. When the server receives multiple simultaneous requests it may spawn a thread to handle each of the requests. The implication of this is important: filters may encounter multiple simultaneous calls to its *HttpFilterProc()*; each occurring on a different thread spawned by IIS. If the filter is handling a common or frequent notification, such as the raw read or send events, it is certain to encounter this behavior.

Resource Management

The filter extension must take appropriate steps to guard static or global resources with synchronization objects, such as critical sections, semaphores, or mutexes. If it does not, the filter will crash and could take the rest of the web server with it. It is important to remember that the filter is a DLL, executing in the context of the IIS server, so failures in this area can be quite disastrous.

It is equally important to avoid programming constructs that guard a single instance of a critical resource with a synchronization object. If there is only a single instance of the resource, properly protecting it with critical sections can turn your ISAPI server into a single-threaded system, substantially impacting the scalability and performance of the server.

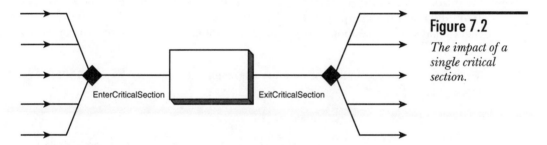

Figure 7.2

The impact of a single critical section.

ISAPI filters must be designed to support N simultaneous threads, where N is substantially greater than 1. Unlike server extensions, filters have the potential to affect all requests to the server. If the filter does not support a sufficient number of concurrent threads, the system will suffer.

 The issues surrounding multi-threaded programming are too complex to cover properly here. I'd recommend you find a good book on Win32's threading and resource management models. Jeffery Richter's book Advanced Windows provides a good overview of the issues and mechanics.

Context Management

It is natural for filters to pass information from one phase of processing a request to another. For example, the authentication filter might want to save information to be recorded in the server log during the log notification call.

Because these functions are performed during separate calls to the filter's *HttpFilterProc()* function, the filter needs a way to save the data across these function calls. Because of the multithreaded nature of the filter, it cannot simply store the data in static variables.

The correct way to manage context data across notifications is to use the HTTP_FILTER_CONTEXT passed as a parameter to *HttpFilterProc()*. The context contains an attribute named *pFilterContext*; this attribute will be available to the filter during each call to *HttpFilterProc()* for a given network session. By storing a pointer to a buffer containing the desired context in this attribute, the filter can ensure its availability for use later in the session.

Memory Management

If a filter will be carrying context data over the life of a session or request, it must take steps to ensure appropriate allocation and deallocation of the memory used. Until the introduction of the SF_NOTIFY_END_OF_REQUEST notification code in IIS 3.0, ISAPI did not provide any explicit support for managing memory on a request-by-request basis; it only supported the management of memory on the basis of a network session.

There are two basic schemes for memory management supported by the ISAPI filter model:

> The *AllocMem()* callback function
>
> The SF_NOTIFY_END_OF_NET_SESSION or SF_NOTIFY_END_OF_REQUEST notification codes

Using AllocMem() for Memory Management

As described earlier, the filter context structure contains a pointer to a function named *AllocMem()*. This function can be used to allocate memory that will live for the duration of the network session. After the SF_NOTIFY_END_OF_SESSION notification is sent to the filter, any memory allocated with this function will be automatically released.

Unfortunately, there are several limitations to this programming model:

◆ There is no way to free the memory manually or to resize an existing block. The only action supported by this memory manager is allocation.

◆ No indication of the size of the buffer is passed automatically. If the filter will be allocating blocks of varying sizes, the filter should store the size of the block allocated within the block for later use.

◆ The use of this function might result in many small allocations and deallocations over the life of the filter. The overhead of these calls, and the heap management required to support them, can be a significant performance drag. Remember that the filter might be called for *every* request to hit the server.

This function is frequently used to allocate memory to pass information from one invocation of the *HttpFilterProc()* to another within the same request. For example, the filter might want to pass data from the preprocess headers notification to the log notification for a request, allocating the memory in preprocess headers and reading it later. The *HttpFilterProc()* for the filter would call *AllocMem()* when it receives the SF_NOTIFY_PREPROC_HEADERS notification, storing the resulting pointer in the allocate memory in the *pFilterContext* attribute of the *HTTP_FILTER_CONTEXT*.

Because the life span of the memory is tied to the life of the network session, it might span multiple requests from the client. This means the *HttpFilterProc()* might be called multiple times for each notification code. If the filter allocates memory each time it receives an SF_NOTIFY_PREPROC_HEADERS notification, multiple blocks will be allocated and will linger until the session ends. This does not constitute a memory leak; the memory will be freed at the end of the network session. It simply means the resource load caused by the use of this function might, in fact, be heavier than expected.

Tip   If a filter is making heavy use of *AllocMem()*, and is heavily used itself, some consideration should be given to adopting a scheme that relies on a static pool of memory. If the level of usage of a site is more manageable, and maximizing performance is not critical, this function can give you easy to use memory management that works, and works reliably.

If you opt to develop your own mechanisms with the end of request or session notification codes, make sure that the mechanism you implement is, in fact, more efficient. It is also important to make sure that any replacement mechanism works as reliably as *AllocMem()*, particularly in heavily multithread settings such as ISAPI filters.

It is frequently to your advantage to use *AllocMem()* for initial development, and replace it later when and if it is warranted. Many sites may make relatively light use of this type memory management, meaning that the replacement of *AllocMem()* with another function is unwarranted or uneconomical.

Tip   The memory allocated in one request might be reused by the filter in the next request in the same session, rather than calling *AllocMem()* independently for each request. If your filter does reuse the block, it must ensure that the buffer is sufficiently large to hold the data for subsequent requests. A common problem is to allocate memory sized to hold data from the initial request and then try to use that buffer for a larger request later in the session.

Using Notifications for Memory Management

Instead of using the *AllocMem()* function to manage memory, a filter can manage it directly. The keys to doing so are the end-of-session and end-of-request notification codes.

As with the *AllocMem()* function, the pointer to the memory can be passed from request to request via the *pFilterContext* attribute of the HTTP_FILTER_CONTEXT structure. A value set in the *pFilterContext* will be passed back to the filter on each subsequent allocation for the session.

If resources are being allocated and deallocated manually, the filter will generally need to indicate that it would like to handle the SF_NOTIFY_END_OF_REQUEST or SF_NOTIFY_END_OF SESSION events. These events can be used to determine if the filter has finished with the memory in question and to release the resources in question.

The SF_NOTIFY_END_OF_REQUEST notification code will be fired at the end of processing for a given request. If the filter chooses to manage memory on a request-by-request basis, it should free the resources used for the request during the handling of this notification. When it does so, it should remember to set the *pFilterContext* attribute back to NULL so subsequent notifications will not attempt to reuse the memory.

The best use of these notifications is for managing access to a static pool of resources. If these notifications are used to trigger calls to *malloc()* and *free()*, or the C++ new and delete operators, they will result in the same problems caused by *AllocMem()*. The overhead of C/C++ heap management will grow substantially after many requests for small blocks of varying size.

Instead, the filter might choose to allocate a number of buffers of fixed sizes, managing access to those buffers itself. The filter can generally implement more efficient management of a pool of fixed-size resources than the generalized run-time memory manager; it can solve a much simpler problem, resulting in much higher performance. When implementing such a scheme, it is important to keep two things in mind:

◆ Thread synchronization objects must adequately protect the data structures used to manage and allocate this static pool of memory.

◆ The pool of buffers must be sufficiently large to allow an adequate number of requests, sessions, and threads to be processed simultaneously. This number should not be one or two, but should be substantially larger.

Building a Filter in C

The best way to understand all the functions described in the chapter to this point is to apply them in a simple filter. This will show the functions in action and help illustrate the actual sequence of events when a request comes into the HTTP server.

The filter implemented here does not contain any functional application logic; see the following chapters for examples of filters that provide tangible functionality. Instead, this filter serves two very limited goals:

◆ It shows a working filter, with a minimal *GetFilterVersion ()* and *HttpFilterProc()*.

◆ It allows the developer to monitor the execution of the filter via the debugger output mechanism.

This filter can be used as a launching point for building functional filters. As mentioned in the beginning of the chapter, see Chapters 8, 9, and 10 for real-world examples of ISAPI filters.

Implementing a Simple Filter

This section describes the implementation of a skeletal filter. It presents each of the major entry points and a number of additional support functions to break down the requests and report them via debug output calls.

Configuring the Filter in GetFilterVersion()

The *GetFilterVersion()* function is extremely simple; it fills in the HTTP_FILTER_VERSION structure to indicate its name, the version of the ISAPI interface it expects to see, and the set of notifications it expects to receive.

LISTING 7.1—IMPLEMENTING GETFILTERVERSION

```
01.BOOL WINAPI
02.GetFilterVersion( PHTTP_FILTER_VERSION pVer  )
03.{
04.    _RPT0(_CRT_WARN,"GetFilterVersion\n");
05.    _RPT1(_CRT_WARN,"\tServerFilterVersion=%lx\n",
06.                (pVer->dwServerFilterVersion));
07.
08.    //
09.    // Set the revision level of the revision of the httpfilt.h
```

continues

LISTING 7.1—IMPLEMENTING GETFILTERVERSION, CONTINUED

```
10.    //    this module was compiled with.
11.    pVer->dwFilterVersion = HTTP_FILTER_REVISION;
12.    //
13.    // Set the name of this filter.
14.    //
15.    strcpy(pVer->lpszFilterDesc,"Test Filter");
16.    //
17.    // Indicate tha we'd like to be added into the chain of
18.    // filters at default priority and would like to be informed
19.    // of all of the standard notifications.
20.    //
21.    pVer->dwFlags = SF_NOTIFY_ORDER_DEFAULT ¦
22.                    SF_NOTIFY_READ_RAW_DATA ¦
23.                    SF_NOTIFY_PREPROC_HEADERS ¦
24.                    SF_NOTIFY_AUTHENTICATION ¦
25.                    SF_NOTIFY_URL_MAP ¦
26.                    SF_NOTIFY_SEND_RAW_DATA ¦
27.                    SF_NOTIFY_LOG ¦
28.                    SF_NOTIFY_END_OF_NET_SESSION ¦
29.                    SF_NOTIFY_ACCESS_DENIED;
30.    //
31.    // Return TRUE to indicate that the module has been
32.    // initialized correctly and should receive events
33.    //
34.    return TRUE;
35.}
```

On line 11, the function sets the version of the ISAPI interface it is designed to support and sets its "name" on line 15. It sets its priority and the set of notifications it expects to handle via lines 21–29; this filter will run at the default priority (low) and would like to see all IIS 2.0 notifications.

 Note The *RPT0()* and *RPT1()* macros used on lines 4 and 5 are defined in the header file crtdbg.h. These macros will send output to the debug window or your debugger when your program is built with debug information, and will compile away to nothing when our program is built for production.

This implementation of *GetFilterVersion()* indicates that it is interested in receiving all notification events; this means that the *HttpFilterProc()* function implemented by this filter will be called for each of these notification funtions.

Implementing HttpFilterProc() for the Sample Filter

The *HttpFilterProc()* implementation is also quite simple; it uses a switch statement to dispatch the incoming notification to the appropriate trace output function.

LISTING 7.2—IMPLEMENTING HTTPFILTERPROC FOR THE SAMPLE FILTER

```
01.DWORD WINAPI
02.HttpFilterProc(PHTTP_FILTER_CONTEXT pFilterContext,
03.             DWORD                notificationType,
04.             LPVOID               pvNotification)
05.
06.{
07.    _RPT2(_CRT_WARN,"HttpFilterProc Context=%p SecurePort=%d \n",
08.                 pFilterContext,
09.                 pFilterContext->fIsSecurePort);
10.    switch(notificationType)
11.    {
12.        case SF_NOTIFY_READ_RAW_DATA:
13.            TraceRawData("SF_NOTIFY_READ_RAW_DATA", pvNotification);
14.            break;
15.        case SF_NOTIFY_PREPROC_HEADERS:
16.            TracePreprocHeaders(pFilterContext,pvNotification);
17.            break;
18.        case SF_NOTIFY_AUTHENTICATION:
19.            TraceAuthentication(pvNotification);
20.            break;
21.        case SF_NOTIFY_URL_MAP:
22.            TraceUrlMap(pvNotification);
23.            break;
24.        case SF_NOTIFY_SEND_RAW_DATA:
25.            TraceRawData("SF_NOTIFY_SEND_RAW_DATA", pvNotification);
26.            break;
27.        case SF_NOTIFY_LOG:
28.            TraceLog(pvNotification);
29.            break;
30.        case SF_NOTIFY_END_OF_NET_SESSION:
31.            _RPT0(_CRT_WARN,"    SF_NOTIFY_END_OF_NET_SESSION\n");
32.            break;
33.        case SF_NOTIFY_ACCESS_DENIED:
34.            TraceAccessDenied(pvNotification);
```

continues

LISTING 7.2—IMPLEMENTING
HTTPFILTERPROC FOR THE SAMPLE FILTER, CONTINUED

```
35.          break;
36.     }
37.     return SF_STATUS_REQ_NEXT_NOTIFICATION;
38.}
```

On line 7, the filter procedure uses the _RPT2 debug output macro to log the
HTTP_FILTER_CONTEXT address and the secure port flag from the
HTTP_FILTER_CONTEXT. The case statement on lines 10–36 is then used to call
the appropriate function to trace the information relevant to each notification code.
The various trace functions called in this case statement each report the data for a
particular notification event to the debugger trace window.

The function returns the SF_STATUS_REQ_NEXT_NOTIFICATION value to
indicate it has not handled the request and the next filter in line should be allowed to
do its work. If there is no filter lower in the filter list, IIS will complete processing for
the event.

TraceRawData() Function

The *TraceRawData()* function is used to report incoming
SF_NOTIFY_READ_RAW_DATA or SF_NOTIFY_WRITE_RAW_DATA requests. The
code is shown in the following listing:

LISTING 7.3—THE TRACERAWDATAFUNCTION

```
01.void TraceRawData(LPCSTR pVerb, LPVOID pvNotification)
02.{
03.     PHTTP_FILTER_RAW_DATA pRawData;
04.     char                  buffer[50];
05.
06.     pRawData = (PHTTP_FILTER_RAW_DATA)pvNotification;
07.
08.     // Copy the first 40 characters of data to a temporary
09.     // buffer to be displayed to the user.
10.     strncpy(buffer,(LPCSTR)pRawData->pvInData,
11.                  min(40,pRawData->cbInData));
12.     buffer[min(40,pRawData->cbInData)]=0;
13.     _RPT4(_CRT_WARN,"    %0s ('%s' DATASIZE=%d BUFFSIZE=%0d)\n",
14.                  pVerb,
15.                  buffer,
16.                  pRawData->cbInData,
17.                  pRawData->cbInBuffer);
18.}
```

This function outputs the amount of data in the buffer, the size of the buffer, and the first 40 bytes of data in the buffer to the debugger output window.

On line 6, the *pvNotification* pointer passed into this function from the *HttpFilterProc()* is cast to a pointer to an HTTP_FILTER_RAW_DATA structure. This is safe because this function is only called for notification types of SF_NOTIFY_READ_RAW_DATA and SF_NOTIFY_SEND_RAW_DATA.

Lines 10 and 11 copy up to 40 bytes of the data from the HTTP_FILTER_RAW structure into a temporary buffer. The function will copy less than 40 bytes if it determines that less then 40 bytes are available in the incoming structure. The number of bytes in this buffer is found by examining *pRawData->cbInData.*

Once the data has been moved to the temporary buffer, it is null terminated on line 12. It is then used in the trace output function and sent to the debugger window via the _RPT4 macro on lines 13-17.

TraceUrlMap() Function

The *TraceUrlMap()* function is used to report SF_NOTIFY_URL_MAP events. The source for the function is:

LISTING 7.4—THE TRACEURLMAP FUNCTION

```
1.void TraceUrlMap(LPVOID pvNotification)
2.{
3.    PHTTP_FILTER_URL_MAP pMap = (PHTTP_FILTER_URL_MAP)pvNotification;
4.    _RPT3(_CRT_WARN,
5.        "    SF_NOTIFY_URL_MAP (URL=%s PATH=%s BUFFSIZE=%0d)\n",
6.        pMap->pszURL,
7.        pMap->pszPhysicalPath,
8.        pMap->cbPathBuff);
9.}
```

The function simply outputs the URL, physical path, and size of the physical pass buffer to the debugger output window.

On line 3, the *pvNotification* pointer passed into this function as a parameter is cast to a pointer to an HTTP_FILER_URL_MAP structure. The structure is then used to generate trace output on lines 4-8.

TraceAuthentication() Function

The *TraceAuthorization()* function outputs incoming authorization requests. The information reported to the debugger window includes the incoming user name, password, and buffer sizes.

LISTING 7.5—THE TRACEAUTHENTICATION FUNCTION

```
01.void TraceAuthentication(LPVOID pvNotification)
02.{
03.    PHTTP_FILTER_AUTHENT pAuth = (PHTTP_FILTER_AUTHENT)pvNotification;
04.    _RPT4(_CRT_WARN,
05.        "    SF_NOTIFY_AUTHENTICATION (USER=%s ULEN=%d PSWD=%s
➥PSWDLEN=%0d)\n",
06.                pAuth->pszUser,
07.                pAuth->cbUserBuff,
08.                pAuth->pszPassword,
09.                pAuth->cbPasswordBuff);
10.}
```

If the authentication scheme in effect is basic or anonymous, the user name and password will be decoded by the time this function is called. The function follows the familiar pattern: the notification structure pointer is cast to the correct type on line 3, and is used to generate trace output on lines 4–9.

TracePreprocHeaders() Function

As described earlier, the HTTP_FILTER_PREPROC_HEADERS structure does not contain data elements directly usable by the filter; instead, it contains pointers to functions that can be used to manipulate the headers for the request.

The *TracePreprocHeaders()* function implemented as part of this example uses the *GetHeader()* pointer to retrieve a header. The source is shown in listing 7.6:

LISTING 7.6—THE TRACEPREPROCHEADERS FUNCTION

```
01.void
02.TracePreprocHeaders(PHTTP_FILTER_CONTEXT pFilterContext,
03.                LPVOID                pvNotification)
04.{
05.    PHTTP_FILTER_PREPROC_HEADERS pHdrs;
06.    TCHAR                        variable[80];
07.    DWORD                        dwVariableLen;
08.
09.    pHdrs = (PHTTP_FILTER_PREPROC_HEADERS)pvNotification;
10.    dwVariableLen = sizeof(variable);
11.
12.    pHdrs->GetHeader(pFilterContext,"version",
13.                    variable,&dwVariableLen);
14.    _RPT1(_CRT_WARN,
```

```
15.          "    SF_NOTIFY_PREPROC_HEADERS (SERVER_PROTOCOL = %s)\n",
16.          variable);
17.}
```

This implementation uses the *GetHeader()* function pointer to retrieve the version special variable; this contains the HTTP protocol version specified on the incoming GET or POST request.

The function begins as the other trace functions do, by converting the *pvNotifcations* pointer to the correct type. This is done on line 9; the resulting HTTP_FILTER_PREPROC_HEADERS pointer is stored in the *pHdrs* variable.

The HTTP_FILTER_PREPROC_HEADERS structure contains a number of function pointers; one of these is the pointer to the *GetHeader() function*. The pointer is used on lines 12 and 13 to actually retrieve the data.

TraceAccessDenied() Function

The *TraceAccessDenied()* function displays information about the SF_TRACE_ACCESS_DENIED request. This structure carries information about the resource the client requested access to and the reason the request was denied.

LISTING 7.7—THE TRACEACCESSDENIED FUNCTION

```
01.void
02.TraceAccessDenied(LPVOID pvNotification)
03.{
04.    PHTTP_FILTER_ACCESS_DENIED pDenied =
05.        (PHTTP_FILTER_ACCESS_DENIED)pvNotification;
06.
07.    char buffer[255];
08.    buffer[0]=0;
09.    if (pDenied->dwReason & SF_DENIED_LOGON)
10.        strcat(buffer,"SF_DENIED_LOGON ");
11.    if (pDenied->dwReason & SF_DENIED_RESOURCE)
12.        strcat(buffer,"SF_DENIED_RESOURCE ");
13.    if (pDenied->dwReason & SF_DENIED_FILTER)
14.        strcat(buffer,"SF_DENIED_FILTER ");
15.    if (pDenied->dwReason & SF_DENIED_APPLICATION)
16.        strcat(buffer,"SF_DENIED_APPLICATION ");
17.    if (pDenied->dwReason & SF_DENIED_BY_CONFIG)
18.        strcat(buffer,"SF_DENIED_BY_CONFIG ");
19.    _RPT3(_CRT_WARN,"    SF_NOTIFY_ACCESS_DENIED (URL=%s PATH=%s
➡REASON=%s)\n",
```

continues

LISTING 7.7—THE TRACEACCESSDENIED FUNCTION, CONTINUED

```
20.              pDenied->pszURL,
21.              pDenied->pszPhysicalPath,
22.              buffer);
23.}
```

The function begins with the usual type cast of the incoming *pvNotification* pointer to the correct type for use by this function.

As described in the HTTP_FILTER_ACCESSS_DENIED structure, the *dwReason* field is a set of single bit flags that described the reason the user's access to the requested resource was denied. Lines 9–18 of the function decode the incoming reason codes by checking to see which bits were set in the mask; the result is a human readable string.

TraceLog() Function

The *TraceLog()* function reports information to be written to the server log. The function is shown in listing 7.8.

LISTING 7.8—THE TRACELOG FUNCTION

```
01.void TraceLog(LPVOID pvNotification)
02.{
03.    PHTTP_FILTER_LOG pLog = (PHTTP_FILTER_LOG)pvNotification;
04.    char buffer[512];
05.    wsprintf(buffer,"    SF_NOTIFY_LOG (ClientHost=%s ClientUser=%s
➥Server=%s Op=%s\n",
06.              pLog->pszClientHostName,
07.              pLog->pszClientUserName,
08.              pLog->pszServerName,
09.              pLog->pszOperation);
10.    _RPT0(_CRT_WARN,buffer);
11.    wsprintf(buffer,"                    Target=%s Params=%s HttpStat=%d
➥Win32Stat=%d)\n",
12.              pLog->pszTarget,
13.              pLog->pszParameters,
14.              pLog->dwHttpStatus,
15.              pLog->dwWin32Status);
16.    _RPT0(_CRT_WARN,buffer);
17.}
```

The data is all in NULL-terminated string or integer form; no special process is required to decode the data. The incoming *pvNotification* pointer is converted to an HTTP_FILTER_LOG pointer on line 3; the pointer is then used to access the data that is to be written to the log.

The *wsprintf()* function is used to create formatted strings containing multiple fields of data on lines 5 and 11; these lines are then sent to the trace window on lines 6 and 12.

Running the Filter

The filter described in this section can be used to see all of the notification events as they are generated by the server. To run the trace output filter and see the activity reported in the debugger output window, do the following:

1. Copy the source code for the project to your computer and perform a debug build.

2. Make sure the World Wide Web publishing service is stopped via the Internet Service Manager.

3. Update the Registry parameter HKEY_LOCAL_MACHINE\CurrentControlSet \Services\W3Svc\Parameters\Filter DLLs to contain the name of this filter ("DemoFilter.dll').

4. Update the debug settings for the project so the executable specified is your installation of inetinfo.exe, and the argument string is -eW3Svc.

5. Start the debugger.

6. Start a web browser and send a request to your server.

As the filter runs, each notification is reported in the debugger output window.

Figure 7.3

The sample filter running in the debugger.

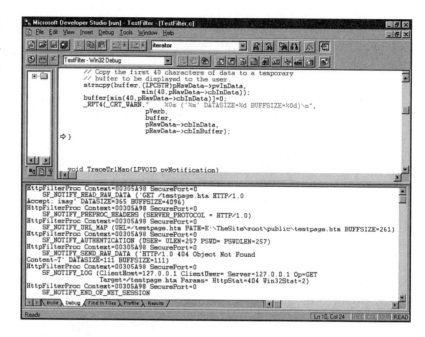

Understanding Filter Output

This section of the chapter shows the data from a sample run of the filter. The data has been reformatted slightly to fit the constraints of the book, and the repeated *HttpFilterProc* headers have been removed to improve readability. This debugger trace output shows the activity that results from a single request from an HTML document named testpage.htm.

LISTING 7.9—SAMPLE TRACE OUTPUT

```
01.GetFilterVersion
02.   ServerFilterVersion=20000
03.
04.HttpFilterProc Context=00305A98 SecurePort=0
05.   SF_NOTIFY_READ_RAW_DATA
06.   ('GET /testpage.htm HTTP/1.0\r\nAccept: imag' DATASIZE=365
➥BUFFSIZE=4096)
07.   SF_NOTIFY_PREPROC_HEADERS
08.   (SERVER_PROTOCOL = HTTP/1.0)
09.   SF_NOTIFY_URL_MAP
10.   (URL=/testpage.htm PATH=c:\inetsrv\wwwroot\testpage.htm BUFFSIZE=261)
11.   SF_NOTIFY_AUTHENTICATION
```

```
12.    (USER= USERLEN=257 PASSWORD= PSWDLEN=257)
13.  SF_NOTIFY_SEND_RAW_DATA
14.    ('HTTP/1.0 200 OK\r\nServer: Microsoft-IIS/2' DATASIZE=222 BUFFSIZE=222)
15.  SF_NOTIFY_SEND_RAW_DATA
16.    ('<!DOCTYPE HTML PUBLIC "-//IETF//DTD HTML' DATASIZE=1178 BUFFSIZE=1178)
17.  SF_NOTIFY_LOG
18.    (ClientHost=127.0.0.1 ClientUser= Server=127.0.0.1 Op=GET
19.     Target=/testpage.htm Params= HttpStat=200 Win32Stat=0)
20.  SF_NOTIFY_END_OF_NET_SESSION
```

This example shows the data that results from a simple retrieval of a single HTML page with no embedded objects. The page is also available without any authentication.

First, the *GetFilterVersion ()* is called and the filter initialized. This is shown in lines 1 and 2. As the *GetFilterVersion()* function is called, it outputs the server's version of the ISAPI filter interface.

The first step in processing the actual request is the receipt of the incoming request. The request can be seen during the SF_NOTIFY_READ_RAW request, when the actual data is read from the network. This is shown on lines 5 and 6. As you can see, this is a simple GET request.

Before conducting further processing, the HTTP server extracts and preprocesses the request headers and calls the *HttpFilterProc()* function with the SD_NOTIFY_PREPROC_HEADERS notification code. In this case, the function simply displays the version number from the GET request; this can be seen on lines 7 and 8.

After headers have been processed, the server maps the incoming URL to a physical file. Next, the server calls the filter function with the SF_NOTIFY_URL_MAP code and gives the filter the opportunity to override the standard mapping. In this case, the filter simply reports the mapping performed by the server.

After the URL has been mapped to a file, the server calls the authentication routine to allow the filter to make any changes required there. This is an anonymous request, so the user name and password fields are empty this can be seen on line 11.

The server now has the physical file to be used to satisfy the request and the user ID and password to be used to validate the client's right to access that file. The server attempts to retrieve the file. If the request requires processing from an extension, the request will be handed off to the extension or script for processing at this time.

After the file is retrieved or the executable items are processed, data is sent to the remote user. The data being transmitted can be seen in this output on lines 13 to 16, on two successive calls to *HttpFilterProc()* for the SF_NOTIFY_SEND_RAW_DATA notification code. In general, the first call contains the HTTP protocol headers, the second contains HTML data that constitutes the response.

After all other processing is complete, the process becomes complete by writing the results to the log. The filter is called on the SF_NOTIFY_LOG notification code and has the opportunity to replace any of the data prior to its being sent to the log. In this case, the data is simply reported to the debug window; this is shown on lines 17–19 of the output.

If this request were being processed by an ISAPI 3.0 server, the *HttpFilterProc()* function would now be called for the new SF_NOTIFY_END_OF_REQUEST notification code. This would notify the filter that the processing for this particular request is complete.

In this example, the client browser was closed immediately after receipt of the desired web page. This ended the network session, causing the server to report the SF_NOTIFY_END_OF_NET_SESSION to the filter. This notification would not have been sent at this time if the browser windows had remained open, because the browser in question and the server each support the "keep-alive" connection option.

MFC Filter Support

The filter presented earlier in this chapter was implemented in C, and worked with the bare ISAPI interfaces. There is an alternative to this: MFC provides classes designed to support the ISAPI filter developer. These classes allow the C++ developer to work at a slightly higher level of abstraction, and avoid some of the details of a normal ISAPI module written in C. The functions MFC provides for the filter developer are:

♦ **CHttpFilter:** base class for filter implementations

♦ **CHttpFilterContext:** a class encapsulating the HTTP_FILTER_PROC structure

The MFC filter mechanisms are much simpler than those provided for server extensions; they do not have a mechanism analogous to PARSEMAPs because there is no need for them. This simplicity is an advantage: because it provides a very thin wrapper around the normal C filter model, it does nothing to get in your way.

Visual C++ 4.x's ISAPI wizard can be used to produce filters. It will prompt for the name of the filter and the set of notifications to be handled by the filter. It will then use this data to generate a correct *GetFilterVersion()* for the filter and a set of virtual function overrides to handle each of the indicated notifications.

CHttpFilter

A filter implemented in MFC will implement a class descending from CHttpFilter:

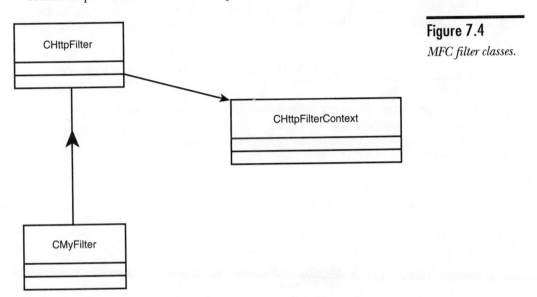

Figure 7.4

MFC filter classes.

The CHttpFilter class converts the two standard entry points for the DLL into virtual functions and handles some parameter mapping to make life more convenient. In your filter extension, you will simply override the virtual functions corresponding to the notifications your filter will handle.

Visual C++ 4.2 provides a wizard that makes this painless; if you generate a filter with the ISAPI wizard, the filter will generate the skeleton of the class for you. This includes a correctly generated *GetFilterVersion()* implementation and virtual function definitions for each handled notification.

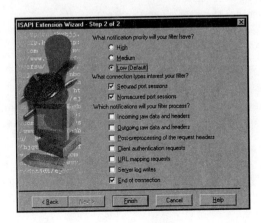

Figure 7.5

The ISAPI wizard in action.

An MFC-based GetFilterVersion() Function

In the MFC filter model, *GetFilterVersion()* is a virtual function implemented in the CHttpFilter class. An acceptable basic implementation is generated for you by the ISAPI wizard. The generated function looks something like the code in listing 7.10:

LISTING 7.10—CMFCSAMPFILTER::GETFILTERVERSION

```
01.BOOL
02.CMFCSampFilter::GetFilterVersion(PHTTP_FILTER_VERSION pVer)
03.{
04. // Call default implementation for initialization
05. CHttpFilter::GetFilterVersion(pVer);
06.
07. // Clear the flags set by base class
08. pVer->dwFlags &= ~SF_NOTIFY_ORDER_MASK;
09.
10. // Set the flags we are interested in
11. pVer->dwFlags |= SF_NOTIFY_ORDER_LOW |
12.                  SF_NOTIFY_SECURE_PORT |
13.                  SF_NOTIFY_NONSECURE_PORT |
14.                  SF_NOTIFY_LOG |
15.                  SF_NOTIFY_AUTHENTICATION |
16.                  SF_NOTIFY_PREPROC_HEADERS |
17.                  SF_NOTIFY_READ_RAW_DATA |
18.                  SF_NOTIFY_SEND_RAW_DATA |
19.                  SF_NOTIFY_URL_MAP |
20.                  SF_NOTIFY_END_OF_NET_SESSION;
21.
22. // Load description string
23. TCHAR sz[SF_MAX_FILTER_DESC_LEN+1];
24. ISAPIVERIFY(::LoadString(AfxGetResourceHandle(),
25.          IDS_FILTER, sz, SF_MAX_FILTER_DESC_LEN));
26. _tcscpy(pVer->lpszFilterDesc, sz);
27. return TRUE;
28.}
```

The function is quite similar to that implemented in the sample C extension, with the exception of the module name being loaded from a resource on line 24.

It is interesting to note that a *GetFilterVersion()* generated by Visual C++ 4.1 does not follow Microsoft's recommendation for the use of the SF_NOTIFY_ORDER_DEFAULT constant when setting the filter's priority. If you select the default priority from the ISAPI wizard, it will generate code that specifies SF_NOTIFY_ORDER_LOW;

this can be seen on line 11. The two values are equivalent at this time, so this does not actually do any harm and will only be a problem if the default priority level changes in the future.

Event-Handling Virtual Functions

In the MFC filter model, the standard ISAPI HttpFilterProc() function is provided by MFC. This function finds your CHttpFilter-derived object, and calls its HttpFilterProc member function. The HttpFilterProc member function then translates the incoming notifications into calls to virtual functions, such as *OnLog()* or *OnAuthentication()*. An MFC filter implements its behavior by overriding one or more of these functions.

Functions for Specific Events

In general, each notification type supported by ISAPI is represented by a virtual function. The functions implemented as of Visual C++ 4.2 are as follows:

TABLE 7.2
The Mapping of Notification Codes to Virtual Functions

Notification Type Code	CHttpFilter member
SF_NOTIFY_AUTHENTICATION	OnAuthentication
SF_NOTIFY_END_OF_NET_SESSION	OnEndOfNetSession
SF_NOTIFY_LOG	OnLog
SF_NOTIFY_PREPROC_HEADERS	OnPreprocHeaders
SF_NOTIFY_READ_RAW_DATA	OnReadRawData
SF_NOTIFY_SEND_RAW_DATA	OnSendRawData
SF_NOTIFY_URL_MAP	OnUrlMap

Each of these functions takes a pointer to a filter context as its first parameter. Any notifications with matching notification structures will also receive a second parameter containing a pointer to that structure.

Two of the notifications are not wrapped with these member functions as of Visual C++ 4.2:

HTTP_FILTER_ACCESS_DENIED

SF_NOTIFY_END_OF_REQUEST

The MFC classes can be easily extended to support these events, but doing so requires changes to the *CHttpFilterProc::HttpFilterProc* function, or an override of this function in a derived class. An example of this process is illustrated in the next section, "Overriding the CHttpFilterProc::HttpFilterProc() Function".

 The ISAPI wizard in Visual C++ 4.2 will fail to generate the OnLog() function override for SF_NOTIFY_LOG events. It will, however, correctly include the override in the assignment to the HTTP_VERSION_FILTER *dwFlags* attribute in the generated *GetFilterVersion()* function.

Overriding the CHttpFilterProc::HttpFilterProc() Function

This function is the point that receives the incoming notifications. The default implementation of the function is a simple switch statement: it determines which function should be called, based on the notification code, and casts the notification structure pointer to the correct type, based on that code.

The only time overriding this function is particularly worthwhile is when a filter needs to handle notifications added to ISAPI that are not yet directly supported by MFC via virtual functions. This can be done quite simply, as follows:

LISTING 7.11—AN OVERRIDEN CHTTPFILTERPROC::HTTPFILTERPROC()

```
01.DWORD CHttpFilterExt::HttpFilterProc(PHTTP_FILTER_CONTEXT pfc,
02.                                 DWORD dwNotificationType,
03.                                 LPVOID pvNotification)
04.{
05.    DWORD dwRet = SF_STATUS_REQ_NEXT_NOTIFICATION;
06.    CHttpFilterContext callCtxt(pfc);
07.
08.    switch (dwNotificationType)
09.    {
10.    case SF_NOTIFY_ACCESS_DENIED:
11.        dwRet = OnAccessDenied(&callCtxt,
12.                            (PHTTP_FILTER_ACCESS_DENIED) pvNotification);
13.        break;
14.    case SF_NOTIFY_END_OF_NET_REQUEST:
15.        dwRet = OnEndOfNetRequest(&callCtxt);
16.        break;
17.    default:
18.        dwRet = CHttpFilter::HttpFilterProc(pfc,dwNotificationType,
19.                                    pvNotification);
```

```
20.        break;
21.    }
22.    return dwRet;
23.}
```

The function handles the two notifications added since ISAPI 1.0 and defers the others to the base class implementation.

The switch statement on lines 8–21 is responsible for selecting the correct behavior based on the notification code received from the server. The case on lines 10-12 handles the new SF_NOTIFY_ACCESS_DENIED notification, and dispatches control to a virtual function to handle the behavior. This pattern is repeated on lines 14–16 for the SF_NOTIFY_END_OF_NET_REQUEST code.

All other cases are handled by the normal MFC supplied version of this function, so on line 18, the base class implementation of *HttpFilterProc()* is called to all other cases via the default clause of the case statement.

> **Note**
>
> As new versions of Visual C++ are released, you should find that the default MFC implementation of the CHttpFilter::HttpFilterProc() function will be expanded to support any new notifications added to ISAPI. If you're using a version of Visual C++ more recent than 4.2, check to see if the codes you need are directly supported.
>
> You should expect to see this pattern repeated over time; new functionality will be introduced into the ISAPI server, and will initially require extra work to allow its use. Subsequent versions of Visual C++ will then be expanded to provide support for the new functions via the MFC wrappers.

CHttpFilterContext Class

The CHttpFilterContext class wraps a pointer to an HTTP_FILTER_CONTEXT. The MFC class provides member functions for each of the function pointers in the HTTP_FILTER_CONTEXT structure. These functions don't provide any capabilities beyond those provided by the function pointer, but simply allow the functions to be called more naturally.

The class also provides access to the underlying HTTP_FILTER_CONTEXT structure. At this point, the HTTP_FILTER_ CONTEXT pointer is generally only used as a parameter to other ISAPI functions and for access to the *fIsSecurePort* attribute. Access to the structure is also provided as a safety valve; if the ISAPI HTTP_FILTER_ CONTEXT is revised between revisions of the MFC support classes, the structure might be manipulated directly to access any added data or functionality.

Summary

Filters can be valuable tools for extending an ISAPI-compliant server; Microsoft has demonstrated this by using filters to implement Active Server Scripting, SSL support, and more. Filters provide a mechanism for altering the behavior of the HTTP server at a fundamental level, allowing your code to monitor and alter the way incoming requests are handled.

Unfortunately, this power comes with a price. Badly written ISAPI filters can wreak havoc with the operation of the server, causing it to run slowly or not at all. It is critical that filters be written to handle multiple simultaneous requests and multiple threads. Each filter must execute as quickly as possible, because additional filters might be fired for every incoming HTTP request.

CHAPTER 8

Enhancing IIS Logging with Filters

T he Microsoft IIS (Internet Information Server) logs enable the webmaster or web developer to log activity on the web site to text files or databases with an ODBC interface. These logs can be extremely useful for a variety of tasks, including site usage analysis, troubleshooting, and load management.

The IIS server records a reasonable variety of useful information; the standard logs are enough to tell you what machines or users are accessing your system, what they are looking at, and what they are doing. Of course, the standard logs do not record everything you might want to know: they are designed to record a workable subset of the data, not everything available.

Rather than designing the server to log everything you might need, Microsoft took the reasonable approach of providing a basic set of information and a mechanism for extending the logs. As you might expect, this mechanism is provided through ISAPI filters.

This chapter will discuss the behavior of the standard log mechanism and describe how to augment or enhance the logs. The chapter will also include a sample MFC-based filter for adding additional fields to the existing log.

The IIS Log

Before altering the operation of the existing IIS log system, it is important to understand how the system works. The IIS log mechanism stores data for more than the HTTP service; it contains information for the FTP and GOPHER services as well. The basic set of information contained in the log is standardized across all three services. The specific set of information contained in the log varies in relation to the place the log data will be stored and the specific format selected.

IIS supports two major options for log output: text files and ODBC databases. Each will be discussed in more detail in the following sections.

Logging to Text Files

The IIS server can be configured to log its operations to a series of text files on the server. These files can take on one of two possible formats: Microsoft IIS's own proprietary format or the more common NCSA log file format.

The Microsoft IIS format (now referred to as the "Standard" format in IIS dialog boxes) contains a superset of the information available in the older NCSA format; it also uses a more convenient file layout. The NCSA format is basically provided for compatibility with older web site management tools, including a variety of public-domain or shareware packages that report on various aspects of web site activity. These are discussed in more detail later in the chapter.

The server can be configured to create new files every day, week, month, or when the size exceeds a user-configured maximum size. The data in the active log file will not be quite up-to-the-minute: IIS buffers data in memory and writes it in batches to improve performance.

 Note Microsoft provides a tool named **convlog** to convert logs from the standard IIS format to the NCSA format, so the choice between the two formats doesn't need to be irrevocable. The tool is included with recent releases of IIS.

IIS Standard Log Files

The standard IIS log file format is a simple CSV (comma separated value) file. It contains a single line of data for each event, with comma-delimited fields containing the data. The set of fields stored in the log is as follows:

♦ **Client IP Address:** the address of the remote client computer, in dotted number form, i.e. "207.207.197.67".

◆ **Client Username:** contains the name of the user requesting the service, or "-". Log entries for HTTP Service (shown as W3SVC) will only contain a username for authenticated remote users.

◆ **Date**

◆ **Time**

◆ **Service Name:** currently one of the following—W3SVC, MSFTPSVC, or GOPHERSVC.

◆ **Computer Name:** the computer name for the server handling the request.

◆ **Server IP Address:** the IP address of the server.

◆ **Elapsed Time:** the time required to complete processing for the request, expressed in milliseconds.

◆ **Bytes Received:** number of bytes received by the server for this request.

◆ **Bytes Sent:** number of bytes transmitted to answer the request.

◆ **Service Status Code:** the service-specific status code. For the HTTP service, this will contain a standard HTTP status code.

◆ **Windows NT Status Code:** the WIN32 status code resulting from handling the request. This will only be a non-zero value if an error occurs during processing.

◆ **Operation Name:** the operation requested by the remote client. For the W3SVC, this will generally be GET or POST.

◆ **Target:** the target of the operation; frequently the URL of the requested resource.

◆ **Parameters:** optional parameters required for the operation. For instance, requests related to server-side imagemaps will have the x and y coordinates of the mouse-click in this field.

A sample record from an IIS 2.0 server is shown below:

```
127.0.0.1, -, 12/18/96, 11:51:16, W3SVC, KCHOME, 127.0.0.1,
➡ 812, 487, 123, 401, 5, GET, /secure/custserv/OrderStatus.html, -,
```

The simple structure of the IIS log file format makes it quite simple to parse, and extend with extra data. It can also be imported into common business tools such as Microsoft Access or Excel for analysis and reporting.

Since this log file format carries more information than the NCSA files (described in the next section), and is easier to parse, it is usually the best choice for logging II activity.

NCSA Log Files

NCSA log files are based on a format developed by the National Center for Supercomputing Applications. The format has been in use for some time and is supported by many different web servers and log analysis tools. The biggest reason to consider the NCSA format is to allow the use of these tools.

The NCSA file format is actually much less expressive than the Microsoft IIS format. It contains fewer fields of information and is somewhat more complex to parse. A sample record in NCSA format is shown in the following lines of code:

```
127.0.0.1 - - [29/Dec/1996:23:15:26 +0000]
➥ "GET /images/Warehouse.gif HTTP/1.0" 200 2327
```

In general, there are only two real reasons to use the NCSA format for logging server activity: Compatibility with existing site-management tools, and compatibility with logs generated by other web servers.

There are many third party tools available that support the NCSA format for log files. Since the IIS server does not come with any tools for analyzing the usage of a site over time, this can be a significant consideration. The data in the logs is not terribly useful without tools to analyze and manage it. Some tools are now available that read IIS standard log files, but far more are available for the NCSA format.

Many web sites are distributed over several physical computers. At some sites, some of the computers may be running HTTP servers other than IIS; these are unlikely to support the standard IIS log file format. The NCSA file format is something of a defacto standard, so it is supported by many web servers. This format may serve a common-denominator across the server in the site, allowing the logs from the various machines to be consolidated.

If the compatibility with specific third-party reporting tools is important to you, or you need to preserve a common format across the machines in a multi-computer site, the NCSA file may be appropriate. If these considerations are not a factor for your site, it will probably be better to use the IIS file format.

Logging to a Database

IIS can log data into any database with an ODBC interface that can be driven from a system DSN (data source name). To configure IIS to log to a database, you'll need to supply the DSN name, a table name, and a username and password for access to the database.

IIS also requires that the database table used to capture the data match a particular design, or schema. A Microsoft SQLServer script that creates a table with the required schema is shown in listing 8.1:

LISTING 8.1—A SQLSERVER CREATE TABLE STATEMENT FOR IIS DATABASE LOGGING

```
01.CREATE TABLE dbo.IISLog
02.(
03.    ClientHost varchar (255) NOT NULL ,
04.    username varchar (255) NOT NULL ,
05.    LogTime datetime NOT NULL ,
06.    service varchar (255) NOT NULL ,
07.    machine varchar (255) NOT NULL ,
08.    serverip varchar (50) NOT NULL ,
09.    processingtime int NOT NULL ,
10.    bytesrecvd int NOT NULL ,
11.    bytessent int NOT NULL ,
12.    servicestatus int NOT NULL ,
13.    win32status int NOT NULL ,
14.    operation varchar (255) NOT NULL ,
15.    target varchar (255) NOT NULL ,
16.    parameters varchar (255) NOT NULL ,
17.)
```

This matches the list of fields shown for standard log files, with one minor exception—the date and time fields are combined into a single *datetime* field.

Logging to the database has some advantages; for example, the data is immediately available for analysis and reporting. On the other hand, logging to the database incurs the overhead of the database engine. The plusses and minuses of hosting the log in the database are discussed in more detail in the next section of this chapter.

Deciding Where and How to Store the Data

IIS gives you a number of options for storing log file data, but at some point you need to decide whether to use database logging, NCSA text files, or IIS log files.

The biggest reason to consider a database is convenience. The data will be available immediately, in a form that can be analyzed and reported by using any number of database reporting tools. This flexibility comes with a price: IIS will become constrained by the throughput of the database engine. Remember, IIS will log all requests to the log: if the log runs slowly, it will impact the performance of the server as a whole. In addition, if the log is stored in the same database as application data, the presence of this data can affect the performance of the site's application.

Text files do not suffer from this problem, as the server buffers data on its way to the log, yielding quite good performance. The text file format might be less convenient for manipulating and managing large amounts of historical data, but loading the data into a database for analysis and long-term storage is a simple process. The IIS format is quite good for this strategy; its comma-delimited fields are ideal for loading the data into a database for later use. The format maximizes the available data and combines it with good performance characteristics and convenient formatting for parsing and reporting.

The NCSA format really only has one advantage: the availability of a large number of third-party utilities designed to facilitate the analysis of these files. Consider looking for tools that support IIS, or use the Microsoft-supplied **convlog** facility to convert the files from IIS log file format to NCSA format.

Filtering Log Events

Although the standard IIS logs are adequate for many needs, they don't always capture all the information you might want or need to see. The designers of IIS were forced to balance the objective of truly comprehensive logging against that of delivering a high-performance web server. Fortunately, there is a mechanism to enable the site developer to change the standard logging behavior by handling the SF_NOTIFY_ ON_LOG notification in an ISAPI filter and altering the data before it is written to the log.

Reasons to Filter Log Events

There are two basic reasons to filter log notification events:

◆ Adding new field to the log.

◆ Modifying or replacing fields written to the log.

There are a number fields that are good candidates for addition to the log. These fields are not as universally applicable as those included in the standard logs, but are often useful in specific cases. They include:

◆ **HTTP_USER_AGENT:** the user agent string can be used to identify the browsers customers are using to visit your web site. This information can be invaluable in deciding which of the latest browser enhancements your site should use. The cross platform, browser independent nature of web based applications is often more theoretical than practical; the newest browser features tend to be vendor specific.

◆ **HTTP_REFERER:** this field indicates the source of the link that was traversed to retrieve the current target. If the current target is an HTML file, this field will contain the URL of the page that contained the link used to retrieve this file. If the target is an embedded graphic or other object, it should contain the name of the host page. The contents of this field are up to the client's browser, so your results may differ somewhat; some browsers do not supply this information.

◆ **UNMAPPED_REMOTE_USER:** this field contains the name of a remote user, prior to any mapping performed by authentication filters. This can be very useful on those sites that use authentication filter; the filter may map many input user names to a single NT username for convenience of administration or security. The standard log mechanism will supply the mapped name; this will allow the log to reflect the name entered by the user.

Other fields can be used; these are simply three of the more commonly used pieces of information.

Adding New Fields to the Log

One of the most common reasons to modify the log is to add additional fields of information not usually tracked by IIS. Unfortunately, IIS does not provide a standard mechanism for adding new fields to the log. The set of fields in the log notification structure is fixed; there is no way to expand the structure.

Fortunately, that is not the end of the story. While there is no way to add new fields to the notification structure, it is possible to get new information into the logs. The answer lies in packing the additional data into an existing field in such a way as to be able to extract it in the future for reporting and analysis. There are techniques that make this reasonably straightforward, particularly for the standard IIS text or database log formats.

Hosting New Fields in the IIS Text Log

The standard IIS log text file format is the simplest to work with when packing new fields into the log. The files are simple CSV (command separated value) files; each of the fields in the log notification structure are sent to the log delimited by commas. The effect of adding a new field to the log can be achieved by adding the value into an existing field, and separating the new data from the existing content with a comma. When the data is written to the log, it will appear to be a new, independent field. This technique will be demonstrated in a sample log filter later in the chapter.

There are some caveats to keep in mind when using this technique:

- The maximum length of any individual field in the notification structure is 256 bytes. All of the virtual fields packed into any physical field in the structure must total no more than 255 characters of data.

- These files depend on commas to delimit the fields within each record. In order to make it practical to parse these records, you should avoid outputting any fields containing commas. If the field contains commas when the value is obtained from the environment or the server, the filter should replace the comma with some other neutral character.

Hosting New Fields when Logging to a Database

Hosting new fields in the database is somewhat more complicated than doing so in a text file. Most of the constraints affecting the standard IIS text file format still apply; the notification structure remains the same. The problem is further complicated by the fact that the IIS server insists that the database table used to hold the log data comply with a particular schema.

With a little work, it is possible to apply the same technique used with the standard text log files; the data can be mapped into existing fields, and delimited with commas. This will allow the filter to combine multiple logical fields of data into a single field in the database record inserted by the filter in a way that can be interpreted later.

In order to use the data in these compound fields, you have two basic options available:

- If the database that will be hosting the log supports trigger, it is possible to write an insert trigger that will extract the additional data added to the field and move it to a new column in the table. For information on this technique, see the documentation for your database server.

- It is fairly simple to write a SQL update statement that will extract the data compound data from one field and use it to update several others. This can be automated if your system supports a scheduler, such as SQL Server's SQL Executive.

 Some books have claimed that additional fields can be added to the database table by simply adding additional comma-separated values to existing fields as described above, and then adding matching columns to the database table. According to these texts, IIS will deposit the additional comma-delimited fields into additional columns in the table *automatically*. This is not the case under IIS 2.0 or 3.0 and the Microsoft SQL Server.

Hosting New Fields in an NCSA Text File

The techniques described for use with IIS standard text files may be used with NCSA text files, but they are generally much less useful in this context. There are several things to keep in mind when considering extensions to the NCSA log format:

◆ The NCSA file format is not comma delimited. It is much harder to place additional information into the file in a way that it can be reliably retrieved to later use.

◆ The only real reason to use this file format is for compatibility with the format used by other servers, or supported by third-party tools. If file format is modified to include multiple logical fields within physical field in the file, it will defeat the purpose of using this format in the first place.

As a general rule, if the basic NCSA format does not meet your requirements, shift to the standard IIS format before adding additional fields via a filter. More fields will be supplied without a filter, and the format will lend itself to extension via a filter if it is necessary to do so.

Note There is a way to log entirely new data: by writing it to an additional external data store. There is nothing to prevent your filter from opening another file, database connect, or other storage mechanism. This generally isn't very useful, because it also requires the filter to provide management of that store. The only case where I have seen it used is in a filter that maintained an external store and logged the number of times particular browsers hit the site. The filter maintained a single record per browser, with fields containing the user agent and a hit count. Space management wasn't a problem, because the total number of different browsers hitting the site was manageable and there was no need to track individual hits, only the gross aggregate number.

Modifying Existing Log Fields

Modifications to the existing IIS fields are quite straightforward; the filter can change the data to whatever is necessary. This is useful when the filter has access to more appropriate sources of information for a field than are normally used by the server.

The best example of modifying or replacing an existing field would be the use the of the UNMAPPED_REMOTE_USER value in place of, or in addition to the standard remote user field. If a site uses an authentication filter to re-map usernames and passwords after submission by the user, it will generally want to use the UNMAPPED_REMOTE_USER field to log the original user name.

There are two limitations to the filter's availability to replace or modify existing field data:

◆ String fields cannot be modified in place. To change a string field of the NOTIFY_LOG structure, replace the existing pointer with a pointer to the updated string.

◆ String lengths should be kept to 255 characters or fewer if database logging will be used.

A Simple Log Filter

This section of the chapter describes the implementation of a simple ISAPI log filter. The filter will record the user agent and referrer fields.

The user agent field contains the browser identification stream reported by remote clients when they request resources from your site. This information is available with every request and can be used to deliver pages optimized for particular browsers. This can be useful information to track; most web sites have limited resources and can use this information to select the browsers to support and the browser features to use.

Many browsers supply the referrer field; it indicates the URL of the page that contained the reference to the page being retrieved. This information can be useful for understanding the path users are taking through a web site. It can also be used to understand how users are finding your site and what links they are using to navigate to it; this is useful for evaluating the effectiveness of advertising or reciprocal links with another site.

Designing the ISAPI Log Filter

This filter will be implemented, using the MFC filter support classes. Writing a filter by using MFC is simply a matter of deriving a class from *CHttpFilter* and implementing the *GetFilterVersion( )* and *OnLog( )* functions.

The only design issue that remains is that of data storage. As described earlier, there is no way to add a truly new field to the ISAPI log; the structure only contains a fixed number of fields, and there is no way to add others. This means the filter must pack the data into existing fields.

In this filter, the two fields will be packed into the *params* field. By default, the *params* field contains the query string of a form-processing GET request, or coordinates selected by a user in conjunction with a server-side image map. The user agent and referrer fields will be prepended to the field, delimited by commas. This preserves the structure of an IIS-formatted text log file and does no harm for database logging. See the section entitled "Adding New Fields to the Log" for more information on this technique.

The data is prepended, rather than appended, because some of the data stored in the parameter field by the IIS server might contain a comma. This is particularly true for entries corresponding to server-side imagemap requests, which contain the X and Y coordinates of the cursor at the time the map was clicked, separated by a comma. Adding these strings to the beginning enables you to find them by extracting the first two comma-delimited values from this field.

If the log is being stored in the database, the parameters column contains the user agent, referrer, and parameters values. If the data is being stored in an NCSA-formatted log, these appear as if they are part of the query string. This makes the data difficult to parse; if you are using NCSA log files, it might be advisable to store the data in some other field.

Implementing CExtraDataFilter::GetFilterVersion()

The *GetFilterVersion()* function can be implemented by the ISAPI wizard for this function. The significant behavior here is setting up the version structure correctly to tell the server the filter is interested in receiving notifications of log events.

The code for this function is shown in listing 8.2.

LISTING 8.2—THE IMPLEMENTATION OF CEXTRADATAFILTER::GETFILTERVERSION

```
01.BOOL
02.CExtraDataFilter::GetFilterVersion(PHTTP_FILTER_VERSION pVer)
03.{
04.    // Call default implementation for initialization
05.    CHttpFilter::GetFilterVersion(pVer);
06.
07.    // Clear the flags set by base class
08.    pVer->dwFlags &= ~SF_NOTIFY_ORDER_MASK;
09.
10.    // Set the flags we are interested in
11.    pVer->dwFlags |= SF_NOTIFY_ORDER_LOW |
12.                     SF_NOTIFY_SECURE_PORT |
13.                     SF_NOTIFY_NONSECURE_PORT |
14.                     SF_NOTIFY_LOG ;
15.
```

continues

LISTING 8.2—THE IMPLEMENTATION OF
CEXTRADATAFILTER::GETFILTERVERSION, CONTINUED

```
16.     // Load description string
17.     TCHAR sz[SF_MAX_FILTER_DESC_LEN+1];
18.     ISAPIVERIFY(::LoadString(AfxGetResourceHandle(),
19.            IDS_FILTER, sz, SF_MAX_FILTER_DESC_LEN));
20.     _tcscpy(pVer->lpszFilterDesc, sz);
21.
22.     return TRUE;
23.}
```

The version structure's *dwFlags* attribute is set in lines 11–14: it indicates that the filter
would like to be inserted into the filter chain at low priority and receive events for
both secured and nonsecured connections when these connections are ready to log
data.

Handling Log Notifications with the OnLog() Function

The active work of the filter is implemented in the *OnLog()* function; it will be called
whenever the filter receives an SF_NOTIFY_LOG event. The implementation of the
function is show in listing 8.3.

LISTING 8.3—THE IMPLEMENTATION
OF CEXTRADATAFILTER::ONLOG

```
01.static const char szSpacer[] = ", ";
02.static const char szEmptyVal[] = "-";
03.static const char szHttpUserAgent[] = "HTTP_USER_AGENT";
04.static const char szHttpRefer[] = "HTTP_REFERER";
05.
06.
07.DWORD
08.CExtraDataFilter::OnLog(CHttpFilterContext* pfc,
09.                        PHTTP_FILTER_LOG    pLog)
10.{
11.     CString outputString;
12.     char    buff[512];
13.
14.     // Get the user agent.  If it's present, move it to the
15.     // output buffer. If not present, use a "-"
16.     DWORD buffSize = sizeof(buffer);
17.     if (pfc->GetServerVariable( szHttpUserAgent,buff,&buffSize))
18.         outputString+=buffer;
19.     else
```

```
20.        outputString+=szEmptyVal;
21.
22.    // insert a ", " separator
23.    outputString+=szSpacer;
24.
25.    // Get the referrer.  if it's present, move it to the output
26.    // buffer. If not present, use a "-"
27.    buffSize = sizeof(buffer);
28.    if (pfc->GetServerVariable( szHttpRefer, buffer, &buffSize))
29.        outputString+=buffer;
30.    else
31.        outputString+=szEmptyVal;
32.
33.    // insert a ", " separator
34.    outputString+= szSpacer;
35.
36.    // add back whatever was in the parameter string.
37.    outputString+= (LPCSTR)pLog->pszParameters;
38.
39.    // figure out how long the buffer is, and AllocMem
40.    // a buffer to hold that much data
41.    DWORD newParamLen = outputString.GetLength()+1;
42.    LPSTR pParamBuffer = (LPSTR)(pfc->AllocMem(newParamLen,01));
43.
44.    // copy the data to the new output buffer
45.    lstrcpy(pParamBuffer,outputString);
46.
47.    // replace the param string with the new one
48.    pLog->pszParameters = pParamBuffer;
49.
50.    return CHttpFilter::OnLog(pfc, pLog);
51.}
```

In lines 1–4, a number of string constants are defined for use in the actual function. These are considered safe because they are read-only constants; non-constant static variables would be a problem in multithreaded code.

In lines 11 and 12, working storage is allocated on the stack for the processing required for each call. The CString *outputString* will be used to accumulate the new value for the parameter attribute. The character array *buffer* will be used to hold the result of calls to *GetServerVariable( )*.

Lines 14–20 are used to retrieve the user agent variable. If the string can be retrieved from the server, it is appended to the output string. If it is not available, a "-" is added instead; this is in keeping with IIS's pattern of using the "-" as a placeholder for missing data. A comma and space are then appended to the string, and the process is repeated for the HTTP_REFERER variable in lines 25–34.

After this processing is complete, the original value of the parameter field is appended to the end of the accumulated output string. This prevents the loss of this value.

Because the filter is not allowed to alter any of the string fields in the HTTP_FILTER_LOG structure directly, it needs to allocate a new buffer to hold the data. Because the data will be needed for a somewhat indeterminate time period, the *AllocMem( )* function is used to allocate memory that will be freed at the end of the network session. In IIS 3.0, it might be preferable to manage a pool of static buffers with SF_NOTIF_END_OF_REQUEST code, but for IIS 2.0, it is much simpler to use this method.

In lines 44–48, the accumulated output string is copied to the new buffer and the *pLog->pszParameters* pointer is updated to point to it. There is no need to free the memory previously pointed to by this attribute; it belongs to the IIS server and will clean up the data.

Finally, in line 50, the function calls the base class implementation of *OnLog( )*; this simply returns the SF_NOTIFY_NEXT_FILTER code.

Using Logging Filters Effectively

When you write logging filters, there are a number of things you should do and a number of things you should not do. Remember a log filter is still a filter, and its performance can materially impact the performance of your server.

Avoiding Time-Consuming Operations

It is important to try to avoid time-consuming operations when implementing a filter. The log filter will be fired for every request processed by the server—even for requests that cannot be satisfied. The filter must avoid operations that add a great deal of overhead to each request.

A classic example of an operation *not* to add to a logging filter is translating client IP addresses to hostnames. The IIS typically populates the client name field of the log with the IP address of the remote client. Most users find hostnames more informative, so there is a desire to replace the IP address of the client with the name of the client machine. Unfortunately, a DNS (Domain Name Service) reverse lookup is required to translate the name, which can take a non-trivial amount of time, particularly on a high-performance web server. This potential for delay makes name translation a poor choice of operations to add to the *OnLog()* function. Unfortunately, an early example of a logging filter implemented exactly this behavior, creating the impression that this was a good idea—it isn't.

A related problem involves operations that might block for some time. A blocking operation is one that prevents the thread from continuing until it is complete. Network operations and other forms of synchronous input or output are often blocking operations; they will block the calling thread from continuing until the I/O request has been serviced. In some cases, this can take an indeterminate period of time; it is difficult to predict how long it may take for an external machine or device to respond to a request.

If an operation blocks during a log operation, the thread on which the function is called will also block. Although the server can spawn a number of new threads to deal with this situation, only a limited number of threads can be productively employed on the server.

The log filter must avoid operations that have the potential to block for indeterminate periods of time. When blocking operations are required, they should be invoked with timeouts, rather then blocking indefinitely until the desired operation is completed. The filter should be written to gracefully degrade if the resources it needs are not available in a timely fashion.

Use Offline Alternatives

An important thing to remember is that the logging filter does not need to do anything. A significant amount of analysis and processing can occur after the fact. The filter only needs to collect data that will not be available at a later time, such as the user agent or referrer; it does *not* need to collect the remote client hostname.

The remote client hostname is a good example of data that can be collected after the fact. Because the server log records the IP address of the remote computer, it's certainly possible to write a program to do the following:

◆ Read the log file

◆ Extract the IP address from each record

◆ Look up the matching host names by calling the DNS

◆ Add the client host name back to the log

This has the advantage of occurring outside the usual flow of request processing. The program can be run during light usage periods or on an entirely different computer.

The important point to remember is that the logging filter should only be used where it is necessary. If the cost of some set of processing can be deferred to a later time, it should be. The filter should only be used to collect data that will not be available after the fact, not to perform analysis or processing better deferred to offline programs.

Summary

Logging filters can be a useful addition to the set of tools available to your web site. These filters offer the opportunity to extend the IIS's log to collect additional information, but should be used with some care to avoid impacting the performance of the server.

CHAPTER 9

Redirecting Based on Client Browsers

This chapter describes techniques for implementing redirectors that are sensitive to the browser used by a client. Redirectors are units of code that redirect a request for one resource into a request for another, based on some information available to the server at the time the request is received. In this chapter, redirectors are used to translate user requests for web pages into equivilant requests for pages tuned to a particular browser. Redirectors are used in a number of other situations as well, including:

◆ **Handling pages that have moved:** by supplying the new location of a page that has moved, the redirector can make the relocation transparent to the client. This is useful when it's necessary to rearrange a site while preserving existing bookmarks.

◆ **Balancing load across servers:** redirectors can be used to distribute requests across multiple machines by altering the hostname specified in the request and issuing a redirection. This is a useful way to use multiple machines to implement a single "virtual" host.

◆ **Directing users to pages optimized for their browsers:** because a string identifying the remote browser travels with every incoming request, the server can take advantage of this to send the user pages designed to work well with the indicated browser.

This chapter discusses the implementation of a redirector based on the capabilities of the user's browser.

Why Redirect Based on the Client's Browser?

In today's world of ActiveX components, Java, JavaScript, VBScript, and plug-ins, it has become increasingly difficult to produce a leading-edge web site without producing some pages that are somewhat browser specific. This leaves the site developer with a choice: optimize the site for one set of browser technologies, or restrict the site to a lowest common denominator feature-set.

Leading Edge versus Lowest Common Denominator

Sites that implement the latest and greatest of technologies can be amazingly attractive, effective sites. Users of these sites can take advantage of all the new features supported by their browsers; this tends to make them appreciate these sites and the browser they selected for their excursion onto the web. Unfortunately, this restricts the optimum use of your site to one or two browsers, leaving a huge number of users unable to experience your site the way you intended. This tends to either eliminate these users from your site entirely or to make the site far less exciting for them.

Of course, a site can be implemented to avoid capabilities that aren't universal. By avoiding Java, JavaScript, plug-ins, stylesheets, and other new techniques, the webmaster can create a site that will work well with almost every browser. Unfortunately, the result can be somewhat stodgy or out of date. Users who've just downloaded the most recent beta of their favorite browser will probably prefer sites that exploit the latest and greatest features.

Sites that provide commercial services often need to take steps to ensure that the widest possible set of customers can use their site effectively. This is particularly true for sites engaged in business-to-business electronic commerce; corporate users tend to lag the rest of the market in the adoption of the latest and greatest in software.

One alternative is to implement multiple versions of some or all of the pages in the site. Although this involves more work, it enables site developers to avoid making an all-or-nothing decision: one version of the site can use leading-edge Internet tools and techniques, and another can be more conservative, appealing to a wider audience.

A simple application of tuning a site to accommodate different browsers can be seen in figures 9.1 and 9.2. Figure 9.1 shows a product catalog page optimized for the Microsoft or Netscape 3.0 browser. It takes advantage of table cell background colors and font control to make the product catalog page more attractive.

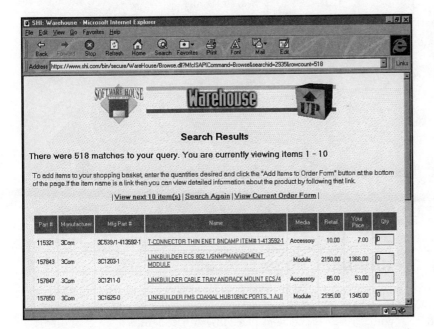

Figure 9.1

A product catalog tuned for the Microsoft Internet Explorer 3.0.

The same site caters to a large number of corporate users who have standardized on the Netscape Navigator 2.0 platform, and are not upgrading as quickly as one might like. The Netscape 2.0 product does not provide as fine a control over typefaces as more modern browsers, and does not support table cell background colors. Rather than force these users to live with pages that don't render correctly, the Software House web site provides pages tuned for this browser; this version of the catalog page is shown in figure 9.2.

Figure 9.2

*A product catalog
tuned for Netscape
Navigator 2.0.*

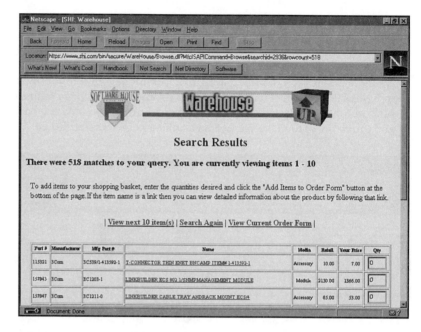

The process of selecting between these two versions of the site is done automatically, based on the identity of the remote user's browser.

Manual of Automatic Page Selection

A technique used on the opening page of many sites allows users to select between a version employing a certain feature versus one that does not. A good example would be the "Shocked" and "Non-Shocked" tags placed by web designers to control the use of the Macromedia Shockwave tool.

Unfortunately, this approach has its own limitations. Because it requires alternate versions of large portions of the site, care must be taken to duplicate pages with links to the modified portions of the site, in addition to the modified pages themselves. Moreover, some users will be confronted with their less-favored status; it is often clear to them that they are not getting the best version of the site. This can create either of two problems: users might choose to go to a different site where their browser is exploited, or they might make an incorrect decision based on a lack of knowledge about their browser.

There is an alternative: silently redirecting users to the correct page based on the browser they use to access the site. Techniques will be presented to accomplish this through either ISAPI filters or extensions.

Redirecting with Filters

An ISAPI filter provides a mechanism for monitoring and potentially changing the file to be returned for any given request. The advantage is that a single piece of code can operate uniformly over an entire site, altering the mapping of incoming requests from one file to another transparently.

The disadvantage is that the code will, in fact, be invoked for each request handled by the site. If only a small percentage of the pages are browser dependent, this imposes overhead on the site that might not need to be incurred.

Using filters for browser redirection is also somewhat limiting in that it requires browser dependencies to be handled consistently across the site. It will be necessary to encode the browser dependency in the URL or directory structure in some fashion so the filter can operate across the site. Although consistency is an admirable goal, it is not always desirable to enforce it this strictly.

Filters are best used for redirectors when many of the pages on the site are browser dependent and when it is acceptable to represent the dependency in the directory structure or the URL.

Redirecting with Extensions

ISAPI extensions can be used to implement redirectors on a small scale. They are best used to distinguish between versions of a page on a case-by-case basis.

For this technique to work, the links between pages affected by the client browser are represented by GET requests rather than standard links. Each of these links can specify two URLs—one to be used if a capability is present, and one if it is not.

When using extensions in this way, the burden of processing is only incurred by those pages that require it. On the other hand, extra work is required when you're building your site. HTML editors will not recognize the invocation of the GET method as a normal link between the two pages and might not be able to invoke site mapping or other similar features.

This technique is best used when the number of pages that should differ is small or when the capability on which the pages are dependent differs from place to place.

Describing Browser Capabilities

Whether your redirector will be based on a filter or an extension, it will need some way to collect information about the client's browser. The method used to describe the client browser can be identical for filters and extensions and can therefore be defined independently.

An important distinction should be made when implementing these redirectors: they should be based on browser capability, not identity. This is a subtle distinction, but an important one.

The site should not be organized into pages for Microsoft Internet Explorer 3.0 or Netscape Navigator 4.0. Instead, it should be modeled in terms of pages that require Java or pages that require VBScript, yielding a much more flexible system that will be more maintainable over time.

Identifying Remote Browsers

The remote browser requesting a given resource can be identified by using the HTTP USER_AGENT request header. The user agent string is usually transmitted with each request and can be conveniently accessed by using the *GetServerVariable()* function in both filters and extensions.

A set of user agent strings is shown in table 9.1. Note that this is only a small sample of the browsers and user agent strings on the net today.

TABLE 9.1
User Agent Strings for Some Popular Browsers

Browser	User agent string
Netscape 2.0 on Win95	Mozilla/2.0 (Win95; I)
Netscape Gold on WinNT	Mozilla/2.0GoldB1 (WinNT; I)
Microsoft IE 3.0	Mozilla/2.0 (compatible; MSIE 3.0B; Windows 95;1024,768)
NetCom Netcruiser	NetCruiser/V2.1

Note	The "Mozilla" name originally identified the Netscape browser; Mozilla is an internal name for Netscape Navigator. Unfortunately, recent versions of the Microsoft Internet Explorer browser also identify themselves as "Mozilla" browsers; they put the actual IE identification later in the string.
	There are historical reasons for this deception. Not very long ago, the Netscape 2.0 browser was *the* state of the art browser. Many sites examined the user agent string to look for "Mozilla/2.0"—if this was found, they served versions of their pages that used Netscape 2 extensions, such as frames, tables, and more. When Microsoft began demonstrating versions of Internet Explorer that also implemented these features, they changed the user agent string to start with the same string to fool sites "optimized for Netscape 2.0" into serving those pages to IE users.

In general, companies are free to have the browser emit anything they like as a part of the user agent string. There are no standards for the construction of these strings. In some cases, the strings identify the operating system hosting the browser, and the screen resolution, and color depth. This information can be quite useful. For example, it can be important to know that the user's Netscape 2.0 browser is running on Windows 3.1, since it does not support Java on that platform, while it does support Java on Win32 platforms.

Building a Browser Capabilities Mechanism

Because the filter and the extension both require knowledge of the capabilities of the client browser, they will share the implementation of the browser capabilities mechanism. The browser capabilities class (*CBrowserCaps*) implemented in the chapter provides a uniform interface that allows the filter to act on the browser's capabilities.

In this section, we'll present a mechanism for identifying a client's browser, and describing the capabilities of that browser for use by the redirector. This will include discussion of:

◆ The requirements for a useful browser capabilities mechanism

◆ The implementation of the browser capabilities manager; responsible for deriving the capabilities of a browser from the HTTP_USER_AGENT string (*CBrowserCapsManager*)

◆ The implementation of a class that describes the capabilites of a particular browser (*CBrowserCaps*)

Requirements

The browser capabilities module must meet the following requirements:

◆ Must encapsulate the process of identifying the browser, given a Filter or Server context object

◆ Must be data-driven; new browsers should be added to the module's repertoire by updating data external to the program. No code changes should be required for this to occur

◆ The mechanism must degrade gracefully; it should answer capabilities questions as intelligently as possible if an "unknown" user agent is encountered

◆ The mechanism must run quite quickly. If the class is used in the context of a redirecting filter, it can be invoked on every incoming request. Overhead must be kept to a minimum

◆ The mechanism must provide a mechanism for the filter or extension to query the availability of given features, including Java, JavaScript, VBScript, Cell Background colors, and more

CBrowserCapsManager Class

This manager class will be responsible for determining the set of capabilities supported by a given browser, as represented by its user agent string. This could be a rather heavyweight object, because it will carry data with it designed to aid in the identification of remote browsers.

Design of CBrowserCapsManager

The *CBrowserCapsManager* class will combine table-based and rule-based approaches to identifying the browser capabilities for a given user agent string. This will enable the manager to be extended by defining values in an external data source, but will allow it to attempt to identify browsers not defined in the data store via code built into the CBrowserCapsManager.

The class will implement an in-memory table of user agents and their associated data. This table will be loaded when the manager is initialized and will remain in memory for the lifetime of the manager object. Although this will occupy a certain amount of memory, it is necessary to obtain the performance required by some of the potential uses of the class. The memory requirements are manageable; if fifty browsers are defined in the table, the table should occupy no more than 5–10 KB of memory.

When attempting to determine the features supported by a particular browser, the manager will first consult this table for a matching definition. If one is not found, it will then attempt to derive capabilities by using an algorithm to detect strings indicative of one of the major browsers.

The manager will support extensibility in two ways:

◆ New definitions can be added to the external data file used to initially load the user agent table

◆ The table load, table look-up, and fallback algorithms will all be implemented by using virtual functions. This will enable any of these operations to be replaced or augmented by overriding the functions in a descendent class

Class Declarations for CBrowserCapsManager

The declaration of the *CBrowserCapsManager* class and the accompanying *SBrowserDef* structure used to represent records in the manager are shown in listing 9.1:

LISTING 9.1—DECLARATION OF CBROWSERCAPSMANAGER

```
01.struct SBrowserDef
02.{
03.               SBrowserDef(string vendor,
04.                          long   capability,
05.                          short  major,
06.                          short  minor);
07.               SBrowserDef();
08.               SBrowserDef(const SBrowserDef& rSrc);
09.    SBrowserDef& operator = (const SBrowserDef& rSrc);
10.
11.    string    m_Vendor;
12.    long      m_Capability;
13.    short     m_Major;
14.    short     m_Minor;
15.};
16.
17.
18.class CBrowserCapsManager
19.{
20.    typedef map<string, SBrowserDef, less<string>,
21.               allocator<SBrowserDef> > UA_TABLE;
22.public:
23.                    CBrowserCapsManager();
24.    virtual         ~CBrowserCapsManager();
25.    virtual void    LoadDefinitions(const char * const fName);
26.    virtual CBrowserCaps GetBrowser(const char * const uAgent);
```

continues

LISTING 9.1—DECLARATION OF CBROWSERCAPSMANAGER, CONTINUED

```
27.
28.protected:
29.                        // override to change the way data is
30.                        // looked up.
31.    virtual bool        Lookup(const char * const uAgent,
32.                                CBrowserCaps& rBrowser) const;
33.                        // Override to change the way browsers
34.                        // are identified if they are not in
35.                        // the table.
36.    virtual bool        Default(const char * const uAgent,
37.                                CBrowserCaps& rBrowser) const;
38.private:
39.    UA_TABLE            m_UserAgents;
40.};
```

Lines 1–15 contain the declaration of the *SBrowserDef* structure. This structure is used as the data element in the user agent table maintained by the manager. It is slightly atypical for a structure to declare and implement member functions, but these are useful to ensure the data can be managed in STL classes effectively. Because the structure contains attributes that are not primitive data types, the copy constructor and assignment operator functions are necessary.

The declaration of the actual class manager begins on line 18. The class declaration begins with a type definition for the data structure that will be used to store the browser definitions loaded from the external file. The data structure is an STL **map<>**; the key will be a string containing the user agent string, and the data will be an instance of the *SBrowserDef* structure.

A standard constructor and destructor are defined for the class; these are empty implementations because the default behavior is acceptable. The destructor is declared to be a virtual function to allow for later specialization.

Note These mechanisms makes use of the STL (the Standard Template Library). This library is the basis of the new standard C++ library, which will soon be part of the ANSI standard for the C++ programming language.

These library provides a wide variety of data structure and fundamental datatype classes. These data structures are much richer and more complete than those provided by MFC. Versions of the library have shipped with Visual C++ 4.0, although early versions are of uneven quality. They are shipped as a part of the standard runtime library in Visual C++ 5.0.

If you are a C++ programmer, you will need to learn to use these classes.

The true external interface to the class is defined on lines 25 and 26. The *LoadDefinitions()* function loads the external data file into memory. The function is overridden to allow the external data source to be changed without changing other details of the implementation. The *GetBrowser()* function retrieves the browser capabilities object corresponding to the user agent string supplied as a parameter. *GetBrowser()* is a virtual function, but it should not be necessary to overload it; the *Lookup()* and *Default()* functions should be overridden instead.

The two functions that actually implement the resolution of user agents to browser capabilities are the *Lookup()* and *Default()* functions. The former retrieves definitions from the user agent table. The latter class handles the cases where the user agent does not correspond to any value loaded from the external file.

Implementing the LoadTable() Function

The *LoadTable()* function is responsible for getting the browser definitions into memory. In this implementation, the definition values are loaded from a simple text file. Each definition occupies a single line in the file; commas separate the fields in the record.

A record takes the form:

```
capabilities,major version,minor version,vendor,user_agent
```

For example, a record might look like this:

```
1023,3,0,Microsoft,Mozilla/2.0 (compatible; MSIE 3.0; Windows NT)
```

In this case, the fields would be as follows:

- ◆ **Capabilities** = 1203 (0x3ff hex); indicates that all current capabilities are present

- ◆ **Major Version** = 3

- ◆ **Minor Version** = 0

- ◆ **Vendor** = Microsoft

- ◆ **User Agent** = Mozilla/2.0 (compatible; MSIE 3.0; Windows NT)

The source code for the supplied implementation of this function is shown in listing 9.2.

LISTING 9.2 - IMPLEMENTATION OF
CBROWSERCAPSMANAGER::LOADTABLE()

```
01.void
02.CBrowserCapsManager::LoadDefinitions(const char * const fName)
03.{
04.     ifstream definitionFile(fName);
05.     if (definitionFile.is_open())
06.     {
07.         long     capability;
08.         short    major;
09.         short    minor;
10.
11.         char     vendor[80];
12.         char     agent[255];
13.
14.         while (!definitionFile.eof())
15.         {
16.             definitionFile >> capability;
17.             if (definitionFile.eof())
18.                 continue;
19.             definitionFile.get();
20.             definitionFile >> major;
21.             definitionFile.get();
22.             definitionFile >> minor;
23.             definitionFile.get();
24.             definitionFile.get(vendor,sizeof(vendor),',');
25.             definitionFile.get();
26.             definitionFile.get(agent,sizeof(agent));
27.             for (char * eos = agent+strlen(agent)-1;
28.                 (agent != eos) && (*eos == ' ');
29.                 eos--)
30.             {
31.                 *eos=0;
32.             }
33.             m_UserAgents[agent]=SBrowserDef(vendor,capability,major,minor);
34.         }
35.     }
36.}
```

The implementation of this function is very straightforward. An input stream for use in processing the file is created on line 4; the stream is then checked to see if it was successfully opened. If so, the function enters a loop from lines 14 to 34, loading a single record per pass through the loop.

The only complication is the loop from line 27 to line 32, which trims trailing blanks from the end of the user agent string. This aids in successfully matching the string to the user agent strings found in incoming requests.

The resulting records are loaded into the user agent table on line 33. If a duplicate record for a user agent is encountered, the previous definition will be replaced.

Implementing the GetBrowser() Function

The *GetBrowser()* function exists primarily to coordinate calls to the *Lookup()* and *Default()* functions. The source for the function is shown in listing 9.3:

LISTING 9.3 - IMPLEMENTATION OF
CBROWSERCAPSMANAGER::GETBROWSER()

```
1.CBrowserCaps
2.CBrowserCapsManager::GetBrowser(const char * const uAgent)
3.{
4.    CBrowserCaps result;
5.    if (!Lookup(uAgent,result))
6.        Default(uAgent,result);
7.
8.    return result;
9.}
```

An object to contain the result of the function is created on the stack on line 4 and is passed to the *Lookup()* function. If it is unable to find a match, the *Default()* function is called in an attempt to come up with some match for the user agent string. The resulting value is then returned to the caller.

Implementing the CBrowserCapsManager::Lookup() Function

The *Lookup()* function is equally straightforward. The STL **map<>** collection used to hold the definition table does most of the work. Listing 9.4 shows the implementation of this function.

 One of the many data structures that are provided by the STL library is the *map*. A *map* is like a dictionary; it provides a structure where a key may be used to retrieve an associated value. Since this is an STL collection, you have ability to decide what the key and the value classes will be. The user agents table is implemented using a map that uses user agent strings as keys, and *SBrowserDef* structures as values.

LISTING 9.4—IMPLEMENTATION OF CBROWSERCAPSMANAGER::LOOKUP()

```
01.bool
02.CBrowserCapsManager::Lookup(const char * const uAgent,
03.                            CBrowserCaps& rBrowser) const
04.{
05.     UA_TABLE::const_iterator i = m_UserAgents.find(uAgent);
06.     if (i != m_UserAgents.end())
07.     {
08.         rBrowser = CBrowserCaps((*i).second.m_Vendor,
09.                              (*i).second.m_Major,
10.                              (*i).second.m_Minor,
11.                              (*i).second.m_Capability);
12.         return true;
13.     }
14.     else
15.         return false;
16.}
```

The function calls the **map<>** collection's *find()* method to get an iterator that points to an entry with a matching key. If none is found, it will point to map<>::end.

If a match is found, the match will be stored in the *rBrowser* parameter and the function will return *true*. If nothing is found, the function will return *false*.

Implementing the CBrowserCapsManager::Default() Function

The *Default()* function is responsible for defining capabilities objects for those browsers not found in the external table. This implementation of the function tries to do something intelligent by looking for patterns that usually correspond to Netscape or Microsoft browsers. The source for this function is found in listing 9.5.

LISTING 9.5—IMPLEMENTATION OF CBROWSERCAPSMANAGER::DEFAULT()

```
01.bool
02.CBrowserCapsManager::Default(const char * const uAgent,
03.                             CBrowserCaps& rBrowser) const
04.{
05.     string          userAgent = uAgent;
06.     string::size_type pos;
07.     string::size_type point;
08.
```

```
09.    string          vendor;
10.    long            capability = 01;
11.    short           major;
12.    short           minor;
13.
14.    // Check for Microsoft's MSIE string, as they might be
15.    // hiding behind a Mozilla ID.
16.    if ((pos=userAgent.find("MSIE"))!=string::npos)
17.    {
18.        point           = userAgent.find('.',pos+4);
19.        string verString = userAgent.substr(pos+4, point-pos);
20.        major           = atoi(verString.c_str());
21.        minor           = userAgent.at(point+1) - '0';
22.        vendor          = "Microsoft";
23.        if (major >= 3)
24.        {
25.            capability = CBrowserCaps::FLAG_ALL;
26.        }
27.        else if (major >=2)
28.        {
29.            capability = CBrowserCaps::FLAG_TABLES |
30.                         CBrowserCaps::FLAG_BGSOUND |
31.                         CBrowserCaps::FLAG_CELL_BG_COLOR;
32.        }
33.    }
34.    else if ((pos = userAgent.find("Mozilla/"))!=string::npos)
35.    {
36.        vendor   = "Netscape";
37.        point    = userAgent.find('/',pos+4);
38.        major    = userAgent.at(point+1) - '0';
39.        minor    = userAgent.at(point+3) - '0';
40.
41.
42.        capability |= CBrowserCaps::FLAG_JAVA |
43.                      CBrowserCaps::FLAG_JAVA_SCRIPT |
44.                      CBrowserCaps::FLAG_FRAMES |
45.                      CBrowserCaps::FLAG_TABLES |
46.                      CBrowserCaps::FLAG_CELL_BG_COLOR |
47.                      CBrowserCaps::FLAG_COOKIES;
48.        if (major >=4)
49.            capability |= CBrowserCaps::FLAG_STYLE_SHEETS;
50.        if (major < 3)
```

continues

LISTING 9.5—IMPLEMENTATION OF
CBROWSERCAPSMANAGER::DEFAULT(), CONTINUED

```
51.            capability &= ~CBrowserCaps::FLAG_CELL_BG_COLOR;
52.        if (userAgent.find("Win16")!=string::npos)
53.            capability &= ~CBrowserCaps::FLAG_JAVA;
54.    }
55.    else
56.    {
57.        vendor = "Unknown";
58.        major  = 0;
59.        minor  = 0;
60.        // Change this line to change your baseline assumptions
61.        // about what capabilities unknown browsers will have.
62.        capability = CBrowserCaps::FLAG_TABLES;
63.    }
64.    rBrowser = CBrowserCaps(vendor,major,minor,capability);
65.    return true;
66.}
```

Lines 14–33 of the function attempt to handle Microsoft Internet Explorer browsers not defined in the table. The function looks for the MSIE string and uses it as an indicator of a Microsoft browser. Existing versions of Internet Explorer follow MSIE with a string containing the version of the browser, so the code attempts to extract the major and minor versions from the user agent string. Given the version number, it is straightforward to set the capabilities flags attribute of the browser definition.

The function continues by repeating this process for the Netscape Browser in lines 34–35. The process is similar; the user agent string is examined for the "Mozilla" name; if it is found, the browser is assumed to be a version of Netscape Navigator. Given the browser name and version numbers, the function can determine the correct capabilities flag. There is one complication: in this case, the operating system platform must be considered as well. The user agent string is checked for the string "Win16," because the Win16 versions of Navigator do not support Java.

Note | This identification process only works if the check for Internet Explorer occurs before the check for Netscape Navigator. This function's check for the Netscape browsers depends on the presence of the Mozilla/2.0 signature in the user agent string.

Since the Microsoft IE 3.0 browser also includes the Mozilla/2.0 signature in its user agent string, we need to check for the MSIE string first. If not, we'll find the Mozilla/2.0 in the Microsoft browser's user agent string, and mistakenly identify it as a Netscape browser.

After an attempt to identify the browser as a Microsoft or Netscape product, it might still be unidentified. At this point, control will fall into the *else* clause on lines 56–63. This code establishes the capabilities to be assumed for unidentified browsers. In this version of the function, the default browser is assumed to support tables but none of the other features on the capabilities manager's list.

CBrowserCaps Class

The *CBrowserCaps* class will be considerably simpler than the manager class. This class is simply responsible for carrying the data describing the capabilities of a browser. Instances of this class are quite lightweight; they can be conveniently passed from function to function to propagate this information to routines that can take advantage of the information.

Before going on to implement the ISAPI filter and ISAPI extension, we will briefly cover:

◆ The design of *CBrowserCaps*

◆ The declaration of the class

◆ The implementation of *CBrowserCaps*

Design of CBrowserCaps Class

As described earlier in the chapter, the browser capabilities mechanism is primarily intended to allow ISAPI filters or extensions to test for the availability of a particular feature in the clients' browser. To that end, the class will provide functions that can be used to query for the availability of a given feature. For example, the class should implement a *SupportsJava()* function that indicates whether or not the browser supports Java.

In addition, the class will also carry the name of the vendor who implemented the browser, along with major and minor version numbers. You should avoid using these functions, but they are provided for those rare instances when they might be needed. For example, it might not always be enough to know a browser supports Java. There are cases where some of the classes provided with the Netscape and Microsoft browsers differ in capabilities.

> **Note**   One specific case where this has been true on my web site has been the need to differentiate between Netscape and Microsoft's browsers due to indifferences in their Java support. Oddly enough, the Microsoft browser provides a more capable implementation of some of the network related classes in the standard Java library than Netscape Navigator.
>
> In this case, it is not enough to know that the remote browser supports Java; I need to know which Java implementation is supported.

Class Declaration

The declaration of the *CBrowserCaps* class is shown in listing 9.6.

LISTING 9.6—DECLARATION OF CBROWSERCAPS

```
01.class CBrowserCaps
02.{
03.public:
04.              enum enCapabilityFlags
05.              {
06.                  FLAG_JAVA          = 0x0001,
07.                  FLAG_JAVA_SCRIPT   = 0x0002,
08.                  FLAG_FRAMES        = 0x0004,
09.                  FLAG_VB_SCRIPT     = 0x0008,
10.                  FLAG_TABLES        = 0x0010,
11.                  FLAG_STYLE_SHEETS  = 0x0020,
12.                  FLAG_BGSOUND       = 0x0040,
13.                  FLAG_CELL_BG_COLOR = 0x0080,
14.                  FLAG_ACTIVEX       = 0x0100,
15.                  FLAG_COOKIES       = 0x0200,
16.                  FLAG_ALL           = 0x03FF
17.              };
18.
19.              CBrowserCaps(string vendor,
20.                           short  majorVer,
21.                           short  minorVer,
22.                           long   capabilities);
23.              CBrowserCaps();
24.              CBrowserCaps(const CBrowserCaps& rSrc);
25.    virtual   ~CBrowserCaps();
26.    CBrowserCaps& operator = (const CBrowserCaps& rSrc);
27.
28.    bool      SupportsJava() const;
29.    bool      SupportsJavaScript() const;
30.    bool      SupportsFrames() const;
31.    bool      SupportsVbScript() const;
32.    bool      SupportsTables    () const;
33.    bool      SupportsStyleSheets() const;
34.    bool      SupportsBgSound() const;
35.    bool      SupportsCellBgColor() const;
36.    bool      SupportsActiveX() const;
37.    bool      SupportsCookies() const;
```

```
38.
39.    string       Vendor() const;
40.    short        MinorVersion() const;
41.    short        MajorVersion() const;
42.
43.protected:
44.private:
45.    string       m_BrowserVendor;
46.    short        m_MajorVersion;
47.    short        m_MinorVersion;
48.    unsigned long m_Capabilities;
49.};
```

The most important characteristic is the representation of the browser's capabilities. Capabilities are stored in an unsigned long and defined by a set of bit flags. The flags for the capabilities are defined in the enumeration on lines 4–17. The capabilities for a browser are defined by ORing together the appropriate flags.

This behavior is hidden from clients of the class. The functions in lines 28–37 can be used to query for the presence of any one of the capabilities.

The remaining functions in the class allow access to the vendor name, major version, and minor version numbers. The class also contains a normal complement of constructors, a destructor, and an assignment operator; these allow the objects to be copied safely.

Implementing CBrowserCaps Class

The implementation of this class is extremely straightforward. The full source code is shown in listing 9.7.

LISTING 9.7—IMPLEMENTATION OF CBROWSERCAPS

```
001.CBrowserCaps::CBrowserCaps(string vendor,
002.                      short   majorVer,
003.                      short   minorVer,
004.                      long    capabilities)
005.          :m_BrowserVendor(vendor),
006.           m_MajorVersion(majorVer),
007.           m_MinorVersion(minorVer),
008.           m_Capabilites(capabilities)
009.{
010.    ;
```

continues

LISTING 9.7—IMPLEMENTATION OF CBROWSERCAPS, CONTINUED

```
011.}
012.
013.CBrowserCaps::CBrowserCaps()
014.{
015.    ;
016.}
017.
018.CBrowserCaps::CBrowserCaps(const CBrowserCaps& rSrc)
019.            :m_BrowserVendor(rSrc.m_BrowserVendor),
020.             m_MajorVersion(rSrc.m_MajorVersion),
021.             m_MinorVersion(rSrc.m_MinorVersion),
022.             m_Capabilites(rSrc.m_Capabilites)
023.{
024.    ;
025.}
026.
027.
028.CBrowserCaps::~CBrowserCaps()
029.{
030.    ;
031.}
032.
033.CBrowserCaps&
034.CBrowserCaps::operator =(const CBrowserCaps& rSrc)
035.{
036.    m_BrowserVendor = rSrc.m_BrowserVendor;
037.    m_MajorVersion  = rSrc.m_MajorVersion;
038.    m_MinorVersion  = rSrc.m_MinorVersion;
039.    m_Capabilites   = rSrc.m_Capabilites;
040.    return *this;
041.}
042.
043.bool
044.CBrowserCaps::SupportsJava() const
045.{
046.    return ((m_Capabilites & FLAG_JAVA)   != 0);
047.}
048.
049.bool
050.CBrowserCaps::SupportsJavaScript() const
051.{
052.    return ((m_Capabilites & FLAG_JAVA_SCRIPT)  != 0);
```

```
053.}
054.
055.bool
056.CBrowserCaps::SupportsFrames() const
057.{
058.    return ((m_Capabilites & FLAG_FRAMES)  != 0);
059.}
060.
061.bool
062.CBrowserCaps::SupportsVbScript() const
063.{
064.    return ((m_Capabilites & FLAG_VB_SCRIPT)  != 0);
065.}
066.
067.bool
068.CBrowserCaps::SupportsTables() const
069.{
070.    return ((m_Capabilites & FLAG_TABLES)  != 0);
071.}
072.
073.bool
074.CBrowserCaps::SupportsStyleSheets() const
075.{
076.    return ((m_Capabilites & FLAG_STYLE_SHEETS)  != 0);
077.}
078.
079.bool
080.CBrowserCaps::SupportsBgSound() const
081.{
082.    return ((m_Capabilites & FLAG_BGSOUND)  != 0);
083.}
084.
085.bool
086.CBrowserCaps::SupportsCellBgColor() const
087.{
088.    return ((m_Capabilites & FLAG_CELL_BG_COLOR)  != 0);
089.}
090.
091.bool
092.CBrowserCaps::SupportsActivex() const
093.{
094.    return ((m_Capabilites & FLAG_ACTIVEX)  != 0);
```

continues

LISTING 9.7—IMPLEMENTATION OF CBROWSERCAPS, CONTINUED

```
095.}
096.
097.
098.bool
099.CBrowserCaps::SupportsCookies() const
100.{
101.    return ((m_Capabilites & FLAG_COOKIES) != 0);
102}
103.
104.
105.string
106.CBrowserCaps::Vendor() const
107.{
108.    return m_BrowserVendor;
109.}
110.
111.
112.short
113.CBrowserCaps::MinorVersion() const
114.{
115.    return m_MinorVersion;
116.}
117.
118.short
119.CBrowserCaps::MajorVersion() const
120.{
121.    return m_MajorVersion;
122.}
123.
124.
125.
```

The constructors for the *CBrowserCaps* class are found on lines 1–25. Three constructors are provided:

◆ The standard constructor, for use when the data required to initialize the attributes of the object is available.

◆ A default constructor; this is mandatory for use with some of the STL collections.

◆ A copy constructor. Since several of the attributes of the class are string objects, we cannot depend on the compiler generated copy constructor.

An assignment operator is implemented on lines 33–41; this function is required for use by the STL map<> collection as well. The compiler generated default implementation of the assignment operator is insufficient since the class contains data elements represented by string objects. These are explicitly copied in the assignment operator.

The remaining functions shown in listing 9.7 are used to provide convenient access to the information encoded in the *m_Capabilities* attribute. Each of these functions using the bitwise AND operator to mask off the bits associated with a particular capability; if the result of this operation is non-zero, the capability is represented in the flag.

Potential Improvements to the Browser Capabilities Mechanism

Currently, if this class is used in multiple extensions, it will load multiple copies of the browser definition table. Ideally, this code could be enhanced to live in a separate DLL or COM object, with a shared copy of the browser definition table.

Implementing a Redirecting Extension

This section describes the implementation of a redirector implemented as an ISAPI extension. This particular redirector is designed to redirect based on the presence or absence of a particular capability. This can be used to insert a single conditional branch in a web site.

For example, a shopping site might contain two versions of its catalog browser: one Java-based, the other implemented in straight HTML forms. The pages could differ quite drastically, so it might be useful to make the link to the search function conditional, taking users of Java-capable browsers to one page and those using browsers that do not support Java to another.

This redirector will be implemented as an MFC-based ISAPI extension. It will implement a single command for requesting conditional redirection. The command might be invoked by a GET method or via a link that uses a GET-style URL.

Requirements

This redirecting extension should operate on three pieces of information:

◆ The name of the capability being tested

◆ The URL to redirect to if the capability is present

◆ The URL to redirect to if the capability is not present

It must be possible to pass all this information via an HTML link; the extension should be driven by these parameters. The extension should be capable of distinguishing between local and remote redirection and should invoke the appropriate operations for each.

Declaring the Extension Class

The first step in understanding the extension class is to examine the class declaration, shown in listing 9.8.

LISTING 9.8—DECLARATION OF THE CREDIREXTEXTENSION CLASS

```
01.class CRedirExtExtension : public CHttpServer
02.{
03.public:
04.                CRedirExtExtension();
05.                ~CRedirExtExtension();
06.
07.     virtual BOOL GetExtensionVersion(HSE_VERSION_INFO* pVer);
08.
09.     void       IfSupported(CHttpServerContext* pCtxt,
10.                            LPCSTR pCapability,
11.                            LPCSTR pIsPresent,
12.                            LPCSTR pIsNotPresent);
13.
14.                DECLARE_PARSE_MAP()
15.
16.private:
17.     CString    GetDefinitionFileName() const;
18.     void       Redirect(CHttpServerContext* pCtxt,
19.                         LPCSTR szUrl);
20.
21.     CBrowserCapsManager m_CapsManager;
22.};
```

The class contains the normal boilerplate for an MFC-based ISAPI extension; it declares constructors, destructors, a PARSEMAP, and an override of *GetExtensionVersion()*. In addition, on line 9 it declares the *IfSupported()* function that will handle the incoming requests for redirection.

The private section of the class (lines 16–21) declares a pair of implementation functions and an instance of the browser capabilities manager. The manager is implemented as a data member of the extension class because its life span is tied to that of the extension object.

Defining the PARSEMAP

The extension currently supports a single command, so the MFC PARSEMAP is reasonably simple. It is shown in listing 9.9.

LISTING 9.9—PARSEMAP FOR THE REDIRECTING EXTENSION

```
1.BEGIN_PARSE_MAP(CRedirExtExtension, CHttpServer)
2.    DEFAULT_PARSE_COMMAND(IfSupported, CRedirExtExtension)
3.    ON_PARSE_COMMAND(IfSupported, CRedirExtExtension,
4.                     ITS_PSTR ITS_PSTR ITS_PSTR)
5.    ON_PARSE_COMMAND_PARAMS("cap yes no")
6.END_PARSE_MAP(CRedirExtExtension)
```

The single supported command is *IfSupported*; it is defined on lines 3 and 4. The command takes three string parameters: *cap*, *yes*, and *no*. The parameters are named on line 5.

Because the extension only supports a single command, it is defined to be the default command on line 2. This enables the function to be invoked without specifying a command name as a part of the URL.

 See Chapter 4, "Basic Form Processing in MFC" for more information on MFC PARSEMAPS, and their role in the implementation of ISAPI extensions in MFC.

Initializing the Redirecting Extension

Before the extension can begin handling commands, it must initialize the browser capabilities manager created previously in the chapter. It must create an instance of *CBrowserCapsManager* and load the external file to initialize the browser table.

The manager is instantiated when the extension object is created. It is initialized after the fact, in an override of the *GetExtensionVersion()* function. The configuration data for this extension will be stored in the Windows Registry; it will be loaded when the HTTP server calls *GetExtensionVersion()* to initialize the extension.

Reading Parameters from the Registry

The only piece of information required to initialize the browser table is the name of the external data store that will be read to load the definitions into memory. Rather than hardcode a name into the extension, the file name should be read from the Windows Registry.

A function that accomplishes this is shown in listing 9.10. Although it is not Internet-related code, it is worthwhile to remember that this type of configuration information should be externalized and should generally be externalized in the Registry.

LISTING 9.10—READING CONFIGURATION INFORMATION FROM THE REGISTRY

```
01.CString
02.CRedirExtExtension::GetDefinitionFileName() const
03.{
04.    CString result;
05.    HKEY    regKey;
06.    DWORD   rc;
07.
08.    rc = RegOpenKeyEx(HKEY_LOCAL_MACHINE,
09.                      _T("Software\\NewRiders\\RedirExt"),
10.                      01,KEY_READ,&regKey);
11.    if (rc == ERROR_SUCCESS)
12.    {
13.        char  valueBuffer[255];
14.        DWORD bufferLen = sizeof(valueBuffer);
15.        DWORD type;
16.
17.        rc = RegQueryValueEx(regKey,_T("DefFile"),01,
18.                             &type,(LPBYTE)&valueBuffer,
19.                             &bufferLen);
20.        if (rc == ERROR_SUCCESS)
21.            result = valueBuffer;
22.        RegCloseKey(regKey);
23.    }
24.    return result;
25.}
```

The configuration data for this extension is stored in the key LOCAL_MACHINE\ Software\NewRiders\RedirExt defined in lines 8–9. It consists of a single value, the name of the external data store. If the key or value is missing from the Registry, this function will return an empty string. This information should be placed in the registry during the installation of the extension.

Implementing the GetExtensionVersion() Function

The *CRedirExtExtension* class overrides the *CHttpServer::GetExtensionVersion()* function, as all MFC extensions do. As usual, the function's chief responsibility is to supply configuration information back to the HTTP server by populating the

HSE_VERSION_INFO structure (see Chapter 4 for more information on this process). The implementation of *CRedirExtExtension::GetExtensionVersion()* can be seen in listing 9.11.

LISTING 9.11—CREDIREXTEXTENSION::GETEXTENSIONVERSION()

```
01.BOOL
02.CRedirExtExtension::GetExtensionVersion(HSE_VERSION_INFO* pVer)
03.{
04.    CString fileName = GetDefinitionFileName();
05.    if (!fileName.IsEmpty())
06.        m_CapsManager.LoadDefinitions(fileName);
07.
08.    // Call default implementation for initialization
09.    CHttpServer::GetExtensionVersion(pVer);
10.
11.    // Load description string
12.    TCHAR sz[HSE_MAX_EXT_DLL_NAME_LEN+1];
13.    ISAPIVERIFY(::LoadString(AfxGetResourceHandle(),
14.            IDS_SERVER, sz, HSE_MAX_EXT_DLL_NAME_LEN));
15.    _tcscpy(pVer->lpszExtensionDesc, sz);
16.    return TRUE;
17.}
```

In addition to the normal duties of a *GetExtensionVersion()* function, this version of *GetExtensionVersion()* is responsible for loading the invoking the browser-capabilities manager's *LoadDefinitions()* function. This function calls *GetDefinitionFileName()* on line 3 to get the name of the file to load. If a filename was retrieved successfully, it is passed to *LoadDefinitions()* on line 6. If no filename is found, the *LoadDefinitions()* function will not be called.

Handling the IfSupported Command

As described earlier, the command is handled by the *IfSupported()* function. This function must accomplish two major tasks:

Determine whether or not the browser implements the requested feature

Issue a redirection to the appropriate page

Checking Browser Capabilities

Two steps are involved in determining which of the two URLs will be used in the redirection.

First, the function needs to acquire a browser capabilities object matching the browser making the request. This is done in lines 11–13 of the function, shown in listing 9.12. The call to *CHttpServerContext::GetServerVariable()* on line 11 acquires the string the browser supplied with the request; the call to *CBrowserCapsManager:: GetBrowser()* on line 13 uses this data to get a browser capabilities object.

Note   The documentation for the *GetServerVariable()* functions in the *CHttpServer* and *CHttpFilter* class doesn't make it clear that you can request variables other than those listed with the function. In fact, you can ask for any of the request header variables by passing the variable name to the function. It is necessary to prefix the variable names with "HTTP_" to retrieve them from IIS.

The implementation of the *IfSupported()* command response function is shown in listing 9.12.

LISTING 9.12—CREDIREXTEXTENSION::IFSUPPORTED()

```
01.void
02.CRedirExtExtension::IfSupported(CHttpServerContext* pCtxt,
03.                             LPCSTR pCapability,
04.                             LPCSTR pIsPresent,
05.                             LPCSTR pIsNotPresent)
06.{
07.    bool  present = false;
08.
09.    char  buff[132];
10.    DWORD buffSize = sizeof(buff);
11.    if (pCtxt->GetServerVariable("HTTP_USER_AGENT",buff,&buffSize))
12.    {
13.        CBrowserCaps browserCaps(m_CapsManager.GetBrowser(buff));
14.
15.        CString capability(pCapability);
16.        capability.MakeUpper();
17.
18.        if (capability == "JAVA")
19.            present = browserCaps.SupportsJava();
20.        else if (capability == "JAVASCRIPT")
21.            present = browserCaps.SupportsJavaScript();
22.        else if (capability == "VBSCRIPT")
23.            present = browserCaps.SupportsVbScript();
24.        else if (capability == "FRAMES")
```

```
25.              present = browserCaps.SupportsFrames();
26.         else if (capability == "STYLESHEETS")
27.              present = browserCaps.SupportsStyleSheets();
28.         else if (capability == "TABLES")
29.              present = browserCaps.SupportsTables();
30.         else if (capability == "ACTIVEX")
31.              present = browserCaps.SupportsActiveX();
32.
33.    }
34.    Redirect(pCtxt, present ? pIsPresent : pIsNotPresent);
35.}
```

After the *IfSupported()* function has acquired a browser capabilities object, it needs to determine which capability the incoming request is testing. The capability name is moved into a *CString* on line 15 and then converted to uppercase, making it easier to test the incoming string against the names assigned to capabilities in this function.

Lines 18–31 test the requested capability name against the names supported by *IfSupported()*; if a match is found, the matching *CBrowserCaps()* function is called to determine if the remote browser supports the desired capability. If no match for the capability name is found, the present flag will retain its original default value of **false**.

Finally, the *Redirect()* function is called on line 34. The present flag is used to decide whether to pass the *pIsPresent* (yes) or *pIsNotpresent* (no) URL to the redirection routine to issue the redirection.

Issuing a Redirection

IIS supports redirection through the *ServerSupportFunction()*. *ServerSupportFunction()*'s behavior is controlled by passing a request code that indicates what operation is being requested from the function. Two of these request codes pertain to redirection:

> HSE_REQ_SEND_URL
>
> HSE_REQ_SEND_URL_REDIRECT_RESP

The HSE_REQ_SEND_URL function handles local redirection. This represents the case in which the original URL and the new URL are present on the same host. In this case, the server does not actually send an HTTP redirect to the client; it simply sends the new resource to the client in place of the one originally requested. This saves the overhead of sending the client a redirect and then processing a new request from that client for the new resource.

The HSE_REQ_SEND_URL_REDIRECT_RESP request code causes IIS to issue an actual HTTP 302 (url redirect) response to the client. This should cause the client to issue a request for the location passed to the *ServerSupportFunction()*. This is necessary if the new destination is on a different server.

This extension will use whichever form of redirection is appropriate. If the destination URL begins with /, the resource is assumed to exist on the same server as the extension DLL, and a local redirect is requested from the server. If the destination URL begins with anything other than /, the function requests a remote redirect instead. This can be seen in listing 9.13.

LISTING 9.13—CR<small>EDIR</small>E<small>XT</small>E<small>XTENSION</small>::R<small>EDIRECTION</small>()

```
01.void
02.CRedirExtExtension::Redirect(CHttpServerContext* pCtxt,
03.                             LPCSTR  szUrl)
04.{
05.    DWORD urlSize = strlen(szUrl)+1;
06.    DWORD operation;
07.
08.    if (szUrl[0] == '/')
09.        operation = HSE_REQ_SEND_URL;
10.    else
11.        operation = HSE_REQ_SEND_URL_REDIRECT_RESP;
12.
13.    pCtxt->ServerSupportFunction(operation,(void*)szUrl,
14.                                &urlSize,NULL);
15.}
```

The actual implementation of the function is quite straightforward. On line 8, the URL is examined to see if it begins with a / character. If it does, the *operation* variable is set to indicate a local redirection; if not, it is set to indicate a remote redirection. This value is then used in a call to *ServerSupportFunction()* on line 13.

 The local redirection is strictly a performance optimization; you could use the remote redirection for both cases. Using local redirection will improve performance when the filter and the destination URLs are all on one server.

Implementing a Redirecting Filter

A redirecting filter has the opportunity to modify the URL that will be used for every request to a web server. The filter can examine each request and alter some or all of the requested URLs, based on the browser being used by the client.

The filter presented in this example is intended for use at a site that hosts many form-oriented pages. The forms in this site can be implemented by using straight HTML 3 forms, VBScript-enhanced forms, or Java Applets. This particular site prefers the VBScript versions of the form, followed by a Java version and then the straight HTML version. The filter is used to decide which version will be used to satisfy the browser's request.

Requirements

The filter must scan all incoming requests from the client for possible redirection. The incoming URL will be checked to see if a node of the name consists of the word "FORM." If so, the filter should replace the string "FORM" with one of the following strings:

◆ **VBS_FRM:** the browser supports VBScript.

◆ **JAVA_FRM:** the browser does not support VBScript, but does support Java.

◆ **HTML_FRM:** the remote browser does not support Java or VBScript, so the server will supply straight HTML forms.

For example, suppose a link on a page refers to the URL /Employment/FORM/Apply.html. The filter should turn this into one of the following URLs, based on the client's browser:

◆ /Employment/VBS_FRM/Apply.html

◆ /Employment/JAVA_FRM/Apply.html

◆ /Employment/HTML_FRM/Apply.html

This manipulation of the URL will enable the site to establish directory structures grouping pages designed to use each of these technologies. It will also enable the site to avoid making duplicates of those pages that are not technology dependent.

This filter operates on pages that are physically present on the server; it is not used to issue remote redirections to other sites.

Selecting Notification Methods for Redirecting Filters

The first step in the implementation of the filter is the selection of the notifications to be used by the filter to do its work. For many filters, this is a fairly trivial process; a logging filter will use the SF_NOTIFY_LOG notification code, and an authentication filter will use the SF_NOTIFY_AUTHENTICATION notification.

 Note For more information on filter notifications, please see Chapter 7, "Understanding ISAPI Filters."

Our example filter falls into a gray area. The most obvious choice for use in this filter is the SF_NOTIFY_URL_MAP. This notification is fired during the process of reconciling an URL with a physical file on the server and could be used to implement this filter.

Upon further examination, the SF_NOTIFY_URL_MAP notification is not the best choice for this job. This notification is delivered to the filter after the URL has been connected to a file. Unfortunately, this means the server has already considered and applied the virtual directory structure for the server; the filter can now only intervene at the physical level. This would require the filter to duplicate the mapping normally performed by the virtual directory mechanism to redirect the request to another file; mapping "C:\inetpub\wwwroot\FORM\default.html" to "d:\inetfiles\JAVA_FRM\default.html".

A better choice for this filter is to handle the SF_NOTIFY_PREPROC_HEADERS event. This event is fired after the server has finished preprocessing headers, but before it has resolved the URL to a file. By changing the requested URL at this point, the filter can still take advantage of the virtual directory mechanism supplied by the server.

This is not a crucial problem, but it is a significant one. Virtual directories give the server a mechanism for spanning multiple physical devices, generally a useful thing to have available.

Design Issues

The redirecting filter does not need to maintain any state information from request to request, so there is no need to handle the SF_NOTIFY_END_OF_NET_REQUEST or SF_NOTIFY_END_OF_NET_SESSION notifications. This also frees the filter from the need to manage memory from request to request.

Like the extension filter described earlier in the chapter, the redirection filter will use the browser capabilities mechanism to identify the browser and its capabilities from the user agent string. This means the filter needs to manage the life span of an instance of *CBrowserCapsManager()*. The filter must also supply the name of an external definition file to the capabilities manager; the file name should be loaded from the Registry.

Declaring the Filter Class

The redirection filter will be implemented by using the *MFC CHttpFilter* class; this means it will implement a descendent class to handle notifications from the server. The class declaration is shown in listing 9.14.

LISTING 9.14—DECLARATION OF CLASS CREDIRFILTER

```
01.class CRedirFilter : public CHttpFilter
02.{
03.public:
04.                 CRedirFilter();
05.                 ~CRedirFilter();
06.
07.    virtual BOOL   GetFilterVersion(PHTTP_FILTER_VERSION pVer);
08.    virtual DWORD  OnPreprocHeaders(CHttpFilterContext* pCtxt,
09.                     PHTTP_FILTER_PREPROC_HEADERS pHdrInfo);
10.
11.private:
12.    CString               GetDefinitionFileName() const;
13.    CBrowserCapsManager m_CapsManager;
14.};
```

The class only requires two functions to participate in the MFC filter mechanism: *GetFilterVersion()* and *OnPreprocHeaders()* (lines 7 and 8, respectively). In addition, it declares a standard constructor, a destructor, and a private implementation function.

Implementing the GetFilterVersion() Function

The redirector class overrides *GetFilterVersion()* in order to indicate that it is interested in handling the SF_NOTIFY_PREPROC_HEADERS event. The filter also uses this function as an opportunity to initialize *m_CapsManager*, an instance of the *CBrowserCapsManager* class described earlier in the chapter. The source for the function is shown in listing 9.15.

LISTING 9.15—IMPLEMENTATION OF
CREDIRFILTER::GETFILTERVERSION

```
01.BOOL
02.CRedirFilter::GetFilterVersion(PHTTP_FILTER_VERSION pVer)
03.{
04.    CString fileName = GetDefinitionFileName();
05.    // If a filename was found in the Registry, use it to
06.    // load the capabilities manager.
07.    if (!fileName.IsEmpty())
08.        m_CapsManager.LoadDefinitions(fileName);
09.
10.    // Call default implementation for initialization
11.    CHttpFilter::GetFilterVersion(pVer);
12.
13.    // Clear the flags set by base class
14.    pVer->dwFlags &= ~SF_NOTIFY_ORDER_MASK;
15.
16.    // Set the flags we are interested in
17.    pVer->dwFlags |= SF_NOTIFY_ORDER_LOW |
18.                     SF_NOTIFY_SECURE_PORT |
19.                     SF_NOTIFY_NONSECURE_PORT |
20.                     SF_NOTIFY_PREPROC_HEADERS;
21.    // Load description string
22.    TCHAR sz[SF_MAX_FILTER_DESC_LEN+1];
23.    ISAPIVERIFY(::LoadString(AfxGetResourceHandle(),
24.            IDS_FILTER, sz, SF_MAX_FILTER_DESC_LEN));
25.    _tcscpy(pVer->lpszFilterDesc, sz);
26.    return TRUE;
27.}
```

With the exception of some reformatting for readability, this function differs very little from an implementation generated by the Visual C++ ISAPI wizard. The only functional alteration is the addition of lines 4–9, which are responsible for managing the initialization of the capabilities manager object with data from an external table.

Implementing the OnPreProcHeaders() Function

The principal work of the filter is done in the overridden *OnPreProcHeaders()* function. The function is called after the HTTP server has preprocessed the headers, but before it has acted on the request. This occurs prior to authentication or URL mapping.

The source code for *CRedirFilter::OnPreProcHeaders()* is shown in listing 9.16.

LISTING 9.16—IMPLEMENTATION OF CREDIRFILTER::ONPREPROCEHEADERS

```
01.static const char szFormWord[] = "/FORM/";
02.static const char szUserAgent[] = "USER-AGENT:";
03.static const char szVBSForm[] = "/VbS_Frm/";
04.static const char szJavaForm[] = "/Java_Frm/";
05.static const char szHTMLForm[] = "/Html_Frm/";
06.
07.DWORD
08.CRedirFilter::OnPreprocHeaders(CHttpFilterContext* pCtxt,
09.                   PHTTP_FILTER_PREPROC_HEADERS pHeaderInfo)
10.{
11.    char  buffer[1024];
12.    DWORD buffSize = sizeof(buffer);
13.
14.    pHeaderInfo->GetHeader(pCtxt->m_pFC,"url",buffer,&buffSize);
15.    char * pPosition = strstr(buffer,szFormWord);
16.    if (pPosition != NULL)
17.    {
18.        char userAgent[255];
19.        char resultBuffer[1024];
20.
21.        buffSize = sizeof(buffer);
22.        pHeaderInfo->GetHeader(pCtxt->m_pFC,szUserAgent,
23.                            userAgent,&buffSize);
24.        CBrowserCaps browserCaps =
25.                    m_CapsManager.GetBrowser(userAgent);
26.
27.        *pPosition = 0;
28.        strcpy(resultBuffer,buffer);
29.        if (browserCaps.SupportsVbScript())
30.            strcat(resultBuffer,szVBSForm);
31.
32.        else if (browserCaps.SupportsJava())
33.            strcat(resultBuffer,szJavaForm);
34.        else
35.            strcat(resultBuffer,szHTMLForm);
36.
37.        strcat(resultBuffer,pPosition+strlen(szFormWord));
38.
39.        pHeaderInfo->SetHeader(pCtxt->m_pFC,"url",
```

continues

LISTING 9.16—IMPLEMENTATION OF
CRedirFilter::OnPreproceHeaders, Continued

```
40.                                resultBuffer);
41.    }
42.
43.    return SF_STATUS_REQ_NEXT_NOTIFICATION;
44.}
```

The *CRedirFilter::OnPreProcHeaders()* function begins its work on line 15 of the listing with a call to the *GetHeader()* function whose address was passed in the HTTP_FILTER_PREPROC_HEADERS notification structure. The function can be used to copy any of the request headers into a user-supplied buffer. In addition to the standard request headers, this function accepts several special variable names, including *url.* In this case, the function will return the URL of the resource being requested by the remote client, excluding the hostname.

The URL is then checked to see if it contains the string /FORM/. If so, one of the directories in the URL must be FORM, and the filter should perform the appropriate substitution. If not, the filter has no work to perform on this request and proceeds to the return statement on line 43 to pass control to the next filter.

If the URL contains a string that needs to be processed by the filter, control proceeds to a second call to the *GetHeader()* function. This time, the filter requests the USER-AGENT: header and feeds the result to the browser capabilities manager. Note that the string used to identify the user agent header is not the same as the string used elsewhere in conjunction with calls to *GetServerVariable()* to retrieve the same data.

After a *CBrowserCaps* object is available, the filter can proceed to build a string containing the result URL. The portion of the source URL found to the left of the /FORM/ string is copied to the result buffer in line 28. The if-then-else statements on lines 29–35 then append a string to the URL that depends on the browser identified by the user agent string. Finally, the portion of the source URL that comes after the /FORM/ string is appended to the URL on line 37.

At this point, the filter has constructed a new URL to use to respond to the browser's request. On lines 39 and 40, the filter calls the *GetHeader()* function, using the pointer passed in the HTTP_FILTER_PREPROC_HEADERS parameter to *OnPreProcHeaders()*. This replaces the URL in the request and causes the server to use this URL for the remainder of processing for the request.

Summary

Redirectors are useful tools for creating a web site that adapts itself to the customer using the site. The chapter describes two ways to do so: with an extension or with a filter. Each of these has advantages and disadvantages.

The extension-based approach is appropriate when there are a small number of browser-sensitive or -dependent pages. This approach is also useful when the criteria used to select between versions differs from page to page; in one situation, the criteria might be support for Java, in another, support for VBScript. The downside to extension-based redirectors is a potential lack of consistency; they do not help establish a uniform structure for managing browser dependencies throughout the site.

The filter-based approach is appropriate where large parts of the site will be dependent on the presence or absence of a particular technology. Because the filter applies across the entire site, it inherently dictates a consistent approach. The downside is that the filter impacts every request to the site in some way. Even in cases where no action is required, the filter will need to examine the requested URL to decide whether to intervene and alter the request. This potential impact should be weighed carefully against the benefits to be derived from use of the filter.

CHAPTER 10

Authentication with Filters

T oday, many sites on the World Wide Web have a need for users to identify themselves to the server. Various sites have many reasons for wanting to know who their users are; for example:

◆ Subscription-oriented sites need to verify the identity of subscribers.

◆ Corporate intranet sites need to secure access to proprietary information.

◆ Many other sites wish to tailor content or services to the preferences of individual users.

The common thread is the fundamental need to identify users in a secure, standardized way.

The HTTP standard defines a mechanism for identifying users, known as *authentication*. HTTP authentication is a challenge/response-based process for validating the user's identity. This mechanism is flexible and extensible, and it underlies the user logon mechanisms throughout the web.

Microsoft implements this standard authentication mechanism in the Internet Information Server. The standard implementation of this mechanism in IIS uses the Windows NT security system to manage users' rights and identifications. This allows the administrators of IIS-based systems to manage their server by using familiar tools, such as the NT User Manager and File Manager, avoiding the need to learn new tools or techniques.

Unfortunately, using these familiar tools is not always the ideal solution. For some systems, the use of the Windows NT User Manager adds to the work of the system's administrator, causing a need to duplicate information that exists elsewhere. In other systems, the number of possible usernames is too large to make administration practical with the existing User Manager.

Microsoft recognized this and provided an escape hatch in the form of authentication filters. These filters can be called each time the server needs to validate a user's identity and right to access, bypassing the need to register all your users in the NT User Manager. This chapter will discuss the implementation of such a filter.

Before embarking on the implementation of a filter, this chapter will provide some background on the underlying mechanisms involved in authentication and security on IIS. This will include:

- ◆ The nature of authentication

- ◆ The standard HTTP 1.1 authentication mechanism

- ◆ The relationship between HTTP authentication and Windows NT Security

Authentication versus Security

Before continuing with the discussion of authentication and filters, it is important to understand what authentication actually is and what role it plays in security. This might seem obvious, but it isn't always so.

Authentication is the process of obtaining and verifying the identity of a user. The authentication mechanism is *not* responsible for determining whether or not the user has access to a particular resource; it is only responsible for establishing the user's identity. This is an important distinction. As you'll see later in the chapter, authentication filters control a user's right to take on a particular role or assume a particular identity; they do not dictate what resources may be accessed by users with that role.

Of course, authentication is the key to building an access control system for a web site. After the server has authenticated a user's identity, that identity might be used by the server to decide whether the user has the right to access a given resource.

Authentication in HTTP 1.1

As described earlier, the HTTP standard defines a mechanism for user authentication. The process defined by the standard is simple, flexible, and extensible. The protocol defines a challenge/response process for verifying a user's identity and right to access the system as described in the next section.

The Challenge/Response Process

The basis of this process is quite straightforward: the user requests some resource that requires authentication, the server challenges the user's right to access the resource, and the user/browser responds with credentials asserting the user's right to the resource. In the HTTP protocol, this might map to the following sequence of events:

1. An anonymous user requests a secured or restricted resource.

2. The server responds with an HTTP 401 "Access denied" message challenging the user's right to access the resource.

3. The browser displays a dialog box, prompting the user for a username and password.

4. The browser resubmits the original request to the server, this time including credentials derived from the user ID and password.

5. The server either accepts the credentials and responds with the requested data or responds with another HTTP 401 "Access Denied."

The following sections walk through the challenge/response process in more detail.

The Initial Request

When someone begins working with a web site, it is generally as an anonymous user. Until making a request that requires access to some resource unavailable to the default user, the user remains in the anonymous state. After a resource unavailable to the anonymous user is requested, the authentication process is initiated.

It is important to understand that the HTTP specification itself does not dictate the circumstances that initiate the process; the previous paragraph describes a common example, but many other scenarios are possible. The HTTP standard only dictates how the server should indicate to the remote client that authentication is required.

For example, the initial request might appear something like the message shown in listing 10.1.

LISTING 10.1—SAMPLE HTTP GET REQUEST
WITHOUT AUTHENTICATION CREDENTIALS

```
01.GET /bin/secure/warehouse/SearchSel.dll? HTTP/1.0
02.Accept: image/gif, image/jpeg, */*
03.Referer: http://localhost/Warehouse/home.html
04.Accept-Language: en
05.UA-pixels: 800x600
06.UA-color: color8
07.UA-OS: Windows NT
08.UA-CPU: x86
09.User-Agent: Mozilla/2.0 (compatible; MSIE 3.0; Windows NT)
10.Host: localhost
11.Connection: Keep-Alive.
```

This initial request will trigger the authentication process because the anonymous user does not have access to the resource shown on line 1: "/bin/secure/warehouse/searchsel.dll."

The Challenge

After the server has determined that authentication is required for access to the resource the user is interested in, it generates a standard HTTP 401 "Access Denied" message. This response tells the remote browser its request has been denied but may be resubmitted with authentication credentials.

A sample response from a server supporting only the basic authentication scheme is shown in listing 10.2.

LISTING 10.2—SAMPLE HTTP 401 ACCESS
DENIED MESSAGE FOR BASIC AUTHENTICATION

```
01.HTTP/1.0 401 Access Denied
02.WWW-Authenticate: Basic realm="localhost"
03.Content-Length: 24
04.Content-Type: text/html
05.
06.Error: Access is Denied
```

This message indicates that the request has been denied via the HTTP 401 status code in the message header, shown here on line 1. The browser should interpret the 401 status code as meaning access is unauthorized but authentication might help. This is different from indicating access to the requested resource is completely forbidden, which would be done via the HTTP 403 status code.

The 401 status code generally indicates that the user has not been authenticated; the server has not yet obtained a set of credentials for the user, so it cannot determine whether or not the remote user should have access to the resource in question.

The 403 status code indicates that the server knows who the remote user is, but that the user in question does not have sufficient priviliges to retrieve the requested resource.

The access-denied message on line 6 is part of the HTTP message body; it contains text the browser can show to the user if it chooses not to attempt authentication. This is typically done after some number of failed attempts to authenticate.

In addition to the bare access-denied message, the response carries a critical set of information on line 2. The server includes a line in the response header for each authentication scheme supported by the server. These schemes (discussed in more detail later in the chapter) represent a method of encoding security credentials for transmission between the browser and the server.

Acting on the Challenge

When the browser receives the access-denied response from the server, it has the right (but not the obligation) to take some action to obtain security credentials and resubmit the request. The browser is not obligated to authenticate and resubmit the request; it simply is told it has the option to do so.

Credentials might be obtained by prompting a user for a username and password or by some other means. For example, some authentication schemes establish user identity by consulting the operating system hosting the browser for the name of the user logged in a local LAN, rather than a new user-id and password. The HTTP standard does not specify what actions the browser should take to obtain security credentials; it merely specifies that the browser has the right to do so and resubmit the request.

The most common response to the "401 Access Denied" message is to display a dialog box to collect the username and password from the user. Once the browser has collected information identifying the user from the user or the underlying network, the browser uses this information to respond to the server's challenge automatically.

Responding to the Challenge by Resubmitting the Request

After the browser has obtained some notion of user-id or password, it resubmits the original request with an additional piece of information: authentication credentials. These are supplied in the request in the form of an additional request header: "Authorization." An example of this is shown in listing 10.3.

LISTING 10.3—A REQUEST CONTAINING AUTHENTICATION CREDENTIALS

```
01.GET /bin/secure/warehouse/SearchSel.dll? HTTP/1.0
02.Accept: image/gif, image/jpeg, */*
03.Referer: http://localhost/Warehouse/home.html
04.Accept-Language: en
05.UA-pixels: 800x600
06.UA-color: color8
07.UA-OS: Windows NT
08.UA-CPU: x86
09.User-Agent: Mozilla/2.0 (compatible; MSIE 3.0; Windows NT)
10.Host: localhost
11.Connection: Keep-Alive
12.Authorization: Basic c2hrbWM6eHh4
```

Line 12 of the listing shows the new header. It contains the encoded credentials and the name of the authentication scheme being used to encode the credentials. Since HTTP is a stateless protocol, it needs to supply these credentials with a new request for the resource. The server does not keep track of what resource was specified in the original request.

Results

After the request is resubmitted to the server, it is processed normally. The server finds the *Authorization* header in the request and attempts to use these credentials to determine the user's identity.

The credentials might not be acceptable to the server; for example, the username and password entered in a browser might not be valid. In this case, the server responds with the same HTTP 401 Access Denied message that began the whole authentication process. The browser then has the option to retry authentication, allowing the user to re-enter username and password, or shifting to another authentication scheme. Many browsers will only allow three attempts to authenticate for any given resource before simply displaying the access-denied message to the user. This behavior is entirely up to the browser and is not dictated by the HTTP standard.

If the credentials supplied with the new request are valid, the server then returns the requested resource.

Impact on Future Requests

After a browser has successfully completed this authentication process for a given server, it generally caches the credentials it used when logging on. It then silently adds these credentials to all requests to the authenticating server for the duration of the user's current browser session.

This addition has important implications for an authentication filter. This behavior means each individual request for a resource from the server after the initial request will include the credentials accepted in the original request. The authentication filter, therefore, should be prepared to revalidate these credentials quickly for subsequent requests.

Authentication Schemes

Authentication schemes are mechanisms used to pass security credentials from a browser to a server. As mentioned earlier, when the web server initiates the authentication process with an HTTP 401 Access Denied response, it includes a list of the authentication schemes supported by the server. A sample response showing this is in listing 10.4.

LISTING 10.4—SAMPLE HTTP 401 ACCESS DENIED RESPONSE FOR MULTIPLE AUTHENTICATION SCHEMES

```
01.HTTP/1.0 401 Access Denied
02.WWW-Authenticate: NTLM
03.WWW-Authenticate: Basic realm="localhost"
04.Content-Length: 24
05.Content-Type: text/html
06.
07.Error: Access is Denied
```

The information in listing 10.4 is critical, because it allows the browser to select a method of obtaining and encoding credentials supported by the server. Thus servers and browsers can innovate by adding new authentication schemes and still negotiate to find a set of protocols supported by each.

The data governing the behavior of the authentication system is carried in a set of new message headers: the WWW-Authenticate records. A WWW-Authenticate record should consist of the following:

◆ **The WWW-Authenticate variable name.**

◆ **The name of the authentication scheme:** examples are *basic* or *NTLM*.

◆ **A realm specification:** this consists of a string of the form *realm=<realm-name>*. The realm name is used to define the space on a server in which a set of credentials is valid. For example, a server might define realms of "sales" or "management" as two discrete regions of the site; credentials obtained in one portion of the site will not be considered valid in the other. IIS generally sets the realm name to the hostname, defining a single authentication space spanning the site.

♦ **An optional list of authentication parameters:** this is a comma-delimited list where each variable takes the form *name=value*. These values are dependent on the authentication scheme in use.

Authentication schemes exist to allow for growth and innovation in the mechanisms used to pass credentials to the server. The HTTP protocol does define one scheme that should be implemented by most browsers, the basic authentication scheme (described later in the chapter). Web servers are free to implement other schemes that improve upon this basic one.

The Basic Authentication Scheme

The basic authentication scheme is included in the HTTP specification. It defines a minimal authentication scheme that is easy to implement and is supported natively by most Internet servers.

Implementing Basic Authentication

The basic scheme transmits encoded usernames and passwords across the network. A server indicates that it supports the basic authentication scheme by including a WWW Authenticate record in the response header, as shown in the following line.

```
WWW-Authenticate: Basic realm="localhost"
```

A request carrying authentication credentials for the basic scheme will contain an Authorization record, as shown in the following line.

```
Authorization: Basic c2hrbWM6eHh4
```

The Authorization record contains the name of the scheme to be used to check the credentials and the encoded form of the credentials themselves. In the HTTP basic scheme, these consist of the username and password (separated by a colon), encoded in the MIME Base-64 format.

This format was originally designed for use in Internet Mail applications; it represents potentially non-printable data in a safe format. This format consists of human-readable characters from a 65-character subset of the ASCII character set. Each character of the encoded data string represents 6 bits of the data originally used to represent the input. Its goal is not to encrypt data but to transmit it in a format that can be safely reproduced by almost any machine. A detailed description of the encoding method can be found in Internet RFC 2045 (available at http://ds.internic.net/rfc/rfc2045.txt).

Basic Authentication Vulnerability

The basic authentication scheme is *not* meant to be a secure mechanism for authentication in and of itself. It is very important to understand that the MIME-64 encoding of the data is just that: a method of encoding (but not encrypting) the data being transmitted. This is a significant difference.

As shown in the previous section, the algorithm for encoding and decoding the username and password is quite straightforward and is not computationally intensive. It will prevent a casual observer from reading usernames or passwords directly from a network monitor, but will not deter any technically competent person. The basic scheme should be considered a method for identifying users, not for truly securing a site; it was never intended to do so.

There is a way around this weakness: combining the basic scheme with the SSL (Secure Sockets Layer). Sessions running under SSL encrypt all the data in the packet in a quite secure fashion. Because HTTP authentication works by embedding headers in messages that are packaged into encrypted packets, the authentication data becomes quite secure. This transforms the basic scheme into a much more secure mechanism. SSL is supported by IIS and by most commercially viable browsers, so it is ubiquitous and useful for the deployment of secure Internet and intranet applications.

 Information about SSL and related encryption technologies supported by Microsoft's Internet Information Server may be found at http://www.microsoft.com/intelev/security/.

The NTLM Authentication Scheme

The IIS and Internet Explorer implement an additional scheme—NTLM authentication. This mechanism improves on the basic authentication scheme in that it does not prompt the user to enter a username and password or transmit them across the network. Instead, it obtains security credentials from the underlying operating system, asking it for the credentials of the user currently logged into the workstation. The browser then transmits a synthesized value across the network, representing the user's security credentials to the server.

This authentication scheme only works if there is an NT or LAN Manager networking domain available. This makes it ideal for use in intranet settings where the underlying network is based on Microsoft servers of some kind, but not particularly useful in Internet applications.

Note The HTTP 1.1 specification indicates that "The realm attribute (case-insensitive) is required for all authentication schemes which issue a challenge." If you look at listing 10.4, you'll see that the WWW-Authenticate record for the NTLM authentication scheme does not contain a realm specification. This isn't a problem today, because IIS is an HTTP 1.0 server, but it is worth knowing. Because the only browsers and servers supporting that scheme are Microsoft products, it doesn't appear to be a major problem.

Authentication and Windows NT Security

Once you understand the basics of HTTP authentication, it is time to look at the way Windows NT and IIS integrate authentication with Windows NT security.

In Windows NT, authentication is basically a process of resolving incoming WWW usernames to NT logons. In the default IIS authentication process, the Window NT user pool is used to authenticate web users. The pool of usernames available for authentication in IIS is the set of users defined in the NT User Manager, and the users' Windows NT passwords are used to validate their right to use the identity.

Warning If your web site employs the basic authentication scheme, there is cause for some concern: Remember, in the basic scheme, user names and passwords are encoded but not encrypted when sent from the browser to the web server. This means Windows NT usernames and passwords for web users are transmitted in an easily decoded form.

Consider using SSL to encrypt the data in transit, or give users different IDs when using your site versus working in the local NT networking domain. Avoid transmitting the local-access user names and passwords over the net in an easily decoded format.

Tip A subject of some confusion is determining which NT security database will be used to authenticate a particular request when the web server is a member of Windows NT domain. If the web server is installed on a primary or backup domain controller, the domain's security database will be used as the default source for usernames and passwords. If the web server is hosted on a server which is not a domain controller, the server's local security database will be used by the web service when authenticating users.

This behavior can be altered by adding a value to the Windows Registry. By adding a value for the key "HKEY_LOCAL_MACHINE\SYSTEM\CurrentControlSet\ Services\W3SVC\Parameters\DefaultLogonDomain" you can specify the main that will be used to authenticate users for your web server.

The Anonymous User

When you configure your IIS site, you are given the option of allowing anonymous web users to access your site. If the site allows anonymous access, it will associate a particular Windows NT user-id with the anonymous user. This NT user-id will be used to determine what resources anonymous users have the right to access on your site.

By default, installing IIS creates a user in the server's local security database of the form *IUSR_<machinename>*. The system administrator can replace the username and password at any time. It is sometimes useful to do so, for example, if your site requires a username in a valid Windows NT domain to handle resources across multiple physical computers.

Security Contexts and IIS

Every request to IIS is resolved by using the context of some Windows NT user. For anonymous users, this is the user assigned in the IIS administrative tool; for authenticated users, this is the Windows NT user associated with the WWW user during the authentication process.

This is true for access to files and for the execution of code. An ISAPI extension invoked in response to a remote user's request will service the request in the context of Windows NT user corresponding to the remote user. For all practical purposes, this means the code is executed as if the remote user was running it from the NT server's console.

This has some useful implications. For example, if an ISAPI module or CGI executable being used to service a request opens a connection to a SQL server database via ODBC, it can use a trusted connection. This means the SQL Server database will grant the extension or CGI program whatever access rights have been defined to be appropriate for that NT user, without the complication of assigning and managing SQL Server passwords in addition to NT usernames and passwords.

NT Access Rights and Authentication

Security in an IIS system is managed by using standard Windows NT access rights. A user's right to retrieve a resource on the server is determined by checking the access rights of the Windows NT user being employed to satisfy the request. If the NT user has access to the requested resource in NT, it will generally have access to it on the web; if it does not, the server will not allow access.

The anonymous user is a slightly special case. If an anonymous request is used to attempt to retrieve a resource, and it does not have access to that resource, it triggers the authentication process. As described earlier, this results in an attempt by the browser to obtain the user's identity and then resubmit the request. If the user is authenticated successfully, the authenticated user's access rights are used to access the requested resource.

Authentication Filters

Now that you have a solid grounding in HTTP authentication and the integration of IIS and Windows NT security, you're ready to implement an authentication filter. The remainder of this chapter describes the semantics, design, implementation, and operation of such a filter.

What Authentication Filters Do

An IIS authentication filter intervenes in the process of mapping the username and password of an Internet user to a Windows NT username and account. The filter performs two basic functions:

- Validates the user's right to access the system based on username and password

- Determines the Windows NT username and password that will be used to determine the user's effective rights on the NT system

The filter is given the username and password entered by the remote user and can deal with them in one of three ways:

- Reject them

- Pass them unmodified

- Change them to a different username and password

Why Use an Authentication Filter?

There are three major reasons why people use authentication filters:

◆ To use usernames and passwords from an existing external system that already implements some form of user identification and password for security

◆ To manage usernames and passwords from a database for convenience or scalability

◆ To implement a role-based security model

Filters Supporting Reuse of Existing Information

A growing number of web sites are being implemented as front ends to existing applications that already implement some security scheme. In these cases, it is much more convenient for the users and administrators of the systems if the usernames and passwords for the two systems can draw from a common source.

The classic example to illustrate this is a system that enables the customers of a bank to access their accounts online. If the bank also provides a voice-response system to perform the same function, it is certainly more convenient if the two systems use a common set of account IDs and PIN numbers for access.

Using Databases for Scalability

There is a fair amount of discussion on the Internet about the suitability of Windows NT domains to manage the user lists for very large web sites. Current opinion is that when a site grows beyond 5,000 to 10,000 users, Microsoft Windows NT domain security is no longer appropriate.

This is partially due to the performance of the Domain server; at this high level, the performance of the security manager built into NT grows somewhat suspect. Microsoft has indicated in some documents that a high-performance server should be able to manage a domain of 40,000 users, but some web site developers in the field are reporting the number to be lower.

Perhaps the more telling argument regards the suitability of the NT User Manager to the task of managing large numbers of users. Many system administrators prefer the power of a database tool for managing quite large numbers of users. These tools simplify searching, maintaining, and reporting on user populations. An authentication filter can allow the administrator to use such tools to maintain the security tables for his or her site.

Implementing Role-Based Security with Filters

On many sites, the security requirements of the site point to a role-based system. Rights to the system are determined by what a user does more than by whom the user is. The system does not need to track the actions of an individual user; it is simply trying to determine the categories of information or functions appropriate for the user.

In such systems, the username and password are employed to determine a user's right to take on a role. This can be modeled in straight Windows NT and IIS by granting all security on the basis of membership in NT User Manager groups and by mapping all Windows NT users into these groups. This is certainly possible, but tends to be inconvenient.

A better alternative might be to create a single Windows NT user ID for each role. For example, there might be a user name for *salesperson* or *cataloguser*. An authentication filter might employ some external source to validate user IDs and passwords, applying one of these role-oriented usernames for access to the underlying system.

The sample presented in this chapter implements this set of features.

Designing and Implementing an Authentication Filter

The remainder of this chapter deals with the implementation of a filter. This filter will do the following:

◆ Validate the user's right to access the system based on username and password

◆ Map this user to a role, replacing the username and password with a username used to model that role in Windows NT

The filter will only be operational for requests using the basic authentication scheme; the NTLM authentication scheme does not provide usernames or passwords in a meaningful way for use by a filter.

Before starting on the design and implementation of the system, a number of operational requirements need to be covered.

Data Storage Requirements

The filter should obtain the set of usernames, passwords, and roles it will be managing from some external data store. The data store will be accessible via ODBC and must behave appropriately in a multi-threaded environment. The system should allow for changes to the set of user IDs while the system is running; it should be possible to add users to the store and have them take effect immediately.

Performance Requirements

The authentication filter will be fired on every resource request, including those for embedded objects such as images, ActiveX controls, or applets. This means each HTML page retrieved by the user could actually cause any number of invocations of the filter.

The authentication filter will also be fired for requests from anonymous users accessing pages that don't require authorization. The filter can safely ignore these anonymous requests, and deferring processing for them to the standard IIS authentication mechanism. Even though these requests can be trivially dismissed, the filter will still see authentication requests for each of these resources as well.

This all points to the fact that the authentication filter must be capable of handling high-throughput operations. It must be very quick to authenticate a user's credentials, so solutions involving searches through text files are not going to be appropriate. Remember that the overhead in this process will contribute to the time required to supply a page to the user. A page with five embedded images will traverse the filter six times, so if the filter takes 1 second to complete the authentication process, it will add 6 seconds to the time required to answer the user's request.

Designing the Filter

The design of this filter is centered on the implementation of three classes:

◆ **CDatabaseManager:** the database manager manages all access to the external data store, using the cache manager to keep performance high.

◆ **CCacheManager:** this class caches valid usernames and passwords in memory after the database manager has retrieved them.

◆ **CAuthFltFilter:** a class derived from *CHttpFilter*. This class handles the interaction with the HTTP server.

The operation of the filter is quite simple. At its simplest, its responsibility is to check incoming usernames and passwords against the database. If a record for the user is located, the role field determines the effective Windows NT username and password for this session.

To meet the performance requirements described earlier, the database will use an in-memory cache to maintain recently used records for rapid access, avoiding the need to re-query the database several times for the retrieval of a page and its dependent objects. Although the database manager might maintain its own cache of recently used objects, the CCacheManager can take advantage of some knowledge of the nature of the objects and how they will be used.

Implementing the Filter

Implementation of the filter will make heavy use of the MFC classes for ISAPI filter support, database access, and concurrency management (thread synchronization). These classes provide a convenient framework for access to these features. With the advent of MFC 4.2, the MFC ODBC support classes are now thread-safe, so there is little or no reason to avoid their use.

Certain pieces of the system will be implemented by using the new standard C++ run-time library classes. These classes provide somewhat more sophisticated data structures than MFC and are now a part of the standard Visual C++ distribution.

As described earlier, the authentication filter's implementation centers on three major classes:

- **CDatabaseManager:** (the database manager)

- **CUserCacheManager:** (the cache manager)

- **CAuthFltFilter:** (a CHttpFilter derivative)

The implementation of the filter adds a pair of additional classes that are less significant. They are as follows:

- **CUserSecurityEntry:** a class that carries information about a user as defined in the database

- **CcacheEntry:** a class that encapsulates a user security entry for use in the cache manager

The relationships between these five classes are shown in the UML class diagram in figure 10.1.

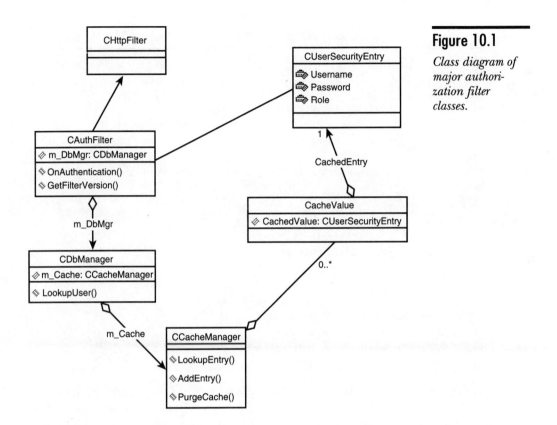

Figure 10.1

Class diagram of major authorization filter classes.

The Database Manager

The database manager is responsible for managing the retrieval of user security records from an ODBC database. The class is narrowly focused on this mission, so the class is quite simple. Its declaration is shown in listing 10.5.

LISTING 10.5—DECLARATION OF CDATABASEMANAGER

```
01.class CDatabaseManager
02.{
03.public:
04.            CDatabaseManager(string connectString,
05.                              bool useCriticalSection=true);
06.    virtual ~CDatabaseManager();
07.
08.    bool    LookupUser(string user, CUserSecurityEntry& entry);
09.
10.protected:
11.private:
12.    void    EnterCriticalSection();
13.    void    ExitCriticalSection();
14.
15.
16.    bool                m_UseCriticalSection;
17.    CUserCacheManager   m_UserCache;
18.    CDatabase           m_Db;
19.    CCriticalSection    m_CriticalSection;
20.};
```

The database manager class uses the MFC *CDatabase* and *CRecordset* classes in its implementation. Starting with Visual C++, these classes are actually thread-safe. If the database used to contain the security records is an Access database, the underlying database engine will not be thread-safe, so the *CDatabaseManager* class must make some provision for thread safety.

Constructing a CDatabaseManager

The constructor of the *CDatabaseManager* class is declared on lines 4 and 5 of listing 10.5. It takes two parameters:

An ODBC connection string

A flag determining whether the class will protect the CDatabase object with a critical section thread synchronization object

The *useCriticalSection* flag value defaults to **true**, because it is less harmful to accidentally enable thread protection than to disable it. It is provided as an option to allow the class to disable the use of protection when not required by the underlying database. Because performance is vital, it is worthwhile to avoid the overhead when protection is not necessary.

The implementation of the constructor is shown in listing 10.6.

LISTING 10.6—THE IMPLEMENTATION OF CDATABASEMANAGER::CDATABASEMANAGER

```
01.CDatabaseManager::CDatabaseManager(string connectString,
02.                                   bool   useCritSection)
03.              :m_UseCriticalSection(useCritSection)
04.{
05.    m_Db.OpenEx(connectString.c_str(),
06.              CDatabase::openReadOnly¦CDatabase::noOdbcDialog
07.              );
08.}
```

The constructor initializes the *m_UseCriticalFlag* attribute in the initializer list on line 3. It then proceeds to open the underlying MFC *CDatabase* object in lines 5 and 6. The database is opened, using the *openReadOnly* flag to enable the underlying database to optimize its access to the data. The *noODBCDialog* flag is also specified, ensuring that the filter will not attempt to display an ODBC logon dialog box if insufficient information is supplied in the connection string. In this case, an exception will be thrown; the filter might handle this itself.

Cleaning up the CDatabaseManager

The destructor of the *CDatabaseManager* class is empty; all the required destruction can be performed automatically. Because the CDatabase object is contained by value, it is destroyed automatically when the CDatabaseManager is destroyed; this has the effect of closing the database connection if it is open.

Retrieving Users from the Database

The LookupUser() member function performs the actual work of the database manager. It retrieves the records for a user from the underlying database. The source code for this function is shown in listing 10.7.

LISTING 10.7—THE IMPLEMENTATION OF CDATABASEMANAGER::LOOKUPUSER()

```
01.bool
02.CDatabaseManager::LookupUser(string          userName,
03.                     CUserSecurityEntry& rEntry)
04.{
05.    bool result=false;
06.
07.    if (!m_UserCache.LookupEntry(userName,rEntry))
08.    {
```

continues

LISTING 10.7—THE IMPLEMENTATION OF
CDATABASEMANAGER::LOOKUPUSER(), CONTINUED

```
09.        EnterCriticalSection();
10.
11.        CSecurityDbRecord rec(&m_Db);
12.        rec.m_strFilter.Format("WebUserName='%0s'",
13.                        userName.c_str());
14.        rec.Open();
15.        if (!rec.IsBOF())
16.        {
17.            rEntry =
18.                CUserSecurityEntry((LPCSTR)rec.m_WebUserName,
19.                            (LPCSTR)rec.m_WebPassword,
20.                            (enRole)rec.m_Role);
21.            m_UserCache.AddEntry(rEntry);
22.            result=true;
23.        }
24.        rec.Close();
25.        ExitCriticalSection();
26.    }
27.    else
28.        result=true;
29.    return result;
30.}
```

The function begins by consulting the cache manager to see if the data for a desired user has already been retrieved and cached. If the cache manager has the desired data, it is used to fill in the return value, and no database access is required.

If the data is not in the cache, the function checks the database. Access to the database is bracketed by calls to *EnterCriticalSection()* and *ExitCriticalSection()* on lines 9 and 25. These two functions are private member functions implemented in the *CDatabaseManager* class; they examine the *m_UseCriticalSection* flag to see if critical sections are required for access to the database. If so, they use the *m_CriticalSection CCriticalsection* object to manage the required thread synchronization.

An MFC recordset object is created on line 11; its filter condition is then specified on lines 12 and 13. The recordset is opened, running the underlying query. If the record is found, it is added to the cache and the record is returned to the caller.

The Cache Manager

The cache manager is responsible for managing an in-memory cache of user security records. As described earlier, the cache manager is required to achieve the level of performance required by the authentication filter.

The cache operates on the assumption that there is a fair degree of proximity of time in the pattern of requests for user security information. This theory is based on the fact that most retrievals of HTML pages requiring authentication will proceed to retrieve a number of embedded objects or subsequent pages, all of which might require authentication using the same credentials.

The user security records in the cache are all given an expiration time; this defaults to 20 minutes from the last time the record is retrieved by the cache manager. The expiration time is used in two ways:

◆ It is used to determine validity of a cached record. After a record has expired, it is removed.

◆ If the cache size exceeds the "soft limit" specified for the maximum number of records to cache, the expiration time is used to purge outdated records from the cache to recover space.

The declaration of the cache manager is shown in listing 10.8.

LISTING 10.8—DECLARATION OF CUserCacheManager

```
01.typedef std::map<string,
02.              CCacheEntry,
03.              std::less<string>,
04.              std::allocator<CCacheEntry> > CACHE_TABLE;
05.
06.
07.class CUserCacheManager
08.{
09.public:
10.        CUserCacheManager();
11.
12.    virtual ~CUserCacheManager();
13.
14.    void    AddEntry(const CUserSecurityEntry& rUser);
15.    bool    LookupEntry(string userName,
16.                    CUserSecurityEntry& rEntry);
17.    void    PurgeCache();
18.
19.protected:
20.private:
21.    CCriticalSection m_CritSection;
22.    CACHE_TABLE      m_Cache;
```

continues

LISTING 10.8—DECLARATION OF CUSERCACHEMANAGER, CONTINUED

```
23.    static const int m_SoftLimit;
24.
25.};
```

The cache manager is built on the data structure defined by the type definition on lines 1–4 of the listing. The data structure is a Standard C++ library *map<>* of strings and *CCacheEntry* objects. This data structure provides the keyed access and the iteration required for the implementation of the cache. The cache's data is managed via one of these maps, declared on line 22 of the listing.

The CCacheManager's public interface consists of three basic functions:

- ◆ **AddEntry():** adds a new entry to the cache
- ◆ **LookupEntry():** retrieves an entry from the cache
- ◆ **PurgeCache():** purges the cache of all expired records

Finally, the cache declares a critical section used to manage concurrent access to regions of code that might modify the collection. Although standard C++ collections are thread-safe, some operations should be constrained.

Adding New Items to the Cache

The *AddEntry()* function is used to add new security records to the cache. The source is shown in listing 10.9.

LISTING 10.9—IMPLEMENTATION OF CUSERCACHEMANAGER::ADDENTRY()

```
01.void
02.CUserCacheManager::AddEntry(const CUserSecurityEntry& rUser)
03.{
04.    m_CritSection.Lock();
05.    try
06.    {
07.        m_Cache[rUser.Key()] = rUser;
08.    } catch(...) {;}
09.    m_CritSection.Unlock();
10.    if (m_Cache.size() > m_SoftLimit)
11.    {
12.        PurgeCache();
13.    }
14.
15.}
```

The entry is added to the collection in lines 4–9. The actual statement adding the code is bracketed by critical section locks and unlocks and a try/catch block. This is intended to protect the data structure from possible corruption and from exiting the block with the critical section lock in place. If the function were allowed to exit with the lock in place, the server would come to a halt while subsequent threads waited for access to the resources guarded by the critical section.

After the item has been added to the collection, the current size of the collection is compared to the preconfigured soft maximum record count. If the count has been exceeded, the *PurgeCache()* function attempts to prune the size of the cache by discarding expired records.

 Note   The maximum record count is referred to as a "soft" limit because the cache manager will allow the cache to grow beyond this limit. The maximum record count is used to trigger behavior that will tend to reduce the size of the cache when the limit is exceeded, but the cache will be allowed to grow beyond the limit.

Retrieving Items from the Cache

The *CCacheManager::LookupEntry()* function retrieves items from the cache. There is a certain amount of intelligence layered onto the bare data structure; entries are checked to see if they have expired before they are returned to the user.

The source for this function is shown in listing 10.10.

LISTING 10.10—IMPLEMENTATION OF
CUSERCACHEMANAGER::LOOKUPENTRY()

```
01.bool
02.CUserCacheManager::LookupEntry(string userName,
03.                               CUserSecurityEntry& rEntry)
04.{
05.    CACHE_TABLE::iterator i = m_Cache.find(userName);
06.
07.    if (i != m_Cache.end())
08.    {
09.        rEntry = (*i).second.CachedValue();
10.        if ((*i).second.IsExpired())
11.        {
12.
13.            m_CritSection.Lock();
14.            try
```

continues

LISTING 10.10—IMPLEMENTATION OF
CUSERCACHEMANAGER::LOOKUPENTRY(), CONTINUED

```
15.            {
16.                m_Cache.erase(i);
17.            } catch(...) {;}
18.            m_CritSection.Unlock();
19.
20.            return false;
21.        }
22.        else
23.            (*i).second.UpdateExpiration();
24.
25.        return true;
26.    }
27.    else
28.        return false;
29.}
```

The function begins by attempting to retrieve the requested user entry on line 5. The *if* statement on line 6 checks the results of the search; if the record is not found, the function has no more work to perform.

If the item is found in the cache, it is checked to see if it has passed its expiration time. If so, it is removed from the collection on line 16. (The usual sentinels protect the removal: the try/catch block and the critical section.) If it has not expired, its expiration time is extended; this should help keep objects that are actively in use by remote clients.

CUserCacheManager::PurgeCache()

The *PurgeCache()* function purges the cache of all expired entries. The client of the class should not need to call this function; it should be invoked sufficiently often by the *AddEntry()* function to keep the cache size at a manageable level.

The details of the implementation of *PurgeCache()* are shown in listing 10.11.

LISTING 10.11—IMPLEMENTATION OF
CUSERCACHEMANAGER::PURGECACHE()

```
01.void CUserCacheManager::PurgeCache()
02.{
03.    m_CritSection.Lock();
04.    try
```

```
05.    {
06.        long currTime = ::GetTickCount();
07.        CACHE_TABLE::iterator i = m_Cache.begin();
08.        while (i != m_Cache.end())
09.        {
10.            if ((*i).second.GetExpiration() > currTime)
11.                i = m_Cache.erase(i);
12.            else
13.                i++;
14.        }
15.    }
16.    catch(...)
17.    {
18.        ;
19.    }
20.    m_CritSection.Unlock();
21.}
```

The usual try/catch block guards the function's inner logic and critical section lock and unlock. The core of the function occurs in lines 6–14 of the listing; it consists of a loop that iterates over the contents of the cache and removes all expired entries.

The function could have been coded to use the *CCacheEntry::IsExpired()* function instead of the explicit comparison made on line 10. The function does not use that function to avoid the overhead of checking the system time inside each call to *IsExpired()*; instead, it depends on the single call to get the current time on line 6.

The Filter Class

The implementation of the filter class is quite simple. The class has only three functions of note:

- ◆ CAuthFltFilter() (the constructor)

- ◆ GetFilterVersion() (MFC ISAPI Filter initialization and configuration function)

- ◆ OnAuthentication() (virtual functions handling authentication requests)

The declaration of the *CAuthFltFilter* class is shown in listing 10.12.

Note Some comments normally generated by the ISAPI wizard have been removed to make listing 10.12 easier to read. The standard ISAPI wizard headers are present in the code on the accompanying CD-ROM.

LISTING 10.12—DECLARATION OF CAUTHFLTFILTER

```
01.class CAuthFltFilter : public CHttpFilter
02.{
03.public:
04.    CAuthFltFilter();
05.    ~CAuthFltFilter();
06.
07.    virtual BOOL GetFilterVersion(PHTTP_FILTER_VERSION pVer);
08.    virtual DWORD OnAuthentication(CHttpFilterContext* pCtxt,
09.                             PHTTP_FILTER_AUTHENT pAuthent);
10.private:
11.
12.    CDatabaseManager m_DbMgr;
13.};
```

The filter contains a database manager; this is initialized in the constructor and available through the life of the filter.

Constructing CAuthFltFilter

The constructor itself does not have any work to do in this implementation. The constructor exists to initialize the database manager by passing it an ODBC connection string. The constructor is shown in listing 10.13.

LISTING 10.13—IMPLEMENTATION OF CAUTHFLTFILTER::CAUTHFLTFILTER()

```
01.CAuthFltFilter::CAuthFltFilter()
02.                 :m_DbMgr("DSN=SecurityDb")
03.{
04.    ;
05.}
```

In this example, the ODBC connection string is hard coded into the filter. For your application, you might wish to change this into a configurable parameter specified in the Registry.

Implementing the GetFilterVersion() function

The implementation of *GetFilterVersion()* can be entirely generated by the Visual C++ ISAPI wizard. The filter version is responsible for indicating to the HTTP server that it is interested in authentication events; the source for the function is shown in listing 10.14.

**LISTING 10.14—IMPLEMENTATION OF
CAUTHFLTFILTER:: GETFILTERVERSION()**

```
01.BOOL
02.CAuthFltFilter::GetFilterVersion(PHTTP_FILTER_VERSION pVer)
03.{
04. // Call default implementation for initialization
05. CHttpFilter::GetFilterVersion(pVer);
06.
07. // Clear the flags set by base class
08. pVer->dwFlags &= ~SF_NOTIFY_ORDER_MASK;
09.
10. // Set the flags we are interested in
11. pVer->dwFlags |= SF_NOTIFY_ORDER_LOW
12.                  | SF_NOTIFY_SECURE_PORT
13.                  | SF_NOTIFY_NONSECURE_PORT
14.                  | SF_NOTIFY_AUTHENTICATION ;
15.
16. // Load description string
17. TCHAR sz[SF_MAX_FILTER_DESC_LEN+1];
18. ISAPIVERIFY(::LoadString(AfxGetResourceHandle(),
19.         IDS_FILTER, sz, SF_MAX_FILTER_DESC_LEN));
20. _tcscpy(pVer->lpszFilterDesc, sz);
21. return TRUE;
22.}
```

The desired notification types are set in the assignment statement on lines 11–14; the filter handles notifications from secure and non-secure connections requesting authentication.

Handling Authentication Requests

The actual work of the filter is performed in the *OnAuthentication()* function. The server calls this function whenever an authentication notification is received. The implementation of the function is shown in listing 10.15.

**LISTING 10.15—IMPLEMENTATION OF
CAUTHFLTFILTER::ONAUTHENTICATION()**

```
01.DWORD
02.CAuthFltFilter::OnAuthentication(CHttpFilterContext* pCtxt,
03.                     PHTTP_FILTER_AUTHENT pAuthent)
```

continues

LISTING 10.15—IMPLEMENTATION OF CAUTHFLTFILTER::ONAUTHENTICATION(), CONTINUED

```
04.{
05.
06.    if (pAuthent->pszUser && (*(pAuthent->pszUser) != 0))
07.    {
08.        CUserSecurityEntry dbEntry;
09.        if (m_DbMgr.LookupUser(pAuthent->pszUser, dbEntry))
10.        {
11.            if (dbEntry.GetNetworkPassword()==pAuthent->pszPassword)
12.            {
13.                strcpy(pAuthent->pszUser,
14.                    dbEntry.GetNtUserId().c_str());
15.                strcpy(pAuthent->pszPassword,
16.                    dbEntry.GetNtPassword().c_str());
17.            }
18.        }
19.    }
20.    return SF_STATUS_REQ_NEXT_NOTIFICATION;
21.}
```

The function begins on line 6 by checking to see if it was somehow handed a null pointer to the username or if the user is the anonymous user. If the anonymous user is being authenticated, the filter should find that the username in the authentication notification structure is an empty string.

If the filter finds a username, it tries to retrieve the user records for this person by calling the database manager's *LookupUser()* function on line 9. If the filter finds a match, it checks to see if the password supplied by the user matches that configured in the database. If so, the username and password appropriate for the user's role is copied into the notification structure, replacing those originally supplied by the user.

The function ends by returning the next notification result code, indicating that the filter has done its work and is ready to continue. As implemented, this filter will not reject failed username and password matches out of hand; it will pass them through to subsequent filters or Windows NT security on the theory that they might be defined elsewhere.

Summary

This chapter has covered the following material:

◆ The underlying authentication mechanism specified by the HTTP specification

◆ The interaction between authentication and the underlying Windows NT security model

◆ The implementation of a simple authentication filter implementing a role based security model

The source code for some trivial classes in the implementation of the filter was not illustrated in the text; please consult the accompanying CD-ROM for the full source code for these ancillary classes.

CHAPTER 11

Advanced Form Processing

This chapter presents an alternative method for handling data from HTML forms. Although the MFC (Microsoft Foundation Class) support for form data via PARSEMAPs is generally quite good, there are a number of situations where they simply do not work very well. This chapter presents a mechnsim for enhancing the MFC support mechanisms, extending them to deal with these situations.

MFC PARSEMAP Limitations

Before launching into the design and implementation of enhancements to MFC, it's worthwhile to review some of the limits inherent in the basic MFC support for form data.

The MFC PARSEMAP mechanism provides a tool for automatically parsing the parameters of incoming requests, translating the parameters to appropriate data types, and dispatching the requests to C++ functions. This is largely managed by defining data structures named PARSEMAPs, which describe the set of commands implemented within an MFC extension DLL and describe the parameters to those commands.

This structure tends to render MFC extension modules somewhat more rigid than might be desirable for some applications. The programming model depends on the fact that the incoming parameters match the PARSEMAPs; it does not react particularly well to cases where the number of fields or data values for those fields vary.

Two situations where this limitation can be a disadvantage are as follows:

◆ Forms that use <select> controls with multiple values. PARSEMAPs expect a field to contain a single value and to be found in the incoming data stream one time. If a <select> element has multiple values selected, the browser sends multiple name=value pairs for the element. This situation also occurs when multiple check boxes are used on a form with the same name.

◆ Forms with variable numbers of fields. Consider the typical shopping cart application. There might be any number of items in the cart, meaning a form might have a variable number of lines of data available to it. Although it is possible to implement a large number of fields with default values to represent the set of possible data elements, this is not terribly convenient. It also imposes an upper limit on the number of occurrences of the field, which might still be inappropriate.

Advantages of the MFC ISAPI Support

Given the limitations of MFC PARSEMAPs detailed in the previous section, you might ask if it is a good idea to use the MFC class library for ISAPI at all. The answer is an unequivocal *yes*. The few situations MFC handles inconveniently do not detract from the many advantages it offers to the form application developer.

First, not all forms fall into one of the trouble areas. Many forms contain a completely predictable set of input elements, with no multi-select option lists or special sets of check boxes. For these forms, the PARSEMAP mechanism is simple, easy to use, and almost ideal. Examples of these forms include many typical form applications, including:

◆ Most questionnaire style forms

◆ Search engine user interfaces

◆ User registration forms

In addition, even in the cases where PARSEMAPs do more harm than good, the rest of the MFC ISAPI support still makes life considerably easier. The *CHttpServerContext* class neatly encapsulates the interface between the developer's extension and the ISAPI interface. The *CHtmlStream* class also provides a convenient mechanism for generating and buffering output, and transmitting it down to the client.

 This chapter presents a mechanism for extending the MFC classes supporting the development of ISAPI extensions. As such, it depends rather heavily on an understanding of the existing MFC classes, especially *CHttpServer* and *CHttpServerContext*. For thorough coverage of these classes, please refer to Chapter 4 of this book, "Basic Form Processing with the MFC."

Designing a Mechanism to Support Flexible Form Content

The first step in extending MFC to handle form data more flexibly is to decide exactly what problems the enhancements will try to solve. This information will be used to define the requirements for these enhancements, which consist of the capabilities that must be provided and the environmental characteristics that must be met. The requirements will lead naturally into the design of the system.

Required Functionalities

In order to provide a more flexible mechanism for handling forms with variable content, the enhancement should provide the following capabilities:

◆ Fields must be addressable by name.

◆ Fields must support multiple values.

◆ Field values must be available in translated form.

◆ The extension must not require the fields to be specified in advance.

◆ The list of fields supplied must be available.

Environmental Characteristics

In addition to providing each of the required capabilities, the extension must be capable of existing in the desired target environment. Some of the required characteristics are as follows:

◆ **Must coexist with PARSEMAPs:** the extension must allow conventional MFC PARSEMAPs to be used within the same extension.

◆ **Must provide a *CHttpServerContext*:** the extension must provide a properly initialized *CHttpServerContext* object to the routines that service a request. The *CHttpServerContext* class is an MFC support class providing a convenient mechanism for building an HTML page in memory; see Chapter 4 for more information.

◆ **Should use STL data structures:** now that Visual C++ 4.x supports the standard C++ library, the extension should use STL for its internal data structures as needed.

The required capabilities and environment characteristics of the extension can be achieved with a fairly straightforward set of classes. The extension will consist of the following:

◆ A set of code for managing the data received as parameters in the request.

◆ A class derived from the MFC supplied *CHttpServer* class to manage the interaction with the rest of the MFC ISAPI extension support.

Note The *CHttpServer* class is provided by MFC as part of its ISAPI extension support. It acts as the base class for user-defined classes that implement a particular extension. For more details, please see Chapter 4.

The set of classes in the design is shown in figure 11.1.

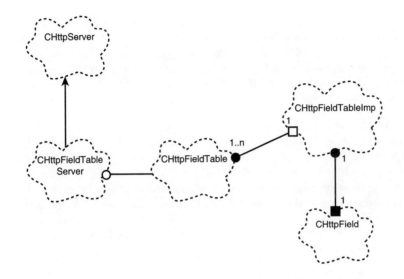

Figure 11.1

*A class diagram
of the classes used
to implement
enhanced forms
support.*

TABLE 11.1
Major Classes in the FieldTable Mechanism

Class	Functionality
CHttpFieldTableServer	Interfaces ISAPI extension
CHttpFieldTable	Manages field data received by the ISAPI extension
CHttpFieldTableImp	Implementation class used by the *CHttpFieldTable*
CHttpField	Manages the data for a single field

The design of each of the classes is discussed in the following sections.

CHttpFieldTableServer Class

This class is derived from the standard MFC *CHttpServer* class. It interfaces with the rest of the MFC ISAPI support code by overriding the *CallFunction()* virtual function; this function is called whenever a request for this ISAPI extension DLL is received.

When a request is received, the following sequence of events will occur:

1. *CHttpFieldTableServer::CallFunction()* is called by the MFC ISAPI support code.

2. *CHttpFieldTableServer::CallFunction()* searches the query string for command name.

3. If a command name is found, the *WillCustomProcess()* virtual function is called. This function is implemented in a class derived from *CHttpFieldTableServer* that implements the logic for a particular ISAPI extension. This function should check the command string, and determine whether or not it will be processed using the field table mechanism. If so, *WillCustomProcess()* should return **true**; otherwise, it should return **false**.

4. *CHttpFieldTableServer::CallFunction()* examines the value returned by *WillCustomProcess()* to determine whether the command will be handled by PARSEMAPs or the field table mechanism. If *WillCustomProcess()* returned **true**, the form data will be parsed into a field table, and the *CustomProcess()* virtual function will be called with the field table as a parameter. The *CustomProcess()* should be overridden by the application's *CHttpFieldTableServer* derived class to implement whatever logic is required by the application. If *WillCustomProcess()* returned **false**, the incoming request will be deferred to the PARSEMAP mechanism for further processing.

CHttpFieldTable Class

The field table class is responsible for managing the set of field data received by the extension for a particular instance of a particular request. The table provides the entire public interface to the field data; the other *CHttpField* classes are strictly for the implementation of this class. It can be thought of as implementing the *facade* design pattern.

> **Note**
>
> Design patterns are a very useful new topic in Object Oriented development. Patterns represent a method for codifying common techniques or architectural constructs that have wide applicability to Object Oriented development. The classic reference work on the subject is *Design Patterns: Elements of Reusable Object-Oriented Software* by Gamma, Helm, Johnson, and Vlissides (the gang-of-four).
>
> The facade design pattern describes a model in which an access to a complex system is provided by a class that provides a facade; a single easy to use interface that masks the complexity of the underlying system. This allows the user of the system to act as if the class was the whole of the modeled system; he or she is freed from needing to learn the intricacies of the underlying system. Instead, they only need to learn how to use the facade.

The field table is only written to as it is created by parsing the parameter stream. After the table has been constructed, it can be viewed as a read-only repository of the data received from the browser.

The field table will implement easy-to-handle copy semantics by defining a copy constructor and assignment operator; the table should be able to be passed by value without incurring a copy of the table.

CHttpFieldTableImp Class

The *CHttpFieldTableImp* class is an implementation artifact; it exists to help the field table class manage the data for the incoming request. Together, the *CHttpFieldTable* and *CHttpFieldTableImp* classes implement the envelope-letter model; the field table object is the envelope that carries the *CHttpFieldTableImp* object.

 Note   An *implementation artifact* is a class that does not appear in the real problem domain. It is an artifact of implementation in that it was created to make implementation possible; external clients of the mechanism will not need to know or care that the class exists.

The implementation object is reference counted. After an instance has been created, multiple field table objects can share it. This enables the field table to implement very low-cost copy operations.

CHttpField Class

The *CHttpField* class is another implementation artifact; it is used in the implementation of the field table, but is not visible to clients. The field class is used to manage the data for a single field on the form. A field can contain multiple values for the form; these values will be maintained in the order in which they are encountered and will be stored as strings.

Using Undocumented MFC to Extend or Enhance MFC

To achieve the level of integration with the rest of the MFC ISAPI support code required to meet the need for coexistence, this code makes use of undocumented components of MFC. This appalls some developers, and overjoys others. Before continuing, it seems worthwhile to touch briefly on the use of undocumented code.

What is Undocumented MFC?

The phrase "undocumented code" has launched articles, books, and arguments. In this chapter, *undocumented MFC code* refers to a number of undocumented members of some otherwise well-documented classes.

Quite a number of classes in the MFC contain undocumented public or protected member functions. This poses something of a quandary; if these member functions are in the public interface of the class, they appear to be available for use. In fact, they are meant for use by other parts of the MFC library. Some of these functions have been documented over time and have entered the officially sanctioned portion of the library.

The bottom line is that the functions do not appear in the MFC documentation; this implies a certain amount of risk.

Risks Versus Rewards of Undocumented MFC Code

When developers build code (ISAPI or otherwise) that uses undocumented parts of MFC, they are trading off some perceived benefit against the risk they bring. Undocumented classes or interfaces are not "blessed" by Microsoft; this means there are no guarantees they will be maintained over time. These interfaces could vanish from one maintenance release to another or—worse yet—subtly shift in meaning.

On the other hand, such interfaces are sometimes the only way to write code that coexists with MFC. The MFC library is not known as the most object-oriented of class libraries; it frequently doesn't expose all the interfaces required to write an adequate extension of an MFC class. Overloading a virtual function in an MFC class frequently requires the developer to cut and paste code from the base implementation of the function. This salvaging of the base implementation of the function frequently brings with it the use of one or more undocumented functions.

In other cases, the undocumented functions or classes are so useful it seems criminal not to take advantage of them. They may perform unique functionality or provide a superior implementation of a common function. When undocumented functions are reused throughout other parts of MFC, making them appear highly unlikely to change over time, there is a temptation to use these interfaces.

Whatever the reason for use of undocumented code, it is important to balance the derived benefit against the risks. At the very least, developers will need to be vigilant about examining each new release of MFC for changes that may impact their code and its use of unsupported features.

Rationale for this Mechanism's Use of Undocumented MFC

In the example in this chapter, both of the aforementioned reasons for using undocumented code apply. One of the requirements for this module is interoperation with MFC, a goal it achieves by extending the *CHttpServer* class. Doing so requires the code to override a virtual function, which tends to require the function to duplicate some of the code from the base class. As is often the case in MFC, this code relies on otherwise undocumented features in MFC.

In addition, the implementation of the *CHttpServer* class involves a number of quite handy functions. For the problem at hand, the most useful is a function named *PreprocessString()*; this function converts a string from the encoded form sent by the browser to a normal ASCII string. Although it is certainly possible to write your own function that duplicates the functionality of this function, it is difficult to see how doing so would be to the developer's advantage. It would not provide greater functionality, or do so in a more efficient way; it would only exist to avoid using the undocumented Microsoft function.

In these two cases, (*CallFunction()* and *PreprocessString()*), the risk of using undocumented MFC seems worthwhile. There's little choice in the first case; this is simply the price of extending MFC. In the second, the function appears unlikely to change, and it serves a real need.

Implementing Enhancements for Handling Variable Form Content

Two sets of code must be implemented to provide the solution described in the "Design" section of this chapter:

The *CHttpServer* extension

The *CHttpFieldData* classes

Each of these bodies of code will be discussed in detail under the headings "Extending the *CHttpServer*" and "Managing the Data with the *CHttpFieldTable* Class."

These mechanisms make heavy use of STL (Standard Template Library). This library is the basis of the new standard C++ library, which will soon be part of the ANSI standard for the C++ programming language.

This library provides a wide variety of data structure and fundamental datatype classes. These data structures are much richer and more complete than those provided by MFC. Versions of the library have shipped with Visual C++ 4.0, although early versions are of uneven quality. They are shipped as a part of the standard runtime library in Visual C++ 5.0.

If you are a C++ programmer, you will need to learn to use these classes.

Extending the *CHttpServer*

The *CHttpFieldServer* class extends the MFC *CHttpServer* class to add support for the new field table mechanism. It is relatively straightforward, implementing a small number of functions and requiring no new data elements. The class declaration for the new class is as follows:

LISTING 11.1—THE HTTPFIELDSERVER.H HEADER FILE

```
01.#if !defined(_HTTPFIELDSERVER_H)
02.#define _HTTPFIELDSERVER_H
03.
04.// include of the field table classes
05.#include "httpFieldTable.h"
06.
07.class CHttpFieldTableServer : public CHttpServer
08.{
09.public:
10.                    // standard virtual destructor
11.    virtual        ~CHttpFieldTableServer();
12.
13.                    // overload of the MFC entry point
14.    virtual int     CallFunction( CHttpServerContext* pCtxt,
15.                            LPTSTR pszQuery,
16.                            LPTSTR pszCommand );
17.
18.                    // pure virtual function definitions
19.    virtual bool    WillCustomProcess(LPTSTR pFuncName) const=0;
20.    virtual void    CustomProcess(CHttpServerContext* pCtxt,
21.                            LPTSTR pFuncName,
22.                            CHttpFieldTable fieldTable)=0;
23.
24.protected:
25.private:
26.                    // internal implementation functions
27.    int             CallCustomProcessFunc(CHttpServerContext* pCtxt,
28.                                LPTSTR pszMethod,
29.                                LPTSTR pszParams);
30.    CHttpFieldTable CreateFieldTable(LPTSTR pszParams) ;
31.};
32.
33.#endif
```

The *CHttpFieldServer* class declares the following items:

◆ **A virtual destructor:** required to allow for proper destruction of descendent classes.

◆ **An overload of the virtual function *CallFunction*:** this is the entry point for integrating the extension with MFC.

◆ **Two pure virtual functions:** these functions provide the mechanism for the *CHttpFieldServer* to recognize and dispatch functions to descendent classes.

◆ **Private implementation functions:** two declared private functions are used in the implementation of the class; these are not exposed to customers of the class, or to derived classes.

> **Note**
>
> Much of the source code in this chapter uses two different data types to refer to Boolean values: BOOL and bool.
>
> BOOL is a type definition provided and used by MFC to represent Boolean values. It is defined via a macro that equates it to an unsigned char. This symbol is basically a notational convenience, to allow the programmer to understand that a particular value is intended to be treated as a Boolean value.
>
> The bool type definition is introduced by the STL/Standard C++ library. It is also used to represent Boolean values, but there is a difference between it and the MFC BOOL datatype. It is a placeholder for the new C++ datatype of the same name, recently adopted by the ANSI standards committee for the C++ language. A number of compilers now directly support this datatype, and more will do so in the immediate future. When the STL is used with these compilers, the native C++ datatype is used.
>
> The same pattern is carried through the constants for Boolean values. The TRUE and FALSE type definitions are provided by MFC; true and false are provided by the STL and the standard C++ datatype.
>
> These two definitions of Boolean constants (TRUE and true, FALSE and false) can generally be used interchangeably. It is important to remember that BOOL and bool do refer to two distinct data types. Variables of type BOOL and bool are not guaranteed to be the same size; they can, and do, occupy differing amounts of memory. They will also be treated as distinct types by the compiler, particularly for matching the types of parameters in function calls.
>
> In this text, the BOOL type is used in pieces of code that have a specific need to interoperate with MFC. All other places that refer to a Boolean value will use the standard bool datatype.

Integrating with MFC via CallFunction

The cornerstone of the class is an implementation of the function
CHttpServer::CallFunction. The MFC framework calls this function once for each
incoming request; the function is called after the entire incoming request has been
received and is available for processing.

The Base Class Implementation

The declaration of the *CallFunction()* member function is as follows:

```
int  CallFunction( CHttpServerContext* pCtxt, LPTSTR pszQuery, LPTSTR
➥pszCommand )
```

The parameters of the declaration are as follows:

- ◆ **pCtxt:** a pointer to a partially initialized server context. When passed to this
  member function, the context does not contain an embedded *CHttpStream*.

- ◆ **pszQuery:** on a GET request, this points to the query string from the ECB
  (extension control block). On a POST request, this points to the form data
  found in the body of the request.

- ◆ **pszCommand:** on a GET request, this is a NULL pointer. For POST requests,
  it points to the query string from ECB.

The default implementation of this function is responsible for finding the name of
the command to be invoked. The command can be specified as part of the URL for
the script or as the first field in the form. Given that the request might be a GET or a
POST request, the command can be found in either the pszQuery or pszCommand
parameter.

After the command is identified, the function attempts to find a matching
PARSEMAP by calling an undocumented implementation function, *LookUp()*. If an
entry can be found, another undocumented function, *CallMemberFunc()*, is called to
parse the parameters, move them onto the stack frame, and call the appropriate
member function.

Simplifying the Extension

The process used to parse the incoming query and identify the function is rather
complex; adding the code for parsing the incoming data and dispatching the appropriate member function is even more complex. Worse, the process depends on a
number of undocumented functions, including some not practical to replace or
reimplement.

This poses a problem for the developer trying to extend the MFC implementation. The *Visual C++ Books Online* documentation suggests that the developer overloading *CallFunction()* should replace it completely and opt out of the PARSEMAP mechanism entirely. This seems to be throwing the baby out with the bath water; the MFC ISAPI support is quite useful. It would be preferable to opt out of the PARSEMAP mechanism on a command-by-command basis, allowing the developer to combine command handlers that use PARSEMAPs with those that don't, and allowing functions to be grouped into DLLs as their functionality dictates.

By making a simplifying assumption or two, it is possible to have the best of both worlds. The bulk of the complexity in the MFC *CallFunction()* routine is the code that looks for the command in the URL or the form data. This code handles both GET and POST requests, and commands that are specified in URL, or the form data via the mfcISAPICommand parameter.

If the extension limits itself to handling commands specified by using the mfcISAPICommand parameter, much of the complexity can be eliminated. Given this restriction, it is also fairly straightforward to write the function so it will forward requests it does not recognize to the base class implementation, thus allowing the use of PARSEMAPs and field tables in the same extension. This assumption is used in the implementation that follows.

Implementing CallFunction()

The source code for this implementation is shown in listing 11.2:

LISTING 11.2—CHTTPFIELDSERVER::CALLFUNCTION

```
01.int
02.CHttpFieldTableServer::CallFunction( CHttpServerContext* pCtxt,
03.                                     LPTSTR pszQuery,
04.                                     LPTSTR pszCommand )
05.{
06.    BOOL    bHandled = FALSE;
07.    int     rc;
08.
09.    LPTSTR pszMethod;
10.    LPTSTR pszParams;
11.
12.    // did the user specify a command via "MfcISAPICommand"?
13.    // Look for end of first parametername via first = sign
14.    LPTSTR pszHiddenCommand = _tcschr(pszQuery, '=');
15.    if (pszHiddenCommand != NULL)
16.    {
```

continues

Listing 11.2—CHttpFieldServer::CallFunction, Continued

```
17.        // Stick a 0 at the position of the first = sign
18.        *pszHiddenCommand = '\0';
19.
20.        // is it there?
21.        if (_tcsicmp(pszQuery, _T("MfcISAPICommand")) == 0)
22.        {
23.            BOOL bNeedToFixParams = FALSE;
24.
25.            // did they have a method, too?
26.            pszMethod = pszHiddenCommand+1;
27.            if (*pszMethod == '\0')
28.                pszParams = pszMethod;
29.            else
30.            {
31.                pszParams = _tcschr(pszMethod, m_cTokenDelimiter);
32.                if (pszParams != NULL && *pszParams != '\0')
33.                {
34.                    // Replace the end of param marker with a
35.                    // null for convenience.
36.                    *pszParams++ = '\0';
37.                    // Keep track of the fact we did so; we
38.                    // might need to put it back later.
39.                    bNeedToFixParams = TRUE;
40.                }
41.            }
42.            // Check to see if this extension would like to process
43.            // this request via field tables.
44.            if (WillCustomProcess(pszMethod) == true)
45.            {
46.                // Call the custom processing function/
47.                rc = CallCustomProcessFunc(pCtxt,pszMethod,pszParams);
48.                bHandled = TRUE;
49.            }
50.            else if (bNeedToFixParams)
51.            {
52.                // If we changed the param structure while
53.                // parsing it, we need to put it back the
54.                // way we found it before handing it to the
55.                // base class implementation.
56.                pszParams—;
57.                *pszParams = m_cTokenDelimiter;
58.            }
```

```
59.          }
60.          // we didn't find the command, or we didn't have
61.          // "MfcISAPICommand", so we'll try to process things
62.          // normally... Put back the = sign we nuked above
63.          *pszHiddenCommand = '=';
64.      }
65.      // If it hasn't been handled yet, hand it off to the base class
66.      if (!bHandled)
67.          rc = CHttpServer::CallFunction(pCtxt, pszQuery,pszCommand );
68.
69.      return rc;
70.}
```

This implementation is fairly straightforward. The function begins by declaring some useful local variables. At line 6, it defines a Boolean variable named *bDefined*, which will be used to keep track of whether the function has handled the request. This will be used later in the function to tell if the base class implementation should be called.

The function continues by checking for the presence of an equals (=) sign in the query string at line 14. The field will be present in the query in the form "MfcISAPICommand=Command" if it has been specified in the form. If the equals sign is found, it is replaced with a null character and the resulting string is compared to "MfcISAPICommand" at line 21. If the string matches, we might have a command to process. The extension can safely check the first parameter, rather than looping through all of them, because the MFC specification for this feature indicates the "MfcISAPICommand" must be the first field or be ignored.

If the command field is found, the variable *pszMethod* is initialized to point to the first character beyond the equals sign. If *pszMethod* points to the NULL character marking the end of the string, there is no method name and there are no parameters. This indicates the user has entered a query consisting of the string "MfcISAPICommand=" and did not specify a command name or parameter string. At this point, it is safe to assume the user does not have a set of parameters to be managed.

If *pszMethod* does not point to a NULL, it points to the first character of the method or command name. In line 31, the function scans for the ampersand (&) character denoting the end of the field. If the ampersand is found, it is temporarily replaced with a NULL character to allow treatment of the command name as a string. A flag is also set to indicate the query string has been modified; this will become important if it is necessary to call the base class implementation of *CallFunction()*.

At line 44, the function is ready to check to see if the descendent class implementing the server would like to process the command. The virtual function *WillCustom-Process()* is called, and is passed the name of the method. The function is declared to be a pure virtual function in the class declaration, so the descendent class must implement it. If it returns **true**, the descendent class will be called on its *Custom-Process()* function via a call to the implementation function *CallCustomProcessFunc()* on line 47. The *bHandled* flag will also be set to indicate the request was handled by this mechanism.

If the *WillCustomProcess()* function returns **false**, the test at line 50 checks to see if the bNeedsToFixParams flag was set earlier in the function. If so, the NULL character placed at the end of the method name is replaced with the ampersand originally found there. Then, at line 63, the function equal sign replaced with a NULL back at line 18 is restored.

Finally, line 66 checks to see if the request has been handled. If not, the *CHttpServer::CallFunction()* member function is called, and passed the original parameters.

 Note All the string manipulation functions used in *CHttpFieldTableServer::CallFunction()* are called via the _tcs macros provided in the C runtime library. These macros correctly handle calls for either Unicode or ASCII builds of the class. All string pointers are declared to be LPTSTRs for the same reason. This is a good practice for code meant for Microsoft NT.

For further implementation on the _tcs macros, please see the documentation in *Visual C++ Books Online*.

Setting Up to Dispatch Commands

The *CallCustomProcessFunc()* implementation function sets things up for a call to the developer's *CustomProcess()* function. The *CallCustomProcessFunc()* function is responsible for completing the initialization of the *CHttpServerContext* object that will be passed to the *CustomProcessFunction()*, and for obtaining a field table. The source is as follows:

LISTING 11.3—CHTTPFIELDSERVER::CALLCUSTOMPROCESSFUNCTION

```
01.int
02.CHttpFieldTableServer::CallCustomProcessFunc(CHttpServerContext* pCtxt,
03.                                              LPTSTR pszMethod,
04.                                              LPTSTR pszParams)
05.{
06.    int nRet = callOK;
07.
08.    ISAPIASSERT(pCtxt->m_pStream == NULL);
09.    pCtxt->m_pStream = ConstructStream();
```

```
10.    if (pCtxt->m_pStream == NULL)
11.        nRet = callNoStream;
12.    else
13.    {
14.        pCtxt->m_pStream->InitStream();
15.        CHttpFieldTable fieldTable(CreateFieldTable(pszParams));
16.        CustomProcess(pCtxt,pszMethod,fieldTable);
17.    }
18.    return nRet;
19.}
```

The *CallCustomProcessFunc()* function begins with an ISAPIASSERT defined to check the stream pointer embedded in the server context to ensure it is NULL. It continues by calling *ConstructStream()* on line 9; this creates a *CHtmlStream* object to be used by the server context. In the MFC implementation of *CallFunction()*, the stream is created in the beginning of the function; this extension defers creation of the stream until it is known whether the field table mechanism will be handling the function. This is necessary to account for the possibility that the extension might call the MFC version of the function, which will expect to find a *CHttpServerContext* with a NULL stream pointer.

CallCustomProcessFunc() checks to see if *ConstructStream()* actually created a stream; if not, the function result code is set to indicate an error. If the stream was created successfully, the stream's *InitStream()* function is called on line 14. This allows for per-instance initialization of the object.

In line 15, a field table object is created and initialized by calling the *CreateFieldTable* member function of this class. The server context, member function name, and field table are then passed to the descendent classes' *CustomProcess* function.

Note The field table created by *CreateFieldTable* is passed by value to the CustomProcess member function. This is safe and efficient because of the implementation of the field table; the data in the table is shared across copies of the table. This is described in more depth in the section "Managing the Data with the *CHttpFieldTable* Class" later in this chapter.

Parsing the Parameters Found in the Incoming Form Data

The parameters are parsed and translated by the private function *CreateFieldTable()*. The source for this function is shown in listing 11.4.

LISTING 11.4—CHttpFieldServer::CreateFieldTable

```
01.CHttpFieldTable
02.CHttpFieldTableServer::CreateFieldTable(LPTSTR pszParams)
03.{
04.    CHttpFieldTable table;
05.
06.    TCHAR szTokens[2];
07.    szTokens[0] = m_cTokenDelimiter;
08.    szTokens[1] = '\0';
09.
10.    LPTSTR pszCurParam = _tcstok(pszParams, szTokens);
11.    LPTSTR pszCleaned;
12.    while (pszCurParam != NULL)
13.    {
14.        LPTSTR pszEquals = _tcschr(pszCurParam, '=');
15.        if (pszEquals!= NULL)
16.        {
17.            *pszEquals = '\0';
18.            _tcsupr(pszCurParam);
19.            pszCleaned = (LPTSTR)PreprocessString(pszEquals+1);
20.            table.addValue(pszCurParam,pszCleaned);
21.        }
22.        pszCurParam = _tcstok(NULL, szTokens);
23.    }
24.    return table;
25.}
```

The *CreateFieldTable()* function begins by creating a field table; the table will bear all responsibility for keeping track of the parameters as they are parsed. The table is created on the stack.

In lines 6–8, the function creates an array of characters and initializes it to contain a one-character NULL-terminated string. The single character is determined by the contents of the *m_cTokenDelimiter*; this is a member of the *CHttpServer* class that contains the character used to delimit elements. By default, this character is an ampersand (**&**). This string will be used as a parameter to _tcstok.

On line 10, the function calls _tcstok (also written *strtok*) to parse the parameter string for strings delimited by the token string. It then enters a loop, processing each of these strings in turn.

Within the loop, each token is scanned for an equals sign, separating the field's name from its value. If the equals sign is found, the name of the field is forced to uppercase via the call to _tcsupr on line 18. The values are processed by calling the base class

PreprocessString() function; this is an undocumented MFC function that translates the string from the "application/x-www-form-urlencoded" encoding scheme to a normal string. The conversion is performed in place, because it is always safe to assume the decoded version will take no more space than its encoded counterpart. The resulting name and value are then added to the field table. Upon exiting from the loop, the table is returned to the caller.

Managing the Data with the CHttpFieldTable Class

The field table class is the heart of the field table extension. The *CHttpFieldTable* class discussed in the previous section exists to facilitate the creation of the field table and its integration with the MFC ISAPI support. The useful and interesting part of the extension comes into play with the field table.

The *CHttpFieldTable* class directly implements a portion of the overall field table functionality; the remainder is implemented in a set of related classes. The implementation of each of these classes is discussed in the next few sections of the chapter, including:

◆ CHttpFieldTable

◆ CHttpFieldTableImp

◆ CHttpField

Additional material in this chapter discusses the treatment of multi-valued fields, and a set of potential enhancements to these classes that you may wish to persue on your own.

CHttpFieldTable Class

The *CHttpFieldTable* class provides the external interface to the field table mechanism. The other two classes in the field table model, *CHttpFieldTableImp* and *CHttpField*, exist to aid in the implementation of this class.

As described earlier in the chapter, the *CHttpFieldTable* class implements a programming model design to allow instances of the class to be passed by value very inexpensively. When copies of a *CHttpFieldTable* object are created, the data in the table is not copied, but is shared between instances. The class implements a mechanism allowing this to occur simply and ensuring destruction of the actual data only when the last reference to it is destroyed. Because of this mechanism, it is generally best to pass field tables by value, rather than passing pointers or references to the structure. This mechanism will make it easy to manage the memory associated with the table.

This mechanism suporting this sharing of values is described in detail later in the chapter.

This section describes the implementatation of the *CHttpFieldTable* class in detail, including:

◆ Type definitions used in *CHttpFieldTable*

◆ The definition of the class

◆ Construction and Copy semantics supported by *CHttpFieldTable*

◆ The process of adding fields and field values to the table

◆ The process of retrieving values and sets of values for specific fields in the table

◆ Retrieving lists of the fields in the table

Type Definitions for CHttpFieldTable Class

The public interface of *CHttpFieldTable* refers to two type definitions:

◆ **FIELD_VAL_ITERATOR:** a STL (Standard Template Library) iterator for field values. This type is actually defined in the HttpField header file; see the section on the CHttpField class for details.

◆ **FIELD_NAME_LIST:** this type is used when providing a list of fields available in a field table. The *typedef* is used for syntactic convenience and to maintain a measure of independence from the actual type used. The actual definition of the type is:

```
typedef vector<string,allocator<string> > FIELD_NAME_LIST;
```

The vector was chosen because the set of fields will be known at the time the collection is generated; the list will be constructed sequentially, and no real flexibility in insertions or deletions is required. It should be possible to change the data structure to a list <string> without making any changes to other parts of the field table.

CHttpFieldTable Class Definition

The class definition for the field table is shown in listing 11.5:

LISTING 11.5—CLASS DECLARATION FOR CHTTPFIELDTABLE

```
01.class CHttpFieldTable
02.{
03.public:
```

```
04.                         // Constructors and destructors
05.                         CHttpFieldTable();
06.                         CHttpFieldTable(const CHttpFieldTable& rSrc);
07.                         ~CHttpFieldTable();
08.
09.                         // Assignment operator
10.     CHttpFieldTable&    operator = (const CHttpFieldTable& rSrc);
11.
12.                         // Value access functions
13.     bool                valueOf(string& rValue,
14.                                 string fieldName,
15.                                 int index=0) const;
16.     FIELD_VAL_ITERATOR valueBegin(string fieldName) const;
17.     FIELD_VAL_ITERATOR valueEnd(string fieldName) const;
18.     int                valueCount(string fieldName) const;
19.
20.                         // Value addition function
21.     void                addValue(string fieldName, string rValue);
22.
23.                         // Get set of field names
24.     FIELD_NAME_LIST*    fieldNames() const;
25.
26.protected:
27.private:
28.                         // Pointer to the actual data
29.     CHttpFieldTableImp* m_pTable;
30.                         // A single static field object
31.     static CHttpField   m_DummyField;
32.};
```

The first set of functions in the class definition contains constructors, a destructor, and an assignment operator. These are used to manage the life span of the field table and the process of creation and destruction. They are described in more detail under the heading "Construction and Copy Semantics."

The second group of functions are used to manipulate the data in the field table by field name. Given a name, they enable the client to access a value, determine the number of values present for that name, or define iterators that can be used to access each of the values in order. If the values are iterated, they will be presented in the order in which they were encountered in the incoming form data.

The *addValue()* function is used by the *CHttpFieldTableServer::CreateFieldTable* function to add values to the field table. It can be called at any time, but it is uncommon to add values to the table after the incoming data stream has been completely parsed.

The *fieldNames()* function generates a list of the fields currently stored in the table. The set of values is projected, using the type defined by the FIELD_NAME_LIST type definition. A pointer to a collection of names is provided to the caller; this is a copy, and the memory becomes the responsibility of the caller.

Two private data elements are defined by the *CHttpFieldTable* class:

◆ **m_pTable:** a pointer to an instance of the *CHttpFieldTableImp* object; this manages the actual data in the table.

◆ **m_DummyField:** a static instance of the *CHttpField* class. This is used by the *valueBegin()* and *valueEnd()* functions to handle the cases when these functions are called with nonexistent fields to provide a null-iterator. Rather than throwing an exception, the dummy field object is used to provide iterators over an empty field. This will yield the desired result; the client will find an empty set of values.

Construction and Copy Semantics

The low-cost copy and shared-data characteristics of the field table class are governed by its constructors, destructor, and assignment operator. Although the *CHttpFieldTableImp* object provides some of the actual behavior, much of it is implemented in the *CHttpFieldTable* class.

The default constructor for the field table is very straightforward. It simply creates an instance of the *CHttpFieldTable*, and uses the result to initialize the m_pTable attribute.

LISTING 11.6—CHTTPFIELDTABLE CONSTRUCTOR

```
CHttpFieldTable::CHttpFieldTable()
{
    m_pTable = new CHttpFieldTableImp;
}
```

The destructor is slightly more interesting; it does not contain a matching delete statement. Instead, it calls the *CHttpFieldTableImp::detach()* function. Because the implementation object is sometimes shared over several copies of the field table, the *detach()* function is responsible for determining when the implementation object can be safely destroyed. The field table is simply responsible for notifying the implementation object that its services are no longer required.

LISTING 11.7—CHTTPFIELDTABLE DESTRUCTOR

```
CHttpFieldTable::~CHttpFieldTable()
{
    m_pTable->detach();
}
```

The copy constructor is reasonably simple; when a table is created as a copy of an existing table, the two tables share a *CHttpFieldTableImp* object. This is performed as follows:

LISTING 11.8—COPY CONSTRUCTOR FOR CHTTPFIELDTABLE

```
CHttpFieldTable::CHttpFieldTable(const CHttpFieldTable& rTable)
{
    m_pTable = rTable.m_pTable;
    m_pTable->attach();
}
```

First, the m_pTable attribute is set to point to the source table's implementation object. The *CHttpFieldTableImp's attach* member function is then called to notify the object of the presence of the new client.

The assignment operator is only slightly more complex. It is used when assigning the set of fields and values in one field table to another field table.

LISTING 11.9—ASSIGNMENT OPERATOR FOR CHTTPFIELDTABLE

```
01.CHttpFieldTable&
02.CHttpFieldTable::operator = (const CHttpFieldTable& rTable)
03.{
04.    if (m_pTable != rTable.m_pTable)
05.    {
06.        if (m_pTable)
07.            m_pTable->detach();
08.        m_pTable = rTable.m_pTable;
09.        if (m_pTable)
10.            m_pTable->attach();
11.    }
12.    return *this;
13.}
```

The differences between the assignment operator and copy constructor stem from differences in the contexts in which they are used.

The assignment operator begins by testing to make sure that a user is not attempting to assign a field table to itself. This test is performed via the *if* statement on line 4. There is no valid reason for a user of this class to do so, but it sometimes happens due to an error in program logic, and it costs little for the class to defend itself from this kind of error.

Since the assignment operator allows the user to assign a new set of values to a field table, it is necessary to release the values that were already in the table. The statement on line 7 accomplishes this; the existing set of values is released before the new values are copied into the field table.

Adding a Value for a Field in the Field Table

Values are added to the collection very easily. The *addValue()* function uses the underlying map's *operator []* function to retrieve a reference to the *CHttpField* object with the desired field name. If a field object with the desired name exists in the collection, a reference to it is returned; if not, one is created and a reference to the new field object is returned.

This is a built-in behavior of the STL map<> class. It requires a default constructor to be present in the *CHttpField* class, because an empty field object will be created prior to the assignment of the value.

LISTING 11.10—CHTTPFIELDTABLE::ADDVALUE

```
void
CHttpFieldTable::addValue(string fieldName, string value)
{
    FIELDTABLE& theMap = m_pTable->getMap();
    theMap[fieldName].addValue(value);
}
```

Retrieving a Single Value from a Field in the Table

As described earlier, the field table supports access to field values, lists of field values, and counts of field values based on field name. The functions that provide this functionality are all fairly similar in their implementation.

The *valueOf()* function allows the client to retrieve a single value based on the name of the field and index of the value. The index parameter defaults to 0; this allows retrieval of the value of single-valued fields quite conveniently, with a statement such as the following:

```
String customerName;
fieldTable.valueOf(customerName,"CUSTNAME");
```

This statement would retrieve the value of a field named "CUSTNAME," and place the result in the variable "customerName." The full source code for this function may be seen in listing 11.11.

LISTING 11.11—CHTTPFIELDTABLE::VALUEOF

```
01.bool
02.CHttpFieldTable::valueOf(string& rValue,
03.                         string fieldName,
04.                         int index) const
05.{
06.    FIELDTABLE& theMap = m_pTable->getMap();
07.    if (theMap.count(fieldName))
08.    {
09.        rValue  = theMap[fieldName].value(index);
10.        return true;
11.    }
12.    else
13.        return false;
14.}
```

The first statement of the function retrieves the map data structure stored in the field table implementation object. The map is then queried to find out whether it contains a field object for the name in question. This query is made prior to attempting to retrieve the value, because the STL map<> data structure will insert an entry into the table if an attempt is made to retrieve a nonexistent key.

Note One of the many data structures that are provided by the STL library is the *map*. A *map* is like a kind of dictionary; it provides a structure where a key may be used to retrieve an associated value. Since this is an STL collection, you have the ability to decide what the key and the value classes will be. The field table uses a map that uses strings as keys, and *CHttpField* objects as values.

If *count()* function returns a nonzero value, the field object is retrieved. It is then asked for the value at the indicated index. The result is stored in the location referred to by rValue, and a Boolean **true** is returned. If *count()* returns zero, then no values for the requested name are present, and the function returns **false**.

Retrieving the Number of Values for a Field

The *valueCount()* function allows users of the field table to determine the number of values that are present for a given field in the table. The implementation of this function is very simple. The basic principle is the same as that of the *valueOf()* function.

LISTING 11.12—CHTTPFIELDTABLE::VALUECOUNT

```
01.int
02.CHttpFieldTable::valueCount(string fieldName) const
03.{
04.    int         result = 0;
05.    FIELDTABLE& theMap = m_pTable->getMap();
06.    if (theMap.count(fieldName))
07.        result = theMap[fieldName].valueCount();
08.    return result;
09.}
```

The map is obtained from the implementation object; count is called to find out if the field is present in the map. If it is present, it is asked for the number of values it contains. The result is then returned to the client.

Retrieving STL Iterators Over the Values of a Field

The two iterator functions are used to retrieve STL begin and end iterators over the set of values for a particular field. The iterators returned are const iterators; they cannot be used to modify the data in the table.

 Note STL iterators provide a mechanism for walking through the set of values in a collection. The begin iterator points to the first value in the collection; the end iterator is one position beyond the end of the collection.

Iterators are a fundamental part of the STL library; any good STL reference should provide a reference on the subject. They can be seen in action in this chapter, in the section "A Sample Field Table Extension."

LISTING 11.13—CHTTPFIELDTABLE ITERATOR FUNCTIONS

```
01.FIELD_VAL_ITERATOR
02.CHttpFieldTable::valueBegin(string fieldName) const
03.{
04.    FIELDTABLE& theMap = m_pTable->getMap();
05.    if (theMap.count(fieldName))
```

```
06.        return theMap[fieldName].begin();
07.    else
08.        return m_DummyField.begin();
09.}
10.
11.
12.FIELD_VAL_ITERATOR
13.CHttpFieldTable::valueEnd(string fieldName) const
14.{
15.    FIELDTABLE& theMap = m_pTable->getMap();
16.    if (theMap.count(fieldName))
17.        return theMap[fieldName].end();
18.    else
19.        return m_DummyField.end();
20.}
```

The only wrinkle in the implementation of these functions is the use of the static dummy field to generate iterators for missing values. Because the iterators are returned by value, there is no way to avoid returning an iterator. The dummy attribute is used to create iterators over an empty set of values when no matching field object can be found for the field name passed as a parameter.

Generating a List of Fields in the Field Table

The field table class provides a mechanism for retrieving a list of the names of all table fields. This function is less useful than might be expected. Most form applications know what fields they expect to process; they are more likely to use the functions that allow access to values by name. The *CHttpFieldTable::fieldNames()* function is useful when debugging; it allows the developer to dump the contents of an incoming request for analysis.

The function is implemented very simply by using an STL algorithm.

LISTING 11.14—CHTTPFIELDTABLE::FIELDNAMES

```
01.string getKeyFunc1( FIELDTABLE::value_type val)
02.{
03.    return val.first;
04.}
05.
06.
07.FIELD_NAME_LIST* CHttpFieldTable::fieldNames() const
08.{
```

continues

LISTING 11.14—CHTTPFIELDTABLE::FIELDNAMES, CONTINUED

```
09.    FIELDTABLE&        theMap = m_pTable->getMap();
10.    FIELD_NAME_LIST* pResult = new FIELD_NAME_LIST;
11.    back_insert_iterator<FIELD_NAME_LIST> out(*pResult);
12.
13.    transform(theMap.begin(),
14.              theMap.end(),
15.              out,
16.              getKeyFunc1);
17.    return pResult;
18.}
```

The *getKeyFunc()* function is a simple unary operation for use in the STL *transform* function; it simply returns the key field from the value pair it receives as a parameter.

The real work of the *fieldNames()* function is performed by the STL *transform()* function. When *fieldNames()* begins, it calls the usual *getMap()* function to get access to the underlying data. It then creates the output data collection and creates a back_insert_iterator on the collection. Finally, it invokes the *transform()* function. The *transform()* function applies *getKeyFunc()* to each element of the map via a pair of iterators and outputs the results to the output collection via the back_insert_iterator.

CHttpFieldTableImp Class

This class is an implementation artifact used to implement the field table. The class implements very little behavior; it manages the life span of the underlying data elements in the field dictionary, providing access to the dictionary on demand.

Type Definitions for CHttpFieldTableImp Class

The field table implementation class only uses one type definition of any note, the FIELDTABLE. The type definition is as follows:

LISTING 11.15—THE FIELDTABLE TYPE DEFINITION

```
typedef map<string,
        CHttpField,
        less<string>,
        allocator<CHttpField> > FIELDTABLE;
```

FIELDTABLE defines the data type used to implement the underlying dictionary of fields. In the current implementation, it is an STL map<>; it uses strings containing field names as keys and *CHttpField* objects as values.

CHttpFieldTableImp Class Definition

As previously indicated, the *CHttpFieldTableImp* class implements very little behavior of its own. The class definition is quite small:

LISTING 11.16—THE CHTTPFIELDTABLEIMP CLASS HEADER

```
01.class CHttpFieldTableImp
02.{
03.public:
04.             CHttpFieldTableImp();
05.    void     attach();
06.    void     detach();
07.    FIELDTABLE& getMap();
08.protected:
09.private:
10.    virtual  ~CHttpFieldTableImp();
11.
12.    long     m_RefCount;
13.    FIELDTABLE m_Map;
14.};
```

The class definition consists of seven items:

◆ **A constructor:** used to initialize the object.

◆ **A destructor:** used to release resources.

◆ **The attach() function:** used in the reference counting mechanism.

◆ **The detach() function:** used in the reference counting mechanism.

◆ **The getMap() function:** provides access to the underlying data structure (*m_Map*).

◆ **m_RefCount:** a data element used to track the number of *CHttpFieldTable* objects using an instance of this class.

◆ **m_Map:** an STL map object used to manage the underlying collection of *CHttpField* objects.

The only item of note in the class declaration is the fact that the destructor is declared to be private. This prevents clients that should use the *detach()* member function from accidentally deleting the object.

Reference Counting

The reference-counting mechanism is implemented through the constructor, attach, and detach member functions.

The constructor simply initializes the m_RefCount attribute to 1 when an instance of the class is created. The assumption is that when the object is created, someone needs it, generating a single use of the object.

LISTING 11.17—CHTTPFIELDTABLEIMP STANDARD CONSTRUCTOR

```
CHttpFieldTableImp::CHttpFieldTableImp()
                :m_RefCount(1)
{
    ;
}
```

The *attach()* member function is equally simple; when called, it increments the reference count. This function is called whenever an additional *CHttpFieldTable* is created that refers to the implementation object.

LISTING 11.18—CHTTPFIELDTABLEIMP::ATTACH

```
01.void
02.CHttpFieldTableImp::attach()
03.{
04.    m_RefCount++;
05.}
```

The detach member function is also quite compact. When a *CHttpFieldTable* object is destroyed, it calls the implementation object's detach member function. The detach member function decrements the reference count, then compares it to zero. When the reference count reaches zero, the object destroys itself via the "delete this" statement.

LISTING 11.19—CHTTPFIELDTABLEIMP STANDARD CONSTRUCTOR

```
void
CHttpFieldTableImp::detach()
{
    m_RefCount — ;
    if (m_RefCount == 0)
        delete this;
}
```

Warning This reference-counting technique works well when used in objects created on the heap. It is important not to try to transplant this implementation to objects created on the stack; the "delete this" statement will have unfortunate consequences if this is on the stack.

This technique is used safely in the implementation of the *CHttpFieldTable* and *CHttpFieldTableImp* classes. The implementation object is managed by the *CHttpFieldTable* object, which always creates it on the heap via the new operator.

CHttpField Class

The *CHttpField* class is responsible for storing the data values for a field in the incoming data stream. This class is basically a thin wrapper around the chosen STL data structures for field data. The class exists to define the exact capabilities required by the rest of the field table mechanism. By defining this class, the extension preserves the option of changing the underlying data structures with little impact on other pieces of the system.

Type Definitions for CHttpField

The field class uses two type definitions to specify the data structures used by the class. The types specify the data structure and an iterator over the data structure. Changing the underlying data structure should be possible simply by changing the type definition.

The first type is the FIELD_VAL_LIST; it defines the data structure used to hold the values. The list is currently implemented by using a vector; the vector was chosen for its efficiency in implementing the direct access of elements required for the *value()* function. The type definition is as follows:

```
typedef vector<string,allocator<string> > FIELD_VAL_LIST
```

The second type is the FIELD_VAL_ITERATOR; it defines an iterator compatible with the value list data structure. The iterator has *const* semantics. The actual type definition is:

```
typedef FIELD_VAL_LIST::const_iterator    FIELD_VAL_ITERATOR;
```

CHttpField *Class Definition*

The *CHttpField* class is rather minimal. It consists of the usual constructors and destructors, with functions for adding, retrieving, and iterating over values.

Listing 11.20—CHttpField Class Header

```
01.class CHttpField
02.{
03.public:
04.
05.                        CHttpField(const char * const pValue);
06.                        CHttpField(const CHttpField& rSrc);
07.                        CHttpField();
08.                        ~CHttpField();
09.
10.    CHttpField&         operator =(const CHttpField& rSrc);
11.
12.    int                 valueCount() const;
13.    string              value(int position=0) const;
14.    void                addValue(string val);
15.
16.    FIELD_VAL_ITERATOR begin() const;
17.    FIELD_VAL_ITERATOR end() const;
18.
19.protected:
20.private:
21.    FIELD_VAL_LIST      m_ValueList;
22.};
```

Construction and Destruction

Two constructors are provided for typical use. The first is used when a field is available, the second when none is available. Because of the behavior of the vector<> used in implementation of the field table, only the latter is currently in use.

An empty destructor is provided in the class (lines 17–20). This function has nothing to do; the standard destruction process will clean up the collection of field values correctly. This destructor is provided as a simple place to set breakpoints during debugging to observe the timing of the destruction of these objects.

Listing 11.21—CHttpField Constructor and Destructor

```
01.// default constructor; doesn't have any work to do.
02.CHttpField::CHttpField()
03.{
04.    ;
05.}
```

```
06.
07.// constructor; used if the field value is known at
08.// the time the field is constructed..
09.CHttpField::CHttpField(const char * const pValue)
10.
11.    m_ValueList.push_back(pValue);
12.}
13.
14.// standard destructor; it could be removed and the compiler
15.// will generate one for us, but this is a convenient place
16.// for breakpoints if trying to test things.
17.CHttpField::~CHttpField()
18.{
19.    ;
20.}
```

Copying a CHttpField object

Support for copying *CHttpField* objects and the data they contain is provided in the usual fashion: via a copy constructor and assignment operator. The source for these functions is shown in listing 11.22.

LISTING 11.22—CHTTPFIELD COPY CONSTRUCTOR AND ASSIGNMENT OPERATOR

```
01.CHttpField::CHttpField(const CHttpField& rSrc)
02.{
03.    back_insert_iterator<FIELD_VAL_LIST> out(m_ValueList);
04.    copy(rSrc.begin(), rSrc.end(), out);
05.}
06.
07.
08.CHttpField& CHttpField::operator =(const CHttpField& rSrc)
09.{
10.    m_ValueList.clear();
11.    back_insert_iterator<FIELD_VAL_LIST> out(m_ValueList);
12.    copy(rSrc.begin(), rSrc.end(), out);
13.    return *this;
14.}
```

The implementations of these functions are only interesting in their use of STL *back_insert_iterators* and the *copy* algorithm. The statement on line 11 constructs a *back_insert_iterator* wrapping the *m_ValueList* collection. This iterator is passed to the *copy()* function on line 12; this will call *copy()* to copy the value list from the source object to this one.

Adding Values to a CHttpField object

Values are added by simply passing the value through to the *push_back* member function of the underlying data structure.

LISTING 11.23—CHTTPFIELD::ADDVALUE

```
01.void CHttpField::addValue(string val)
02.{
03.    m_ValueList.push_back(val);
04.}
05.
```

This function is a good candidate for conversion to an inline member function, because it simply wraps a single function call to the value list's *push_back()* function.

> **Note** Declaring a function to be an inline function allows the compiler to transplant the code in the function to sites where the function is called. This can have positive performance implications, because it allows the compiler to omit the generation of a function call for the inline function. It does have some negative implications as well; because the code from the inline function will be transplanted to the sites of calls to the function, it tends to increase the size of the code somewhat.
>
> Judicious use of inlining can drastically improve the performance of a program, while indiscriminate use of these functions can bloat the program while delivering little performance. It's generally a good idea to build your code without inlining, then profile the code to look for opportunities to improve performance by inlining small, frequently called functions.

Retrieving Single Values from a Field

Single values are retrieved quite easily. The field is retrieved at the index passed in the position parameter. The position defaults to 0 if none is supplied in the call; this is appropriate for single-valued fields.

LISTING 11.24—CHTTPFIELD::VALUE

```
string CHttpField::value(int position) const
{
    return m_ValueList.at(position);
}
```

Multivalued Fields

Fields with multiple values are supported by three functions: the *valueCount()* function and the two iterator functions. Like the other members of this class, they are simply pass-throughs to the underlying data structure. The implementations are as follows:

LISTING 11.25—CHTTPFIELD FUNCTIONS FOR MULTIPLE VALUES

```
01.int CHttpField::valueCount() const
02.{
03.    return m_ValueList.size();
04.}
05.
06.FIELD_VAL_ITERATOR CHttpField::begin() const
07.{
08.    return m_ValueList.begin();
09.}
10.
11.FIELD_VAL_ITERATOR CHttpField::end() const
12.{
13.    return m_ValueList.end();
14.}
```

Possible Enhancements to the Field Table Mechanism

The classes in the field table mechanism provide a number of opportunities for enhancements, or tuning, in light of differing requirements. Two are described here for consideration:

◆ **Inlining of member functions:** all the member functions shown in this class are minimal enough to be effectively inlined. They are not specified this way because they have not been shown to represent a large amount of overhead and are easier to use in a debugging environment as out-of-line functions.

◆ **Lower-cost single-valued fields:** the current implementation of this class does not distinguish between fields with single or multiple values. The class uses a vector to store all data; single-valued fields simply have a single element in the vector. It would be possible to recode the class to use a single string field for single-valued fields, creating a vector later if needed. This would increase the complexity of the code somewhat; there is a tradeoff between size of code and size of the data.

Using the CHttpFieldTableServer Class in an ISAPI Extension

This section illustrates how to use the *CHttpFieldTableServer*. It presents simple directions for integrating the field table server with an ISAPI extension generated by the ISAPI Extension Wizard, and then presents an example of a working extension.

Converting an MFC ISAPI Extension to Use the FieldTable Classes

Converting an extension from a standard MFC PARSEMAP-based ISAPI extension to one that supports both PARSEMAPs and field tables is a simple process. To accomplish this, follow the steps described here.

In the header file for the extension class:

1. Add an include directive to include the file httpFieldServer.h.

2. Change the base class for the extension from *CHttpServer* to *CHttpFieldTableServer*.

3. Add declarations for the two required virtual functions, *WillCustomProcess()* and *CustomProcess()*.

After modifying the extension class header file, you need to make the following changes to the C++ source file for the extension class:

1. Modify the BEGIN_PARSE_MAP macro to specify *CHttpFieldTableServer* in place of *CHttpServer*.

2. Modify the *GetExtensionVersion* implementation to invoke *CHttpFieldTableServer::GetExtensionVersion* in place of *CHttpServer::GetExtensionVersion*.

3. Add implementations of the two required virtual functions, *WillCustomProcess()* and *CustomProcess()*.

4. Modify the BEGIN_MESSAGE_MAP macro invocation to point to *CHttpFieldTableServer*. This will not affect the code in any way, but is a bookkeeping convenience for the Class Wizard.

A Sample Field Table Extension

This extension implements a single verb through the field table mechanism: *Dump*. When the extension receives the dump command, it responds with a page that shows the contents of the data stored in the field table for the incoming form.

This section will show the source code for the two virtual functions for custom processing and the function responsible for processing the dump command. It will also show a sample input form and the response generated for that form.

The Virtual Functions

The first of the two virtual functions is the *WillCustomProcess()* function. This function should return **true** if the extension would like to use field tables to process the command, and **false** if it would like to use the default parse table processing. The implementation of this function is straightforward:

LISTING 11.26—AN IMPLEMENTATION OF WILLCUSTOMPROCESS

```
bool
CSampleExtension::WillCustomProcess(LPTSTR pFuncName) const
{
    if (_tcsicmp(pFuncName,_T("DUMP"))==0)
        return true;
    else
        return false;
}
```

The second virtual function is the *CustomProcess()* function. It is called by the field table server extension after a request has been received and the field table created. It will be called for any command request for which the *WillCustomProcess* member function returns **true**. It can handle the request itself or delegate it to another function; the latter is generally cleaner. In this case, it delegates the request to a function named *DumpFieldData*.

LISTING 11.27—A CUSTOMPROCESS IMPLEMENTATION

```
void
CSampleExtension::CustomProcess(CHttpServerContext* pCtxt,
                                LPTSTR pFuncName,
                                CHttpFieldTable fieldTable)
{
    if (_tcsicmp(pFuncName,_T("DUMP"))==0)
        DumpFieldData(pCtxt,fieldTable);
}
```

The *DumpFieldData()* function looks quite a bit like a standard MFC ISAPI command handler. The biggest difference between this function and a standard MFC function is that the *DumpFieldData()* function receives its parameters via a field table instead of a set of C++ data types.

LISTING 11.28—CSAMPLEEXTENSION::DUMPFIELDDATA

```
01   void
02   CSampleExtension::DumpFieldData(CHttpServerContext* pCtxt,
03                                   CHttpFieldTable      fieldTable)
04   {
05       // Output headers
06       StartContent(pCtxt);
07       WriteTitle(pCtxt);
08
09       *pCtxt << _T("<h1>Output All fields </h1>\r\n");
10       *pCtxt << _T("<table>\r\n");
11
12                        // Get set of field names
13       FIELD_NAME_LIST*  pNames = fieldTable.fieldNames();
14       string            value;
15       int               valueCount;
16
17       // Iterate over the set of field names
18       for (FIELD_NAME_LIST::iterator i = pNames->begin();
19            i != pNames->end();
20            i++)
21       {
22           // output the first (or only) value for the field.
23           *pCtxt << _T("<tr><td>") << (*i).c_str() << _T("</td>");
24           fieldTable.valueOf(value,*i);
25           *pCtxt << _T("<td>") << value.c_str() << _T("</td></tr>\r\n");
26           // check to see if there are any more.
27           valueCount = fieldTable.valueCount(*i);
28           if (valueCount > 1)
29           {
30               // If so, output them as well
31               for (int ctr=1;ctr<valueCount;ctr++)
32               {
33                   *pCtxt << _T("<tr><td> </td>");
34                   fieldTable.valueOf(value,*i,ctr);
35                   *pCtxt << _T("<td>") << value.c_str() << _T("</td>
➡</tr>\r\n");
```

```
36                }
37            }
38        }
39        // delete the list of names
40        delete pNames;
41
42        // close the table
43        *pCtxt << _T("</table>\r\n");
44
45        // end the body and page
46        EndContent(pCtxt);
47 }
```

The function starts very typically; in lines 6 and 7, it generates the standard start-of-page HTML. On lines 9 and 10 it outputs a page heading and opens a table.

On line 13, the function requests a list of field names from the field table. It might be important to note that the name list is not sorted in any particular order; although the list of values for a field will be maintained in the order in which it is received, the fields themselves are in random order.

Line 18 begins the for-loop that will be used to generate the output for each of the fields; the loop extends through line 38. The loop uses STL iterators over the field name list to control the loop.

The field name and the first (or only) field value are displayed in the table by lines 23–25. Line 24 retrieves the first value from the field via a call to the *valueOf()* function.

The function then checks to see if any additional values are available for the field. If the call at line 27 indicates more than one value present for the field, use the loop from lines 31–36 to output any additional values. This inner loop uses a for-loop and counter to walk through the values; passing the counter to the *valueOf()* function retrieves the values from the table. This loop could also have been implemented with the field value iterator functions.

Finally, lines 42–46 close the table and output the usual end-of-page HTML tags to complete the response.

The Field Table Extension in Action

As an example, consider an input form that looks like the one in figure 11.2:

Figure 11.2

A sample input form.

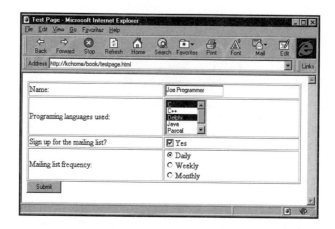

The form consists of the following elements:

◆ A text input field (name = name)

◆ A select tag allowing multiple selections (name = Languages)

◆ A check box (name = maillist; value = ON)

◆ A set of radio buttons (name = frequency)

When this form is filled out as shown in figure 11.2 and submitted for processing, the extension generates a page that looks like figure 11.3.

Figure 11.3

Response to the sample form.

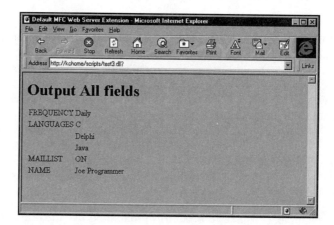

Summary

This chapter has presented the design and implementation of a set of classes to extend MFC's support for form data. This extension can coexist with PARSEMAPs, improving support for some types of data. The extension is not meant to be a complete replacement for the mechanisms built into MFC, but to augment them in situations they do not handle quite as well as others.

CHAPTER 12

ISAPI Programming Using Borland Delphi 2.0

Although C++ is usually the language used in ISAPI programming, ISAPI presents a language-neutral interface. Any development tool that can produce a 32-bit DLL that exports functions with "C" linkage can be used to create ISAPI extensions and filters.

Because Borland Delphi 2.0 easily satisfies these requirements and has many compelling features, it is a logical candidate for ISAPI development. This chapter discusses how to use Delphi effectively in this context.

All ISAPI programmers, whether using Delphi or not, will find important information in this chapter. Because Delphi does not include any framework (such as Visual C++'s MFC) to ease ISAPI programming, you'll have to deal with ISAPI at a lower level than you'll see in the rest of this book. Reading this chapter will provide you with important knowledge about what is going on at a lower level. This is invaluable regardless of your choice of programming language.

Advantages to Using Delphi

Borland Delphi 2.0, using the Object Pascal programming language, is a competent object-oriented development environment. Many developers are currently using this tool, and many have a great deal invested in existing code.

Although most ISAPI developers seem to be using C++ today, it's certainly not a requirement. If you are already comfortable using Delphi, you might prefer also to do your ISAPI development in this environment. The cost of buying C++ compilers or other new software and training developers in that new environment, particularly one with as many hidden traps as C++, might well be prohibitive.

If you have time and effort invested in existing Delphi code, it might not be cost effective to move to another environment. If you continue developing in Delphi, you might be able to reuse much of your existing code.

Many corporations are using Delphi for their internal development today. If you've already written a Human Resources application in Delphi, and now want to provide employees with access to benefits information through the Intranet, you may well be able to reuse some of that existing application in your ISAPI application.

Bear in mind that the ISAPI environment might place different demands on your programs than running as a stand-alone executable. In particular, ISAPI is fundamentally multithreaded. Much existing code is not designed to be executed in a multithreaded environment.

Delphi Limitations with ISAPI

When you began Delphi development you paid money for—and invested significant time learning—a very rich tool. It is a powerful development environment consisting of the Object Pascal language, a suite of visual programming tools, a robust component architecture, a database engine, and a library of components, many of which are integrated with that database engine.

When programming in ISAPI, many of the elements of this rich tool are either irrelevant or inoperable, as described in the following sections.

No User Interface in ISAPI Programs

All the visual components created with Delphi are useless in ISAPI. The user interface in an ISAPI application is actually the data being sent to the client's browser, which becomes the web page that the client views. Components such as radio buttons and combo boxes have no place in ISAPI programs.

In fact, without some very special considerations, it is illegal for any ISAPI extension or filter to have windows. The Windows NT operating system considers it a security breach to allow *service* code to interact with the address space of the *user*. Some special applications, such as those employing DDE communications, require the ISAPI extension to communicate through the Windows message queue. Ways do exist to work with such requirements, but it is beyond the scope of this chapter.

Database Problems

The BDE (Borland Database Engine) was not designed for the requirements of ISAPI programming. Its limitations will exclude its use from most real-world web applications.

The first problem is a design limitation. The BDE only supports a maximum of 32 connections per process. Only the most popular web sites consistently demand more database resources than this, but the chances are good that any site with a substantial number of users will exceed this limit from time to time.

The second problem is less clear, but just as significant for many developers. Many people, including the author, have reported problems with the BDE when running in the context of an ISAPI extension. Difficulty connecting to databases and corrupted data have been experienced.

You don't need to let this scare you away from developing your extensions in Delphi. There are still ways to gain database access. In particular, several excellent components are available that allow access to databases through ODBC. These solutions can be very effective at what they were designed for, but might not allow you to use any existing Delphi database access code in your work. One component that has been reported to work well is ODBCExpress from DataSoft (Pty) Limited. You can get more information about this from their web page:

```
http://www.adam.co.za/odbcexpress/
```

Lack of an Application Framework for ISAPI Applications

Delphi enables the programmer to create a simple Windows application in minutes by drawing the desired user interface and writing just a small amount of code. Your code executes within a framework supplied by Delphi, so all standard functionality is automatically provided unless you choose to override it.

Unfortunately, Borland has not yet delivered any analogous framework to handle the "dirty work" in an ISAPI application. This chapter will help you overcome this deficit by presenting a framework to handle the protocol of communicating with the server and automate the retrieval and parsing of request parameters and cookies.

Delphi versus C++ ISAPI Programming

To successfully communicate with the server through the API, you must understand how the dialog, which Microsoft has documented for the C++ programmer, appears from the Delphi side of the fence.

Although on the surface the languages are different, there is really a striking similarity. This is probably because both languages are object-oriented derivatives of languages (C and Pascal) that were originally cousins in that they were designed to support structured programming.

After you translate the API from C/C++ terms to Object Pascal, the rest is easy. The differences you notice are those you're probably already accustomed to as a Delphi developer.

Data Type Correspondence

The most obvious difference between Delphi and C++ is the way information is passed. The languages support similar data types, but their names are different. Both languages are strongly typed, but differ in the way values can be cast from one type to another. The function call linkage differs, as well. A translation of Microsoft's C++ header files is given in the following listing (as well as included on the CD-ROM in the file \projects\chap12\ISAPIExt.pas). Using this, you won't have to worry about these differences at all.

Borland has released their own port of the header used for developing ISAPI extension applications. The unit presented in listing 12.1 is somewhat simpler to use and highly recommended by the authors of this book. Borland has not released a translation of the Httpfilt unit for implementing ISAPI filters.

- ◆ **Fundamental data types:** although similar types are supported, they have different names. For example, when C++ refers to a *BOOL*, this is actually a type of integer and does not correspond to Delphi's *Boolean* type. Similarly, Delphi has the *PChar* type, which corresponds to C++'s *char**.

- ◆ **Type casting:** owing to Object Pascal's heritage as a strongly typed language, it can be more difficult to convert a value from one type to another. The semantics of some ISAPI function calls, however, demand an object to be passed by reference in some cases, but a *nil* value to be passed in other cases. The translated ISAPI units presented in the chapter's example differ chiefly from Borland's in that they are written to make this easier without casting.

- ◆ **Function call linkage:** the C language always passes variables to functions by value; when pass-by-reference is needed, the programmer must pass the address.

Object Pascal, on the other hand, can explicitly pass the variable by reference. Thus, where C thinks it's passing pointers, Object Pascal can use the *var* or *const* modifiers.

Unavailability of MFC or Other Framework

Despite the fact that Object Pascal is typically thought of as a higher-level language than C or C++, most of the programming in this chapter is at a lower level than you will see elsewhere in this book. The programming examples elsewhere all rely on services provided by the MFC (Microsoft Foundation Classes). Although Delphi, like Visual C++ via MFC, provides a robust framework for implementing Windows GUI applications, no such help is available for ISAPI applications.

Because of this, you will learn the mechanics of parsing the values passed in a GET or POST request and gain a better understanding of how other aspects of ISAPI programming and the HTTP (HyperText Transfer Protocol) work.

Writing an ISAPI Application with Delphi

Writing an ISAPI application involves communicating with the web server by using a protocol specified by Microsoft. Following this protocol, the server loads your DLL and calls the prescribed entry point when a request is received. You can call back into the server to retrieve the data sent with the request and to send data back to the client.

Writing an ISAPI application successfully requires knowledge of the HTTP specification. This describes such things as the types of requests that might be made, how data is encoded, and how to respond to requests. The current version of the HTTP specification is 1.0 and is described in RFC 1945. Version 1.1 is currently being considered. Both of these documents are included on the companion CD-ROM.

The ISAPIExt Unit

The first requirement for working with ISAPI is to provide definitions for all elements of the protocol. Borland supplies these definitions, but they are somewhat incomplete. In addition, the way Borland has chosen to declare some of the function calls requires typecasting, making their library inconvenient to use. Listing 12.1 shows a unit that improves on Borland's definition.

LISTING 12.1—PROJECTS/CHAP12/ISAPIEXT.PAS

```
001   unit ISAPIExt;
002   {
003    declares the interface for ISAPI extension applications
004    Portions copyright (c) 1996  Borland International
005   }
006
007   interface
008
009   uses
010      SysUtils,
011      Windows,
012      Classes;
013
014   const
015      HSE_VERSION_MAJOR       =   1;      // major version of this spec
016      HSE_VERSION_MINOR       =   0;      // minor version of this spec
017      HSE_LOG_BUFFER_LEN      =  80;
018      HSE_MAX_EXT_DLL_NAME_LEN = 256;
019
020   type
021      HCONN = THandle;
022
023   const
024      // the following status codes may be
025      // returned by HttpExtensionProc
026      HSE_STATUS_SUCCESS                  = 1;
027      HSE_STATUS_SUCCESS_AND_KEEP_CONN    = 2;
028      HSE_STATUS_PENDING                  = 3;
029      HSE_STATUS_ERROR                    = 4;
030
031      // Values representing requests for services
032      // from the ServerSupportFunction.
033      //  Values from 0 to 1000 are reserved
034      HSE_REQ_BASE                        = 0;
035      HSE_REQ_SEND_URL_REDIRECT_RESP      = ( HSE_REQ_BASE + 1 );
036      HSE_REQ_SEND_URL                    = ( HSE_REQ_BASE + 2 );
037      HSE_REQ_SEND_RESPONSE_HEADER        = ( HSE_REQ_BASE + 3 );
038      HSE_REQ_DONE_WITH_SESSION           = ( HSE_REQ_BASE + 4 );
039      HSE_REQ_END_RESERVED                = 1000;
040
041      //
```

```
042    //  Microsoft-specific extensions
043    //
044    HSE_REQ_MAP_URL_TO_PATH                    = (HSE_REQ_END_RESERVED+1);
045    HSE_REQ_GET_SSPI_INFO                      = (HSE_REQ_END_RESERVED+2);
046
047
048    //
049    // passed to GetExtensionVersion
050    //
051  type
052    PHSE_VERSION_INFO = ^THSE_VERSION_INFO;
053    THSE_VERSION_INFO = packed record
054      dwExtensionVersion: DWORD;
055      lpszExtensionDesc: array [0..HSE_MAX_EXT_DLL_NAME_LEN-1] of Char;
056    end;
057
058
059  type
060    TGetServerVariableProc = function ( hConn:      HCONN;
061                                        VariableName: PChar;
062                                        Buffer:     Pointer;
063                                        lpdwSize: LPDWORD ):
064    BOOL; stdcall;
065
066    TWriteClientProc = function ( ConnID:     HCONN;
067                                  Buffer:     Pointer;
068                                  lpdwBytes: LPDWORD;
069                                  dwReserved: DWORD ):
070    BOOL; stdcall;
071
072    TReadClientProc  = function ( ConnID:     HCONN;
073                                  Buffer:     Pointer;
074                                  lpdwSize: LPDWORD ):
075    BOOL; stdcall;
076
077    TServerSupportFunctionProc = function ( hConn: HCONN;
078                                   HSERRequest:  DWORD;
079                                   Buffer:       Pointer;
080                                   lpdwSize:     LPDWORD;
081                                   lpdwData type: LPDWORD):
082    BOOL; stdcall;
083
```

continues

LISTING 12.1 PROJECTS/CHAP12/ISAPIEXT.PAS, CONTINUED

```
084    //
085    // passed to extension procedure on a new request
086    //
087  type
088
089    PEXTENSION_CONTROL_BLOCK = ^TEXTENSION_CONTROL_BLOCK;
090    TEXTENSION_CONTROL_BLOCK = packed record
091      cbSize: DWORD;                // size of this struct.
092      dwVersion: DWORD;             // version info of this spec
093      ConnID: HCONN;                // Connection handle
094      dwHttpStatusCode: DWORD;      // HTTP Status code
095                                    // null terminated log info
096      lpszLogData: array [0..HSE_LOG_BUFFER_LEN-1] of Char;
097      lpszMethod: PChar;            // REQUEST_METHOD
098      lpszQueryString: PChar;       // QUERY_STRING
099      lpszPathInfo: PChar;          // PATH_INFO
100      lpszPathTranslated: PChar;    // PATH_TRANSLATED
101      cbTotalBytes: DWORD;          // Total bytes received
102      cbAvailable: DWORD;           // bytes available in buffer
103      lpbData: Pointer;             // pointer to buffer
104      lpszContentType: PChar;       // Content type of client data
105
106      GetServerVariable:    TGetServerVariableProc;
107      WriteClient:          TWriteClientProc;
108      ReadClient:           TReadClientProc;
109      ServerSupportFunction: TServerSupportFunctionProc;
110    end;
111
112    // constants received by the TerminateExtension function
113    // (if one is provided)
114  const
115    HSE_TERM_ADVISORY_UNLOAD = 1;
116    HSE_TERM_MUST_UNLOAD     = 2;
117
118    //
119    //  these are the prototypes that must be exported from the extension DLL
120    //
121
122    // function GetExtensionVersion( var Ver: THSE_VERSION_INFO ): BOOL;
➥stdcall;
```

```
123  //  function HttpExtensionProc( var ECB: TEXTENSION_CONTROL_BLOCK ):
➥DWORD; stdcall;
124  //  function TerminateExtension( dwFlags: DWORD ): BOOL; stdcall;
125
126  implementation
127
128  end.
```

There are two important differences between the unit in listing 12.1 and the one supplied by Borland:

◆ **TerminateExtension entrypoint:** Borland's unit omits this function (as described on line 124) and the constants used by the function (on lines 112–116).

◆ **Function parameters:** the parameters of the callback functions declared on lines 60–82 differ in declaration, although in practice they amount to the same thing. Borland's declarations require pass-by-reference, which makes it difficult to pass *nil* as the actual value; listing 12.1 sidesteps the problem by declaring parameters of type *LPDWORD*.

Providing ISAPI Application Entry Points in DLLs

Your application must contain two special functions and an optional third. You can see sample declarations for these functions in the comments on lines 122–124 of listing 12.1.

The GetExtensionVersion() Function

This is a very simple function. Its only purpose is to specify the version of ISAPI the DLL was implemented for and to give a description of the extension. The server calls when the DLL is first loaded. This occurs the first time a request is made for the DLL, just before *HttpExtensionProc()* is called for the first time. All you need to do is to reply with the constants *HSE_VERSION_MAJOR* and *HSE_VERSION_MINOR*, defined on lines 15–16 of listing 12.1.

When the function is called, a *THSE_VERSION_INFO* record (defined on lines 53–56 of listing 12.1) is passed by reference into the function. Your job in implementing the function is to fill in the fields of this record. Listing 12.2 shows a typical implementation:

LISTING 12.2—SIMPLE GETEXTENSIONVERSION() IMPLEMENTATION

```
1   function
2   GetExtensionVersion (var pVer : THSE_VERSION_INFO):
3   BOOL; export;  stdcall;
4   begin
5     pVer.dwExtensionVersion := MAKELONG( HSE_VERSION_MINOR,
6                                          HSE_VERSION_MAJOR );
7     StrPCopy( pVer.lpszExtensionDesc, 'Sample ISAPI extension' );
8     result := TRUE;
9   end;
```

Fulfilling the responsibility of the *GetExtensionVersion()* function requires doing three things:

1. Encoding the major and minor version numbers (defined on lines 15 and 16 of listing 12.1) and placing the resulting DWORD value into the field that identifies the expected version number

2. Copying a description to the field *lpszExtensionDesc* (limited in length to *HSE_MAX_EXT_DLL_NAME_LEN* characters)

3. Returning a *TRUE* value

Although this is all the function needs to do, you're welcome to do more if necessary. In particular, this is a great place to perform any initialization that isn't appropriate within the *initialization* sections of your code.

For example, you may want to load configuration information at this point, or open a pool of database connections for later use.

The *GetExtensionVersion()* function is called to act on behalf of the server; it will be executing within the system security context. This provides you with complete access to the system for your initialization activities, such as reading from the registry.

The HttpExtensionProc Function

The HttpExtensionProc function is the real meat of your extension. The server calls this function every time a request is made for the extension. When called, it will be passed a *TEXTENSION_CONTROL_BLOCK* record (defined on lines 90–110 of listing 12.1) by reference. This structure (usually referred to as the ECB for short) contains information you will need for servicing the request and callback function pointers, which you can call to do or get anything else you require.

Listing 12.3 contains the logic necessary to handle a request for a "Hello, World!" web page. Used in conjunction with the *GetExtensionVersion()* function shown in listing 12.2, you'll have the complete implementation of a traditional "Hello, World!" for ISAPI.

LISTING 12.3—SIMPLE HTTPEXTENSIONPROC() IMPLEMENTATION

```
01  function
02  HttpExtensionProc (var pECB : TEXTENSION_CONTROL_BLOCK):
03  DWORD; export; stdcall;
04  const
05    CrLF = ^M^J;
06  var
07    outstr: String;
08    dwLen: DWord;
09  begin
10    // set the status and the content type headers;
11    // IIS will supply reasonable defaults for
12    // everything else
13    outstr := '200 OK' + CrLf
14              + 'Content-Type: text/html';
15    // set the ECB's status field
16    pECB.dwHttpStatusCode := 200;
17    // send the headers
18    pECB.ServerSupportFunction( pECB.ConnID,
19                                HSE_REQ_SEND_RESPONSE_HEADER,
20                                PChar(outstr),
21                                NIL, NIL );
22
23    outstr := '<HTML><BODY>Hello, world!</BODY></HTML>';
24    dwLen := Length(outstr);
25    // send the body of the reply
26    pECB.WriteClient( pECB.ConnID,
27                      PChar(outstr),
28                      @dwLen, 0 );
29    result := HSE_STATUS_SUCCESS
30  end;
```

Fulfilling the responsibility of the *HttpExtensionProc()* function requires doing two things:

1. Filling in the ECB's *dwHttpStatusCode* field to indicate the status of the request processing. This is described in detail later in the section "Sending Headers." You can see an example on line 16 of listing 12.3.

2. Returning an appropriate result code. The values are defined on lines 26–29 of listing 12.1, and you can see it in action on line 29 of listing 12.3. Typically, you will use a value of *HSE_STATUS_SUCCESS*. The legal values are defined on lines 26–29 of listing 12.1; for more information on them, see Appendix A.

Any useful application is going to require more work than this, though. Most significantly, you will want to provide some output to send to the user. Before you can actually do this, you must send the necessary HTTP headers, as done in lines 10–21 of listing 12.3. Lines 23–28 send the "Hello, World!" message to the user. This is all explained in greater detail in the section "Sending Data Back to the User."

Unlike *GetExtensionVersion()* and *TerminateExtension(),* the HttpExtensionProc function acts on behalf of the user; that is, it is called from the security context of the user issuing the request. This will typically be *IUSR_machinename* if the user is allowed anonymous access, or it might be the user's personal profile in other security schemes.

The TerminateExtension() Function

Unlike the other two entry point functions, *TerminateExtension()* is optional. If present, it is called when the server wants to unload the DLL. One of two values (defined on lines 115–116 of listing 12.1) will be passed in the following:

◆ A value of *HSE_TERM_ADVISORY_UNLOAD* that asks permission to unload the DLL. A return of TRUE will allow this to occur

◆ A value of *HSE_TERM_MUST_UNLOAD* that forces the DLL to clean up and prepare to be unloaded

Like *GetExtensionVersion(), TerminateExtension()* acts on behalf of the server, so it's allowed to do virtually anything necessary.

Using the ECB to Interact with the Server

In a typical ISAPI extension, the lion's share of the work is done in *HttpExtensionProc()* or the functions it calls. It's unable to do its work in a vacuum, however. One of the parameters that the server passes into the function is a reference to an Extension Control Block, which is a sort of Swiss army knife with gadgets you can use to get the data you need and send the results to the user.

There are a few different types of things included in the ECB. It has several data fields, some of which deliver information to you and some of which you fill in to return data to the server. It also has a few callback functions—pointers to functions with which you can retrieve values or send data. The following table provides descriptions of the most important of these fields (see Appendix A for a complete description).

TABLE 12.1
Important Members of the Extension Control Block

Name	Type	Description
ConnID	Handle; Input	A handle that identifies the connection to the server. This is actually useless to you, but is required as a parameter when calling any of the callback functions
dwHttpStatusCode	DWORD;	Enables you to communicate the status of the Output request when returning from HttpExtensionProc. The value you placed here will be stored in the server's log
lpszMethod	PChar; Input	A pointer to a null-terminated string that indicates the type of request, such as *GET* or *POST*
lpszQueryString	PChar; Input	A pointer to a null-terminated string that contains the actual query. This is only defined for *GET* requests
cbTotalBytes	DWORD; Input	The total number of bytes sent for a *POST* request
cbAvailable	DWORD;	The total number of bytes that have been received for a *POST* request so far
lpbData	Pointer;	A pointer to the data sent in a *POST* request
GetServerVariable	Callback	Retrieves the value of the server variable or header you request
WriteClient	Callback	Sends the contents of a buffer to the user
ReadClient	Callback	Reads additional data from the user
ServerSupportFunction	Callback	Provides a number of miscellaneous functions, determined by the value of the *dwHSERequest* parameter. This is most often used for sending response headers, but also provides such services as redirection

Retrieving Header Information and Server Variables

Server variables and header information such as cookie values are not directly available to the extension while processing in the *HttpExtensionProc()* function. This data can be easily retrieved, however, by employing the *GetServerVariable()* callback function. A pointer to this function is given in the ECB. By specifying the name of the variable or header, you can retrieve a string containing the value.

A typical call looks like this:

```
success := pECB.GetServerVariable( pECB.ConnID, 'REMOTE_HOST',
                                   @myBuffer, @myBufferLen );
```

This call retrieves the value of the REMOTE_HOST variable. The value is placed into the specified buffer and terminated with a null character to produce a value that can be read as a string. Either of two conditions might cause the function call to fail:

> The value requested is not available.

> The buffer is not long enough to hold the value.

In these cases, the function returns FALSE; otherwise TRUE is returned.

Interpreting Requests

The first thing you're likely to want to do when *HttpExtensionProc()* is called to service a user's request is to determine just what that request is. How this information is sent depends on whether the request method is *GET* or *POST*.

GET Requests

The content of a *GET* request is sent as part of the URL. IIS provides a bit of help by parsing the URL for you. The request data itself is available to you in two ways:

> You can retrieve it directly from the ECB through the *lpszQueryString* parameter.

> You can request its value from the *GetServerVariable()* callback function.

Either source is correct.

POST Requests

It's potentially more difficult to retrieve the value of a *POST* request. This is the price of the greater flexibility and carrying capacity of this method. Retrieving the request is usually as easy as dereferencing the *lpbData* field of the ECB. This buffer has a limited, fixed size (defaulting to 48 KB), and extremely large requests might overflow it, requiring some special consideration.

If there is any chance the size of the incoming request could exceed the capacity of the buffer, you should check the buffer and request size. These values are sent in the ECB as *cbTotalBytes* and *cbAvailable*, respectively. If the total size of the request is greater than the number of available bytes (which would equal the size of the buffer, if it were filled), you will have to retrieve the data in the *lpbData* buffer, retrieve the extra data that didn't fit into the buffer, and concatenate the two values.

The extra data can be retrieved with the *ReadClient()* callback function. A pointer to this function is given in the ECB. Call this function and pass the *ConnID* supplied in the ECB, a buffer you allocate (of sufficient size to contain the result of the request), and the number of bytes you'd like to have retrieved.

 Do not request more bytes than the difference between *cbTotalBytes* and *cbAvailable* indicates are waiting. Doing so will cause the call to block until either sufficient bytes to complete the request become available or the connection is closed.

Separating Request Fields

The data in a request usually consists of the names and values of fields in an HTML form on a web page. Having retrieved the entire request, you still need to parse it to get out the individual field names and values. The HTTP specification dictates that fields in the request be separated by ampersands and that each field consist of an optional field name, an equals sign, and an optional value. By scanning the request string for these delimiters, you can easily break up the request into name/value pairs.

When you parse these values, you should keep in mind there is no guarantee that field names within a request will be unique. In particular, the values of an HTML form's *<SELECT MULTIPLE>* field are each sent as separate fields with the same name. If this is a possibility, you must be prepared to handle multiple valued fields. In fact, MFC's default processing fails to handle this situation; Chapter 11, "Advanced Form Processing," describes how to solve this problem in C++.

 Although there is no mention of this in the HTTP specification, many browsers will add an extra carriage return/linefeed combination at the end of any *POST*ed data. Because any white space or control characters should have been URL-escaped (as described in the next section), you can (and should) normally trim these characters from the request.

For a practical example of parsing a request, turn to the section "Parsing the Request" in Chapter 13, "Using the Delphi ISAPI Application Framework."

Cross
Reference

URL Encoding

After you have received and parsed the request, it's probably still not usable. In order to transmit it, the user's browser should have encoded the request by escaping any special characters in it. The process changes spaces to plus signs, and other characters outside the set of alphanumerics and a few other characters to escape codes. The escape code consists of a percent sign followed by the two-digit hexadecimal representation of the character's ASCII value.

For example, suppose that the string *Hello, World!* needs to be transmitted. The browser needs to replace the punctuation and spaces with characters that can safely be sent in an HTTP request. In this case, the result would be *Hello%2C+World%21*.

You must reverse this process for both the names and values of the fields.

Cross Reference

To see practical examples of functions that encode and decode strings in this way, turn to the section "Handling URL-Escaped Data" in Chapter 13.

Sending Data Back to the User

After you have retrieved, parsed, and decoded the request and performed any application-specific processing necessary, you will need to respond to the user. This is actually a two-step process. First, the response headers must be sent to the user, an easily overlooked step because it's invisible to the user, but critical nonetheless. Second, you send the body of the response. The body isn't strictly required, but the blank pages that result will satisfy few applications.

Sending Headers

Before the user's browser can handle the body of the response, it must get a description of what it's about to receive. This description consists of a line indicating the version of the HTTP protocol being used and the status of the request, followed by a series of headers, each separated by a carriage return/linefeed combination. Each header consists of the header name, a colon, and the value of the header.

You should assemble the headers into a string buffer and use the *ServerSupportFunction()* callback function with a dwHSERequest value of *HSE_REQ_SEND_RESPONSE_HEADER* to send it off. A pointer to this function is provided in the ECB. The header string you send is assumed to be a null-terminated string. The following code shows a typical call to the function:

```
pECB.ServerSupportFunction( pECB.ConnID, HSE_REQ_SEND_RESPONSE_HEADER,
                  PChar(outstr), NIL, NIL );
```

Before sending the request, IIS will parse your header string and add any additional headers necessary. However, the intelligence of this feature is somewhat limited. To ensure the desired output, there are a few things you should watch for when creating your header strings:

◆ **Always send the HTTP status code:** this should be the first line of the header. Assign the same value to the ECB field *dwHttpStatusCode*. The legal values are defined in the HTTP specification and can be found in Appendix C. This will typically be "200," which signifies OK.

◆ **Never send the HTTP protocol version:** the protocol requires this to be sent (along with the status code) as the first line of the response. IIS understands this and will automatically prepend your header strings with the correct value if one is not supplied. You should allow IIS to specify the version of HTTP it will be communicating with.

◆ **Always send a Content-Type header:** there's no way the server can know what value this should take, so you will have to supply it yourself. This is typically a string such as *Content-Type: text/html*.

◆ **Do not end your header string with a line end:** IIS will append one automatically. An extra line end results in the browser misinterpreting any headers IIS appends. The browser will think that they're part of the body and display them at the top of the web page.

 Although not required, sending a *Content-Length* header is a good idea. If the user's browser receives this, it can give the user feedback on the progress of the request. Unfortunately, you frequently will not know the actual length until you complete a lengthy process of actually determining all the data to send. In cases like these, you're probably better off not sending this header.

Figure 12.1 shows a typical response header string, as well as the actual header string sent by IIS:

Sent to ServerSupportFunction	Sent by ServerSupportFunction to User	**Figure 12.1**

`200 OK`
`Content-Type: text/html`
	`HTTP/1.0 200 OK`
	`Content-Type: text/html`
	`Server: Microsoft-IIS/2.0`
	`Date: Sun, 03 Nov 1996 18:30:26 GMT`
		IIS adds additional headers as necessary.

Technically, it's possible to send the headers by using the *WriteClient()* function rather than *ServerSupportFunction()*; the user's browser can't tell which function was called. Resist the temptation to do this! It might interfere with the operation of any ISAPI filters, and you lose the benefit of IIS's automatic generation of additional required headers.

You should check the value returned by *ServerSupportFunction()*. A TRUE value indicates a successful operation. An unsuccessful operation—indicated by a FALSE return—means the request could not be completed for some reason. If this occurs, you will generally be unable to do anything else useful for the user, so your best bet is to abort the request handling, clean up, and return from the *HttpExtensionProc*.

Sending the Response Body

After the headers have been sent, you can send the body of the response. This is done with the *WriteClient()* callback function. A pointer to this function is given in the ECB. This function can be called as many times as you like while servicing a request.

Unlike the header string you sent with *ServerSupportFunction()*, the data you send here cannot be assumed to be a null-terminated string. It might be binary data such as a GIF or JPEG image. This means you must supply the length of the data to be sent, as well as a pointer to the buffer itself. The following code shows a typical call:

```
dwLen := Length(datastr);
pECB.WriteClient( pECB.ConnID, PChar(datastr), @dwLen, 0 );
```

Each call will be sent to the user directly, so if the response consists of a dynamically generated web page, for example, you might be able to improve the perceived performance by sending blocks of data as they are generated rather than waiting until the entire response page is built.

If you will be sending the response in many parts, you should check the value returned by *WriteClient()*. A TRUE value indicates a successful write. An unsuccessful write, indicated by a FALSE return, means the data could not be sent to the user for some reason—most likely because the connection has been terminated. Whatever the cause, you will be saving resources by aborting the request handling, cleaning up, and returning from the *HttpExtensionProc()*. You won't be doing anyone any good by sending data to an unreachable user.

Persistent State Information: Using Cookies

It is frequently desirable to store information about someone currently using your site. This might simply be to track the user's identity, or it might be something more complicated such as a "shopping basket" to track the items a user has decided to purchase from an online catalog. Unfortunately, the very nature of the HTTP protocol will not allow storing such information. For all practical purposes, each request is entirely independent and is received and serviced independently. There is no state information or context available to relate the current request with past or future requests.

Some programmers have circumvented the problem by dynamically adding hidden fields to each page to send the data back to the server with each request. This solution has many disadvantages. It's cumbersome to implement each link as a form submission rather than a simple anchor. It's inefficient to insert these fields dynamically onto every page. And it might be horribly insecure to transfer some data through insecure connections.

Netscape devised a solution to alleviate these problems, which they refer to as "cookies." Not all browsers support the feature, but most do, including Netscape Navigator and Microsoft Internet Explorer. By using this scheme, a user's browser manages the persistent information. The server sends a cookie to the browser to manage, and the browser sends it back as appropriate.

Information you expect to need again when servicing subsequent requests is sent to the user in a header field. The browser returns it (when appropriate, as discussed later, in the section "Setting a Cookie") as a header sent to the server along with requests. The server might optionally specify that the information expire after some period, that it only be sent with requests for some subset of the pages in a site, and that it only be transmitted over a secure connection.

This scheme is not foolproof. Not all browsers support cookies. If they are supported, the browser—or the user—might choose to delete any cookies currently being held, as it deems necessary (for example, to free storage space). A browser also might not delete a cookie when it is set to expire. If cookie usage becomes excessive, throughput might be affected adversely.

Retrieving the Value of a Cookie

Cookies can be retrieved by getting the value of the *HTTP_COOKIE* header (see the section "Retrieving Header Information and Server Variables" earlier in this chapter for information on doing this). The value returned will contain all the cookies sent, similar to the way the query string is assembled. A typical value returned looks like this:

```
CookieName1=CookieValue1; CookieName2=CookieValue2
```

A semicolon and a space (as contrasted to ampersands in the query string) separate cookies. The name and value are separated by an equals sign.

The next section recommends that you encode cookies before sending them. If you do this, you will obviously need to decode them before use.

Setting a Cookie

Before setting any cookies, you must understand a number of things. There are several attributes you can specify to control when the cookies are sent back to the server, and there are a number of limitations to their use.

Naturally, you don't want all the cookies the user's browser is managing to be sent to all the servers the user connects to. This would waste bandwidth, and more importantly, could pose a serious security problem. To avoid this, the server sends a domain name as part of the cookie. A cookie will be returned only to the domain specified when the cookie is sent. Because the domain name defaults to the current host name if it's omitted, and a server is only allowed to send a value of a domain name to which it belongs, this is rarely used explicitly. It will almost always work the way you want it to without any intervention on your part.

A cookie can be set to expire at a certain time. If no expiration time is sent, the cookie will expire and be deleted at the end of the session—when the browser is shut down. If an expiration time is sent, the cookie is said to be *persistent*, signifying the value is valid until the time specified. As previously noted, the cookie might still be deleted before then, so you can't count on its presence. The time must always be specified for the GMT time zone, with the following format, where *Day* is a three-letter abbreviation for the weekday and *Mon* is a three-letter abbreviation for the month:

```
Day, DD-Mon-YYYY HH:MM:SS GMT
```

Here is an example of a valid cookie expiration time:

```
Sun, 03-Nov-1996 18:30:26 GMT
```

A path can be specified to limit the applicability of a cookie to a subset of the pages of a site. A cookie will only be sent to the server with a request if that request is at or below the specified path. A value of / (forward slash) is the most general path: a cookie with this value will be sent along with all requests for this site.

The attribute *secure* might be added if the cookie should only be sent over secure connections (that is, through a connection that's using the Secure Sockets Layer). This attribute has no value.

The values of the attributes described here (as appropriate), together with the cookie's name and value, are sent to the user's browser in a *Set-Cookie* header (see the section "Sending Headers" earlier in this chapter for information on sending headers). Many *Set-Cookie* headers might be sent with a single response if there are many cookies needing to be set. A request with all attributes set (which will rarely happen—this is just for illustration) looks like this (except it should all be on a single line):

```
Set-Cookie: MyCookie=MyValue; expires=Sun, 03-Nov-1996 18:30:26 GMT;
path=/; domain=mysite.com; secure
```

In this example, the name of the cookie is *MyCookie*; its value is *MyValue*. No particular encoding is dictated for the cookie's name or value. However, something is clearly needed to ensure the string can be parsed by looking for delimiting semicolons. The URL-escaping described previously in the section "URL Escaping" will be sufficient, particularly because you already need to write a function for it to decode the input requests.

If the user's browser receives a cookie with the same name and path as an existing cookie, the new one will overwrite the original. You can use this to delete cookies whose values are made obsolete, by sending new ones with an *expires* attribute whose value has already passed.

Note that cookies with the same name can exist for multiple levels in the path. For example, suppose a cookie named *MyCookie* with a value of *General* is sent to the user with a path of /, and another cookie of the same name is sent with a value of *Specific* and a path of */mydirectory*. When the user makes a request whose path is at or below */mydirectory* (such as */mydirectory/somepage.htm*), *two* cookies will be sent to the server. The header would look like this:

```
Cookie: MyCookie=Specific; MyCookie=General
```

When multiple cookies with the same name are sent, the cookies at a more specific path will be returned to you before those at a more general path.

The Netscape cookie specification gives several limitations to the use of cookies. It's not safe to count on any particular browser supporting this exactly as written. The following maximums are specified:

◆ A browser should be able to store a total of 300 cookies (overflow is to be deleted on a least-recently-used basis).

◆ A cookie should not exceed a length of 4 KB, including its name and value (the value can be trimmed to fit, if necessary).

◆ A browser should be able to store up to 20 cookies per server or domain (overflow is to be deleted on a least-recently-used basis).

Writing an ISAPI Filter

ISAPI filters can also be implemented in Delphi. Borland does not supply a unit defining the filter interface. It is, however, available on the Internet. See the companion CD-ROM for links to the site where Borland makes this unit available for download.

Just as with writing an ISAPI application, there is very little difference between the implementation of filters in C++ and in Delphi. Chapter 7, "Understanding ISAPI Filters," will provide a good start toward implementing one in Delphi.

Summary

Delphi is a practical tool for ISAPI development. There are many reasons to use the language, most significantly that you might have a large amount of code already implemented in Delphi.

If you choose to use Delphi, you need to be aware of some differences between Delphi and the C++ development that is much more widely documented, both in this book and elsewhere. You will need a unit to supply the definitions of the ISAPI interface. Delphi does not include a framework (such as MFC) to handle the details of ISAPI programming. You will need to either learn the details of ISAPI at a deeper level than would be required otherwise, or use the framework for ISAPI applications presented in Chapter 13.

The web server expects certain functions to be present in an ISAPI application DLL. It will call *GetExtensionVersion()* when the DLL is first loaded and *HttpExtensionProc()* each time a request needs to be serviced. Your ISAPI application needs to interact with the Extension Control Block passed to *HttpExtensionProc()*. This provides callback functions you can use to retrieve the request and other variables. You use other callback functions to send headers back to the user, as defined in the HTTP specification. After the headers have been sent, you can send the contents of your response to the user.

It can be cumbersome to manage all these details. The following chapter presents a complete framework for developing ISAPI application in Delphi, which will greatly simplify the development process for you if you choose to use Delphi.

CHAPTER 13

Using the Delphi ISAPI Application Framework

O ne of the goals of this chapter is to overcome a deficiency suffered by Delphi developers, compared to C++ developers, in the programming of ISAPI extensions. C++ developers enjoy the help of the MFC class library in developing ISAPI extensions.

MFC provides many useful services for developers of ISAPI extensions. It determines which functions should be called for handling a request, it handles all communications between the server and the user's browser, and it parses form requests (within limitations described in Chapter 11, "Advanced Form Processing"). Most of this work is pure drudgery—by freeing the developer from having to deal with it personally, MFC supports greater productivity. Clearly, Delphi developers would benefit from the availability of such a library.

This chapter presents a library for Delphi developers:

◆ The goals of the framework will be laid out.

◆ You'll be shown how the framework can help you to write a simple ISAPI extension.

◆ A practical example that converts between Fahrenheit and Celsius temperatures will be presented.

◆ You'll see how to use the framework for more sophisticated tasks such as handling cookies.

◆ The inner workings of the framework will be explored.

After reading this chapter you'll be able to use it to speed and simplify development of your own ISAPI extensions. The complete source code is included on the companion CD-ROM in the directory \projects\chap13\ISAPIExtension.

Design Goals

The goal of the library presented in this chapter is to provide a framework that enables the creation of ISAPI extensions with a similar degree of ease, and at a similar level of abstraction, as Microsoft's MFC does for C++ developers.

This is not to say that the library emulates MFC in any way. MFC capitalizes on some features of C++ not enjoyed in Delphi. Likewise, a framework for Delphi can exploit features of Delphi not shared by C++. In particular, parse maps employing function overloading and stream output using overloaded operators are not applicable to Delphi. On the other hand, some aspects of the Delphi object model allow a cleaner object-oriented solution than would be possible in C++.

Cross
Reference

The following tasks are sufficiently automated to allow you to create a full-featured ISAPI extension, even if you are unfamiliar with the details discussed in Chapter 12, "ISAPI Programming Using Borland Delphi 2.0":

◆ Invocation of the user's code as determined by the request, including support for multiple requests within a single extension

◆ Automatic retrieval of the request, regardless of its method (POST or GET)

◆ Automatic parsing of form fields in the request, including decoding URL-escaped strings and handling of multiply valued fields

◆ Retrieval of field values by name and index

◆ Retrieval of headers and server variables by name

◆ Setting the status of the request

◆ Sending status and headers

◆ Reading and writing from/to the client

◆ Setting cookies

◆ Retrieving cookies, including parsing and decoding their names and values and providing access to them by name as with form requests

These features are provided with minimal overhead. An extension built with this framework should present a reasonable footprint and provide a reasonable level of performance, considering the functionality implemented by the extension.

Using the ISAPI Application Framework

A library having all of the features outlined in the previous section is bound to need some explanation. This section introduces you to the concepts you'll need to exploit the framework.

The concepts that will be presented in this section include:

◆ Creating a project that uses the framework

◆ Calling your extension from an HTML form

◆ Writing a class to handle requests for your extension

◆ How the framework's services are exposed to you

◆ Retrieving the values that a user entered into a form

◆ Retrieving server variables and information from the request's headers

◆ Sending headers back to the user

◆ Working directly with a request's parameters and cookies

◆ Sending data to the client

◆ Handling exceptions in your code

Creating a New Project for Your Extension

Create a new project by copying the source code from your companion CD-ROM. A complete set of source code without any request handlers (discussed later) can be found in the directory \projects\chap13\ISAPIExtension. The following list shows the files that make up the framework; you will need to add them to your project.

ISAPIExtension.dpr	HTTPServer.pas	HTTPSrvrCtxt.pas
ISAPIExtension.pas	ISAPIExt.pas	MultiValList.pas
HTTPUtilities.pas	RequestHandler.pas	RequestHandlerRegistry.pas

You will want to rename the project file (currently named ISAPIExtension.dpr), of course.

 You might find it helpful to put this project into Delphi's object repository. This excellent feature of Delphi can be quite helpful in organizing your work to promote code reuse. If you are a programmer who's been around for a while, you surely have a collection of useful code you have written over the years. The object repository will enable you to track and reuse this code base with ease.

Preparing HTML Forms with the ISAPICOMMAND Field

The first step in implementing an application with this framework is to decide for which requests it is to be invoked. These requests must be given names, which will be incorporated into the HTML pages issuing the request, and must be coded into the ISAPI extension so requests can be delegated to the correct part of your code.

Any request must include a field named *ISAPICOMMAND*, whose value is set to the name of the request. For example, if a form is meant to be handled by the ISAPI extension DLL myext.dll, and the name of the request is *MYREQUEST*, the form should look something like this:

```
<FORM METHOD=POST ACTION="myext.dll">
  <INPUT TYPE=HIDDEN NAME="ISAPICOMMAND" VALUE="MYREQUEST">
  <! Collect some more input >
</FORM>
```

Both the name of the field (*ISAPICOMMAND*) and its value (the name of the request, *MYREQUEST* in this case) are case-sensitive.

If the ISAPICOMMAND field is not specified, or a request handler with the specified name cannot be found, the user receives an error message and a web page containing the message Command not specified by *ISAPICOMMAND*.

Writing and Registering a Class to Handle Requests

A single extension may handle many different requests. Each one is written separately, and encapsulated in a class written specifically for that purpose. This class is referred to as a request handler. A base class, *ReqHandler*, is provided; your request handler must descend from this class. The framework delegates the various requests to their appropriate handler classes by instantiating an object of the corresponding class and executing a method implemented by the individual request handler.

For example, if you're writing an extension to handle all of the user management functions on your web site, you might decide to provide separate requests within it for changing the user's password and for changing the user's email address. For the former you might create a request handler class called PasswordReqHandler, which is to be invoked when the extension receives an ISAPICOMMAND value of CHANGEPASSWORD. For the latter, you might create a request handler called AddressReqHandler, which is to be invoked when the extension receives an ISAPICOMMAND value of CHANGEADDRESS.

To make this work for your request handler, you must do five things:

1. Create a new unit in which you will implement your request handler, and add it to the project.

2. Provide a uses clause that includes the necessary units (ISAPIException, RequestHandlerRegistry, HTTPSrvrCtxt, RequestHandler).

3. Define a class that descends from *ReqHandler*.

4. Override the virtual function execute, where you will actually put the code that handles the request.

5. Provide an initialization section that calls the virtual function *doRegister*, passing the name of the request.

Step 1 is just what you'd do to add a new class to any Delphi project.

Step 2 provides access to the framework itself. You can see an example on lines 9–18 of listing 13.1. This is necessary so your request handler can access the classes, functions, and variables the framework defines for you.

 In your own code, you must be sure to place these files in the uses clause before any reference to your request handler or any file that uses your request handler.

The order is important because the request handler registration mechanism depends on the creation of a global request-handler registry object *before* the definition of any request handlers themselves. Delphi executes the initialization sections of the program's units in the order in which the units appear in the *uses* clause. The registry must be created before any request handlers attempt to add themselves to it.

Step 3 defines your new class as a request handler, thus providing the implementation of functions to handle interaction with the framework's request dispatcher and registration of your request handler. It also enables the framework to handle all requests in a uniform fashion, as a generic *ReqHandler*. This is done on lines 20–25 of listing 13.1.

Step 4 is implemented on lines 30–37 of listing 13.1. You can put here whatever code is necessary to handle the request.

Step 5 adds the request name and a reference to your class into a global table. This global table is where the framework's request dispatcher looks up the name of any request it receives. The information that the request dispatcher finds will determine what request handler class to create and call to handle the request. You can see an example on lines 40–41 of listing 13.1. The mechanics of this process are described in much more detail in the section "Class Registration and the Object Factory."

 You will find it easier to organize your request handlers if you keep one in each unit. In addition to keeping your code better organized, this makes it easier to see the relationship between each request handler and its request name.

Ever since Kernighan and Ritchie, tradition has dictated that a new programming paradigm be demonstrated through a program that displays "Hello, World!". This chapter is no exception. Listing 13.1 shows a complete request handler that will, when requested, return a web page containing the message "Hello, World!".

LISTING 13.1—\PROJECTS\CHAP13\MYREQUESTHANDLER.PAS—A SIMPLE REQUEST HANDLER IMPLEMENTATION

```
01   unit MyRequestHandler;
02
03   {
04     simple example of a request handler
05   }
06
07   interface
08
09   uses
10     SysUtils,
11     Windows,
12     Classes,
13     // the next four units import
14     //      the framework's definitions
15     ISAPIException,
16     RequestHandlerRegistry,
17     HTTPSrvrCtxt,
18     RequestHandler;
```

```
19
20  type
21    MyReqHandler = class(ReqHandler)
22      function
23      execute:
24      Boolean; override;
25    end;
26
27  implementation
28
29  { ================================================= }
30  function
31  MyReqHandler.execute:
32  Boolean;
33  begin
34    m_ServerContext.writeClient(
35          '<HTML><BODY>Hello, world!</BODY></HTML>' );
36    result := true;
37  end;
38
39  { ================================================= }
40  initialization
41    MyReqHandler.doRegister('MYREQUEST');
42
43  end.
```

Compare listing 13.1 with listing 12.3 in Chapter 12. Each unit accomplishes the same task, displaying a simple *Hello, World!* page on the user's browser. The code in listing 13.1, which uses the framework, is almost 50% longer than that in listing 12.3, which does it by hand. This shows there is a small overhead associated with using this framework.

This overhead is insignificant when you consider two factors:

> With the exception of four lines (34–36 and 41), listing 13.1 is completely boilerplate. Listing 12.3, on the other hand, is almost entirely hand-coded for the purpose of printing "Hello, World!".

> The cost of an object-oriented framework is always exaggerated by a program that doesn't use the features of that framework. When you start to take advantage of its request-parsing capability, you will find a dramatic decrease in the relative amount of code you must write.

The HTTPServerContext Object

In the previous section, you derived your request handler from a base class so the framework can easily handle your code. It probably hasn't been evident yet, but you will realize a significant benefit from this as well. It allows the server to give you access to a HTTPServerContext object, which provides most of the services that will make your job easier.

This object is an instance of the class *HTTPServerContext*. The framework creates it before your request handler is called, and passes it to your request handler after its creation. It's a protected member of the *ReqHandler* class, so you have access to it through the m_ServerContext member of your request handler class.

The *HTTPServerContext* object manages the entire interaction with ISAPI's ECB. You can call functions in your m_ServerContext member to get most of the functionality that's available through the ECB and its callback functions, as well as some additional conveniences, without needing to deal with connection IDs and other details.

If all of these relationships between the objects seem confusing, you can see it all diagrammed in figure 13.3.

The functions in *HTTPServerContext* that you can call for various services are described in table 13.1.

TABLE 13.1
Members Functions of HTTPServerContext

Function	Description
getClientData	Retrieves any data that was sent in the client data buffer. In a *POST* request, this will be the request query string.
getRequestString	Retrieves the request query string. This will automatically retrieve it from the QUERY_STRING variable or the client data buffer as appropriate for the type of request.
getServerVariable	Returns a server variable or header value as requested.
retrieveServerVariable	Retrieves a server variable or header value as requested into a string variable.
setStatus	Sets the status of the HTTP response.
setMIMEType	Sets the MIME type of the response.
addHeader	Adds a response header string.

Function	Description
aendHeaders	Sends the status and header information to the client.
wasHeaderSent	Returns TRUE if the headers have already been sent to the client for this request.
writeClient	Sends a string to the client.
writeClientBinary	Sends a binary buffer of a given size to the client.
getParameterValue	Retrieves the value of specified instance (normally 0) of the specified request field.
getParameterValueCount	Returns the number of values available for the specified parameter.
getCookieValue	Retrieves the value of specified instance (normally 0) of the specified cookie.
getCookieValueCount	Returns the number of values available for the specified cookie.
setCookie	Adds a cookie to the headers to be sent to the client.
dumpParameterTable	For debugging purposes; generates an HTML-formatted table listing all variables in the request and all their values.
dumpCookieTable	For debugging purposes; generates an HTML-formatted table listing all cookies sent by the client and all their values.
getParameterList	Returns a TMultiValList object containing all of the parameters and their values.
getCookieList	Returns a TMultiValList object containing all the cookies and their values.
retrieveECB	Retrieves the ECB the server submitted with the request. This is useful for functions not directly supported by the framework, such as redirection.

These functions will be discussed in greater detail in the following sections.

Retrieving the Values for a Form's Fields

You can retrieve the value of any field sent in the request by calling *m_ServerContext*. The *getParameterValue()* function takes as parameters the name of the parameter, the index of the value of the parameter, and a string to put the value into. The function returns TRUE if the value was found, or FALSE otherwise.

The name of the parameter is case sensitive. The index will almost always be zero, but as noted in the "Separating Request Fields" section in Chapter 12, multiple values are sometimes supplied for a field, particularly with *<SELECT MULTIPLE>* fields.

The HTML specification does not require a name to be provided for all fields of a form. In these cases, the server will receive a value without any corresponding name. For example, if the form looks like the following, one field (in addition to the ISAPICOMMAND) will be retrieved:

```
<FORM METHOD=POST ACTION="myext.dll">
  <INPUT TYPE=HIDDEN NAME="ISAPICOMMAND" VALUE="MYREQUEST">
  <INPUT TYPE=TEXT>
</FORM>
```

In cases where values are encountered without names, the framework assigns a default name to them. The value of the default name is determined by the value of the constant string *HTTPUtilAnonymousItemName*, which is defined in the unit HTTPUtilities. The value of this constant is set to *ANONYMOUS*. If multiple unnamed fields are encountered, they are added as additional values to the *ANONYMOUS* parameter. The first one will be at index 0, the next at index 1, and so forth. More complex applications can be handled easily as well. Chapter 11, discusses an application involving a table listing an order for merchandise. Each line item making up the order has an entry field that the user can alter to change the quantity of the item to be ordered. Because you won't know ahead of time the number of items the user will order, you won't know how many values will be received for the quantity field.

The server context object provides a function called *getParameterValueCount()* that will help you solve this problem. This function will return the number of values that are supplied for a given parameter name. Using the number returned, you can examine each value for the parameter by incrementing the *index* parameter of *m_ServerContext. getParameterValue()* in a loop.

The framework will already have taken care of parsing the request string and decoding any URL-escaped strings, as described in the sections "Separating Request Fields" and "URL Escaping" in Chapter 12. Note that the decoding is performed on both the name and the value.

Retrieving Header Information and Server Variables

Two functions give you access to the values of header information and server variables: *retrieveServerVariable()* and *getServerVariable()*. Usually you will use *retrieveServerVariable()*. This takes as parameters the name of the value to retrieve and a string variable to put the value into. If the value is found, the function will return TRUE; otherwise, FALSE.

Because some values are always present (always supplied by the server), a function *getServerVariable()* is supplied for convenience. This takes only the name of the variable as a parameter and returns the value of the variable as a string directly. You should only use this function if you can be certain the variable will be found; the results are undefined otherwise.

Sending Headers to the Client

Some aspects of managing the headers are automated, but the user still has to manage the details if anything is out of the ordinary. For example, if you're sending an image you'll need to specify a MIME type other than the default of *text/html*. Or, you may want to prevent the user's browser from caching the data you send because of its dynamic nature. You'd accomplish this by sending an additional header, *Expires*, with a date that's already past.

For these cases, the framework provides functions for setting the request status, setting the MIME type, adding headers, and eventually sending them to the user's browser.

If you look at listing 13.1, you won't see anything done with headers. As this is a very simple request to handle, everything is left to the default, which consists of a status of OK being sent along with a *Content-Type* of *text/html*.

The header information is automatically transmitted, if necessary, when the body of the response is written to the client, because this is the last opportunity to send the headers. Trying to send headers after part of the body has been sent results in an exception being raised. Before the body is sent, the framework checks to see if any headers have been sent. If not, it checks to see if any headers are waiting to be sent. If any are waiting, it sends them; otherwise, it constructs the default headers and sends them.

Setting the HTTP_STATUS

The first line of the response must indicate the status of the request. This value must also be placed into the ECB for return to the server, as described in the "Sending Headers" section in Chapter 12.

Cross Reference

When your request handler is called, the request status is initialized to a default value of OK. These values are enumerated in the ISAPIException unit. The legal values correspond with those defined in the HTTP 1.0 specification and described in Appendix C, "HTTP Status Codes."

They are represented in the framework as follows:

Legal Values for the Status of a Request

OK	REDIR_MULTIPLE_CHOICE	ERR_BAD_REQUEST
CREATED	REDIR_MOVED_PERMANENT	ERR_UNAUTHORIZED
ACCEPTED	REDIR_MOVED_TEMPORARY	ERR_FORBIDDEN
NO_CONTENT	REDIR_NOT_MODIFIED	ERR_NOTFOUND
		ERR_INTERNAL

Warning Most of these values do not make sense under ordinary circumstances, so make sure you understand the implications of any values you set.

You can change the status value by calling the procedure *m_ServerContext.setStatus()*. You should do this before any headers are sent to the user. The *setStatus()* function will store the status code so that the appropriate values and their corresponding strings will be reflected in the headers that are eventually sent. At the time the status is sent to the user, the status value will be copied to the ECB's dwHttpStatusCode field for proper communication with the server.

Changing the Content-Type

The framework will automatically generate a Content-Type header for you. Its value comes from the MIME type defined in the server context object at the time the headers are sent.

The default value of this is text/html, but you can change this easily by calling m_ServerContext.setMIMEType.

Adding Other Headers

You might find it necessary to add additional headers of your own. For example, if you know the exact length of the body of your response, you might want to add a Content-Length header. This can be done simply by calling the *addHeader()* member function, passing a string containing the header as a parameter. The string should *not* contain any line end characters.

Attempting to add a header after any headers have already been sent is illegal and raises an EISAPIException exception.

Sending the Headers

Any headers, whether supplied by you or the defaults, will automatically be sent just before any of the body is written, if they haven't been already. You can, however, force the headers to be sent at any time prior to your first write of actual data to the client. Calling the *sendHeaders()* function does this. No parameters are needed.

Attempting to send the headers after they have already been sent once is illegal and raises an EISAPIException exception.

There is probably only one circumstance that will call for manually sending the headers; otherwise, the automatic behavior should be sufficient. If the data to be sent will take a long time to generate, you may want to send the headers first so that the user can see that the server is responding to the request.

Getting Direct Access to Parameters and Cookies

The server context object will manage the lists of parameters and cookies for you. When the server context object receives requests for values, it simply delegates the request to the appropriate value list object.

Sometimes, however, you might need to interact directly with the value list. Chapter 11 describes applications in which the number of parameters to be received aren't known ahead of time. In one of these applications there is a page whose contents can be customized for each user. Because you don't know the names of the fields that might be on this form, or even how many fields there will be, you'll need to retrieve the parameter list itself and step through the list one parameter at a time.

Cross Reference

There are two functions you can call to obtain access to these lists:

◆ *getParameterList()* returns the list containing all the parameters sent in the request

◆ *getCookieList()* returns the list containing all the cookies the user's browser sent

The lists returned by these functions are references to objects belonging to the class *TMultiValList*. This class is defined in the unit MultiValList.pas, which must be included in the *uses* clause of any unit that employs them.

Don't forget the framework owns and manages these lists for you. Under no circumstances should you try to free the objects returned by *getParameterList* or *getCookieList*.

Table 13.3 lists the functions you can use to work with TMultiValList objects:

TABLE 13.2
Functions Supported by TmultiValList

Method	Description
procedure addItem (const itemname: String; itemvalue: String);	Adds a name/value pair to the list. If the name const did not previously exist, it is added and given the single value provided. If an item already existed with that name, the given value is appended to the end of its value list.
function retrieveItem (const itemname: String; index: Integer); Boolean;	Places an item value into the *itemval* parameter, normally 0, indicates which value to use from the value list for the item named by the *itemname* parameter. Returns **TRUE** on success or **FALSE** on failure (due to an unfound item name or insufficient values for the index specified).
function retrieve NumberedItem(itemnum: Integer; index: Integer; var itemval: String) : Boolean;	Places an item value into the *itemval* parameter. The index parameter, normally 0, indicates which value to use from the value list of the item given by the *itemnum* parameter. Returns **TRUE** on success or **FALSE** on failure (due to insufficient items or values for the specified numbers).
function retrieveName Index (const itemname: String; var Integer): Boolean;	Places the number of the item named by *itemname* into the itemnum: itemnum parameter. Returns **TRUE** on success or **FALSE** on failure (due to the name being unfound).
function getItemCount: Integer;	Returns the number of items in the list.
function getValueCount (itemnum: Integer): Integer;	Returns the number of values defined for the item at index *itemnum*.

Method	Description
`function dumpList(const heading: String ): String;`	Returns a string containing all the items with all of their values. The list has HTML formatting to display as a table. The *heading* parameter is used as a heading in the table. This is useful for debugging.

In the example application previously mentioned, you'd probably want to call the *getValueCount()* function to determine how many parameters were received. You'd then call the *retrieveNumberedItem()* function within a loop to retrieve each parameter in turn.

Writing Data to the Client

The framework makes writing data to the client one of the simplest tasks to accomplish. This is good because it's one you will use very often. All that needs to be done is to call the *writeClient()* function, passing the string to be written as a parameter.

Calling this function will send any headers (if they haven't been already) to the client. Make sure you have set all of the necessary headers (and cookies, because they're really headers as well) before you try to send any data.

This function is intended only for sending string data, which is what you will probably be doing most often. If you need to send binary data, refer to the section "Writing Binary Data to the Client," later in this chapter.

The *writeClient()* function will raise an EISAPIBadWrite exception object if the write is unsuccessful. If there is any cleanup work to be performed before your request handler is destroyed, you should handle this exception and then re-raise it. Otherwise, you can safely allow the framework to catch the exception and destroy your request handler for you. Either way, there's no sense continuing your own processing, because there is no way to communicate your results to the client (see the section "Sending Data Back to the User" in Chapter 12 for further explanation). Exception handling is discussed in greater detail in the next section.

Handling Exceptions

Many of the functions the framework provides for you sometimes encounter conditions they cannot handle, generally because of erroneous input from the user or from your request handler itself. The framework responds to these conditions by raising an exception of type EISAPIException, which is derived from *Exception*. You can catch such an exception just as you would catch any other exception in Delphi. You can also raise them yourself if appropriate.

The framework will catch any exceptions you don't, or any exceptions you raise yourself. If the exception the framework catches is of type *EISAPIException*, it can provide better feedback to the user, because of the two ways *EISAPIException* differs from the base Exception:

♦ **Setting the request status:** the framework's exception class provides an additional property, *Status*, which contains the HTTP request status code to be reported to the user, should this exception be caught by the framework.

♦ **Providing a message to the user:** the semantics of the base class's *Message* property is enhanced. A message in an *EISAPIException* is understood to be a message to the user. When creating an *EISAPIException* yourself, this message should be formatted in HTML, suitable for placing on the returned web page.

The constructor for *EISAPIException* requires an additional parameter, status, which is the request status previously mentioned.

When the framework catches an exception, it builds a response by using either the values defined in the *EISAPIException* or, if the exception is not of that type, a set of hard-coded defaults. It consults with the *HTTPServerContext* to see if headers have been written yet; if not, it sends appropriate headers that reflect the information provided in the exception object. It then sends the message that was determined.

One other type of exception is defined. It is named *EISAPIBadWrite* and derives directly from *EISAPIException* without adding any additional attributes or behavior. The only case in which an exception object of type *EISAPIBadWrite* will be raised is the failure of *sendHeaders()* or one of the two *writeClient()* functions. If you don't handle this exception, the framework will catch it for you, but nothing will be sent to the user, because the connection is presumed to have been lost. This is generally the desired behavior.

If, however, there is any cleanup to be performed—that is, if you have dynamically allocated any resources, such as memory or objects, or opened any files—the framework can't do it for you. You should be sure to either handle this exception yourself (generally with a *finally* block) or arrange for your destructor to do the cleanup when the framework destroys the request handler.

Exception handling by the framework is discussed in greater detail later, in the section "The Exception Architecture."

Building a Simple Request Handler

You now have all the tools you need to build a simple request handler. This section will show how it all fits together by implementing one in its entirety. This sample will give you the opportunity to see many of the features of the framework in action.

The application described is a temperature converter from Fahrenheit to Celsius and vice versa. The user can enter a temperature, indicate the direction in which it needs to be converted, and submit the request. This will all be done in an ordinary HTML form. A request handler will be implemented to receive that request, which will retrieve and check the fields sent from the form, perform the calculation, and build a page to present the response.

The Temperature Conversion Request

You need an HTML page to issue the request in the first place. It needs to have a form on it to collect all the data your request handler is going to need to complete the request, including the name of the request. Listing 13.2 presents an HTML page that fits the bill for this purpose.

LISTING 13.2—THE HTML PAGE THAT
ISSUES THE CONVERTTEMPERATURE REQUEST

```
01  <!DOCTYPE HTML PUBLIC "-//W3C//DTD HTML 3.2//EN">
02
03  <HTML>
04  <HEAD>
05    <TITLE>Temperature Converter</TITLE>
06  </HEAD>
07
08  <BODY BGCOLOR=FFFFE0>
09    <H1>Temperature Converter</H1>
10    <FORM METHOD=GET ACTION="tempconv.dll">
11    <INPUT TYPE=HIDDEN NAME="ISAPICOMMAND" VALUE="CONVERTTEMPERATURE">
12    <TABLE>
13      <TR>
14        <TD ALIGN=RIGHT>
15          Temperature to convert:
16        </TD>
17        <TD>
18          <INPUT TYPE=TEXT ALIGN=RIGHT NAME="TEMPERATURE" VALUE="0">
```

continues

```
19          </TD>
20        </TR>
21        <TR>
22         <TD ALIGN=RIGHT>
23           Conversion direction:
24         </TD>
25         <TD>
26           <INPUT TYPE=RADIO NAME="DIRECTION" VALUE="C" CHECKED>
27           Fahrenheit to Celsius<BR>
28           <INPUT TYPE=RADIO NAME="DIRECTION" VALUE="F">
29           Celsius to Fahrenheit<BR>
30         </TD>
31        </TR>
32        <TR>
33         <TD COLSPAN=2 ALIGN=CENTER>
34           <INPUT TYPE=SUBMIT>
35         </TD>
36        </TR>
37       </TABLE>
38       </FORM>
39
40    </BODY>
41    </HTML>
```

The form spans lines 10–38. Line 10 specifies the name of the ISAPI extension to be sent the request (tempconv.dll) and the type of query to be issued. The latter is not important; the framework will automatically handle either GET or POST. Line 11 is the magic hidden field, which gives the framework the information necessary to dispatch the request to the appropriate request handler. In this case, it specifies a request handler named CONVERTTEMPERATURE. Don't forget that the name and value of this field are case-sensitive, along with the names of any other fields in the form. Lines 18, 26, and 28 provide fields to collect the other parameters required by the request handler.

Figure 13.1 shows what the web page looks like when the user views it.

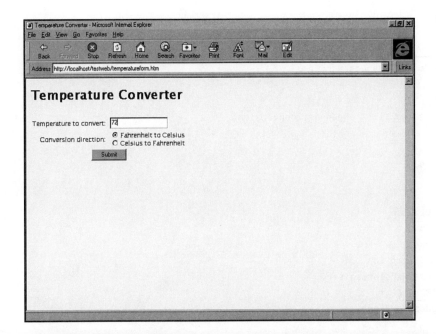

Figure 13.1

Web page making the CONVERT TEMPERATURE request.

The Temperature Conversion Request Handler

This section offers an implementation of a request handler that can service the request made by the HTML page in listing 13.2. To accomplish this, the request handler uses a number of the features of the Delphi ISAPI framework discussed in the section "Using the Delphi ISAPI Application Framework."

The section "Writing and Registering a Class to Handle Requests" lists five requirements for creating a request handler. Listing 13.3 shows a temperature conversion request handler in which all of these steps have been executed.

Step 1 is accomplished by creating the file. Lines 9–16 accomplish step 2. This is boilerplate code you can simply copy into any request handler's unit. A class named *TempConvRH* is derived from *ReqHandler* on lines 19–23, satisfying step 3. The bulk of this unit, lines 28–115, implement step 4, the overridden virtual function *execute*. Finally, to satisfy step 5, line 119 registers the request handler when the extension is loaded.

LISTING 13.3—THE REQUEST HANDLER FOR THE TEMPERATURE CONVERSION

```
001   unit TempConvRequestHandler;
002
003   {
004    perform celsius/fahrenheit conversions
005   }
006
007   interface
008
009   uses
010     SysUtils,
011     Windows,
012     Classes,
013     ISAPIException,
014     RequestHandlerRegistry,
015     HTTPSrvrCtxt,
016     RequestHandler;
017
018   type
019     TempConvRH = class(ReqHandler)
020       function
021       execute:
022       Boolean; override;
023     end;
024
025   implementation
026
027   { ===================================================== }
028   function
029   TempConvRH.execute:
030   Boolean;
031   var
032     intemperaturestr, outtemperaturestr, direction: string;
033     fromstr, tostr, outstr: string;
034     intemperatureval, outtemperatureval: Real;
035     dchar: Char;
036     dummy: Integer;
037     returncode: Boolean;
038   begin
039     result := TRUE;
040     try
```

```
041     // both input temperature and direction are required
042     if not (m_ServerContext.getParameterValue(
043                     'TEMPERATURE', 0, intemperaturestr )
044             AND m_ServerContext.getParameterValue(
045                     'DIRECTION', 0, direction ) ) then
046       begin
047         raise EISAPIException.Create(
048                     'Missing parameters in request',
049                     ERR_BAD_REQUEST );
050       end;
051
052     // convert the input string to a number
053     Val( intemperaturestr, intemperatureval, dummy );
054
055     dchar := direction[1];
056
057     case dchar of
058       'F':  // celsius to fahrenheit
059             begin
060               outtemperatureval :=
➥intemperatureval*9/5+32;
061               fromstr := ' Celsius';
062               tostr   := ' Fahrenheit';
063             end;
064       'C':  // fahrenheit to celsius
065             begin
066               outtemperatureval :=
➥(intemperatureval-32)*5/9;
067               fromstr := ' Fahrenheit';
068               tostr   := ' Celsius';
069             end;
070       else  // anything else is illegal
071             begin
072               raise EISAPIException.Create(
073                     'Invalid direction specified',
074                     ERR_BAD_REQUEST );
075             end;
076     end;
077
078     // turn the result into a string
079     Str( outtemperatureval:4:1, outtemperaturestr );
080
```

continues

LISTING 13.3—THE REQUEST HANDLER FOR THE TEMPERATURE CONVERSION, CONTINUED

```
081     // build the response page dynamically
082     outstr := '<HTML><BODY><H1>Temperature Converted</H1>'
083             +intemperaturestr+fromstr+' = '
084             +outtemperaturestr+tostr
085             +'</BODY></HTML>';
086
087     // send it to the user
088     m_ServerContext.writeClient( outstr );
089
090 except
091    on Exc: EISAPIException do
092      begin
093        // if the error was an EISAPIException we can use
094        // the status and message in the exception object
095        m_ServerContext.setStatus( Exc.Status );
096        m_ServerContext.writeClient( '<HTML><BODY><H1>'
097                +'Temperature Not Converted</H1>'
098                +'Error processing conversion request: '
099                +'<BR>'+Exc.Message
100                +'</BODY></HTML>' );
101      end;
102    else
103      begin
104        // we can only give a generic error message here
105        m_ServerContext.setStatus( ERR_BAD_REQUEST );
106        m_ServerContext.writeClient( '<HTML><BODY><H1>'
107                +'Temperature Not Converted</H1>'
108                +'Error processing conversion request'
109                +'</BODY></HTML>' );
110      end;
111    end;
112
113 end;
114
115 { ================================================== }
116 initialization
117   TempConvRH.doRegister('CONVERTTEMPERATURE');
118
119 end.
```

Figure 13.2 depicts the page that the request handler sends back to the user in response to a temperature conversion request.

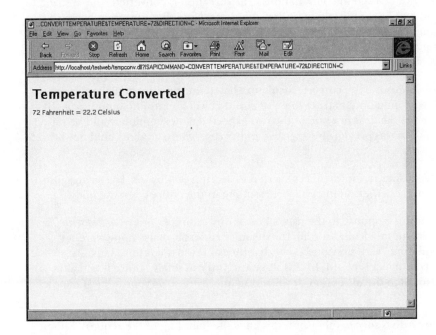

Figure 13.2

Web page sent as a response from the TempConvRH request handler.

This small application requires two pieces of information: a temperature to convert and an indication of the direction in which the conversion should be performed (Fahrenheit to Celsius or vice versa). Both items are required; if either is missing, the process cannot proceed.

This application combines the retrieval of the values with the check for their presence into a single operation, implemented on lines 42–45. This is a conditional statement consisting of two calls to *m_ServerContext.getParameterValue*, one for each of the required parameters. If values are successfully found for both calls, they will be placed into the variables intemperaturestr and direction.

On the other hand, if either function call fails—perhaps because the request was lacking the requested field—the condition will evaluate TRUE. This results in creating and raising an *EISAPIException* object on lines 47–49. It is created with a message describing the problem and an appropriate status, to give the user a better understanding of what went wrong. The function will catch this exception on line 91, where it creates a web page in response, containing a message based on the one it caught, but with some additional text.

Lines 53 and 55 convert from the string values that were retrieved to types usable for the purposes at hand. The input temperature is converted from a string to a real number so it can be used in computations. The direction is converted from a string to a single character by simply taking its first character. Note that the string having a 0 length would result in a range error being thrown. If this were to occur, the exception would be caught at line 102. Here again a web page is created to inform the user of the answer; in this case, however, the error message is less specific.

Lines 57–76 determine the correct calculation based on the direction character, perform the computation, and set some strings that will go into the output page. If the direction character is not one of the two expected, an exception would be raised. This works just as was previously described in the case where a value could not be found.

Now that the answer is known, it's converted to a string on line 79. The strings just built are strung together on lines 82–85, resulting in the entire response body.

Line 88 sends this response to the user's browser by calling *m_ServerContext.writeClient*. This results in automatically sending the default headers because none were set explicitly and none were previously sent. If either of these operations fails, an *EISAPIBadWrite* object is raised. In this situation, you can safely ignore it and allow the framework to catch the exception. It will automatically destroy your request handler and return.

Whether the write is successful or not, this ends the handling of the request. Either the *execute()* function will return or the stack will be unwound to handle the exception. One way or another, control returns to the framework, which calls your destructor and returns from the HttpExtensionProc() call.

Advanced Issues

The preceding sections have presented all the tools necessary for writing basic ISAPI extensions by using the framework. In the following section, you will see some more complex features, used less frequently but useful enough to include in the framework, nevertheless.

The HTTPUtil Utility Class

The *HTTPUtil* class defines a number of functions and procedures used internally by the framework and also available to your request handlers. These functions have more general use outside of ISAPI extensions, so were not included in *HTTPServerContext* class as you might otherwise expect. This allows them to be used in other applications. In particular, you might find them useful in writing ISAPI filters in Delphi.

> **Note**
> Utility classes aren't used very often in Delphi, but are more familiar to C++ programmers. These classes are never meant to be instantiated—you should never call their constructors. In fact, the constructor for the *HTTPUtil* class has been declared private to prevent anyone from calling it.
>
> All the functions and procedures in a utility class are declared at a class scope. This means they don't act on a particular instance of a class, but act as global functions instead. You call a function through the name of the class, for example, *HTTPUtil.encodeURL(myvariable)*. The advantage of utility classes is you can better organize your code. Functions, procedures, and even variables that need to be available globally but are related by a common subject matter can be gathered into a utility class. This prevents pollution of the global namespace, thereby avoiding function name clashes in large projects.

The services that are provided by the *HTTPUtil* class include:

◆ **Encoding and decoding URL-escaped values:** encodes strings for safe use as an URL and decodes strings that have been encoded

◆ **Converting Date/Time types:** converts a Delphi TDateTime object to a string in the appropriate format for use in cookies and other HTTP applications

◆ **Parsing requests and cookies:** parses HTTP request strings and cookies into lists of values

◆ **Converting status codes:** converts a status code selected from an enumeration into the value and string that is required by HTTP protocol

Encoding and Decoding URL-Escaped Values

The section "URL Escaping" in Chapter 12 describes possible encoding for the contents of a request string. You might need to decode these strings on your own or, more likely, encode strings for use as URLs within the pages your request handler generates.

Two functions are provided for this purpose: *decodeURL* and *encodeURL*. The former converts an encoded value to normal text; the latter takes a string of normal text and returns an encoded string. Here are examples of calling each function:

```
encodedstring := HTTPUtil.encodeURL( normalstring );
normalstring  := HTTPUtil.decodeURL( encodedstring );
```

Any errors encountered by these functions raises an *EISAPIException* object.

Converting TDateTime Values

HTTP specifies a special format for representing timestamps. There are several occasions when you might want to use such a value. For example, it's useful for cookies (see the sections "Setting a Cookie" in Chapter 12 and "Reading and Writing Cookies" in this chapter) and for headers such as the Expires header, which forces the user's browser to refresh a page after some time.

The function *convertDateTime()* takes a *TDateTime* as a parameter and returns a string with the proper representation of the provided value. For example:

```
datestring := HTTPUtil.convertDateTime( mydatetimeval );
```

 The function expects the TDateTime value it receives to be in Greenwich Mean Time. Make sure you provide any necessary conversion for your time zone before calling this function.

Parsing Request Strings and Cookies

The *HTTPUtil* class defines the functions *parseRequest()* and *parseCookie()* to extract lists of values from a string. These are the functions the framework uses, but you can call them yourself if necessary. There are a couple of reasons you might want to do this. First, if you're writing a filter, you won't have the benefit of the framework to do it for you. Second, the framework has these functions automatically perform URL decoding; if this is inappropriate, you can call these functions with a parameter that turns the decoding off.

Here are examples of calling the functions:

```
myfieldlist := HTTPUtil.parseRequest( requeststring, mydecodeflag );
mycookielist := HTTPUtil.parseCookie( cookiestring, mydecodeflag );
```

Each call returns an object of type *TMultiValList*, which is defined in the unit MultiValList.pas. You would then retrieve values from this object by calling its member function retrieveItem rather than by calling *m_ServerContext.getParameterValue* or *m_ServerContext.getCookieValue*.

Any errors encountered by these functions raise an *EISAPIException* object. Errors might result from improperly formed strings, which should not happen in normal use.

Converting Internal Status Codes

The framework uses the procedure *HTTPUtil.convertStatusCodes* to generate the HTTP result string from the internal *HTTP_STATUS* value. There isn't usually any reason for you to call this function on your own, because the framework always generates this part of the header automatically. If you're using the HTTPUtil class for writing filters, you might want to use it.

The function takes three parameters: the input HTTP_STATUS value and two parameters for output. The output parameters include an integer that receives the actual value defined by the HTTP specification and the string that corresponds with the value.

For example, the following results in a value of 200 in *mycode* and a value of 200 OK in *mycodestring*:

```
HTTPUtil.convertStatusCodes( OK, mycode, mycodestring );
```

Reading and Writing Cookies

The framework incorporates features that allow you to set cookies with relative ease and to access the values of the cookies retrieved by the client as simply as the values of the fields sent in the request.

For more information on the use of cookies, see the section "Persistent State Information: Using Cookies" in Chapter 12.

X
Cross
Reference

Reading Cookies with the Framework

The values of cookies can be retrieved by calling the *getCookieValue()* function in the HTTPServerContext object. This works in exactly the same way as the *getParameterValue()* function. The only difference is that internally the values are retrieved from the cookies sent with the request headers rather than from the request body.

You should always check the value returned by *getParameterValue()*, and with this function it's doubly important. There is *always* a significant possibility of not being able to retrieve the value of a cookie you sent, because some browsers don't support cookies yet. Even if your user's browser does support them, there is no guarantee the browser or even the user won't delete the cookie.

Note that this feature does not require any additional overhead in processing a request until it's actually used. The framework does not attempt to retrieve and parse the cookie string until the first time a cookie value is requested. Thus, if you never try to get the value of a cookie, you will never incur the cost of parsing it. Don't assume that you can use cookies indiscriminately, though. The cost of transmission will still be incurred regardless of whether this function parses the string or not.

Writing Cookies with the Framework

A cookie can be set with a single call to the setCookie function in the HTTPServerContext object. Here's an example:

```
m_ServerContext.setCookie( 'MyCookie', mycookievalue,
                           '', '/', '', false );
```

The first parameter gives the name of the cookie, which is what you will request to retrieve its value from *getCookieValue()*. It must have a length greater than zero, or an EISAPIException will be raised. The second parameter gives the value of the cookie; this is what will be returned by *getCookieValue()*.

The third parameter gives the domain and will almost always be a null string. The fourth parameter gives the path and can be null if no path is to be specified. The fifth parameter can also be null, or a string formatted according to the HTTP specification for dates, specifying the expiration time. You can call *HTTPUtil.convertDateTime* to create the string from a Delphi TDateTime value (see the section "Converting TDateTime Values" earlier in this chapter for more information). The final parameter is a Boolean. A **TRUE** value indicates the cookie should only be transferred over secure connections; you will usually use a value of **FALSE**.

Keep in mind that cookies are sent to the user in the form of headers; therefore, any cookies must be added (by using the setCookie() function in HTTPServerContext) before the headers are sent to the user and before any of the body of the response has been written. An EISAPIException will be raised if this is done out of sequence.

Writing Binary Data to the Client

The function you will normally use to send data to the user is *writeClient()*; however, this is only appropriate for sending string data. A more general-purpose function is provided as well. The function *writeClientBinary()* enables you to send arbitrary binary data by accepting as parameters a pointer to a buffer and the length of the data to be sent from that buffer. The distinction is to prevent any confusion due to nulls embedded in the input data.

As with its partner *writeClient()*, the failure of *writeClientBinary()* raises an EISAPIBadWrite object.

This function also calls *sendHeaders()* automatically if they have not yet been sent.

Accessing the ECB Directly for Special Functions

Some functions have not been added to the framework. For example, no provision has been made to provide access to the ECB's *ServerSupportFunction()* to perform tasks such as redirection. You can get direct access to the ECB for your own purposes by calling *m_ServerContext.retrieveECB*.

Call this function with a single parameter, a PEXTENSION_CONTROL_BLOCK, as defined in ISAPIExt.pas. When the function returns, the parameter will have been filled with a pointer to the ECB.

A complete description of the extension control block can be found in Appendix A, "ISAPI Functions, Structures, and Constants."

How the Delphi ISAPI Application Framework Works

ISAPI's interface definition is designed specifically to be language neutral. This is both an advantage and a liability. It's an advantage in that it opens a great potential user base; however, it complicates the use of the strengths of any particular language. Specifically, no provision is made for object-oriented languages such as Delphi. The interface your extension exposes is forced to "lower itself" to operating on a procedural paradigm.

The Delphi ISAPI application framework provides an interface between the procedural interface called by the web server and an object-oriented design a Delphi developer should be more comfortable with.

The challenge in the design of the framework is an apparent contradiction between the intent of the ISAPI interface and the principles of object-oriented design. The web server calls a global function to perform a particular action in the absence of any application-related state information. This is at odds with important object-oriented design principles.

There are areas in particular that present the object-oriented designer with a challenge:

◆ **De-emphasizing procedures:** the ISAPI server's means of interaction with your extension is by calling a function. This is in opposition to the object-oriented goal of de-emphasizing functions in favor of describing objects and the ways they interact.

◆ **Elimination of global data:** ISAPI calls a globally defined function, and its stateless nature encourages you to store any application information globally. In defining objects and the attributes they are built from, an object-oriented designer tries to move information out of the domain of the program and into the domain of the objects being defined.

This framework uses a fairly straightforward design to bridge the procedural and object-oriented paradigms. Two basic design concepts are employed:

Encapsulation of the functions and data necessary to complete normal tasks through the Extension Control Block sent by the server provides a basic partitioning of responsibilities

Dynamic registration of polymorphic request-handler functors provides the ability to dispatch requests to an extensible set of handlers

The class diagram in figure 13.3 depicts the significant features of the framework's design and how they relate to each other.

Figure 13.3

UML class diagram framework's classes.

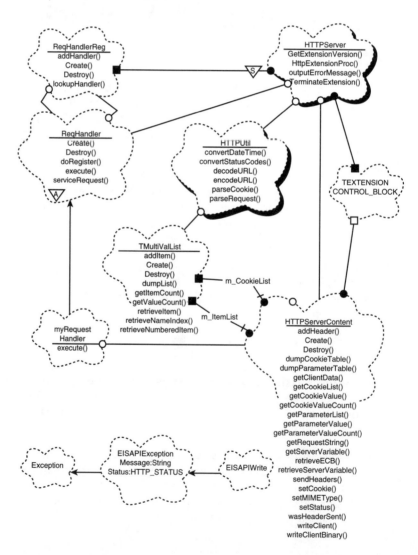

Request Handlers as Functors

The first contradiction to resolve is between the server's call to the extension to perform a particular action and the object-oriented designer's desire to work in terms of objects rather than actions. The solution presented here requires some compromise, but does so with an idiom used commonly by many object-oriented developers.

A functor is a class describing the execution of an action instead of a more traditional class describing an actual object. This seems to be a contradiction of object-oriented design, but the concept is actually very useful. For designers, functors provide clean and simple solutions to some problems otherwise requiring very complex mechanisms. For programmers, functors are also useful for simplifying code.

The use of a functor allows a process to be described in a generic way, independent of some details that might vary depending on the circumstances. The functor performs the variable part of the process. At run-time, the program determines the specific course of action needed and creates a functor meant to handle that particular circumstance. This object (functor) is then passed to the generic process, which instructs the functor to do its thing when appropriate.

An excellent example of the use of functors is the C++ Standard Library. Here, the developer can implement functors that perform comparisons. Because the criteria for comparing two objects might differ depending on the context, functors can be written to make comparisons based on name, weight, voltage, price, or whatever is applicable to the particular objects under consideration.

 Although not used in this capacity here, the functor idiom is also useful to simplify callbacks to member functions within your classes.

The syntax and use of method pointers is cumbersome and prone to error. The difficulty results because a member function implicitly has an extra parameter, self, which indicates the identity of the object on which the method is to act. Ensuring that your callback function will always be called with an appropriate self pointer can be a major headache.

By using functors, you can easily avoid the issue altogether. Rather than calling through a function pointer that is passed into the object or function, the caller simply calls a function (which you would agree upon ahead of time) in the functor.

The functor you pass in would be previously created and initialized with the information necessary to complete its task. Frequently this means a pointer to the object that's creating it. In fact, it might be even simpler to make the calling object the functor itself, and pass its own self pointer as the functor.

The process of handling an HTTP request is a perfect candidate for implementation as a functor because of the following characteristics:

◆ The framework needs to be able to treat all request handlers in a generic fashion. Introducing a base type for the request handler that implements all chores of the functor allows the framework to treat all request handlers as instances of that base type, once they have been constructed.

◆ The identity of the function to be called to service a particular request is not known when the framework is built. That is, the whole point of the framework is to be extensible, so it is not practical to hard-code a correspondence between incoming requests and request handlers.

◆ The identity of the request handler to be invoked can be easily determined at runtime from the value of the incoming ISAPICOMMAND field. If a registration facility is provided, an appropriate request handler can be created easily. (This is described in detail in the next section.)

The resolution to all of this is to create a base class for all request handler functors. This is named *ReqHandler()*, defined in the unit RequestHandler.pas, and its public interface is shown in the following code.

```
ReqHandler = class
  public
    constructor Create;
    destructor  Destroy; override;
    function    execute: Boolean; virtual;
    function    serviceRequest( var srvrctxt:
                    HTTPServerContext ): Boolean; virtual;
    class procedure doRegister( ISAPICommandStr:
                    String ); virtual;
end;
```

As a functor, there needs to be a predetermined protocol for its client (the framework) to invoke its functionality. Calling the *serviceRequest()* method does this here. This method takes as a parameter an *HTTPServerContext* object, which provides the interface to the server functions that the request handler will need to do its job. After *serviceRequest()* has taken care of this, it calls the virtual function *execute*, which you override to implement your own request handler.

Class Registration and the Object Factory

Using functors to handle the requests relies on a facility for dynamically determining the identity of the request handler that is intended to handle the request. It goes on to assert that after these requirements are fulfilled, creating an object of the appropriate type is simple. Delphi offers some nifty features that really simplify this.

In short, the objective is to provide the following features:

◆ A registry object that can do two things. It must record the identity of request handlers and the ISAPICOMMAND strings that lead to invocation of those request handlers. It must also be able to return the identity of a request handler, given an ISAPICOMMAND string.

◆ A mechanism that can be used by request handlers to dynamically add themselves to the registry.

◆ A means of constructing the proper request handler, given its identity as retrieved from the registry.

The Request Handler Registry

The first requirement is to provide a registry to keep track of which requests should invoke which functors. The class library shipped with Delphi is fairly rich and contains a class that is perfect for this purpose: *TStringList*. This class saves a string (which is where the ISAPICOMMAND will be stored) and an associated datum.

The registry class (*ReqHandlerReg*, defined in the unit RequestHandlerRegistry.pas) is a very simple wrapper around this class. It adapts the *TStringList* for the desired semantics. Here is the class's public interface:

```
ReqHandlerReg = class
  public
    constructor Create;
    destructor  Destroy; override;
    { add a request handler to the list }
    procedure addHandler( const instr: String; data: Pointer );
    { return the datum associated with the string (nil if not found) }
    function lookupHandler( const instr: String ): Pointer;
end;
```

A request handler can be added to the registry by passing the ISAPICOMMAND string and the datum identifying the request handler to *addHandler*. Conversely, calling *lookupHandler* with the string to search for can retrieve a request handler's identity; the result will be *nil* if the string is not found.

A single global reference to a ReqHandlerReg is declared. The initialization section of the unit containing this declaration (the same one that defines the class) has a statement that creates an instance of the class and assigns it to this global variable.

Naturally, the global instance must be deleted later to prevent a memory leak. The ISAPI protocol provides a convenient way to implement this. The function

TerminateExtension is called with a value of *HSE_TERM_MUST_UNLOAD* when the extension DLL is about to be unloaded. This happens to be a good time to free the registry. Listing 13.4, which contains an excerpt from the file HTTPServer.pas, shows how this is done.

LISTING 13.4—THE TERMINATEEXTENSION() FUNCTION IN HTTPSERVER.PAS

```
01  function
02  TerminateExtension( dwFlags: DWORD ):
03  BOOL; export; stdcall;
04  begin
05    if dwFlags = HSE_TERM_MUST_UNLOAD then
06      begin
07        // when the DLL is to be unloaded,
08        // the registry must be freed
09        theRegistry.Free;
10      end;
11    result := TRUE;
12  end;
```

This simple function is invoked by the server when the extension DLL is to be unloaded. All the function needs to do is free the registry object, which it does on line 9.

Self-Registering Classes

The first issue to be addressed here is defining exactly the identity of a request handler. Delphi has a wonderful way of expressing this (which saves most of the trouble of implementing a class factory, as a C++ programmer would be forced to do): the class type can be stored in a class reference variable.

Along with the definition of the class *ReqHandler*, found in the unit RequestHandler.pas, a definition of the type *TReqHandlerClass* is provided as well:

```
TReqHandlerClass = class of ReqHandler;
```

A variable of this type can store the identity of a request handler—the actual class type of any class derived from *ReqHandler*. What's more, a class reference variable can be used to call the class' constructor (or any accessible class function). Thus, this value provides the means to construct a new object of the same type that generated it.

If the datum stored in the registry is used to hold a *TReqHandlerClass*, the identity of the class can be associated with the ISAPICOMMAND and stored in the registry and later retrieved.

The second issue to address here is how to provide automatic, dynamic registration of all defined request handlers. Once again, Delphi provides a few nifty features that make the job much easier than it would be in C++. These features are a better definition of initialization order and a somewhat different object model.

Delphi guarantees the initialization code in your application's units will be performed in the order in which the units appear in the project's uses clause (and the uses clauses of those units, and so on). Capitalizing on this feature, the framework can assume that a global request handler registry object is created early in the initialization process and that any request handlers are initialized *after* that. Thus, the initialization section of the unit defining the request handler can be used to dynamically add the request handler to the registry as the unit is initialized.

The automatic part, enabling one-line boilerplate registration, relies on the same element of Delphi's object model that enables the use of class reference variables to call constructors. As it turns out, any class method also has a *self* pointer, which is a class reference variable—the very thing used to identify the class for the registry.

As a result of all this, the unit defining your request handler only needs a single line in its initialization section to accomplish the registration. For a practical example in context, see lines 116–117 of listing 13.3. Here is a general example of the registration statement:

```
TMyReqHandler.doRegister('MYREQUEST');
```

In this statement, *TMyReqHandler* is the name of the class implementing the request handler, and *MYREQUEST* is the *ISAPICOMMAND* string that will be sent to invoke your request handler. This statement calls the class function *doRegister*, defined by the base class *ReqHandler*. This function, cut from the file RequestHandler.pas, is shown in listing 13.5.

LISTING 13.5—THE REQHANDLER.DOREGISTER() PROCEDURE IN REQUESTHANDLER.PAS

```
01   class procedure
02   ReqHandler.doRegister( ISAPICommandStr: String );
03   var
04     classref: TReqHandlerClass;
05   begin
06     { since this is a virtual function, the self pointer
07       will reference the actual class type }
08     classref := self;
09
10     { save this class reference in the registry }
11     theRegistry.addHandler( ISAPICommandStr, classref );
12   end;
```

This function simply gets the self pointer as a TReqHandlerClass variable, adding the pointer and the specified string to the registry.

Creating Request Handlers Dynamically

Of the whole process through which request handlers register themselves, this is the simplest part. Here's what must be done:

1. Ask the registry for the datum stored for the requested ISAPICOMMAND. This is done on line 29 of listing 13.6.

2. Cast that value to a *TReqHandlerClass*. This is done on line 33 of listing 13.6.

3. Use the *TReqHandlerClass* to call the appropriate request handler's constructor. This is done on line 34 of listing 13.6.

The code to implement this is in the *HttpExtensionProc()* function, located in the *HTTPServer.pas* unit. Listing 13.6 presents the function here.

LISTING 13.6—THE HTTPEXTENSIONPROC() FUNCTION IN HTTPSERVER.PAS

```
01   function
02   HttpExtensionProc (var pECB : TEXTENSION_CONTROL_BLOCK):
03   DWORD; export; stdcall;
04   var
05      classref:      TReqHandlerClass;
06      CommandName:   String;
07      tempptr:       Pointer;
08      handler:       ReqHandler;
09      servercontext: HTTPServerContext;
10      returncode:    Boolean;
11      headerswritten: Boolean;
12   begin
13      headerswritten:= FALSE;
14      returncode    := FALSE;
15      servercontext := nil;
16
17      try
18        try
19          servercontext := HTTPServerContext.Create( @pECB );
20
21          { retrieve the command that should have
22             been passed here in the request }
```

```
23        if servercontext.getParameterValue( ISAPICommandString,
24                                             0,
25                                             CommandName ) then
26      begin
27        { if we found it, look for the class reference
28          in the handler registry }
29        tempptr := theRegistry.lookupHandler( CommandName );
30        if tempptr<>nil then
31          begin
32            { instantiate a new handler of the given type }
33            classref := tempptr;
34            handler := classref.Create;
35            try
36              { ask the handler to service the request }
37              returncode :=
38                  handler.serviceRequest( servercontext );
39            finally
40              { always make sure we know if the headers
41                were sent, so we can send them if necessary
42                before our error message }
43              headerswritten := servercontext.wasHeaderSent;
44              handler.Free;
45            end;
46          end
47        else
48          begin
49            raise EISAPIException.Create(
50                      '<HTML><BODY><H1>Command not supported: '
51                      +CommandName+'</H1></BODY></HTML>',
52                      ERR_BAD_REQUEST);
53          end;
54      end
55    else
56      begin
57        raise EISAPIException.Create(
58                  '<HTML><BODY><H1>Command not specified by '
59                  +ISAPICommandString+'</H1></BODY></HTML>',
60                  ERR_BAD_REQUEST);
61      end;
62
63  finally
64    servercontext.Free;
65  end;
```

continues

LISTING 13.6—THE HTTPEXTENSIONPROC() FUNCTION IN HTTPSERVER.PAS, CONTINUED

```
66
67    except
68      on EISAPIBadWrite do
69        begin
70          { nothing necessary here }
71        end;
72      on Exc: EISAPIException do
73        begin
74          returncode := outputErrorMessage( pECB,
75                                            headerswritten,
76                                            Exc.Status,
77                                            Exc.Message );
78        end
79      else
80        begin
81          returncode := outputErrorMessage( pECB, headerswritten,
82                          ERR_INTERNAL,
83                          '<HTML><BODY><H1>An internal processing '
84                          +'error occurred while handling '
85                          +'your request</H1></BODY></HTML>' );
86        end;
87    end;
88
89    if returncode then
90      result := HSE_STATUS_SUCCESS
91    else
92      result := HSE_STATUS_ERROR;
93  end;
```

The meat of this function is easily obscured by all of the error handling logic. The important part of the function starts on line 23, where the ISAPICOMMAND string is retrieved. Line 29 retrieves the command's associated data from the registry, and line 33 converts it to a *TReqHandlerClass*. Line 34 uses that reference to the type of the request handler to create a new instance of that request handler. Finally, lines 37–38 invoke the request handler.

As in many applications, dealing with errors drives a small amount of code for actually implementing the desired functionality up to a 93-line listing. Here are the things that can go wrong:

◆ **The command string isn't found:** this is detected on line 23 and handled on lines 55–61 of listing 13.6.

◆ **The class reference variable is incorrect:** if the value retrieved from the registry is not a valid reference to a request handler class, the code on line 33 will raise an exception that is handled on lines 46–79.

◆ **The request handler cannot be constructed:** if the constructor for the request handler fails (due to insufficient memory, for example), the code on line 34 will raise an exception that is handled on lines 46–79.

◆ **The request handler fails to handle an internal exception:** the exception handler might raise an exception but not handle it internally. If this occurs, it will be caught in one of the three handlers on lines 68–76, depending on the type of exception.

In any of these cases, the user must be informed that an error occurred. Assembling an appropriate string and passing it to the function outputErrorMessage accomplishes this.

Retrieving Input Data

Perhaps the most significant service the framework performs is to encapsulate code providing easy access to HTML form fields sent with a request.

There is quite a bit of code in place to facilitate this feature. It is located in the HTTPServerContext object (in unit HTTPSrvrCtxt.pas) and HTTPUtil utility class (in unit HTTPUtilities.pas). The implementation is fairly straightforward, but there is a bunch of it. This section describes how that code works.

Getting the Request String

The first part of retrieving input data is to get the raw request string. As described in the section "Interpreting Requests" in Chapter 12, the type of request must first be retrieved. This determines the source of the request string. Once that is known, the data is actually retrieved from the appropriate source.

To retrieve the request string, use the function *HTTPServerContext.getRequestString()*, shown here in listing 13.7.

LISTING 13.7—THE HTTPSERVERCONTEXT.GETREQUESTSTRING() FUNCTION IN HTTPSERVERCONTEXT.PAS

```
01  function
02  HTTPServerContext.getRequestString: String;
03  begin
04    { depending on the request method, retrieve the data }
```

continues

LISTING 13.7—THE HTTPSERVERCONTEXT.GETREQUESTSTRING() FUNCTION IN HTTPSERVERCONTEXT.PAS, CONTINUED

```
05    if GetServerVariable('REQUEST_METHOD') = 'POST' then
06      begin
07        { from the request buffer }
08        result := getClientData;
09      end
10    else
11      begin
12        { or from the query string sent as part of the URL }
13        result := GetServerVariable('QUERY_STRING');
14      end;
15  end;
```

HTTPServerContext.getRequestString() first retrieves the value of the server variable *REQUEST_METHOD* and checks its value (line 5). If this indicates a *POST* request, on line 8 the function retrieves the data from the client data buffer (described later); otherwise it's assumed to be a *GET* request, and on line 13 the data is retrieved from the server variable *QUERY_STRING*.

Either way, the resulting string is returned from the function.

The implementation of the *getClientData()* function, which retrieves the data of a POST request, isn't much more complicated. It's shown here in listing 13.8.

LISTING 13.8—THE HTTPSERVERCONTEXT.GETCLIENTDATA FUNCTION IN HTTPSERVERCONTEXT.PAS

```
01  function
02  HTTPServerContext.getClientData: String;
03  begin
04    { don't retrieve again if we've already done it }
05    if m_ClientDataRetrieved = FALSE then
06      begin
07        { copy the data from the ECB buffer into our string }
08        m_ClientData := StrPas(m_pECB.lpbData);
09        m_ClientDataRetrieved := TRUE;
10      end;
11    result := m_ClientData;
12  end;
```

The function begins by checking a Boolean flag in the server context object to see if the data has already been retrieved. If so, the retrieval is not performed again. Otherwise, the buffer is copied into a string in the server context object and returned.

Perhaps it seems silly to bother checking whether the data has been retrieved already. Why not just retrieve it anyway? Retrieving it might necessitate one possible enhancement to the framework. In Chapter 12, the section "Post Requests" mentions that IIS by default allocates a buffer of 48 KB for the request data. In some very rare applications this might be insufficient, for example, when uploading files.

In these cases, you will need to enhance the class HTTPServerContext for the purpose. The *getClientData()* is defined *virtual* to enable this. Your *getClientData()* function will first need to retrieve the data stored in the buffer. Then compare the values of *cbTotalBytes* and *cbAvailable* in the Extension Control Block (stored by the HTTPServerContext object in the variable *m_pECB*). If the total number of bytes is greater than the number available, you will need to allocate a buffer for the difference and call *m_pECB.ReadClient* to get the remainder.

For extremely large requests, you might even prefer to allocate a smaller buffer than the remainder requires. This is possible; you just have to call *m_pECB.ReadClient* repeatedly. Remember on the last call not to ask for more than is available or you will be stuck waiting for more data to be transferred.

Parsing the Request

The parsing routines are implemented in the utility class HTTPUtil (defined in HTTPUtiltity.pas), because they are generally useful outside of the framework as well.

The process of parsing a request breaks into three high-level steps:

1. Scanning the request for the characters that delimit fields in the request, and for characters that separate field names from their values

2. Extracting the field names and values

3. Decoding the names and values of the fields. In the interest of efficiency, no parsing is done until the first time the server context object is asked to return the value of a parameter, which you accomplish by calling the server context object's *getParameterValue()* function. In the case of fields in the request, this turns out not to make any practical difference, because the very first thing the framework does is request the value of the ISAPICOMMAND field to determine which request handler to use. In the case of cookies, though, this can turn out to be a significant savings. The source code to *HTTPServerContext.getParameterValue()* is shown in listing 13.9.

LISTING 13.9—THE HTTPSERVERCONTEXT .GETPARAMETERVALUE() FUNCTION IN HTTPSERVERCONTEXT.PAS

```
01  function
02  HTTPServerContext.getParameterValue(
03                          const paramname: String;
04                                index:     Integer;
05                          var   paramval:  String
06                                        ):
07  Boolean;
08  begin
09    result := false;
10
11    { if we haven't got the structure containing all of
12      the param/values yet, do it now }
13    if m_ItemList = nil then
14      begin
15        buildParamList;
16      end;
17
18    result := m_ItemList.retrieveItem( paramname,
19                                       index,
20                                       paramval  );
21  end;
```

The first thing this function does is check to see if the parsing has been done yet. It determines this on line 13 by seeing if the *m_ItemList* object is initialized yet. Even if no parameters were found in the parse, an empty item list would be present. If it's not there, on line 15 the function *buildParamList()* will be called to retrieve the request and parse it.

Now that there is an item list, on line 18 the function asks it to retrieve the requested value. An indication of the success of this operation will be returned by *getParameterValue()*.

The function *buildParamList()* is also trivial. It's placed in a separate function just because the same code would otherwise be repeated multiple times in the program. The code for this function is shown in listing 13.10.

LISTING 13.10—THE **HTTPSERVERCONTEXT.BUILDPARAMLIST()** FUNCTION IN **HTTPSERVERCONTEXT.PAS**

```
1 procedure
2 HTTPServerContext.buildParamList;
3 begin
4   m_ItemList:=HTTPUtil.parseRequest( getRequestString,
5                                      FALSE );
6 end;
```

This function does nothing other than call *getRequestString* to obtain the request and call the parse function.

The HTTPUtil utility class actually does the parsing. To parse a request string, *HTTPUtil.parseRequest* is called. It is passed the request string and a flag indicating whether URL-encoded data should be decoded (the framework always uses TRUE; you can call this yourself if you need different behavior). A reference to a newly created TMultiValList is returned. This object will contain all the names found and the values corresponding to those names.

The function *HTTPUtil.parseRequest* doesn't do much of anything; it just delegates to *HTTPUtil.parseGeneral*. The one piece of information it adds is the delimiter character: it knows that fields in the request are separated by ampersands. Because the same general pattern is used for sending both requests and cookies with the exception of the delimiter character and some white space, the same code can be used for both.

The implementation of *HTTPUtil.parseGeneral* is shown in listing 13.11.

LISTING 13.11—THE **HTTPUTIL.PARSEGENERAL()** FUNCTION IN **HTTPUTILITIES.PAS**

```
01  class function
02  HTTPUtil.parseGeneral( const instr:    String;
03                         decodeflag: Boolean;
04                         delimchar:  Char    ):
05  TMultiValList;
06  var
07     itemlist:      TMultiValList;
08     cursor,
09     len:           Integer;
10     itemnamestart,
11     itemnamelen,
12     itemvalstart,
13     itemvallen:    Integer;
```

continues

```
14  begin
15    { whatever happens, the user will at least get
16      an empty list }
17    itemlist := TMultiValList.Create;
18    Result   := itemlist;
19
20    len      := Length(instr);
21
22    cursor       := 0;
23    itemnamestart := 0;
24    itemvalstart  := 0;
25    itemnamelen   := 0;
26    itemvallen    := 0;
27
28    while cursor < len do
29    begin
30      if PChar(instr)[cursor] = delimchar then
31        begin
32          itemvallen := cursor - itemvalstart;
33          addItem( PChar(instr), decodeflag,
34                   itemlist,
35                   itemnamestart,
36                   itemnamelen,
37                   itemvalstart,
38                   itemvallen );
39          cursor       := cursor+1;
40          { next item starts at the *next* character }
41          itemnamestart := cursor;
42          itemnamelen   := 0;
43          itemvalstart  := cursor;
44          itemvallen    := 0;
45        end
46      else if PChar(instr)[cursor] = '=' then
47        begin
48          { this signals the end of the item name;
49            compute its length. The value starts at
50            the *next* character }
51          itemnamelen := cursor - itemnamestart;
52          cursor      := cursor+1;
53          itemvalstart:= cursor;
```

```
54          end
55       else
56         begin
57           { examine the next character }
58           cursor       := cursor+1;
59         end;
60     end;
61
62     { the last item should have ended without a
63       delimiter. As in that case above, calculate the
64       length of the value, and add the item. However,
65       if zero items were present in the request, we
66       don't want to add a spurious item; that's
67       what the if statement is checking for }
68     if cursor>itemvalstart then
69       begin
70         itemvallen := cursor - itemvalstart;
71         addItem( PChar(instr), decodeflag,
72                     itemlist,
73                     itemnamestart,
74                     itemnamelen,
75                     itemvalstart,
76                     itemvallen );
77       end;
78   end;
```

HTTPUtil.parseGeneral() actually implements the first step of the parsing process that was previously outlined. The first thing the function does, on lines 17–18 of listing 13.11, is to create a new TMultiValList and assign it to the result. This function is guaranteed to return such a list; if no valid data is found, the list returned will simply be empty.

The function then calculates the length of the request, and on line 28 it enters a loop, checking the value of each character in turn. Lines 30 and 46 in this loop check for special delimiting characters. Equals signs (identified by line 46) separate the name and value of a parameter, so when one is encountered, any text between the current position and the preceding delimiter must be the name of the field. When a parameter delimiter character, which was passed into the function as a parameter, is found (by line 30), any text between the last equals sign and the current position must be the value.

Having calculated the boundaries of the name and value, *addItem()* is called on line 33. This gets passed to the string being parsed, the offsets of the name and values as calculated, the decode flag, and the TMultiValList the parameter is to be added to.

This loop continues through the entire string. After it's completed, there might be one last parameter left to record. This will always be the case unless there were *no* parameters in the string, which line 68 checks for. If there was at least one parameter, the string end is taken as a delimiter and the resulting parameter is added by *addItem()* as well. The job of *addItem()*, shown in listing 13.12, is to actually extract and decode the name and value strings and add these to the value list, which is the second and third major steps of the parsing process.

LISTING 13.12—THE HTTPUTIL.ADDITEM() PROCEDURE IN HTTPUTILITIES.PAS

```
01  class procedure
02  HTTPUtil.addItem( const instr:        PChar;
03                           decodeflag:    Boolean;
04                     var   itemlist:      TMultiValList;
05                           itemnamestart,
06                           itemnamelen,
07                           itemvalstart,
08                           itemvallen:    Integer
09                   );
10  var
11    itemname,
12    itemvalue: String;
13    temppchar: PChar;
14    tempint:   Integer;
15
16  begin
17    { compute maximum size necessary for buffer }
18    tempint := itemnamelen;
19    if itemvallen > tempint then
20      tempint := itemvallen;
21    temppchar := StrAlloc( tempint+1 );
22
23    try
24      { set the name string: if we didn't get a name,
25        use the anonymous string }
26      if (itemnamelen > 0) then
27        begin
28          StrLCopy( temppchar, instr+itemnamestart,
29                    itemnamelen );
30          itemname := temppchar;
31        end
32      else
```

```
33        begin
34          itemname := HTTPUtilAnonymousItemName;
35        end;
36
37      if decodeflag then
38        begin
39          { when handling cookies, the name might
40            be preceded by white space }
41          itemname := decodeURL( TrimLeft(itemname) );
42        end;
43
44      { set the value string: if we didn't get
45        a name, use an empty string }
46      if (itemvallen > 0) then
47        begin
48          StrLCopy( temppchar,
49                    instr+itemvalstart, itemvallen );
50          itemvalue := temppchar;
51        end
52      else
53        begin
54          itemvalue := '';
55        end;
56
57      if decodeflag then
58        begin
59          { trim off the trailing newline that some browsers
60            send. Can't do this if not decoding, because
61            the user might want this stuff }
62          itemvalue := decodeURL( TrimRight(itemvalue) );
63        end;
64
65      itemlist.addItem( itemname, itemvalue );
66
67    finally
68      StrDispose( temppchar );
69    end;
70  end;
```

The addItem() function begins on lines 18–20 by calculating the size necessary for a buffer. It uses the buffer copy strings from the parse string and allocates the buffer (on line 21) with a size sufficient to accommodate the larger of the name and value strings. Note that the function must be sure to release the memory upon completion;

this is done on line 68 within a *try...finally* block to ensure against a memory leak even in an exception situation.

The name is the first string the function considers, beginning on line 26. If the length of the name is greater than zero, addItem copies the name from the parse string. A name is required, so if the length is zero it supplies a default. This value is determined by a constant defined at the top of the unit. If the decode flag is set to true, any leading white space is trimmed and *decodeURL* is called to do the decoding. The trimming is necessary because cookies are actually delimited by a semicolon followed by a space, but simplifying this to just a semicolon and later trimming the space allows a tremendous simplification of the scanner in *parseGeneral*.

The value is considered next, beginning on line 46. Just as with the name, the string is copied from the parse string if the length is non-zero. In this case, however, a zero length simply results in a null string. Also, if the decode flag is set, any white space is trimmed from the right side before calling the decoding routine. Here the trimming is necessary for a completely different reason—because some browsers append an additional newline to the request string in a *POST* request, although the HTTP specification does not provide for this.

After the name and value strings have been set, they are added to the item list.

Handling URL-Escaped Data

Functions are provided in the *HTTPUtil* utility class for decoding and encoding URL-escaped data. Each of these takes a single parameter—the string to be converted—and returns the converted string as the result. Incorrect input data raises an *EISAPIException* exception object.

Decoding the Data

The third and final step in the request parsing process (outlined at the beginning of the previous section) is to decode the URL-encoded data. Listing 13.13 shows the function *HTTPUtil.decodeURL()*, which transforms URL-encoded data to regular text.

LISTING 13.13—THE HTTPUTIL.DECODEURL()
FUNCTION IN HTTPUTILITIES.PAS

```
01   class function
02   HTTPUtil.decodeURL( const instr: String ):
03   String;
04   var
05     outbuf: PChar; { buffer to build the result string into }
06     inpos, outpos, inlen: Integer;
07   begin
```

```
08    inlen  := Length( instr );
09    outbuf := StrAlloc( inlen+1 );
10    Result := '';
11
12    try
13      inpos := 0;
14      outpos:= 0;
15      { for each character in input string }
16      while inpos < inlen do
17        begin
18          case PChar(instr)[inpos] of
19            '+': { convert plus to space }
20                  outbuf[outpos] := ' ';
21            '%': { % + 2 hex chars convert to char given
22                    by that ascii value }
23                  if inpos > inlen-2 then
24                    begin
25                      raise EISAPIException.Create(
26                            'Error in URL-escaped value',
27                            ERR_INTERNAL);
28                    end
29                  else
30                    begin
31                      outbuf[outpos] := Chr( hexByte2Int(
32                                        PChar(instr)[inpos+1],
33                                        PChar(instr)[inpos+2] )
34                                             );
35                    { skip the 2 hex digits }
36                      inpos := inpos+2;
37                    end;
38            else { pass the character through }
39                  outbuf[outpos] := PChar(instr)[inpos];
40          end;
41          inpos  := inpos+1;
42          outpos := outpos+1;
43        end;
44      { put a terminator on output buffer }
45      outbuf[outpos] := Chr(0);
46      Result := String( outbuf );
47
48    finally
49      StrDispose( outbuf );
50    end;
51  end;
```

The goal of this function is to take an encoded string like *Hello%2C+World%21* and remove the encoding that was used to allow transmission of special character. The resulting string should look like this: *Hello, World!*

The logic of this function is quite simple. Two integers are declared, *inpos* and *outpos,* which track the current offset in the input and output strings, respectively. A buffer is created to build the result string into. Here a PChar string is used, rather than a Pascal-style string, for efficiency. This enables the function to directly place each character in turn, instead of having to repeatedly scan to the end of a string to append and resize the string vector if necessary.

The *decodeURL()* function loops through the input string. Depending on the value of the current character of the input string, various actions are taken. If a plus sign is found, it is transformed to a space in the output. If a percent sign is found, the next two characters should be hex digits; the character represented by the ASCII value given by those two digits is placed on the end of the output string and the input counter is incremented by 2. This (together with the later default increment of 1) causes the whole 3-character block to be passed. Finally, if the input character is anything else, it is duplicated in the output string. The offsets of both the input and output are incremented.

After the loop has completed, a null character is placed after the last character in the output buffer, making it a legal string. This string is copied to the result. Finally, the buffer is released.

The two hex digits mentioned previously are converted to an integer by *hexByte2Int,* another function in HTTPUtil.

Encoding the Data

Just as it's necessary to decode any request received, the complementary function must be provided for encoding cookies and for encoding requests that are to be placed as links in an output web page. Listing 13.14 shows the function *HTTPUtil.encodeURL,* which transforms regular text to URL-escaped data.

LISTING 13.14—THE HTTPUTIL.ENCODEURL() FUNCTION IN HTTPUTILITIES.PAS

```
01  class function
02  HTTPUtil.encodeURL( const instr: String ):
03  String;
04  var
05    outstr: String;
06    inpos, inlen: Integer;
07  begin
```

```
08    inlen := Length( instr );
09
10    try
11      outstr := '';
12      { for each character in the input }
13      for inpos := 0 to inlen-1 do
14        begin
15          case PChar(instr)[inpos] of
16            { these characters can pass through }
17            '0'..'9','A'..'Z','a'..'z',':','@','/':
18                outstr := outstr + PChar(instr)[inpos];
19            { space is changed to '+' }
20            ' ': outstr := outstr + '+';
21            { else convert to escape sequence by appending
22              a '%' followed by the hex ascii value }
23            else outstr := outstr + '%' +
24                    IntToHex( Ord(PChar(instr)[inpos]), 2 );
25          end;
26        end;
27
28    except
29      else raise EISAPIException.Create(
30                          'Error creating URL-escaped value',
31                          ERR_INTERNAL);
32    end;
33    result := outstr;
34  end;
```

The goal of the function *HTTPUtil.encodeURL()* is to take a text string like *Hello, World!* and replace any special characters with substitutes that are legal in HTTP requests. This means changing spaces to plus signs, and converting most non-alphanumeric characters to escaped values consisting of a percent sign followed by the two-digit hexadecimal ASCII value of the character. The output should look like this: *Hello%2C+World%21.*

The function *HTTPUtil.encodeURL()* is even simpler than *decodeURL()*, which implements the reverse of this function. In *encodeURL()*, the function simply loops through the input string. Depending on the value of the current input character, appropriate text is appended to the output string.

One difference between this function and *decodeURL()* is that the latter places characters into an output buffer, keeping track of the current offset into that buffer. It's not as efficient for *encodeURL()* to do this, because the size of the buffer can't be calculated beforehand—the length depends on the number of characters that need to represented by hex codes. Instead, *encodeURL()* simply appends to a Pascal-style string. Although the result will be less efficient than *decodeURL()*, it will probably be called far less often and therefore not make much difference.

The logic of *encodeURL()* is simply to perform a loop, examining each character in the input. A case statement causes the correct action to be taken, depending on the value of the character. The characters that can be safely placed in an URL (alphanumerics and a few others) are simply appended to the output string as they are. Space characters result in appending a plus sign to the output string. Anything else results in appending a percent sign followed by two hex digits that give the ASCII value of the input character.

Storing Name/Value Data

The framework needs a way to store and retrieve parameters and cookies. This is somewhat more complex, because any particular parameter or cookie can have multiple values.

Cross Reference

For more information on storing and retrieving parameters and cookies, see the sections "Separating Request Fields" and "Setting a Cookie" in Chapter 12.

In addition, it is sometimes useful to access values in the item's list of values by index numbers rather than names to simplify processing some pages.

Here are the requirements that should be met to satisfy the needs of the ISAPI Application Framework:

◆ Multiple items must be stored.

◆ Multiple values for a given item must be stored.

◆ The ordering of items within the list must be preserved; the first one inserted must appear first in the list, and so on.

◆ The ordering of the values defined for an item must be preserved; the first one inserted must appear first in the list, and so on.

◆ The user (the request handler) must be able to retrieve items and their values by name or number.

◆ The user must be able to obtain the number of items in the list as well as the number of values defined for a given item.

Listing 13.15 shows declaration of the class TMultiValList, which satisfies all these requirements.

**LISTING 13.15—DECLARATION OF CLASS TMULTIVALLIST
IN MULTIVALLIST.PAS**

```
01   TMultiValList = class
02     public
03       constructor
04       Create;
05
06       destructor
07       Destroy; override;
08
09       { add a name/value pair to list }
10       procedure
11       addItem ( const itemname:  String;
12                 const itemvalue: String );
13
14       { get the nth value for the requested item name;
15         returns TRUE if found, otherwise FALSE }
16       function
17       retrieveItem ( const itemname: String;
18                            index:     Integer;
19                      var   itemval:  String ):
20       Boolean;
21
22       { get the nth value for the requested item number;
23         returns TRUE if found, otherwise FALSE }
24       function
25       retrieveNumberedItem (     itemnum: Integer;
26                                  index:   Integer;
27                            var itemval: String ):
28       Boolean;
29
30       { get the number of the named item }
31       function
32       retrieveNameIndex ( const itemname: String;
33                           var   itemnum:  Integer ):
34       Boolean;
35
36       { get the number of items currently defined }
37       function
38       getItemCount:
39       Integer;
40
```

continues

LISTING 13.15—DECLARATION OF CLASS TMULTIVALLIST IN MULTIVALLIST.PAS, CONTINUED

```
41     { get the number of values currently defined
42       for the named item }
43     function
44     getValueCount ( itemnum: Integer ):
45     Integer;
46
47     { for debug purposes; returns an HTML-formatted
48       table containing all of the items and
49       their values }
50     function
51     dumpList( const heading: String ):
52     String;
53
54   protected
55     m_ItemList:   TStringList;
56
57   private
58
59   end;
```

The implementation behind the interface in listing 13.15 is less complicated than you might expect, thanks to the rich class library Borland ships with Delphi. The class *TStringList* provides a large part of the necessary logic. It can be used as a dictionary or map container—meaning it can look up a value and return an associated object, just as a dictionary returns a definition for a given word. In this case, the name of the item, as a string, must be stored in addition to a list of the values defined for that item.

Now a means of storing the list of values must be devised. A *TStringList* works well here. A regular *TList* object would probably be more efficient, because the additional data pointer in the *TStringList* is wasted in this case; however, the *TStringList* is far more convenient, because it manages the memory used by the strings it stores. If you were to use a *TList*, the framework would need to take care of allocating strings as they're added to the list and freeing them when the list is freed.

The resulting data structure consists of a *TStringList* object with a string and a pointer for each item in the list. Each of these pointers refers to another *TStringList* containing a string for each value of the item that points to the list. Figure 13.4 shows the structure that results from this.

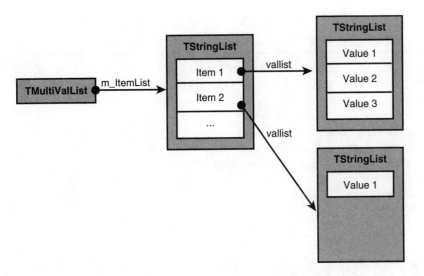

Figure 13.4

The structure of a TmultiValList object.

There is still one bit of memory management to be taken care of with this scheme. The outer *TStringList* (the one holding the items themselves) needs to traverse the list and delete the inner lists (the ones holding the values). This is necessary because TStringList only manages the strings it contains, not data pointers associated with those strings—it can't manage pointers because it doesn't know the type of object the pointer refers to.

All instances of a *TMultiValList* contain a list, even if no items have yet been added to the list. The constructor must allocate this list and assign it to the member variable *m_ItemList*.

As the name indicates, the *addItem()* procedure will add an item to the list. This is illustrated in listing 13.16.

LISTING 13.16—THE TMULTIVALLIST.ADDITEM() PROCEDURE IN MULTIVALLIST.PAS

```
01  procedure
02  TMultiValList.addItem ( const itemname:  String;
03                          const itemvalue: String );
04  var
05     vallist: TStringList;
06     tempint: Integer;
07  begin
08     { get a list to put the value into }
09
```

continues

```
10    { search for an existing item with this name }
11    if NOT retrieveNameIndex( itemname, tempint ) then
12      begin
13        { if there wasn't already one with the
14          same name, create it now }
15        vallist := TStringList.Create;
16        m_ItemList.AddObject( itemname, vallist );
17      end
18    else
19      begin
20        vallist := m_ItemList.Objects[tempint]
21                          as TStringList;
22      end;
23    { either way, we've now got a list }
24
25    { set the value string }
26    vallist.Add( itemvalue );
27  end;
```

This function must obtain a list to add the value to. If the item name is already in the item list, the list of that item's values should be used. Otherwise, a new list must be created. Line 11 of listing 13.16 calls *retrieveNameIndex()*, a function that searches for an item with the specified name. If one is found it puts the index of that item into a variable parameter and returns **TRUE**; if the name is not among the strings in the list, **FALSE** is returned.

If no item exists with the given name, the conditional expression on line 11 evaluates **TRUE**. This allows control to pass to line 15, where a new value list is created. The item name is then appended to the item list, with an associated datum equal to a pointer to the newly created value list.

If an item does exist with the given name, the statement at line 20 will be executed instead. This uses the index of the existing item (retrieved by *retrieveNameIndex*) to obtain a pointer to that item's value list.

Either way, the variable *vallist* now points to a list associated with the specified item. All that's left to do is append the value to that list. This is done on line 26 of listing 13.16.

Many of the other member functions work similarly; that is, they call a function to locate the value list associated with the item name and manipulate that list by using the methods and properties of *TStringList* to accomplish the task at hand. The function to locate the item *retrieveNameIndex* is trivially simple as well. It consists of very little besides a call to *TStringList.indexOf* to find the requested string in the list.

As mentioned previously, you need to provide memory management for the value list. You can see how the memory is allocated and stored on lines 15–16 of listing 13.16. When the *TMultiValList* is destroyed, the memory that was allocated must be freed to prevent a memory leak. Naturally, this is done in the destructor of *TMultiValList*, shown in listing 13.17.

LISTING 13.17—THE TMULTIVALLIST.DESTROY() METHOD IN MULTIVALLIST.PAS

```
01  destructor
02  TMultiValList.Destroy;
03  var
04     vallist: TStringList;
05     i:        Integer;
06  begin
07     if m_ItemList <> nil then
08       begin
09         vallist := nil;
10         for i:= 0 to m_ItemList.Count-1 do
11           begin
12             try
13               vallist:= m_ItemList.Objects[i] as TStringList;
14             except on Exception do
15               vallist:= nil;
16             end;
17             vallist.free;
18           end;
19         m_ItemList.free;
20         m_ItemList := nil;
21       end;
22     inherited Destroy;
23  end;
```

This function loops through each item in the item list. For each item, the associated data pointer is retrieved on line 13 of listing 13.17. Line 17 then frees the list object the pointer refers to. The *TStringList* manages the strings itself. Having emptied the item list, it's now safe to free the list itself without fear of a memory leak. This is done on line 19.

Finally, the *TMultiValList* must clean itself up by calling the destructor of its parent.

Holding and Sending Headers

An ISAPI extension author would rather worry about the contents of the page to be sent than the headers demanded by the HTTP protocol. The framework tries to automate this as much as possible for the application programmer. Under the majority of conditions, the headers can be generated automatically; however, when the default headers are inappropriate, it's important that the programmer is able to override the default behavior easily.

Overriding the default behavior is necessary in several circumstances. For example, if you're sending an image you'll need to specify a MIME type other than the default of text/html. Or, you may want to prevent the user's browser from caching the data you send because of its dynamic nature. You'd accomplish this by sending an additional header, *Expires*, with a date that's already past.

The main part of the header transmission process is essentially self contained in the sendHeaders() function. There is a separate mechanism for creating cookie headers, because they require process to put them into the correct format.

Sending Headers

A request handler might send the headers explicitly by calling the *sendHeaders()* function in the server context object. Because headers must be sent before any response data is sent to the client, the function writeClient will call *sendHeaders()* automatically if it hasn't been done already.

The information automatically generated for the user is the request status (based on the value the user sets in the server context object, which defaults to OK), the MIME type (with a default value of text/html), and any cookies the user has set.

The result status header is always generated dynamically at the time the headers are sent, based upon the current value of m_HTTPStatus at the time the headers are sent. This allows the user to simply call the server context object's *setStatus()* function if a different value must be sent.

Similarly, the Content-Type header is generated dynamically. The value that will be generated is determined by a variable stored in the server context object. You can call the object's *setMIMEType* procedure to alter this value.

Cookies are tracked separately from the rest of the headers. When the headers are sent, the headers necessary to set the requested cookies will be appended to the other headers. Setting a cookie has no effect whatsoever on the rest of the headers to be sent. The exception is any headers that are actually cookies manually added to the header list—cookies with duplicate names will supersede the preceding definition.

The procedure that sends the headers, *HTTPServerContext.sendHeaders*, is shown in listing 13.18.

Listing 13.18—The HTTPServerContext.sendHeaders() Procedure in HTTPSrvrCtxt.pas

```
01  procedure
02  HTTPServerContext.sendHeaders;
03  const
04    CrLF = ^M^J;
05  var
06    outstr, statstr : String;
07  begin
08    { can't send them twice! }
09    if (m_HeadersSent = false) then
10      begin
11        { make the full header string }
12        HTTPUtil.convertStatusCodes( m_HTTPStatus,
13                                     m_pECB.dwHttpStatusCode,
14                                     statstr);
15
16        { report the status as the beginning of the header
17          (IIS will automatically prepend the HTTP version) }
18        outstr := statstr+CrLf;
19
20        { provide the MIME type also }
21        outstr := outstr+ 'Content-Type: '
22                  + m_MIMEType;
23
24        { if there are any additional headers to send }
25        if Length( m_Headers ) > 0 then
26          begin
27            { then add them to the header string }
28            outstr := outstr + CrLf + m_Headers;
29          end;
30
31        { if there are any cookies to send }
32        if Length( m_Cookies ) > 0 then
33          begin
34            { then add them to the header string }
35            outstr := outstr + CrLf + m_Cookies;
36          end;
37
38        if not m_pECB.ServerSupportFunction( m_pECB.ConnID,
39                         HSE_REQ_SEND_RESPONSE_HEADER,
40                         PChar(outstr),
```

continues

```
41                              NIL, NIL ) then
42          begin
43              raise EISAPIBadWrite.Create(
44                      'sendHeaders failed',
45                      OK );
46          end;
47        m_HeadersSent:=true;
48      end
49    else
50      begin
51        raise EISAPIException.Create(
52              'Attempt to send headers out of sequence',
53              ERR_INTERNAL );
54      end;
55  end;
```

Although the function in listing 13.18 is called sendHeaders(), the actual transmission of the header data is only half of its job. Before it can send the headers, the function must assemble the complete header block from the various parts the server context object has been storing. These parts include:

◆ HTTP status code

◆ MIME content type

◆ Any user-specified headers

◆ Cookies generated by the *setCookie()* function

The first part of the header to be generated is the status code. The function *HTTPUtil.convertStatusCodes* performs this service. Given one of the framework's internal status codes, an HTTP status value is retrieved, along with the textual description of that status code. The latter function is called on line 12. This description becomes the first line of the headers to be output. On the second line of the output, the status description is repeated as the value of a *Result* header.

The next header to be appended to the string is the *Content-Type*, on line 21.

Any user-defined headers are added by lines 25–29. The condition on line 25 is necessary to prevent extra line ends from being sent. Because line ends act as header terminators, and two consecutive line ends are interpreted by the user as the termination of the entire header block, care must be taken only to insert a delimiter when there is a header to delimit. Otherwise the two line ends will not be read by the browser and might be displayed to the user as screen garbage. This same issue is dealt with by the functions *addHeader()* and *setCookie()*. These functions automatically insert line ends between the existing data and new entries as they're added.

Cookies generated by the framework get the same treatment as the user-defined headers. This occurs on lines 32–36.

Line 38 transmits the header block that was just generated. The *ServerSupportFunction()* callback provided in the Extension Control Block does this. If the operation is unsuccessful, there's no sense continuing (the most likely reason for a failure is a loss of communication with the user). Line 46 creates and raises an *EISAPIBadWrite* object. See the next section, "The Exception Architecture," for more information on these exceptions.

The headers can only be sent once per request. *HTTPServerContext* contains a Boolean variable, *m_HeadersSent*, which is initialized as FALSE but changed to TRUE on line 47 of listing 13.18 after the headers have been sent.

Trying to resend headers is impossible, and trying to add header information (via *addHeader*) or set a cookie (via *setCookie*) is nonsensical after the headers have been sent. To prevent this from occurring, each of these functions checks the value of *m_HeadersSent* when called. If any of these functions determine that the headers have already been sent, they will raise an *EISAPIException* object.

Generating Cookie Headers

The *setCookie()* function, shown in listing 13.19, takes information about the desired cookie from the caller and builds a header that sets the described cookie in the user's browser.

The description of the cookie is given by the values of the function's six parameters. Of these, the *cookiename* parameter must have a non-zero length. You can pass null strings for the values of *cookieval*, *domain*, *path*, and *expiry*. The Boolean parameter secure must be defined, of course.

LISTING 13.19—THE HTTPSERVERCONTEXT.SETCOOKIE PROCEDURE IN HTTPSRVRCTXT.PAS

```
01  procedure
02  HTTPServerContext.setCookie( const cookiename: String;
03                               const cookieval:  String;
04                               const domain:     String;
05                               const path:       String;
06                               const expiry:     String;
```

continues

LISTING 13.19—THE HTTPSERVERCONTEXT.SETCOOKIE PROCEDURE IN HTTPSRVRCTXT.PAS, CONTINUED

```
07                                    secure:    Boolean
08                          );
09  const
10    CrLF = ^M^J;
11  var
12    headerstr, tempstr: String;
13  begin
14    if (m_HeadersSent = false) then
15      begin
16        if Length(cookiename)<1 then
17          begin
18            raise EISAPIException.Create(
19                  'Attempt to set cookie without a name',
20                  ERR_INTERNAL );
21          end;
22
23        headerstr := 'Set-Cookie: ';
24
25        { URL-encode the name of the cookie
26          and add it to the string }
27        tempstr   := HTTPUtil.encodeURL( cookiename );
28        headerstr := headerstr + tempstr + '=';
29
30        { URL-encode the value and add it to the string }
31        tempstr   := HTTPUtil.encodeURL( cookieval );
32        headerstr := headerstr + tempstr;
33
34        if Length( expiry ) > 0 then
35          begin
36            headerstr := headerstr + '; expires=' + expiry;
37          end;
38
39        if Length( path ) > 0 then
40          begin
41            headerstr := headerstr + '; path=' + path;
42          end;
43
44        if Length( domain ) > 0 then
45          begin
46            headerstr := headerstr + '; path=' + domain;
47          end;
```

```
48
49        if secure then
50          begin
51            headerstr := headerstr + '; secure';
52          end;
53
54        if Length(m_Cookies) > 0 then
55          begin
56            { add a new line to terminate preceding header }
57            m_Cookies := m_Cookies + CrLf;
58          end;
59
60        m_Cookies := m_Cookies + headerstr;
61      end
62    else
63      begin
64        { can't send headers more than once! }
65        raise EISAPIException.Create(
66              'Attempt to set cookies out of sequence',
67              ERR_INTERNAL );
68      end;
69
70  end;
```

The *setCookie()* function first checks that its invocation is valid. Line 14 verifies that the headers have not yet been sent. Line 16 verifies that the cookie has been given a name. Either of these errors will result in an exception being raised.

Now that the function knows it can safely proceed, it begins to assemble a Set-Cookie header from the data sent to it. The first thing to do is set the header name, on line 23. Lines 27–32 encode the cookie's name and value in the same way an URL would be encoded. The Netscape specification for cookies does not require this type of encoding or any other; it does, however, note that some sort of encoding is advisable. Because an acceptable encoding scheme is already defined and implemented, it makes sense to use it rather than inventing a new scheme. This holds true so long as the same encoding scheme is used for encoding and decoding. If all of your code uses the ISAPI Application Framework, or at least uses the standard URL-encoding/ decoding, this will work out fine.

Lines 34–47 check the value of each of the other string parameters in turn. For any string parameter found with a value defined, its value will be added to the cookie header, preceded by the name of that attribute. Finally, lines 49–52 add a secure specification if required.

The cookie header has now been generated. Lines 54–58 add it to the list of cookie headers to be sent. If any are already present, a line end is added to separate the last cookie header from the new one to be added.

The Exception Architecture

In Delphi, the preferred means of handling errors—particularly those that logically result in a termination of the task—is not by passing return codes. Instead, an exception object should be raised. This provides two significant benefits:

◆ An exception can be handled at the level of abstraction that understands it. Intermediaries need not carry the baggage of error reporting, so long as they are well behaved in the presence of exception.

◆ The use of exception both simplifies and improves the management of resources in the presence of errors.

The degree to which the ISAPI interface can enable exceptions is extremely limited by the fact that it is language neutral—it must be usable by languages that do not support exceptions. The Delphi ISAPI framework attempts to provide an interface that enables exception handling for its users.

There are three elements to the support provided by the framework:

◆ Defining a set of exception objects meaningful to the domain of ISAPI requests

◆ Introducing code to raise exceptions when the server returns error codes, as well as errors internal to the framework

◆ Providing code surrounding the invocation of the request handler so any exception not handled by the request handler (or caused by it) can be dealt with properly

Exception Objects

The framework includes a unit called *ISAPIException.pas.* This unit provides definitions for the framework's two exception objects as well as for the enumeration of possible status codes. The two exception objects are *EISAPIException* and *EISAPIBadWrite.*

EISAPIException is derived from Delphi's base exception object, *Exception.* It adds to the base class an additional property, Status. This takes a value of type *HTTP_STATUS,* which is defined here as well. The value placed in the Status property should be appropriate for the situation that precipitated the creation of the exception object, because it will be sent to the user if the request handler does not handle the exception itself.

An additional convention is added to the base class as well, although this isn't embodied in the code. The string put into the Message property should be suitable for sending to the user, and this could mean providing HTML formatting tags within it. In contrast, the messages defined in any of Delphi's predefined exception types will not be sent to the user, because they are assumed to be either inappropriate for users to read or not interpretable by a web browser.

The framework derives an additional exception class, *EISAPIBadWrite*, from *EISAPIException*. No additional attributes or behavior is defined for this class. Its purpose is simply to provide a means for exception handlers to differentiate various types of exceptions.

Both exception classes, *EISAPIException* and *EISAPIBadWrite*, are shown in listing 13.20.

LISTING 13.20—THE UNIT ISAPIEXCEPTION.PAS

```
01  unit ISAPIException;
02
03  {
04    defines EISAPIException, the class used for
05    exceptions within the ISAPI framework
06
07    defines HTTP_STATUS, an enumerated type
08    giving the status of the HTTP request
09  }
10
11  interface
12
13  uses
14    SysUtils,
15    Windows,
16    Classes;
17
18  type
19    HTTP_STATUS = (
20                  OK,
21                  CREATED,
22                  ACCEPTED,
23                  NO_CONTENT,
24                  REDIR_MULTIPLE_CHOICE,
25                  REDIR_MOVED_PERMANENT,
26                  REDIR_MOVED_TEMPORARY,
```

continues

LISTING 13.20—THE UNIT ISAPIEXCEPTION.PAS, CONTINUED

```
27                    REDIR_NOT_MODIFIED,
28                    ERR_BAD_REQUEST,
29                    ERR_UNAUTHORIZED,
30                    ERR_FORBIDDEN,
31                    ERR_NOTFOUND,
32                    ERR_INTERNAL
33                );
34
35    { Exception object used by the ISAPI framework }
36    EISAPIException = class(Exception)
37    protected
38      FStatus: HTTP_STATUS;
39      FLogMsg: String;
40    public
41      constructor
42      Create(const Msg: string; status: HTTP_STATUS );
43
44      property
45      Status: HTTP_STATUS read FStatus write FStatus;
46
47    end;
48
49    EISAPIBadWrite = class(EISAPIException);
50
51  implementation
52
53  constructor
54  EISAPIException.Create( const Msg:    string;
55                                  status: HTTP_STATUS );
56  begin
57    inherited Create( Msg );
58    FStatus := status;
59  end;
60
61  end.
```

Lines 36–47 of listing 13.20 show the declaration of *EISAPIException*. Notice line 45, where the HTTP_STATUS value is defined as a property, allowing easy access for the class' clients. Lines 53–59 implement *EISAPIException*'s constructor, its only method. This function simply initializes the object's member data to the values passed to the constructor.

On line 49, *EISAPIBadWrite* is declared. Since it adds no additional behavior to its base class, nothing else needs to be declared or defined.

Raising Exceptions

The objects and functions comprising the framework will raise exceptions in four situations:

- ◆ Error codes returned from calls to the ECB callback functions

- ◆ Incorrect usage of the framework, such as attempting to set a cookie after headers have already been sent

- ◆ Invalid data, such as errors in the encoding of data in the request string

- ◆ Internal processing errors, such as inability to create an object due to insufficient memory

In all these situations, the Status and Message properties of the exception object raised will be set to meaningful values.

Most errors will result in raising an exception of type *EISAPIException,* because the situation should be reported to the user (if it's not caught and handled internally). Some exceptions, those that indicate an inability to communicate with the user, result in raising an *EISAPIBadWrite* object. By drawing a distinction between these two, both the request handler and the framework can avoid the expense of sending a notification that will not—due to the very nature of the error—be received.

Catching Exceptions

The first line for catching exceptions is of course within the request handler. This is essential if there are any local, dynamically allocated resources. Failure to catch and handle the exception with a *try...finally* block so the resources can be freed will result in a resource leak.

In many cases, catching the exception will be unnecessary. If all dynamic resource allocation is handled in the constructor of an object and released in its destructor, leaks can be avoided automatically. The framework will always destroy the request handler after completion or after it catches an exception (see lines 39–45 of listing 13.6). If all dynamic resources are owned by the request handler, or by objects that are owned by the request handler in turn, they will be deleted automatically as part of the destruction of the request handler.

If the request handler does not handle the exception, the framework will. Lines 67–87 of listing 13.6 do this. There are three separate handlers in this block of code:

- In the case of an *EISAPIBadWrite* exception, nothing can be done; the handler is empty but must be present to prevent its being caught by a handler for one of its base classes.

- Any other *EISAPIException* results in generating a page to notify the user; the contents of the page are based on the Status and Message properties of the exception object.

- Any other exception results in generating a page to notify the user; in this case a generic, hard-coded message is used with a Status of ERR_INTERNAL because no better information is available.

The error page resulting from these is generated and sent by a function called *outputErrorMessage()*, shown in listing 13.21. This function requires the Extension Control Block so it can call the functions necessary to send the following information:

- A Boolean indicating whether headers have already been sent to the user (it can't be done twice!)

- The status that should be sent in the header

- The message that should be sent

If possible, a header will be sent with the desired HTTP status. This can only be done if no headers have yet to be sent. On line 43 of listing 13.6, the framework will always check to see if the request handler wrote the headers. The function *outputErrorMessage()*, shown in listing 13.21, uses this to determine whether it can safely send its own headers.

LISTING 13.21—THE OUTPUTERRORMESSAGE() FUNCTION IN HTTPSERVER.PAS

```
01  function
02  outputErrorMessage( var pECB:         TEXTENSION_CONTROL_BLOCK;
03                      headerswritten: Boolean;
04                      status:         HTTP_STATUS;
05                      Message:        String ):
06  Boolean;
07  const
08    CrLF = ^M^J;
09  var
10    statstr, outstr: String;
11    dwLen: DWord;
12  begin
13    Result := TRUE;
14    try
```

```
15    { if no headers have been written yet,
16      spit out some appropriate ones }
17    if NOT headerswritten then
18      begin
19        HTTPUtil.convertStatusCodes( status,
20                                     pECB.dwHttpStatusCode,
21                                     statstr);
22        outstr := statstr + CrLf + 'Status: ' + statstr
23                + CrLf + 'Content-Type: text/html';
24        Result := pECB.ServerSupportFunction( pECB.ConnID,
25                                    HSE_REQ_SEND_RESPONSE_HEADER,
26                                    PChar(outstr),
27                                    NIL, NIL );
28      end;
29    { output the message that was specified }
30    if result = TRUE then
31      begin
32        dwLen := Length(Message);
33        result := pECB.WriteClient( pECB.ConnID,
34                                    PChar(Message),
35                                    @dwLen, 0 );
36      end;
37    except
38      else // just catch the exception; too late to fix it now!   end;
39  end;
```

You can see the function check if the headers have been written on line 17. If they have not been, lines 19–27 provide a minimal amount of functionality for sending headers. More is unnecessary: there's no sense in sending cookies, for example, if there was an error generating them in the first place.

The remainder of listing 13.21 is fairly minimal, because the root of the problem might be insufficient memory or some other situation that will prevent doing anything more fancy. All that is done is to send the headers, if appropriate, and then send the message that was passed in.

Summary

Delphi is a practical tool for ISAPI development, but Delphi programmers are handicapped in developing ISAPI applications by a lack of any application framework.

There are many reasons to use the language, most significantly that you might have a large amount of code already implemented in Delphi.

A complete framework suitable for developing commercial-quality ISAPI applications in Delphi is presented in this chapter. By using this framework, a developer can create request-handler objects that are invoked to service a request. These request handlers can rely on a wide range of services to automate retrieving and parsing requests—sending headers, sending the response, and sending, retrieving, and parsing cookies.

CHAPTER 14

Debugging ISAPI Filters

Debugging of any kind is often an intuitive process. Quite often when working on a bug, the programmer suddenly sees what the problem is without going through any rational procedure. That's when writing software is the most fun.

There are other instances, however, when rational procedures and good programming habits can save a lot of time, especially when the bug pops up months after the program is out in the real world. The best way to fix a bug is to write the code with as few bugs as possible in the first place. Therefore, this discussion will begin by listing a few things to watch out for when designing an ISAPI application.

Reentrancy

Reentrancy is a common problem in ISAPI applications and DLLs in general. Suppose you're writing an extension that needs to maintain some kind of global variable. Quite often solo programmers are in a rush. It's easier to create a global variable than to continually pass parameters to functions and assign return values. For instance, suppose you allocate some memory at the beginning of a program and don't need to deallocate it until the end of a program. Listing 14.1 gives an example of code that will get you in trouble:

LISTING 14.1—DONTDOTHIS.C

```
//  Purpose: ISAPI DLL designed to cause problems
01. #include <windows.h>
02. #include <httpext.h>
03.
04. CHAR * pMemBlock = NULL;
05.
06. DllExport DWORD HttpExtensionProc (EXTENSION_CONTROL_BLOCK *pECB)
07. {
08.
09.   // Allocate 1000 bytes of memory
10.   if( ! pMemBlock = ( CHAR * ) GlobalAlloc ( GPTR, 1000) ) )
11.   {
12.     return HSE_STATUS_ERROR;
13.   }
14.
15.   DoSomethingWithMemory();
16.
17.   GlobalFree( pMemBlock );
18.
19.   return HSE_STATUS_SUCCESS;
20.
21. } // End of Program.
```

Normally this would be fairly innocuous even if it is bad coding. In a DLL, however, this code has a problem. Because ISAPI DLLs are reentrant, the value of pMemBlock could be changed at line 15 by another thread running through the same code. Then, whatever information pMemBlock is pointing to will be lost and there will be a memory leak. The first thread could also deallocate the memory used by the second thread and cause a General Protection Fault. This bug will only occur when one thread interrupts another in the middle of the code so it will seem to crash randomly.

A better way to write this code would be to create the memory pointer as a stack variable as shown on line 8 of listing 14.2.

LISTING 14.2—MAYBEDOTHIS.C

```
//  Purpose: ISAPI DLL hoping to avoid problems
01 #include <windows.h>
02 #include <httpext.h>
03
04
05 DllExport DWORD HttpExtensionProc (EXTENSION_CONTROL_BLOCK *pECB)
06 {
07
08   CHAR * pMemBlock = NULL;
09
10   // Allocate 1000 bytes of memory
11   if( ! pMemBlock = ( CHAR * ) GlobalAlloc ( GPTR, 1000) ) )
12   {
13     return HSE_STATUS_ERROR;
14   }
15
16   DoSomethingWithMemory( pMemBlock );
17
18   GlobalFree( pMemBlock );
19
20   return HSE_STATUS_SUCCESS;
21
22 } // End of Program.
```

Because the stack of a DLL is always the stack of the calling program, you can be sure that multiple threads of MaybeDoThis.DLL will never be pointing at the same location in memory. Be sure not to use static variables, because they are stored in the global data segment of a DLL and not in the stack segment.

Critical Sections in Code

Another common reentrancy problem is the issue of critical sections in code. Suppose your program needs to number invoices sequentially and that you are storing the numbers in a file. You have to open the file, read the number, increment it, and then write it back to the file. You don't want a second thread to interrupt the first one after the number has been read in but before the incremented number has been written back out. The result would be two invoices with the same number. In such a situation, you need to use some kind of locking mechanism so the second thread knows to wait until the first thread has finished the critical section.

One way to lock out other threads is demonstrated in listing 14.3.

LISTING 14.3—INCREMENTNUMBER.C

```
01.  CRITICAL_SECTION    gCS;  //use InitializeCriticalSection when loading
➥DLL, use DeleteCriticalSection when unloading DLL
02.int  GenerateNumber( void )
03.{
04.
05.     int ticket;
06.     CHAR * out_string;
07.
08.     EnterCriticalSection(&gCS);
09.
10.
11.     ticket = GetPrivateProfileInt("Section_name",    // section name
12.                                   "Last_ticket",      // key name
13.                                   1,                  // default return value
14.                                   "INI_FILE_NAME"     // ini filename
15.                                  );
16.     if (ticket == 1)
17.     {
18.         //error reading ini file
19.     }
20.     else
21.     {
22.         ticket++;
23.         wsprintf( out_string, "%d", ticket);
24.     WritePrivateProfileString(
25.             "Section_name",      // section name
26.             "Last_ticket",       // key name
27.             out_string,          // string to add
28.             "INI_FILE_NAME"      // ini filename
29.                             );
30.     }
31.     LeaveCriticalSection(&gCS);
32.
33.     return ticket;
34.}
```

When the DLL containing the code in listing 14.3 is loaded it should initialize the critical section object with the *InitializeCriticalSection()* function. The *GenerateNumber()* function uses *EnterCriticalSection()* to keep other threads from interrupting all code up to the *LeaveCriticalSection()* function. The number is then retrieved from the file, incremented, and written back to the file.

Memory Leaks

Memory leaks are especially bad problems in ISAPI applications because they are usually running 24 hours a day, seven days a week on web servers with (hopefully) millions of people visiting the site. DontDoThis.c in listing 14.1 has an example of a possible memory leak, but not a very likely one. Most often, they occur in applications when resources of any kind are allocated but not deallocated. They usually don't show up as a lack of memory. Instead, *other* applications begin to crash when *they* start running out of memory. This is fortunate for you as a programmer, because you can just blame the problem on someone else! If you prefer to take responsibility for yourself, the Run-Time Debug Libraries discussed later in the chapter are quite helpful.

Debugging Under Windows NT

There are a lot of strategies for debugging ISAPI filters and extensions. Some are presented in the following sections, with explanations, so you can choose one that meets your particular needs.

Stepping Through Your Code in a Debugger

Because IIS is a service and only reacts to web browsers, it is not quite as easy to debug as a regular Windows API program. As a service, IIS runs in the local system account, which means it runs in an impersonated security context and there is no desktop. As a result, you usually won't have the security rights necessary to debug it.

Setting Up for Debugging

If you are writing an ISAPI extension, the easiest way to run IIS under a debugger is to use the Windows NT User Manager to grant "Act as Part of the Operating System" rights to your user account. This procedure is detailed in the series of steps that follows. Of course, you are advised not to do this on a production server.

1. In the NTAS 4.0 User Manager, pull down the Policies menu and select User Rights.

2. The User Rights Policy dialog box appears. Make sure the Show Advanced User Rights checkbox is checked.

3. From the Right list, select Act as Part of the Operating System.

4. Click on Add button to add yourself to the list of users granted that right.

Loading the Web Server in the Debugger

Because ISAPI applications are by definition DLLs, you need to set up your debugger to execute IIS as a console application before your code will be reached. You can accomplish this by doing the following:

1. Turn off all Internet Services (WWW, FTP, and Gopher) by using the IIS Service Manager or the Services Control Panel.

2. In Visual C/C++ 4.x, pull down the Build menu and choose Settings.

3. Click the Debug tab in the Project Settings dialog box.

4. Choose the General category. In the Executable for Debug Session field, type the location of the IIS executable file on your computer (usually **C:\WINNT\SYSTEM32\INETSRV\INETINFO.EXE**).

5. In the Program Arguments field, type **-e W3SVC**. This tells IIS to execute the WWW service.

Set breakpoints wherever you need to in your code. When you execute the program, you will get an annoying message asking if you are sure you want to debug an executable that has no debugging information in it. You do. Now you need to launch your browser and pull up the page containing the form you are going to debug. When you click on the Submit button for the form, the debugger breaks at the appropriate line in your code.

Some features of IIS do not behave correctly when IIS runs as a console application. In this case, you will want to take a different approach to running it under your debugger. You can debug IIS as a service by first starting it as a service and using PVIEW (which comes with Visual C++) or TLIST (from the NT Resource Kit) to get the process ID of INETINFO.EXE. Then attach your debugger to the running process. You will need to use *DebugBreak()* function statements in your code to cause the debugger to break in your code.

Debugging with the OutputDebugString( ) Function

Another way to debug ISAPI applications is to use the Win32 function *OutputDebugString()*, which sends any string you want to the debug monitor. You can use DBMON (part of the Win32 SDK) or some other program that shows debugging output to display the strings on the screen as your application runs. Again, the problem is that IIS runs in the local system security context, whereas DBMON runs in the context of the account you logged on to NTAS with. Fortunately, Microsoft provides a fix for this.

A fix is necessary to view ISAPI debug output with DBMON, because the DLL runs in the local system account while DBMON runs in the logged-in user account. Starting with the Win32 SDK for Windows NT 4 beta 2, DBMON creates a NULL DACL and passes the security attributes to both CreateEvent calls and the CreateFileMapping call. You can modify DBMON yourself if you do not have the current SDK. The following code shows how to make a NULL DACL:

LISTING 14.4—FROM MICROSOFT KNOWLEDGE BASE

```
01. SECURITY_ATTRIBUTES sa;    SECURITY_DESCRIPTOR sd;
02.
03. sa.nLength = sizeof(SECURITY_ATTRIBUTES);
04. sa.bInheritHandle = TRUE;
05. sa.lpSecurityDescriptor = &sd;
06.
07. if(!InitializeSecurityDescriptor(&sd,
08. SECURITY_DESCRIPTOR_REVISION))
09.   return;   // Handle errors
10. if(!SetSecurityDescriptorDacl(&sd, TRUE, (PACL)NULL, FALSE))
11.   return;   // Handle errors
12.
13. // You may now pass &sa to CreateEvent and CreateFileMapping
```

Debugging with the MessageBox( ) Function

You can use the *MessageBox()* function from the Win32 API to display information by including the two constants MB_SERVICE_NOTIFICATION and MB_TOPMOST in the nType parameter. Without these two flags, *MessageBox()* won't work inside a service, because there is no desktop at that security level. The flags tell the operating system to display the information on the logged-in user's desktop. In general, *MessageBox()* should only be used for debugging purposes and not as a regular part of your program.

Tips for Easier Debugging

Here are a few hints to make your life easier when debugging:

1. Change the Output file name of your DLL to reflect the location it will need to be in when running under IIS. Remember that the DLL needs to reside wherever the HTML source code makes a request for it, usually somewhere underneath the C:\INETPUB\SCRIPTS directory.

2. Turn off caching of DLLs in IIS. This won't matter while running IIS under your debugger, because IIS will stop and start as you stop and start debugging. But it will matter when you are going through compile iterations, tweaking little things about your DLL, because IIS will keep your DLL loaded in memory unless you tell it not to. To turn caching off, set the following key to 0 in the Windows NT registry:

```
1. HKEY_LOCAL_MACHINE
2.     System
3.        CurrentControlSet
4.          Services
5.            W3SVC
6.              Parameters
7.                CacheExtensions
```

   There is no way to change the loading behavior of ISAPI filters, so you must stop IIS, copy the new version of the filter over the old one, and restart IIS to re-load it.

3. Turn off the loading of pictures in your browser or create HTML files with no references to pictures when debugging ISAPI filters. Each graphic generates a new request to the server that will interrupt your debugging session making it difficult to debug the filter.

Debugging with ISMOKE.EXE

One way to debug ISAPI extensions is to use ISMOKE.EXE, a small Win32 program that is part of the IIS SDK. ISMOKE will load a DLL into memory, create an EXTENSION_CONTROL_BLOCK, and call HttpExtensionProc. ISMOKE comes in source code form you will have to compile, which means you can make any modifications to it you need to.

ISMOKE is limited to debugging ISAPI extensions and is not useful for debugging ISAPI filters. It is not recommended for heavy-duty debugging, because you have to type in any parameters the way they would be passed by a browser to the web server; however, it is handy for writing extensions and watching their output.

To use ISMOKE.EXE, set ISMOKE.EXE as the executable in your compiler, put breakpoints in your code, and start debugging. The Query field should contain the information your DLL expects to get, such as *VARIABLE1=Hi There&VARIABLE2= Good Bye*. The Method field allows you to choose between GETting, POSTing, and PUTting the data. The DLL field should contain the name of your DLL, and so far this author has found it doesn't work unless the Loaded field is checked. Click on the Submit button when you are ready. When your extension is done executing, the output will appear in the Extension Output window. This is fairly self-explanatory.

Debugging with CGIWRAP

Another approach, similar to ISMOKE, is to use the CGIWRAP example that comes with the IIS SDK. It was designed for running ISAPI DLLs as if they are executables so they can be executed anywhere a CGI Script executable can be run. If the environment variables are set correctly, CGIWRAP will work from the command line instead of from within IIS. Of course, ISMOKE and CGIWRAP won't simulate everything about IIS, but you can step through your code from within them.

Making It Airtight

After you have a working ISAPI DLL, the next step is to make it work reliably. IIS has a self-protection mechanism that handles exceptions fairly well, but it is always better to have a solid application. There is nothing worse than finding out your web server hasn't been working for the last eight hours.

The best preventive medicine this author has found is to step through every single line of code. If programmers never had to deal with adverse circumstances, their lives would be wonderful (okay, some programmers' lives would be wonderful). It seems as though 90 percent of any program is dealing with all the things that might happen. Most of the things you write code for do not happen during the normal running of a program, but when your program hits the road and an adverse condition happens, the code you wrote to deal with that condition crashes because it has never been executed in the lab. Here is an example:

LISTING 14.5—NORMALLYWORKS.C

```
01 int NormallyWorks ( void )
02 {
03
04   char * pString;
05
```

continues

LISTING 14.5—NORMALLYWORKS.C, CONTINUED

```
06    // Allocate 1000 bytes of memory
07    pString = ( CHAR * ) LocalAlloc ( LPTR, 1000);
08    if( ! pString );
09    {
10      return 0;
11    }
12    DoSomethingWithString( pString );
13
14    return 1;
15
16 } // End of Program.
```

Most of the time, *NormallyWorks()* performs fine, but one day, for some reason, the memory allocation fails. On that day, the program crashes because you accidentally put a colon at the end of line 8—which means line 10 will never be executed—and the program still goes to line 12 where *DoSomethingWithString()* crashes because it has a bad pointer. Of course, this is an error a modern compiler would pick up, but you get the idea. The point is, use the debugger to cause every exception to the general flow of your program, and watch how the program handles the disruptions. For example, after executing line 7 of listing 14.5, you could alter the value of pString to 0 and you would notice that you never get to line 10.

ASSERT Statements

ASSERT statements are another great debugging tool. ASSERT statements test the validity of a statement such as *pMemory != NULL* before you use *pMemory* in your program. ASSERT statements won't slow down your program, because they are only executed when _DEBUG or a similar variable is defined.

It is a good idea to sprinkle ASSERT statements liberally throughout your code. It is an especially good idea to use ASSERT statements to test the validity of a pointer in your code before you use the pointer. ASSERT statements can also be used to make sure integers are within the appropriate boundaries or strings are the right length.

LISTING 14.6—USE OF ASSERT STATEMENTS

```
01 int SelfTesting ( void )
02 {
03
04    char * pMemory1;
05    char * pMemory2;
```

```
06
07    pMemory1 = ReturnPointerToMem( NULL );
08
09    ASSERT( pMemory1 != NULL );
10
11    pMemory2 = ReturnPointerToMem( pMemory1 );
12
13    ASSERT( (pMemory2 != NULL) && (pMemory1 != NULL));
14
15    DoSomethingWithMemory( pMemory1, pMemory2 );
16
17    return 1;
18
19 } // End of Program.
```

You might be surprised at the number of problems that get caught by using ASSERT statements. In general, they alert you to the problem the minute it appears. So many bugs that seem to happen later in the program are really the result of something that occurred earlier. It can take a while to fix these kinds of bugs.

Run-Time Debug Libraries

The Run-Time Debug Libraries are particularly good for catching other problems with pointers. NULL pointers cause exceptions, but quite often memory gets overwritten by errant pointers. The Run-Time Debug Libraries check memory buffers and test for overruns.

One of the best ways to catch memory leaks is to use the Run-Time Debug Libraries. To use them in Visual C++ 4.x, do the following:

1. First, choose the Settings command under the Build menu.

2. In the C++ tab, choose Category, Code Generation.

3. Under Use Run-Time Library, choose Debug Multithreaded DLL.

4. Then compile and link again.

Listing 14.7 shows some sample code provided by Microsoft that can aid you in catching memory leaks:

Listing 14.7—Microsoft Code for Using Run-Time Debug Libraries

```
01.#define WIN32_LEAN_AND_MEAN
02.    #include <windows.h>
03.
04.    #if 1     // change to #if 0 to turn off mem check
05.
06.    DWORD g_dwTotal;
07.
08.    //
09.    // Call MemAlloc just as you would call HeapAlloc
10.    //
11.
12.    LPVOID MemAlloc (HANDLE hHeap, DWORD dwFlags, DWORD dwSize)
13.      {
14.      LPVOID p;
15.
16.      p = HeapAlloc (hHeap, dwFlags, dwSize);
17.      if (p)
18.        g_dwTotal += dwSize;
19.
20.      return p;
21.      }
22.
23.    BOOL MemFree (HANDLE hHeap, DWORD dwFlags, LPVOID p)
24.      {
25.      DWORD dwSize;
26.      BOOL bReturn;
27.
28.      dwSize = HeapSize (hHeap, dwFlags, p);
29.      bReturn = HeapFree (hHeap, dwFlags, p);
30.
31.      if (dwSize != 0xffffffff && bReturn)
32.        g_dwTotal -= dwSize;
33.
34.      return bReturn;
35.      }
36.
37.    void DumpBytesInUse (void)
38.      {
39.      TCHAR szMsg[256];
40.
```

```
41.       wsprintf (szMsg, "Bytes in use: %u\r\n", g_dwTotal);
42.       OutputDebugString (szMsg);
43.       }
44.
45.    #else
46.
47.    #define MemAlloc HeapAlloc
48.    #define MemFree HeapFree
49.    #define DumpBytesInUse(x)
50.
51.    #endif
```

If you suspect memory overruns by your application are crashing IIS, you can also rewrite your DLLs to use an alternate heap by using the *HeapCreate()*, *HeapAlloc()*, and *HeapFree()* functions in listing 14.7 for all memory allocations.

Providing Error Messages

Another thing that will help you when your DLL is in production is to use good error messages. Ideally, an error message gives the name of the program, the line number in the code where the problem is, what the problem is, and some sort of statement in the native language of the user to let them know what to do. Error messages such as "Cyclic Redundancy Hyper-Interpolated Bit Swapping Checkpoint Exception" or "Error in Program" will waste a bunch of your time on the phone with someone.

A better error message would be "The server was unable to process your request. Try again in five minutes. Technical Support Information: ISAPI.DLL was unable to allocate memory at line 115 of ISAPI.C." You can use compiler programs and define statements to simplify the task of creating effective error messages.

Stress Testing

It's a good idea to devise a stress-testing strategy for your DLL. If you have traced through every line of the code, you have already discovered many of the bugs that would occur when your program is confronted with unusual circumstances, but you might find more with stress-testing. It's not as easy to stress-test an ISAPI application as it is to test a stand-alone program, because ISAPI applications are run under a web server that might have its own trouble in difficult situations.

Here are some tests you might think about running:

1. Because reentrancy is a problem, write a small program that makes multiple, simultaneous requests to your DLL. (See the Hammer program in the text that follows.) Running two web browsers and clicking on Submit simultaneously probably won't do it.

2. Test how your DLL handles getting bad data. First of all, any good program should clearly tell the user what was done incorrectly and what to do the next time. This will help prevent technical support calls later. Beyond a simple blank field, you might write a program to send data in a blatant effort to bring down your DLL. Your DLL should be bullet-proof in terms of parsing incoming data and ready for any contingency. The Internet has plenty of hackers who want to see if they can bring down someone's system.

3. Test how your software runs in low-memory, low-resource circumstances. Most compilers provide tools for using up resources artificially for testing purposes.

4. Test how your program works under a continuous heavy load. This can be done by setting up some kind of test and letting it run nonstop for a week. This isn't as much of an issue for ISAPI DLLs as it is for a regular application, because ISAPI DLLs by their nature usually perform a small task and then quit very quickly. Anything that needs to maintain state information, or needs to keep records or sequential information, could have bugs that only appear after running nonstop for a while.

5. If your software is for commercial release, test it on a variety of hardware configurations. It is always interesting to see how a program works on a 386-16 with 16 MB of RAM. Problems related to timing and synchronization will definitely start to show up!

6. Use the Hammer application included at the end of this chapter in listing 14.8 and on the CD-ROM. It will throw as many requests at your server as you tell it to.

7. Check the WWW Consortium Library at http://www.w3.org/pub/WWW/Library/. They have a variety of tools for web site creation and testing.

Of course, most programmers do not have a lot of time to spare, so the testing cycle usually lasts about 10 minutes and happens right before the last Federal Express truck leaves. A good way to deal with this limitation is to automate the test procedure with a tool such as Visual Test. At the very least, it is helpful to run your program through a written checklist before you consider it to be solid. Then after every small change in your program, run the tests to be relatively sure you haven't caused a new problem.

Stress Testing with Hammer

Listing 14.8 contains the code for a small command line program that you can use for stress testing your DLL's and your web server in general. It takes three arguments, the number of times to send the HTTP request to the server, the name of a file containing the query to be sent to the server, and the name of the server. It sends the queries in rapid succession in an effort to bombard the server.

LISTING 14.8—HAMMER.C- CONTAINS CODE FOR POUNDING ON AN ISAPI DLL

```
001./*
002.*
003.*
004.* HAMMER.C- Contains for pounding on a ISAPI DLL
005.*
006.* Written 1996 Jim Clemens - Electronic Storefronts, Inc.
007.*
008.*
009.* First argument is number of times to submit data
010.* Second Argument is name of file to send down the pipe
011.* Third argument is server name
012.*
013.* File should contain complete query like:
014.          GET //Scripts/ISAPI.DLL?name=Fred&Address=1000 Lincoln
015.* Make sure file has a CRLF at the end.
016.*
017.* Sample Command Line:
018.*     Hammer 25 test.txt yourserver.com
019.*
020.*/
021.
022.
023.
024.
025.
026.#include <windows.h>
027.#include <winsock.h>
028.#include <stdio.h>
029.#include <io.h>
030.#include <fcntl.h>
031.
032.
033.BOOL SocketReady( SOCKET hSocket );
034.SOCKET ConnectWebServerSocket( LPSTR lpszHostName );
035.int SendWebQuery( SOCKET nSocket, LPSTR lpszQuery );
036.BOOL RecvWebResponse( SOCKET nSocket );
037.char * GetDataFromFile( char * file_name );
038.
039.
```

continues

Listing 14.8—HAMMER.C- Contains
Code for Pounding on an ISAPI DLL, Continued

```
040.#define WINSOCK_VERSION 0x0101   // Program requires Winsock version 1.1
041.#define PF_INET_LENGTH     4      // Length of Long for internet
042.#define NO_FLAGS           0      // No special flags specified
043.#define WEB_PORT          80      // Well-known port for Web's HTTP protocol
044.#define MAX_RECV_BUFFER  20000    // Size of buffer to recieve web pages
045.#define REPLY_WAIT_TIME    5       // Number of seconds to wait for a reply
046.#define DEFAULT_PROTOCOL   0      // No protocol specified, use default
047.
048.
049.WSADATA wsaData;            // Winsock implementation details
050.
051.char response_buffer[ MAX_RECV_BUFFER ];
052.
053.void main( int argc, char * argv[] )
054.{
055.    int number_of_hammers;
056.    int counter;
057.    char * file_name;
058.    char * server_name;
059.    char * data_to_send;
050.    int number_of_sends = 0;
061.    int number_of_responses = 0;
062.    SOCKET * pSocketHandles;
063.
064.    if (argc < 4)
065.    {
066.        printf( "Syntax = HAMMER HammerCount FileName ServerName" );
067.        return;
068.    }
069.
070.    number_of_hammers = atoi( argv[1] );
071.    if (number_of_hammers < 1)
072.    {
073.        printf( "You must hammer at least ONE time!" );
074.        return;
075.    }
076.
077.    file_name = argv[2];
078.    server_name = argv[3];
079.
080.    if (WSAStartup(WINSOCK_VERSION, &wsaData))
081.    {
```

```
082.        /* error */
083.            printf( "Unable to load WSOCK32.DLL" );
084.            return;
085.    }
086.
087.    pSocketHandles = malloc( sizeof( SOCKET ) * [ccc]number_of_hammers );
088.    if (pSocketHandles == NULL)
089.    {
090.        WSACleanup();
091.        printf( "Can't allocate enough Memory to Hammer.");
092.        return;
093.    }
094.
095.    for (counter = 0; counter < number_of_hammers; counter++)
096.    {
097.        /* connect to server */
098.        pSocketHandles[ counter ] = ConnectWebServerSocket(server_name );
099.        if (pSocketHandles[ counter ] == SOCKET_ERROR)
100.        {
101.            /* The server may not handle more connections than this */
102.            number_of_hammers = counter;
103.            break;
104.        }
105.    }
106.
107.    if (number_of_hammers < 1)
108.    {
109.        printf( "Unable to connect to server" );
110.        free( pSocketHandles );
111.        WSACleanup();
112.        return;
113.    }
114.
115.    data_to_send = GetDataFromFile( file_name );
116.
117.    if (! data_to_send)
118.    {
119.        for ( counter = 0; counter < number_of_hammers; counter++)
120.        {
121.            closesocket( pSocketHandles[ counter ] );
122.        }
123.        WSACleanup();
124.        free( pSocketHandles );
```

continues

LISTING 14.8—HAMMER.C- CONTAINS
CODE FOR POUNDING ON AN ISAPI DLL, CONTINUED

```
125.          printf( "Cant open Data File." );
126.          return;
127.      }
128.
129.      for (counter = 0; counter < number_of_hammers; counter++)
130.      {
131.          /* Send data to server */
132.          if (SendWebQuery( pSocketHandles[ counter ],data_to_send) != -1 )
133.          {
134.              number_of_sends++;
135.          }
136.      }
137.
138.      for (counter = 0; counter < number_of_hammers; counter++)
139.      {
140.          /* Get Responses */
141.          if (RecvWebResponse( pSocketHandles[ counter ]) > 0)
142.          {
143.              number_of_responses++;
144.          }
145.      }
146.
147.      free( pSocketHandles );
148.      free( data_to_send );
149.      WSACleanup();
150.      printf( "Server Hammered!  %d Queries Sent, %d Good responses.",
151.          number_of_sends, number_of_responses);
152.      return;
153.}
154.
155.
156.
157.BOOL SocketReady( SOCKET hSocket )
158.{
159.      fd_set read_set;
160.      fd_set write_set;
161.      fd_set except_set;          // Sets for select function
162.      struct timeval tv;          // Timeout values for select
163.      int socket_count;
164.
165.      /* Wait in seconds for recv function */
```

```
166.    tv.tv_sec  = REPLY_WAIT_TIME;
167.    tv.tv_usec = 0;
168.
169.    FD_ZERO( &read_set );
170.    FD_ZERO( &write_set );
171.    FD_ZERO( &except_set );
172.
173.    FD_SET( hSocket, &read_set );
174.
175.    socket_count = select( 1, &read_set, &write_set, &except_set, &tv);
176.    if (socket_count == 1)
177.        {
178.        /* if our socket isn't ready for reading */
179.        if (! FD_ISSET( hSocket, &read_set ))
180.            {
181.            return FALSE;
182.            }
183.        return TRUE;
184.        }
185.    return FALSE;
186.}
187.
188.
189.SOCKET ConnectWebServerSocket( LPSTR lpszHostName )
190.{
191.
192.    LPHOSTENT pHostEnt;                    // Internet host information
➥structure
193.    SOCKADDR_IN sockAddr;                  // Socket address structure
194.    int nConnect;                          // Socket connection results
195.
196.    SOCKET nServerSocket = INVALID_SOCKET;
197.
198.    if (! (pHostEnt = gethostbyname(lpszHostName)))
199.        {
200.        return INVALID_SOCKET;
201.        }
202.
203.    nServerSocket = socket( PF_INET, SOCK_STREAM, IPPROTO_TCP    );
204.
205.    if ( nServerSocket == INVALID_SOCKET )
206.        {
207.        return INVALID_SOCKET;
```

continues

LISTING 14.8—HAMMER.C- CONTAINS
CODE FOR POUNDING ON AN ISAPI DLL, CONTINUED

```
208.        }
209.    // Configure the socket
210.    // Define the socket address
211.    sockAddr.sin_family = AF_INET;
212.    sockAddr.sin_port = htons(WEB_PORT);    // WEB_PORT = 80
213.    sockAddr.sin_addr = *((LPIN_ADDR)*pHostEnt->h_addr_list);
214.
215.    // Connect the socket
216.    nConnect = connect( nServerSocket, (LPSOCKADDR)&sockAddr,
➥sizeof(sockAddr));
217.
218.    if ( nConnect == SOCKET_ERROR )
219.        {
220.        return INVALID_SOCKET;
221.        }
222.
223.    return ( nServerSocket );
224.
225.}
226.
227.
228.int SendWebQuery( SOCKET nSocket, LPSTR lpszQuery )
229.{
230.
231.    int nCharSent;                         // Number of characters
➥transmitted
232.
233.    nCharSent = send( nSocket, lpszQuery, strlen( lpszQuery ), NO_FLAGS);
234.
235.    if (nCharSent == SOCKET_ERROR)
236.        {
237.        closesocket( nSocket );
238.        return -1;
239.        }
240.    return nCharSent;
241.}
242.
243.
244.
245.BOOL RecvWebResponse( SOCKET nSocket )
246.{
```

```
247.    unsigned short nCharRecv;                // Number of characters
received
248.    fd_set read_set;
249.    fd_set write_set;
250.    fd_set except_set;                       // Sets for select
function
251.    struct timeval tv;                       // Timeout values for
select
252.    int socket_count;
253.    BOOL quit_loop;
254.     BOOL server_response = FALSE;
255.
256.    /* Wait in seconds */
257.    tv.tv_sec  = REPLY_WAIT_TIME;
258.    tv.tv_usec = 0;
259.
260.    nCharRecv = 0;
261.    quit_loop = FALSE;
262.
263.    while (quit_loop == FALSE)
264.    {
265.     /* make sets for select function null to start */
266.        FD_ZERO( &read_set );
267.        FD_ZERO( &write_set );
268.        FD_ZERO( &except_set );
269.
270.        FD_SET( nSocket, &read_set );
271.
272.        socket_count = select( 1, &read_set, &write_set, &except_set,
&tv );
273.        if (socket_count == 1)
274.        {
275.            /* if our socket isready for reading */
276.            if ( FD_ISSET( nSocket, &read_set ))
277.              {
278.                nCharRecv = recv( nSocket, response_buffer,
279.                    MAX_RECV_BUFFER, NO_FLAGS);
280.                  response_buffer[ nCharRecv ] = 0;
281.                if (nCharRecv > 0)
282.                   {
283.                        if (( strstr( response_buffer, "</html>") !=
NULL ) ||
```

continues

LISTING 14.8—HAMMER.C- CONTAINS
CODE FOR POUNDING ON AN ISAPI DLL, CONTINUED

```
284.                                    ( strstr( response_buffer, "</HTML>") !=
➥NULL ))
285.                        {
286.                            /* we're done */
287.                            quit_loop = TRUE;
288.                            server_response = TRUE;
289.                        }
290.                    }
291.                    else
292.                    {
293.                        quit_loop = TRUE;
294.                    }
295.                }
296.            }
297.            else
298.            {
299.                /* Nothing came in */
300.                quit_loop = TRUE;
301.            }
302.
303.    } /* end while loop */
304.
305.    closesocket( nSocket );
306.
307.    return server_response;
308.}
309.
310.
311.char * GetDataFromFile( char * file_name )
312.{
313.    int fh;
314.    int length;
315.    char * buffer;
316.    int bytesread;
317.
318.    /* set file mode to binary */
319.    _fmode = _O_BINARY;
320.
321.    fh = _open( file_name, _O_RDONLY );
322.    if (fh == -1)
323.    {
```

```
324.        return NULL;
325.    }
326.    length = _filelength( fh );
327.     buffer = malloc( length + 1 );
328.     if (! buffer)
329.     {
330.         _close( fh );
331.         return NULL;
332.     }
333.
334.     bytesread = _read( fh, buffer, length );
335.     if (bytesread < length)
336.     {
337.         _close( fh );
338.         free( buffer );
339.         return NULL;
340.     }
341.
342.     _close( fh );
343.    return buffer;
344.
345.}
346.
```

Hammer allocates the memory for holding the socket handles for each query. It opens a socket for each query and then sends the contents of the file specified on the command line to the web server. It waits for a response containing the </HTML> tag and tabulates the number of successful requests and successful responses.

You can use Hammer to pound continuously on your server by putting it inside a batch file with an endless loop. If you are really into stressing your server, you can get several copies running at once and leave them going all day. You can use the Windows NT performance monitor to see how hard your server is actually working.

Summary

Hopefully this chapter has given you enough tips for debugging your ISAPI DLL's and debugging techniques in general that you can produce successful and robust ISAPI applications with a minimum of effort. Had this book existed when the author began writing ISAPI extensions, his life would have been greatly enhanced and he would have had a lot fewer irate customers wondering why their scripts weren't written yet! God knows he didn't make any money writing the book, so his only satisfaction will be knowing that he made someone's life easier (with the exception of the editor whose life he shortened a bit).

ISAPI Functions, Structures, and Constants

This appendix defines the functions and data used by the ISAPI interface. These functions and data consist of the following:

◆ The DLL entrypoint functions that the web server calls

◆ The callback functions that can be invoked while processing calls from the server

◆ The special structures that contain the data that's exchanged

◆ Any constants defined to convey special information

Extensions

One of the two types of ISAPI components are extensions. ISAPI extensions provide vertical slices of functionality, implementing the complete servicing of a particular HTTP request.

The following sections provide the definitions relating to ISAPI extensions.

DLL Entrypoints

An ISAPI extension is implemented as a DLL. This DLL must present at least two, and an optional third, functions for the web server to call. The functions are described in the following sections.

GetExtensionVersion( ) Function

Syntax:

```
BOOL WINAPI GetExtensionVersion( HSE_VERSION_INFO  *pVer );
```

The web server calls this function immediately before the first time that an extension defined in the DLL is called.

The purpose of the call is to allow the server to verify that the extension version is supported. However, it also provides the author of an extension an excellent opportunity to perform any initialization necessary.

A return value of *TRUE* indicates success; *FALSE* indicates failure.

This function is sent a pointer to a *HSE_VERSION_INFO* structure, described in table A.1.

TABLE A.1
Members of the HSE_VERSION_INFO Structure

Name	Type	Description
dwExtensionVersion	DWORD; Output	The extension should place information here describing the ISAPI version that is implemented. Typically this will be done with a statement like this: pVer->dwExtensionVersion= MAKELONG (HSE_VERSION_MINOR,HSE_VERSION_MAJOR); These constants are defined in the extension header files.

Name	Type	Description
lpszExtensionDesc	char; Output	The extension should copy a string describing the extension into this buffer. The size of the buffer, and thus the maximum length of the string, is given by *HSE_MAX_EXT_DLL_ NAME_LEN*.

HttpExtensionProc() Function

Syntax:

```
DWORD WINAPI HttpExtensionProc( EXTENSION_CONTROL_BLOCK *pECB );
```

The web server calls this function for each request that is made for this extension's services.

The extension may return any of the four following values:

- ◆ **HSE_STATUS_SUCCESS:** all processing has been completed.

- ◆ **HSE_STATUS_SUCCESS_AND_KEEP_CONN:** all processing has been completed, but further interaction is expected so the connection should not be disconnected; this should only be used in conjunction with sending a keep-alive header.

- ◆ **HSE_STATUS_PENDING:** processing is *not* complete; the extension will complete the processing asynchronously and alert the server via a call to *ServerSupportFunction()* with a value of *HSE_REQ_DONE_WITH_REQUEST* when complete.

- ◆ **HSE_STATUS_ERROR:** processing has been aborted due to an error.

The function is passed a pointer to an EXTENSION_CONTROL_BLOCK structure, described in table A.2.

TABLE A.2
Members of the EXTENSION_CONTROL_BLOCK Structure

Name	Type	Description
cbSize	DWORD; Input	The size of this structure
dwVersion	DWORD; Input	The version of the spec

continues

TABLE A.2, CONTINUED
Members of the EXTENSION_CONTROL_BLOCK Structure

Name	Type	Description
ConnID	HCONN; Input	Handle to the connection that is being serviced; must be passed as a parameter when invoking any of the callback functions
dwHttpStatusCode	DWORD;	Place the HTTP Status code here before returning from HttpExtensionProc. See Appendix C for possible values
lpszLogData	char; Out	Buffer to receive a null-terminated string of log information. The size of the buffer, and thus the maximum length of the string, is given by *HSE_LOG_BUFFER_LEN*
lpszMethod	char *; Input	Pointer to a string naming the method of the request. Equivalent to the value of the variable *REQUEST_METHOD*
lpszQueryString	char *; Input	Pointer to a string containing the query of a *GET* request. Equivalent to the value of the variable *QUERY_STRING*
lpszPathInfo	char *; Input	Pointer to a string path requested. Equivalent to the value of the variable *PATH_INFO*
lpszPathTranslated	char *; Input	Pointer to a string path requested, after translating to the server's physical path. Equivalent to the value of the variable *PATH_TRANSLATED*
cbTotalBytes	DWORD; Input	The total number of bytes in the request
cbAvailable	DWORD; Input	The number of bytes available in the *lpbData* buffer
lpbData	LPBYTE Input	Pointer to a buffer containing the data of a *POST* request
lpszContentType	char *; Input	Pointer to a identifying the MIME content type of the request. Equivalent to the value of the variable *CONTENT_TYPE*

Name	Type	Description
GetServerVariable	Callback; Input	Pointer to a function that can be used to retrieve the values of server variables; see the description that follows
WriteClient	Callback; Input	Pointer to a function that can be used to write data to the client; see the description that follows
ReadClient	Callback; Input	Pointer to a function that can be used to retrieve data from the client; see the description that follows
ServerSupport Function	Callback; Input	Pointer to a function that supports various other operations; see the description that follows

TerminateExtension( ) Function

Syntax:

```
BOOL  WINAPI    TerminateExtension( DWORD dwFlags );
```

This function is optional. If present, the web server will call it to warn that the DLL is about to be unloaded.

This function is very helpful to manage resources, when necessary. When this function is called with a value of HSE_TERM_MUST_UNLOAD, the extension may take the opportunity to release all of the resources that it has allocated.

Return a value of *TRUE* if it's now okay to unload the DLL, or *FALSE* otherwise. The return value is ignored if the value passed to the function is *HSE_TERM_MUST_UNLOAD*.

The function will be passed one of the two following integer values:

◆ **HSE_TERM_ADVISORY_UNLOAD:** the server would like to unload the DLL; return *TRUE* if this is okay, or *FALSE* otherwise.

◆ **HSE_TERM_MUST_UNLOAD:** the server is *going* to unload the DLL now. The extension has no choice but to perform any necessary cleanup and return.

Callbacks

The functions described in the following sections can be called by an extension during the processing of the *HttpExtensionProc()* function. The server sends pointers to these functions to the extension through the Extension Control Block.

GetServerVariable() Function

Syntax:

```
BOOL (WINAPI * GetServerVariable) ( HCONN   hConn,
                                    LPSTR   lpszVariableName,
                                    LPVOID  lpvBuffer,
                                    LPDWORD lpdwSize );
```

An extension can call this function to obtain the value of server variables and any headers received with the request. The server variables that can be retrieved are listed in Appendix D. Header values can be retrieved by requesting the name of the header, capitalized and prepended with the string *HTTP_*. For example, requesting *HTTP_COOKIE* retrieves the contents of the *Cookie* header.

The function returns a Boolean value indicating the success of the request. If successful, the value is *TRUE*. The request can fail due to an invalid connection handle, an invalid variable requested, or insufficient space in the destination buffer. In the latter case, the required amount of space can be determined by looking at the variable pointed to by the *lpdwSize* parameter.

The parameters to the GetServerVariable() function are listed in table A.3.

TABLE A.3
GetServerVariable() Parameters

Name	Description
hConn	The connection handle that was passed to *HttpExtensionProc()* in the Extension Control Block structure
lpszVariableName	A pointer to a null-terminated string giving the name of the variable to be retrieved
lpvBuffer	A pointer to a buffer to receive the variable's value
lpdwSize	A pointer to the size of the buffer pointed to by *lpvBuffer*; if the request fails due to insufficient buffer space, the variable that is pointed to will be altered to the necessary buffer size

WriteClient() Function

Syntax:

```
BOOL (WINAPI * WriteClient)  ( HCONN    ConnID,
                               LPVOID   Buffer,
                               LPDWORD  lpdwBytes,
                               DWORD    dwReserved );
```

An extension calls this function to send the body of the response to the client.

A Boolean value is returned, indicating the success of the request is returned. If the operation was successful, the value will be *TRUE*.

The parameters to the WriteClient() function are listed in table A.4.

TABLE A.4
WriteClient() Parameters

Name	Description
hConn	The connection handle that was passed to *HttpExtensionProc* in the Extension Control Block structure
Buffer	A pointer to a buffer containing the data to write
lpdwBytes	The number of bytes that should be written from the buffer pointed to by *Buffer*
dwReserved	*Reserved for future use*

ReadClient() Function

Syntax:

```
BOOL (WINAPI * ReadClient)  ( HCONN    ConnID,
                              LPVOID   lpvBuffer,
                              LPDWORD  lpdwSize );
```

An extension calls this function to read additional data from the client, particularly when the request buffer is full and more data remains.

This can be determined by examining the values of the *cbAvailable* and *cbTotalBytes* fields in the Extension Control Block. If the latter is greater, then there is more data that should be retrieved by a call to *ReadClient*.

A Boolean value is returned, indicating the success of the request returned. If the operation was successful, the value will be *TRUE*.

The parameters to the ReadClient() function are listed in table A.5.

TABLE A.5
ReadClient() Parameters

Name	Description
hConn	The connection handle that was passed to *HttpExtensionProc()* in the Extension Control Block structure
lpvBuffer	A pointer into which the data read from the client should be stored
lpdwSize	The number of bytes that should be transmitted to the user from the buffer pointed to by *Buffer* (and therefore a number less than or equal to the size of the buffer); upon return, this value will be changed to contain the number of bytes actually read

ServerSupportFunction() Function

Syntax:

```
BOOL (WINAPI * ServerSupportFunction)( HCONN   hConn,
                                       DWORD   dwHSERequest,
                                       LPVOID  lpvBuffer,
                                       LPDWORD lpdwSize,
                                       LPDWORD lpdwDataType );
```

This function performs other miscellaneous functions not covered by the three previously covered callback functions.

A Boolean value is returned, indicating the success of the request returned. If the operation was successful, the value is *TRUE*.

The parameters to the ServerSupportFunction() function are listed in table A.6.

TABLE A.6
ServerSupportFunction() Parameters

Name	Description
hConn	The connection handle that was passed to *HttpExtensionProc()* in the Extension Control Block structure
dwHSERequest	A constant value indicating the operation to be performed
lpvBuffer	Pointer to a buffer; meaning varies depending upon *dwHSERequest*
lpdwSize	Pointer to a doubleword; its meaning varies depending upon *dwHSERequest*
lpdwDataType	Pointer to a doubleword; its meaning varies depending upon *dwHSERequest*

The operation performed by the ServerSupportFunction() function, and the meaning of the parameters, depends upon the value of the parameter *dwHSERequest* as defined in the following list:

◆ **HSE_REQ_SEND_URL_REDIRECT_RESP:** redirects the client browser to an URL at another site. Sends a *302* response to the client, and redirects it to the URL null-terminated string pointed to by *lpvBuffer*. *lpdwSize* points to a doubleword containing the length of this string. *lpdwDataType* is ignored.

◆ **HSE_REQ_SEND_URL:** redirects the client browser to an URL on this server. The client does not know that it's been redirected. Instead, the server internally re-issues a request for the specified URL to itself. The URL is communicated as a null-terminated string pointed to by *lpvBuffer*. *lpdwSize* points to a doubleword containing the length of this string. *lpdwDataType* is ignored.

◆ **HSE_REQ_SEND_RESPONSE_HEADER:** sends response headers to the client. The string containing the headers is passed in the buffer pointed to by *lpvBuffer*. *lpdwSize* points to a doubleword containing the length of this string. *lpdwDataType* is ignored. The string should be null terminated, immediately preceded by a newline.

◆ **HSE_REQ_DONE_WITH_SESSION:** notifies the server that asynchronous processing of a request is complete. This processing would have begun with HttpExtensionProc() returning a value of *HSE_STATUS_PENDING*. The values of *lpvBuffer*, *lpdwSize*, and *lpdwDataType* are ignored.

- **HSE_REQ_MAP_URL_TO_PATH:** maps a logical path to a physical path. The transformation occurs in place, in the buffer pointed to by *lpvBuffer*. *lpdwSize* points to a doubleword containing the length of this string. *lpdwDataType* is ignored.

- **HSE_REQ_GET_SSPI_INFO:** retrieves security information: the *lpvBuffer* is filled in with the context handle and the variable pointed to by *lpdwDataType* is filled in with the credential handle.

Filters

The second of the two types of ISAPI components are filters. ISAPI filters provide horizontal slices of functionality, implementing a single facet of the processing for *all* requests.

The following sections provide the definitions relating to ISAPI filters.

DLL Entrypoints

An ISAPI filter is implemented as a DLL. This DLL must define two functions for the web server to call. The functions described in the following sections are those called by the web server.

GetFilterVersion() Function

Syntax:

```
BOOL WINAPI GetFilterVersion( HTTP_FILTER_VERSION * pVer );
```

The web server calls this function immediately before the filter DLL is loaded.

The purpose of the call is to allow the server to verify that the extension version is supported, and to allow the filter to indicate the events that it would like to receive. However, it also provides the author of an extension an excellent opportunity to perform any initialization necessary.

A return value of *TRUE* indicates success. A return value of *FALSE* indicates that the filter was unable to initialize; the DLL is unloaded and the filter will never be called.

This function is sent a pointer to a *HSE_VERSION_INFO* structure, described in table A.7.

TABLE A.7
Members of the HSE_VERSION_INFO Structure

Name	Type	Description
dwServerFilterVersion	DWORD; Input	The version of the specification used by the server. The version of the current header file is *HTTP_FILTER_REVISION*
dwFilterVersion	DWORD; Output	The version of the specification used by the extension. The version of the current header file is *HTTP_FILTER_REVISION*
lpszFilterDesc	char *; Output	The extension should copy a string describing the filter into this buffer. The size of the buffer, and thus the maximum length of the string, is given by *HSE_MAX_FILTER_DESC_LEN*
dwFlags	DWORD; Output	A masked doubleword that gives the combination of events in which the filter is interested and its desired notification priority. See the following list of values

The value of the *dwFlags* field in table A.7 is constructed by performing a logical OR of the values corresponding with the desired notifications. Setting a bit in this way will cause the server to call the filter each time a corresponding event occurs. The filter notification flags are listed in table A.8.

TABLE A.8
Filter Notification Flags

Name	Description
SF_NOTIFY_SECURE_PORT	Notification requested for sessions on secure ports only
SF_NOTIFY_NONSECURE_PORT	Notification requested for sessions on non-secure ports only

continues

TABLE A.8, CONTINUED
Filter Notification Flags

Name	Description
SF_NOTIFY_READ_RAW_DATA	Notification requested for all raw data reads (i.e., data the server reads from the client). The headers and data have not yet been separated
SF_NOTIFY_PREPROC_HEADERS	Notification requested following the server preprocessing the incoming request headers
SF_NOTIFY_AUTHENTICATION	Notification requested when the server is authenticating the client
SF_NOTIFY_URL_MAP	Notification requested when the server is mapping a logical path to a physical path
SF_NOTIFY_ACCESS_DENIED	Notification requested when the server is about to send an access denied response to the client
SF_NOTIFY_SEND_RAW_DATA	Notification requested when the server is sending raw data to the client
SF_NOTIFY_LOG	Notification requested when the server is writing data to its log
SF_NOTIFY_END_OF_NET_SESSION	Notification requested when the client's session is ending
SF_NOTIFY_ORDER_HIGH	The filter will be notified with high priority, before medium or low priority filters
SF_NOTIFY_ORDER_MEDIUM	The filter will be notified with medium priority
SF_NOTIFY_ORDER_LOW	The filter will be notified with low priority
SF_NOTIFY_ORDER_DEFAULT	The filter will be notified with the default priority

HttpFilterProc() Function

Syntax:

```
DWORD
WINAPI
HttpFilterProc(
    HTTP_FILTER_CONTEXT *      pfc,
    DWORD                      NotificationType,
    VOID *                     pvNotification
    );
```

The server calls this function whenever an event occurs for which the filter requested notification.

There are six constants that the filter is allowed to return describing the way in which it handled the event. These are described in table A.9.

TABLE A.9
Filter Return Constants

Name	Description
SF_STATUS_REQ_FINISHED	The filter has handled the request; the server may disconnect the session
SF_STATUS_REQ_FINISHED _KEEP_CONN	The filter has handled the request; the server should keep the session alive, if appropriate
SF_STATUS_REQ_NEXT _NOTIFICATION	The next filter in line should be allowed to process the event
SF_STATUS_REQ_HANDLED _NOTIFICATION	The event has been handled; do not continue to pass the event to subsequent filters
SF_STATUS_REQ_ERROR	An error occurred; the server should notify the client
SF_STATUS_REQ_READ_NEXT	Used only in conjunction with SF_NOTIFY_ READ_RAW_DATA; indicates that the session parameters are being negotiated and that the data read should not be passed through

When the server calls your filter to notify it of an event, a number of parameters are sent to allow you to determine the nature and context of the event. These parameters to the function are listed in table A.10.

TABLE A.10
HttpFilterProc() Parameters

Name	Description
pfc	A pointer to an HTTP_FILTER_CONTEXT structure
NotificationType	A doubleword containing a value indicating the type of event that the filter is being notified of. These values correspond to those set in *GetFilterVersion()*, enumerated in table A.8
pvNotification	A pointer to a notification structure. The actual type of this structure is determined by the value of the *NotificationType* parameter. These structures are described later in this section

The first of the parameters sent to your filter's HttpFilterProc() function is a pointer to a HTTP_FILTER_CONTEXT structure. This contains several pieces of information that help you to determine the context in which the function was called. More importantly, it also contains pointers to several callback functions that you'll need to interact with the server and the client. The filter context structure is described in table A.11.

TABLE A.11
The HTTP_FILTER_CONTEXT Structure

Name	Type	Description
cbSize	DWORD; Input	The size of this structure
Revision	DWORD; Input	The revision of the ISAPI specification the server implements
ServerContext	PVOID; Input	Private information used by the server
ulReserved	DWORD; Input	Private information used by the server
fIsSecurePort	BOOL; Input	TRUE when the event was triggered by a request on a secure port

Name	Type	Description
pFilterContext	PVOID; Input/ Output	A pointer to anything the filter wants; this value will be sent to the filter on subsequent requests from this connection; the memory it points to should be freed by the filter when it receives an *SF_NOTIFY_END_OF_NET_SESSION* notification
GetServerVariable	Callback; Input	Pointer to a function that can be used to retrieve the values of server variables; see the description that follows
AddResponseHeaders	Callback; Input	Pointer to a function that can be used to add an additional header to an outgoing response; see the description that follows
WriteClient	Callback; Input	Pointer to a function that can be used to write data to the client; see the description that follows
AllocMem	Callback; Input	Pointer to a function that the filter can use to allocate memory that the server will automatically free when the request is completed
ServerSupportFunction	Callback; Input	Pointer to a function that supports various other operations; see the description that follows

ISAPI defines six different structures that may be sent to HttpFilterProc() in its *pvNotification* parameter. The type of structure can be determined by examining the *NotificationType* parameter. Table A.12 shows the correspondence between notification types and notification structures. Note that the HTTP_FILTER_RAW_DATA structure serves double duty, being used for both SF_NOTIFY_READ_RAW_DATA and SF_NOTIFY_SEND_RAW_DATA notifications.

TABLE A.12
The Relationship Between Notification Types and Notification Structure

Notification Type	Notification Structure
SF_NOTIFY_ACCESS_DENIED	HTTP_FILTER_ACCESS_DENIED
SF_NOTIFY_AUTHENTICATION	HTTP_FILTER_AUTHENT
SF_NOTIFY_LOG	HTTP_FILTER_LOG
SF_NOTIFY_PREPROC_HEADERS	HTTP_FILTER_PREPROC_HEADERS
SF_NOTIFY_READ_RAW_DATA	HTTP_FILTER_RAW_DATA
SF_NOTIFY_SEND_RAW_DATA	HTTP_FILTER_RAW_DATA
SF_NOTIFY_URL_MAP	HTTP_FILTER_URL_MAP

The following sections present the definitions of the structures.

HTTP_FILTER_ACCESS_DENIED

When HttpFilterProc() is passed a NotificationType parameter equal to SF_NOTIFY_ ACCESS_DENIED, then the parameter pvNotification is a pointer to a structure of type HTTP_FILTER_ACCESS_DENIED. The members of the HTTP_FILTER_ ACCESS_DENIED structure are described in table A.13.

TABLE A.13
The HTTP_FILTER_ACCESS_DENIED Structure

Name	Type	Description
pszURL	char *; Input	The URL that was requested
pszPhysicalPath	char *; Input	The physical path of the resource
dwReason	DWORD Input	A bitmapped field indicating what type of access was denied. The possible values are: *SF_DENIED_LOGON* *SF_DENIED_RESOURCE* *SF_DENIED_FILTER* *SF_DENIED_APPLICATION* *SF_DENIED_BY_CONFIG*

HTTP_FILTER_ACCESS_AUTHENT

When HttpFilterProc() is passed a NotificationType parameter equal to SF_NOTIFY_
AUTHENTICATION, then the parameter pvNotification is a pointer to a structure of
type HTTP_FILTER_AUTHENT. The members of the HTTP_FILTER_AUTHENT
structure are described in table A.14.

TABLE A.14
The HTTP_FILTER_AUTHENT Structure

Name	Type	Description
pszUser	char *; Input/Output	A pointer to a null-terminated string containing the name of the user to be authenticated; or a null string for anonymous logons. This value may be altered by the filter
cbUserBuff	DWORD; Input	The length of the buffer pointed to by *pszUser*; guaranteed to be at least *SF_MAX_USERNAME* bytes
pszPassword	char *; Input/Output	A pointer to a null-terminated string containing the password of the user to be authenticated. This value may be altered by the filter
cbPasswordBuff	DWORD; Input	The length of the buffer pointed to by *pszPassword*; guaranteed to be at least *SF_MAX_PASSWORD* bytes

HTTP_FILTER_LOG

When HttpFilterProc() is passed a NotificationType parameter equal to
SF_NOTIFY_LOG, then the parameter pvNotification is a pointer to a structure of
type HTTP_FILTER_LOG. The members of the HTTP_FILTER_LOG structure are
described in table A.15.

TABLE A.15
The HTTP_FILTER_LOG Structure

Name	Type	Description
pszClientHostName	const char *; Input/Output	The name of the client's host
pszClientUserName	const char *; Input/Output	The user name of the client
pszServerName	const char *; Input/Output	The name of the server the client is connected to
pszOperation	const char *; Input/Output	The HTTP command type that is being executed
pszTarget mand	const char *; Input/Output	The target of the HTTP com-
pszParameters	const char *; Input/Output	Any parameters passed to the command
dwHttpStatus	DWORD Input/Output	The HTTP status code
dwWin32Status	DWORD Input/Output	The Win32 error code

 The character string pointers in this structure refer to *constant* strings. You cannot alter the contents of these strings. You can, however, alter the pointers themselves.

If you choose to do this, you must allocate the memory for the new, replacement strings with calls to the *AllocMem()* callback function.

HTTP_FILTER_PREPROC_HEADERS

When HttpFilterProc() is passed a NotificationType parameter equal to SF_NOTIFY_PREPROC_HEADERS, then the parameter pvNotification is a pointer to a structure of type HTTP_FILTER_PREPROC_HEADERS. The members of the HTTP_FILTER_PREPROC_HEADERS structure are described in table A.16.

TABLE A.16
TABLE A.16
The HTTP_FILTER_PREPROC_HEADERS Structure

Name	Type	Description
GetHeader	Callback; Input	A pointer to a function used to retrieve the value of a specified header; see the description in the section "Callbacks" for more information
SetHeader	Callback; Input	A pointer to a function used to change the value of, or to delete, a specified header; see the description in the section "Callbacks" for more information
AddHeader	Callback; Input	A pointer to a function used to add a new header; see the description in the section "Callbacks" for more information
dwReserved	DWORD	Reserved

HTTP_FILTER_RAW_DATA

When HttpFilterProc() is passed a NotificationType parameter equal to either SF_NOTIFY_READ_RAW_DATA or SF_NOTIFY_SEND_RAW_DATA, then the parameter pvNotification is a pointer to a structure of type HTTP_FILTER_RAW_DATA. The members of the HTTP_FILTER_RAW_DATA structure are described in table A.17.

TABLE A.17
The HTTP_FILTER_RAW_DATA Structure

Name	Type	Description
pvInData	PVOID; Input/Output	A pointer to the data buffer; contrary to the name of the member, this data could be either incoming or outcoming data, depending upon the type of notification
cbInData	DWORD; Input	The number of bytes in the buffer pointed to by *pvInData*
cbInBuffer	DWORD; Input	The size of the buffer pointed to by *pvInData*
dwReserved	DWORD	Reserved

HTTP_FILTER_URL_MAP

When HttpFilterProc() is passed a NotificationType parameter equal to SF_NOTIFY_URL_MAP, then the parameter pvNotification is a pointer to a structure of type HTTP_FILTER_URL_MAP. The members of the HTTP_FILTER_URL_MAP structure are described in table A.18.

TABLE A.18
The HTTP_FILTER_URL_MAP Structure

Name	Type	Description
pszURL	const char *; Input	A pointer to a constant, null-terminated string containing the URL to be mapped
pszPhysicalPath	char *; Input/Output	A pointer to a buffer to receive the physical path representing the URL given in *pszURL*; this string can be modified as necessary
cbPathBuff	DWORD; Input	The size of the buffer pointed to by *pszPhysicalPath*

Callbacks

While processing the HttpFilterProc() function, a filter often needs to interact with the server, or to read data from, or write data to, the user. A number of callback functions are provided for this purpose. The addresses of these functions are provided in the HTTP_FILTER_CONTEXT structure that is passed to the filter by the server, or in the HTTP_FILTER_PREPROC_HEADERS structure when the filter is notified of a SF_NOTIFY_PREPROC_HEADERS event.

GetServerVariable() Function

Syntax:

```
BOOL (WINAPI * GetServerVariable) (
     struct _HTTP_FILTER_CONTEXT * pfc,
     LPSTR                         lpszVariableName,
     LPVOID                        lpvBuffer,
     LPDWORD                       lpdwSize
     );
```

A filter may call this function to obtain the value of server variables and any headers received with a request. The server variables that can be retrieved are listed in Appendix D. Header values may be retrieved by requesting the name of the header, capitalized and prepended with the string *HTTP_*. For example, requesting *HTTP_COOKIE* can retrieve the contents of the *Cookie* header.

A Boolean value indicating the success of the request is returned. If successful, the value will be *TRUE*. The request can fail due to an invalid connection handle, an invalid variable requested, or insufficient space in the destination buffer. In the latter case, the required amount of space can be determined by looking at the variable pointed to by the *lpdwSize* parameter.

The parameters to the GetServerVariable() function are listed in table A.19.

TABLE A.19
GetServerVariable() Parameters

Name	Description
pfc	The *HTTP_FILTER_CONTEXT* structure from which the callback function's pointer was obtained
lpszVariableName	A pointer to a null-terminated string giving the name of the variable to be retrieved
lpvBuffer	A pointer to a buffer to receive the variable's value
lpdwSize	A pointer to the size of the buffer pointed to by *lpvBuffer*; if the request fails due to insufficient buffer space, the variable that is pointed to will be altered to the necessary buffer size

AddResponseHeaders() Function

Syntax:

```
BOOL (WINAPI * AddResponseHeaders) (
    struct _HTTP_FILTER_CONTEXT * pfc,
    LPSTR                         lpszHeaders,
    DWORD                         dwReserved
    );
```

This function adds headers to the response that will be returned to the client. Contrast this with the callback function *AddHeader()*, which adds headers to the *incoming* request for processing by the server.

A Boolean value is returned, indicating the success of the request returned. If the operation was successful, the value will be *TRUE*.

The parameters to the AddResponseHeaders() function are listed in table A.20.

TABLE A.20
AddResponseHeaders() Parameters

Name	Description
pfc	The *HTTP_FILTER_CONTEXT* structure from which the callback function's pointer was obtained
lpszHeaders	The *HTTP_FILTER_CONTEXT* structure from which the callback function's pointer was obtained
dwReserved	Reserved

WriteClient() Function

Syntax:

```
BOOL (WINAPI * WriteClient)  (
      struct _HTTP_FILTER_CONTEXT * pfc,
      LPVOID                        Buffer,
      LPDWORD                       lpdwBytes,
      DWORD                         dwReserved
      );
```

A filter calls this function when it needs to send data back to the client.

A Boolean value is returned, indicating the success of the request returned. If the operation was successful, the value will be *TRUE*.

The parameters to the WriteClient() function are listed in table A.21.

TABLE A.21
WriteClient() Parameters

Name	Description
pfc	The *HTTP_FILTER_CONTEXT* structure from which the callback function's pointer was obtained

Name	Description
Buffer	A pointer to a buffer containing the data to be sent
lpdwBytes	The number of bytes to be sent from the buffer pointed to by *Buffer*
dwReserved	Reserved

AllocMem() Function

Syntax:

```
VOID * (WINAPI * AllocMem) (
        struct _HTTP_FILTER_CONTEXT * pfc,
        DWORD                         cbSize,
        DWORD                         dwReserved
        );
```

This function allocates blocks of memory for filters. Memory allocated in this manner will be managed by the server: it is automatically freed upon completion of the request. This is essential for use in such tasks as altering the contents of the data received in a *SF_NOTIFY_SEND_RAW_DATA* request.

The function returns a pointer to a block of memory of the requested size.

The parameters to the AllocMem() function are listed in table A.22.

TABLE A.22
AllocMem() Parameters

Name	Description
pfc	The *HTTP_FILTER_CONTEXT* structure from which the callback function's pointer was obtained
cbSize	The number of bytes that must be allocated
dwReserved	Reserved

ServerSupportFunction()

Syntax:

```
BOOL (WINAPI * ServerSupportFunction) (
    struct _HTTP_FILTER_CONTEXT * pfc,
    enum SF_REQ_TYPE             sfReq,
    PVOID                        pData,
    DWORD                        ul1,
    DWORD                        ul2
    );
```

This function allows for additional functionality not covered by the other callback functions.

A Boolean value is returned, indicating the success of the request returned. If the operation was successful, the value will be *TRUE*.

The parameters to ServerSupportFunction() are listed in table A.23.

TABLE A.23
ServerSupportFunction() Parameters

Name	Description
pfc	The *HTTP_FILTER_CONTEXT* structure from which the callback function's pointer was obtained
sfReq	A constant identifying the requested operation; see the following list for details
pData	A pointer to data to be used to satisfy the request
ul1	A DWORD whose meaning varies depending upon the operation requested
ul2	A DWORD whose meaning varies depending upon the operation requested

ServerSupportFunction() performs different actions depending upon the value supplied for the second parameter, *sfReq*. In addition, the meaning of the remaining parameters differs according to this value. The values allowed for *sfReq* are listed here:

- ◆ **SF_REQ_SEND_RESPONSE_HEADER:** causes a complete HTTP response header to be sent. *pData* points to a null-terminated string containing an HTTP status string; if NULL, *200 OK* will be used. *ul1* is a pointer to a null-terminated string containing additional header data; if NULL, a line end will be used.

◆ **SF_REQ_ADD_HEADERS_ON_DENIAL:** causes additional headers to be added to a request if the server denies the request. pData is a pointer to a null-terminated strung which should contain one or more header lines terminated by a line end.

◆ **SF_REQ_SET_NEXT_READ_SIZE:** used only when processing a *SF_NOTIFY_READ_RAW_DATA* event, in conjunction with a return code of *SF_STATUS_READ_NEXT* from HttpFilterProc. *ul1* is the desired number of bytes from the next read.

◆ **SF_REQ_SET_PROXY_INFO:** indicates that the request is a proxy request. *ul1* contains the proxy flags to set: a value of 0x00000001 indicates that this is a proxy request.

GetHeader() Function

Syntax:

```
BOOL (WINAPI * GetHeader) (
     struct _HTTP_FILTER_CONTEXT * pfc,
     LPSTR                        lpszName,
     LPVOID                       lpvBuffer,
     LPDWORD                      lpdwSize
     );
```

The pointer to this function is provided in the HTTP_FILTER_PREPROC_HEADERS structure, and as a result is only available while processing a SF_NOTIFY_PREPROC_HEADERS event.

The GetHeader() function retrieves the value of the specified header in the request. It does not retrieve the values of outgoing headers in a response.

A Boolean value is returned, indicating the success of the request returned. If the operation was successful, the value will be *TRUE*.

The parameters for the GetHeader() function are listed in table A.24.

TABLE A.24
GetHeader() Parameters

Name	Description
pfc	The HTTP_FILTER_CONTEXT structure from which the callback function's pointer was obtained

continues

TABLE A.24, CONTINUED
GetHeader() Parameters

Name	Description
lpszName	The name of the header to retrieve, including the trailing colon. Use the values *method*, *url*, and *version* to retrieve those portions of the request line
lpvBuffer	A pointer to a buffer to receive the value of the requested header
lpdwSizeofBuffer	The size of the buffer pointed to by *lpvBuffer*; returns with the length of the retrieved string, including the null terminator

SetHeader() Function

Syntax:

```
BOOL (WINAPI * SetHeader) (
    struct _HTTP_FILTER_CONTEXT * pfc,
    LPSTR                         lpszName,
    LPSTR                         lpszValue
    );
```

The pointer to this function is provided in the HTTP_FILTER_PREPROC_HEADERS structure, and as a result is only available while processing a SF_NOTIFY_PREPROC_HEADERS event.

The SetHeader() function can be used to either change the value of a header in a request or to delete the header altogether. It cannot be used to alter outgoing response headers.

A Boolean value is returned, indicating the success of the request returned. If the operation was successful, the value will be *TRUE*.

The parameters for the SetHeader() function are listed in table A.25.

TABLE A.25
SetHeader() Parameters

Name	Description
pfc	The *HTTP_FILTER_CONTEXT* structure from which the callback function's pointer was obtained

Name	Description
lpszName	A pointer to a null-terminated string containing the name of the header to be altered
lpszValue	A pointer to a null-terminated string containing the new value for the header. If this points to a null string (*not* a null pointer!) then the header will be deleted

AddHeader() Function

Syntax:

```
BOOL (WINAPI * AddHeader) (
      struct _HTTP_FILTER_CONTEXT * pfc,
      LPSTR                         lpszName,
      LPSTR                         lpszValue
      );
```

The pointer to this function is provided in the HTTP_FILTER_PREPROC_HEADERS structure, and as a result is only available while processing a SF_NOTIFY_PREPROC_HEADERS event.

The AddHeader() function allows additional headers to be added to a request, as if the client had sent them. It does *not* add additional headers to an outgoing response.

A Boolean value is returned, indicating the success of the request returned. If the operation was successful, the value will be *TRUE*.

The parameters to the AddHeader() function are listed in table A.26.

TABLE A.26
AddHeader() Parameters

Name	Description
pfc	The *HTTP_FILTER_CONTEXT* structure from which the callback function's pointer was obtained
lpszName	A pointer to a null-terminated string containing the name of the header to be added
lpszValue	A pointer to a null-terminated string containing the value for the new header

Creating a System
Data Source Name

Microsoft's IIS (Internet Information Server) runs as a system service. Because the server is not running on behalf of a user, it (as well as ISAPI extensions and filters that it might call) is unable to connect to the database through a standard User DSN (Data Source Name).

Version 2.5 of the ODBC (Open Database Connectivity) specification introduced a new feature called the System DSN. A system service may connect to a database through a System DSN. This appendix describes how to create a System DSN.

Adding a System Data Source Name

The following numbered procedure takes you through the necessary steps to add a System DSN, enabling IIS services to connect to a database.

> **Note** The following instructions and figures apply to ODBC 3.0 running on Microsoft NT 4.0, the current versions at the time of this writing. This version of the ODBC driver is installed with Microsoft Office 97, Visual C++ 5.0, and a number of other products.

1. Ensure that the installed version of ODBC is at least version 2.5. You can check this by opening the ODBC object in the Control Panel and selecting *Help*. If necessary, you can install the appropriate ODBC Drivers and Administrator software as follows:

   a. Open *Internet Information Server Setup* in the Microsoft Internet Server program group.

   b. Click *Add/Remove...* to add the ODBC components, and enter the correct path for the IIS installation directory.

   c. Check the *ODBC Drivers & Administration* box and click *OK*.

2. Open the ODBC object in the Control Panel.

3. Select the *System DSN* tab (depicted in fig. B.1).

Figure B.1

List of System DSNs.

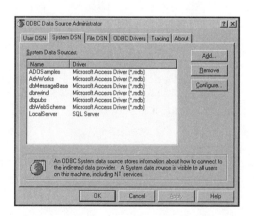

4. Click the *Add...* button to get the Create New Data Source dialog (see fig. B.2).

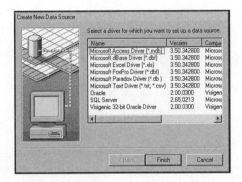

Figure B.2

Create New Data Source dialog.

5. Select from the list the driver that will access your data.

6. Click the *Finish* button to configure the data source. The resulting dialog will vary depending upon the driver selected.

Configuring an Access System Data Source Name

Following Step 6, in the previous list for adding a System DSN and selecting the Microsoft Access Driver, you will see a dialog box (pictured in fig. B.3) that asks you to set up the data source. If you are setting up a DSN for a data source other than Access, the dialog box that you see will be different.

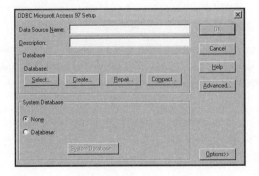

Figure B.3

ODBC Microsoft Access 97 Setup.

These are the steps necessary to configure an Access 97 data source:

1. Enter the desired Data Source Name and a description.

2. Click the *Select...* button in the *Database* group.

3. Locate the file containing the desired database and click OK. Note that the file must be accessible to the ultimate user of the database. For example, if IUSR_*machinename* cannot access the file, then an anonymous web user will not be able to use the database.

4. Click *OK* (the other buttons and the **System Database** group aren't generally used).

Configuring a SQL Server System DSN

Following Step 6 in the previous list for adding a System DSN, and selecting the SQL Server driver, you will see a dialog box (pictured in fig. B.4) that asks you to set up the data source.

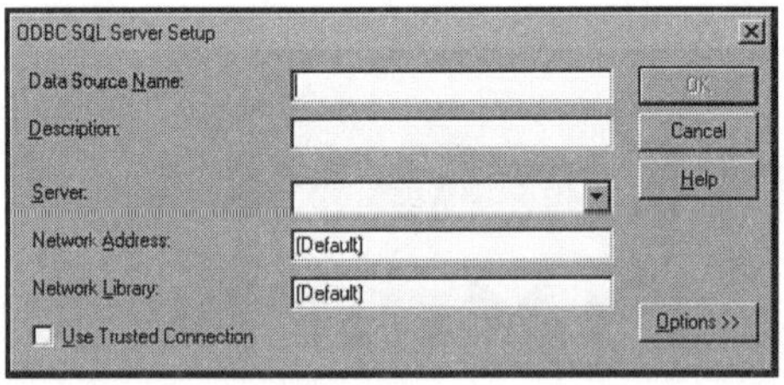

Figure B.4

ODBC SQL Server Setup.

ODBC SQL Server Setup		
Data Source Name:		OK
Description:		Cancel
Server:		Help
Network Address:	[Default]	
Network Library:	[Default]	
Use Trusted Connection		Options >>

These are the steps necessary to configure a Microsoft SQL Server data source:

1. Enter the desired Data Source Name and a description.

2. Select the desired server from the Server combobox.

If you are accessing a database on a server other than the machine on which IIS is located, you should look at Microsoft's Knowledge Base article Q149425. This contains important information regarding the integration of IIS and NT authentication.

This article is accessible on the Microsoft Developer's Network Library CD, or on Microsoft's web site (www.microsoft.com) by searching for the article number.

3. Click *OK*.

After completing these steps you should have a datasource configured so that applications running on your web site can successfully interact with the database on behalf of your users.

HTTP Status Codes

T his appendix describes the status codes, as defined by the HTTP 1.0 specification, which can be returned in response to an HTTP request. The user's browser interprets these codes in order to present success (or warning) messages. Your ISAPI programs will need to return these values, although the MFC framework does it automatically for its users.

The HTTP request status codes consist of a three-digit numeric code followed by a textual description. The first digit of the numeric code determines the *class* of the response as described in the following list:

- ◆ **1** Informational

- ◆ **2** Successful

- ◆ **3** Redirection

- ◆ **4** Client Error

- ◆ **5** Server Error

The remaining two digits of the code denote the status number within the class. These numbers are strictly defined by the HTTP 1.0 specification.

Unlike the numeric codes, the descriptive phrases provided in the following list are only recommendations; you can substitute your own phrases as appropriate. For example, if your site has non-English speaking users, you may want to provide messages in a different language.

Table C.1
Status Codes

Status Code	Description
1xx Informational	There are no informational codes defined; this class is reserved for future use.
2xx Successful	The request was successfully received, understood, and accepted.
200 OK	The request was successful; the information requested is returned as appropriate for the request.
201 Created	The request successfully created a new resource.
202 Accepted	The request has been accepted for processing, but that processing has not yet been completed. This should not be taken to imply that a future response will be sent upon completion; there is no provision for such a response.
204 No Content	The request has been fulfilled, but the result did not result in any new data.
3xx Redirection	The request cannot be fulfilled without further assistance by the user agent.
300 Multiple Choices	The requested resource can be obtained at one or more other locations. The body of the response should include a list of these locations from which the user (or his agent) can choose. If one is preferred it should be specified by a *Location* header which the user agent can automatically retrieve the resource.
301 Moved Permanently	The requested resource has permanently moved to a new URL. The body of the response should include a hyperlink to the new location. That location should also be specified by a *Location* header which the user agent can both automatically retrieve the resource and update the user's bookmarks if possible.

Status Code	Description
302 Moved Temporarily	Similar to *301*. However, since the move is temporary, the user's bookmarks should not be updated.
304 Not Modified	The request is accepted, but the data has not changed since the timestamp specified in the request's *If-Modified-Since* header.
4xx Client Error	The request could not be satisfied, apparently due to an error on the part of the client.
400 Bad Request	The request was syntactically incorrect and could not be understood; the client should modify the request before resending it.
401 Unauthorized	The user must be authenticated before the request can be accepted. The response must also contain a *WWW-Authenticate* header with an appropriate *challenge*. If the request already included *Authorization* credentials, then those credentials were refused.
403 Forbidden	The request was understood but the server refuses to fulfill it. The client should not attempt to retry; *Authorization* will not help.
404 Not Found	The server could not locate the requested resource.
5xx Server Error	The request could not be satisfied due to an error in the server.
500 Internal Server Error	The server detected an unexpected internal error while processing the request.
501 Not Implemented	The server does not support the functionality necessary to service the request.
502 Bad Gateway	While acting as a gateway or proxy, the server received an invalid response from the upstream server.
503 Service Unavailable	The request can not be serviced due to temporary overloading or maintenance.

Server Variables

I n this appendix, you'll find a complete list of the names of
variables that can be retrieved from the server with the
GetServerVariable( ) callback function. The values of these variables
provide important information about the server itself and about the
connection with the remote user.

The values of headers can be retrieved as well, by requesting the
(uppercase) name of the header prepended with the string *HTTP_*.
For example, you can retrieve the value of the *Cookie* header by
requesting *HTTP_COOKIE*.

The following table describes the server variables that IIS defines:

TABLE D.1
Server Variables

Variable Name	Description
ALL_HTTP	All of the HTTP header fields
AUTH_TYPE	The type of authorization in effect. The value will be *BASIC* if the user has been authenticated by the user; otherwise it will not be present
CONTENT_LENGTH	The number of bytes in the request
CONTENT_TYPE	The MIME type of the request information. A typical value is *application/x-www-form-urlencoded*
GATEWAY_INTERFACE	The CGI revision. With IIS 2.0 this should be CGI/1.1
LOGON_USER	The user's Windows NT account, if authenticated
PATH_INFO	The path alias of the script before translation into the physical path. A typical value might be */Scripts/MyApp/Page1.idc*
PATH_TRANSLATED	The physical path of the script. A typical value might be *C:\InetPub\scripts\myapp\page1.idc*
QUERY_STRING	For a GET request, this will contain a list of field names and their values; for a POST request, this will not be present
REMOTE_ADDR	The IP address of the client
REMOTE_HOST	The hostname of the client (or the IP address if the name is not available)
REMOTE_USER	The user name, if any, supplied by the client and authenticated by the server
REQUEST_METHOD	The HTTP request method. Usually either *GET* or *POST*

Variable Name	Description
SCRIPT_NAME	The name of the script being executed, for example, */Scripts/MyApp/Page1.idc*
SERVER_NAME	The server's hostname (or IP address if unavailable)
SERVER_PORT	The TCP/IP port on which the request was received
SERVER_PORT_SECURE	A flag indicating if the request was made on a secure port: 1 if secure, 0 if not
SERVER_PROTOCOL	The name and version of the protocol of the request, usually *HTTP/1.0*
SERVER_SOFTWARE	The name and version of the server software. For IIS 2.0, the value is *Microsoft-IIS/2.0*
URL	The URL of the request

APPENDIX E

Commonly Used Headers

When an HTTP request or response is sent in a dialog between the client's browser and the server, the message consists of three main parts:

1. **Request or Response Line**

   ◆ **For Requests:** in the case of a request, a line containing the type of request, the URL requested, and the HTTP version being used

   ◆ **For Responses:** in the case of a response, an identification of the HTTP version being used and a status code (as enumerated in Appendix C)

2. **Optional Headers:** each header describes an aspect of the message. The most common ones are described in the accompanying table

3. **Message Body:** the actual message, preceded by a blank line

The headers in the message are optional. Each one that is given is placed on its own line, in the form

```
header-name: header-value
```

You can see practical examples of the construction of headers in Chapter 12.

The headers sent in HTTP communications fall into four types:

◆ **General:** used with requests or responses

◆ **Entity:** refers not to the request or response itself, but to the data that is transferred with it

◆ **Request:** applies to the request, and should only be used in requests

◆ **Response:** applies to the response, and should only be used in responses

The following table lists and describes some of the commonly used headers.

COMMON HEADERS

Name	Type	Description
Accept	request	Enumerates the MIME types that can be accepted in response to the request
Allow	entity	Enumerates the methods that are allowed on the entity requested; invalid as part of a POST entity
Authorization	request	Provides authentication credentials to the server for the user
Connection	general	A value of keep-alive requests that the TCP connection between client and server be kept alive after the request is fulfilled. If this is used, a Content-Length must be specified, since the broken connection is what would otherwise flag the end of the transmission
Content-Encoding	entity	Indicates any additional encoding that has been applied to the resource beyond what is specified by the Content-Type header. This allows, for example, a bitmap to be zipped
Content-Length	entity	Gives the (decimal) length of the entity's body
Content-Type	entity	Indicates the MIME type of the entity
Cookie	request	Lists the cookies that the client has associated with this URL

Name	Type	Description
Date	general	Indicates the date and time at which the message was originated; for example, Sun, 01 December 1996 14:00:00 GMT
Expires	entity	Indicates the date and time in which the entity should be considered obsolete. This is used primarily for managing the client's cache
From	request	Gives the email address of the user making the request
Host	request	Gives the host name or IP address of the client
If-Modified-Since	request	Makes the request conditional; if the requested information has not changed since the specified date/time, the server may respond with a 304 status indicating that the data has not changed
Last-Modified	entity	Indicates the date/time in which the entity is believed to have been modified last. The meaning of this is application-defined
Location	response	Gives an URL indicating the exact location of the requested resource; used most often in conjunction with redirection responses (see Appendix C for more information)
Pragma	general	Specifies implementation-specific behavior. One common use is with a value of no-cache, which indicates that the requested resource should not be cached
Referer	request	Gives the address of the resource that sent the client here, usually the URL of the page containing the link to this resource
Server	response	Identifies the server software. Microsoft IIS 2.0 uses a value of Microsoft-IIS/2.0
Set-Cookie	response	Sends new cookies to the client
User-Agent	request	Identifies the client's software
WWW-Authenticate	response	Used in conjunction with a 401 status response. It includes at least one challenge indicating the required authentication scheme

What's on the CD?

The CD that's included with this book contains a number of things that you, as an ISAPI developer, should find useful. Naturally, the source code for all of the samples in the book are included. In addition, there are development tools, documentation, complete ISAPI components, and ISAPI-related World Wide Web links provided to put you on the right track for developing your own ISAPI extensions and filters.

Source Code

Complete projects for all the samples in the book are provided. With the right tools (see the sections "Hardware Requirements" and "Software Requirements" in the Introduction) you should be able to build any of these projects immediately.

Development Tools

The following table lists a set of tools included on the CD-ROM to help you develop and debug your applications.

Tool Name	Description
webAction	webAction is a product from classTools, Inc. The product consists of a set of tools that allows you improve the performance of legacy CGI code. Its primary goal is to help you develop new applications that enjoy the same performance gains, using a development environment that you're already familiar with, such as Visual Basic or Borland Delphi 2.0. An additional advantage is speedier application development when using their library of high-level functions.
Tornado	Tornado has a number of similarities to webAction in that it is designed to allow integration of programs written in Visual Basic and other languages. However, it was developed with some different goals in mind. The most significant difference is that webAction emphasizes rapid development of new applications (through the use of libraries and custom OLE automation interfaces); Tornado emphasizes leveraging existing applications and site administration.
WebHub	WebHub, from HREF Tools Corp., follows a rather different approach than the previous two tools. Although some capability is provided for creating applications without writing code, WebHub is designed primarily for developing interactive web applications in Borland Delphi

Documentation

Aside from the information that this book provides about ISAPI development itself, you'll need to understand some more fundamental information. The documents listed in the following table provide detailed information on publishing in HTML and about the protocols used by web servers and browsers.

Document Name	Description
The HTML Reference Library	The HTML Reference Library is a complete reference for HTML in Windows Help format. It explains all of the standard tags, plus the extension currently supported by Microsoft and Netscape. There is also a table comparing the tags supported by Microsoft Internet Explorer, Netscape Navigator, and Spry Mosaic.
RFC 1945	"Hypertext Transfer Protocol — HTTP/1.0," specifies the HTTP/1.0 protocol, the most common protocol currently in use for carrying World Wide Web communications.
RFC 2068	"Hypertext Transfer Protocol — HTTP/1.1," specifies the HTTP/1.1 protocol, the eventual replacement to HTTP/1.0.
RFC 1738	"Uniform Resource Locators (URL)," defines how URLs are to be formed.
RFC 1630	"*Universal Resource Identifiers in WWW*: A Unifying Syntax for the Expression of Names and Addresses of Objects on the Network as used in the World-Wide Web."
RFC 1521	"*MIME (Multipurpose Internet Mail Extensions) Part One*: Mechanisms for Specifying and Describing the Format of Internet Message Bodies," also applies to the bodies of HTTP requests.
RFC 822	"Standard for the Format of ARPA Internet Text Messages," complements MIME definition of RFC 1521.

ISAPI Components

Also included on the CD are the Online Eventlog Viewer and preview versions of two commercial ISAPI components, AuthentiX and DefaultX, that you can plug right into your server to see the benefits of ISAPI.

Component Name	Description
AuthentiX	AuthentiX provides more control over your server's authentication than is available through the built-in mechanisms.
DefaultX	DefaultX allows your server to have multiple default pages, and script-based default pages.
Online Eventlog Viewer	This online event log viewer allows you to view what's happening on your server from home or other remote location. This is handy when a user calls with problems in the middle of the night.

Web Links

The field of Internet development changes so quickly that it's impossible to give you the most up-to-date information all of the time. The following table provides some web links that you should find helpful in keeping on top of the latest developments.

Site Name	URL	Description
The World Wide Web Consortium	http://www.w3.org/pub/WWW/	The main page of the World Wide Web Consortium (W3C), a body which provides a "repository of information about the World Wide Web for developers and users, especially specifications about the Web"
HTTP - Specifications, Drafts and Reports	http://www.w3.org/pub/WWW/Protocols/Specs.html	Information from the World Wide Web Consortium (W3C) regarding the HTTP protocol
Linked RFCs	http://www.pmg.lcs.mit.edu	Search engine for locating RFCs. This enables you to locate the official specifications for the information you need
Nexor RFC Index Search Form	http://pubweb.nexor.co.uk/public/rfc/index/rfc.html	Another RFC search engine

Site Name	URL	Description
Microsoft Developer Network Online	http://www. microsoft.com/msdn/ default.htm	Microsoft's outlet for information aimed at developers
Microsoft Site Builder Workshop Mailing Lists	http://www. microsoft.com/ workshop/resource/ mail-f.htm	Microsoft-maintained mailing lists through which developers can support each other (notice the ISAPI and Denali lists, in particular)
Microsoft Internet Server API Documentation	http://www. microsoft.com/ win32dev/apiext/ isalegal.htm	Microsoft's own published ISAPI documentation
The Common Gateway Interface	http://hoohoo. ncsa.uiuc.edu/cgi/	Documents the Common Gateway Interface (CGI) standard for interactive web development
The HTML Reference Library	http://subnet. virtual-pc.com/ ~le387818/	The official site for the HTML Reference Library, the current version of which is provided on this CD. Check here for updates as the HTML specification evolves
The ISAPI Developer's Site	http://rampages. onramp.net/~steveg/ isapi.html *(to be moved to* http://www. isapideveloper.com*)*	Semi-official site hosting the ISAPI FAQ and other important information for anyone using ISAPI
Unauthorized Site Builder	http://www. sitebuilder.net/	Contains information for developers of web sites using Microsoft tools

INDEX I

MACMILLAN COMPUTER PUBLISHING USA

A VIACOM COMPANY

Technical
---- Support:

If you need assistance with the information in this book or with a CD/Disk
accompanying the book, please access the Knowledge Base on our Web
site at **http://www.superlibrary.com/general/support**. Our most
Frequently Asked Questions are answered there. If you do not find the
answer to your questions on our Web site, you may contact Macmillan
Technical Support **(317) 581-3833** or e-mail us at **support@mcp.com**.